Digital History

Digital History

A Guide to Gathering, Preserving, and Presenting the Past on the Web

DANIEL J. COHEN AND
ROY ROSENZWEIG

PENN

University of Pennsylvania Press

Philadelphia

10   9   8   7   6   5   4   3   2   1

Published by
University of Pennsylvania Press
Philadelphia, Pennsylvania 19104-4112

Library of Congress Cataloging-in-Publication Data

Cohen, Daniel J.
    Digital history : a guide to gathering, preserving, and presenting the past on the Web / Daniel J. Cohen and Roy Rosenzweig.
        p. cm.
Includes bibliographical references (p.) and index.
ISBN-13: 978-0-8122-1923-4 (pbk. : alk. paper)
ISBN-10: 0-8122-1923-6 (pbk. : alk. paper)
    1. History—Computer network resources.   2. Internet. History—Computer-assisted instruction.   3. History—Methodology.   4. History—Research. I. Title.

D16.117.C64 2005
004.67'8—dc 22

                                                                              2005048451

To our friends and colleagues at the Center for History and New Media and the American Social History Project, from whom we learned everything we know about digital history

Contents

Introduction: Promises and Perils of Digital History   1

1. Exploring the History Web   18

2. Getting Started: The Nature of Websites, and What You Will Need to Create Yours   51

3. Becoming Digital: Preparing Historical Materials for the Web   80

4. Designing for the History Web   108

5. Building an Audience   141

6. Collecting History Online   160

7. Owning the Past? The Digital Historian's Guide to Copyright and Intellectual Property   189

8. Preserving Digital History: What We Can Do Today to Help Tomorrow's Historians   220

Some Final Thoughts   247

Appendix: Database Software, Scripting Languages, and XML   249

Notes   261

Index   301

Acknowledgments   315

Introduction

Promises and Perils of Digital History

Step back in time and open the pages of the inaugural issue of *Wired* magazine from the spring of 1993, and prophecies of an optimistic digital future call out to you. Management consultant Lewis J. Perleman confidently proclaims an "inevitable" "hyperlearning revolution" that will displace the thousand-year-old "technology" of the classroom, which has "as much utility in today's modern economy of advanced information technology as the Conestoga wagon or the blacksmith shop." John Browning, a friend of the magazine's founders and later the executive editor of *Wired UK*, rhapsodizes about how "books once hoarded in subterranean stacks will be scanned into computers and made available to anyone, anywhere, almost instantly, over high-speed networks." Not to be outdone by his authors, *Wired* publisher Louis Rossetto links the digital revolution to "social changes so profound that their only parallel is probably the discovery of fire."[1]

Although the *Wired* prophets could not contain their enthusiasm, the techno-skeptics fretted about a very different future. Debating *Wired* Executive Editor Kevin Kelly in the May 1994 issue of *Harper's*, literary critic Sven Birkerts implored readers to "refuse" the lure of "the electronic hive." The new media, he warned, pose a dire threat to the search for "wisdom" and "depth"—"the struggle for which has for millennia been central to the very idea of culture."[2]

Some historians—on both the right and the left—also saw deep trouble ahead. In November 1996, the conservative Gertrude Himmelfarb offered what she called a "neo-Luddite" dissent about "the new technology's impact on learning and scholarship." "Like postmodernism," she complained, "the Internet does not distinguish between the true and the false, the important and the trivial, the enduring and the ephemeral. . . . Every source appearing on the screen has the same weight and credibility as every other; no authority is 'privileged' over any other." A year later, the Marxist historian of technology David Noble found himself standing beside Himmelfarb in the neo-Luddite crowd, although not surprisingly he spotted the cyber-threat coming from a different direction. "A dismal new era of higher education has dawned," he wrote in a paper called "Digital Diploma Mills: The Automation of Higher Education." "In future years we will look upon the wired remains of our once great democratic higher education system and wonder how we let it happen."[3]

More than a decade into the promised "digital revolution," the cyberenthusiasts and the techno-skeptics have both turned out to be poor prophets of the future. Universities and libraries still stand. Culture has not crumbled. Paradise has not arrived. But to decide that neither utopia nor dystopia beckons should not lead to the comfortable conclusion that nothing has changed or will change. Driven by the rapid emergence and dissemination of computers, global computer networks, and new digital media, change—though not revolution—surrounds us. Our daily habits of finding the news and weather, buying books, and communicating with colleagues and loved ones have permanently changed.

Even the ancient discipline of history has begun to metamorphose. In the past two decades, new media and new technologies have challenged historians to rethink the ways that they research, write, present, and teach about the past. Almost every historian regards a computer as basic equipment; colleagues view those who write their books and articles without the assistance of word-processing software as objects of curiosity. History teachers labor over their PowerPoint slides as do sixth graders preparing for History Day. Email and instant messaging have broadened circles of communication and debate among dispersed historical practitioners, scholars as well as amateur enthusiasts.

Nowhere are the signs of change for historians more evident than on the World Wide Web. Yahoo's web directory currently lists 32,959 history websites. Even this vast catalog greatly underestimates the pervasiveness of the past online, not including, for example, the tens of thousands of online syllabi for history courses. In the past decade, historians with interests ranging from ancient Mesopotamia to the post–Cold War world have enthusiastically embraced the web. Virtually every scholarly journal duplicates its content online (though not always openly), and almost every history course has its syllabus posted on the web. Virtually every historical archive, historical museum, historical society, historic house, and historic site—even the very smallest—has its own website. So does just about every reenactment group, genealogical society, and body of historical enthusiasts.

This book emerges in response to these dramatic changes. Just ten years ago, we would not have imagined the need for "a guide to gathering, preserving, and presenting the past on the web." Indeed, few of us knew the web existed. Even the editors of *Wired* ignored it in their inaugural issue.[4] Ten years ago, *we* would have been objects of curiosity, if not derision, if we had proposed such a project. Today, the need for it seems self-evident.

To offer such a volume implicitly puts us on the other side of the fence from neo-Luddite historians like Noble and Himmelfarb. We obviously believe that we gain something from doing digital history, making use of the new computer-based technologies. Yet although we are wary of the conclusions of the techno-skeptics, we are not entirely enthusiastic about the views of the cyber-enthusiasts either. Rather, we believe that we need to critically and soberly assess where computers, networks, and digital media are and aren't useful for historians—a category that we define broadly to include amateur enthusiasts, research scholars, museum curators, documentary filmmakers, historical society adminis-trators, classroom teachers, and history students at all levels. In what ways can digital media and digital networks allow us to do our work as historians better?

This introduction briefly sketches seven qualities of digital media and networks that potentially allow us to do things better: capacity, accessibil-ity, flexibility, diversity, manipulability, interactivity, and hypertextuality (or nonlinearity). We also talk about five dangers or hazards on the information superhighway: quality, durability, readability, passivity, and inaccessibility. This scorecard of possibilities and problems seems, on balance, to suggest a digital future worth pursuing. We thus align our-selves with neither the wild-eyed optimists nor the gloomy pessimists but rather with the camp known as "techno-realists" who seek, in the words of computer scientist and social theorist Phil Agre, to analyze "case by case the interactions between technology and institutions through which the action really unfolds."[5] Doing digital history well entails being aware of the technology's advantages and disadvantages, and how to maximize the former while minimizing the latter.

The first advantage of digital media for historians is storage *capacity*—digital media can condense unparalleled amounts of data into small spaces. A 120-gigabyte hard drive that sells for $95 and weighs about a pound can hold a 120,000-volume library. Because historians love data and archival sources, they have great interest in this ability to condense large amounts of data into tiny amounts of space. Historians who would like to make considerable quantities of primary sources available over the web quickly learn that storage space is perhaps the smallest expense they face.

The most profound effect, however, may be on tomorrow's historians. The rapidly dropping price of data storage has led computer scientists like Michael Lesk (a cyber-enthusiast to be sure) to claim that in the future, "there will be enough disk space and tape storage in the world to store everything people write, say, perform, or photograph." In other words, why delete anything from the current historical record if it costs so little save it? How might our history writing be different if all historical evidence were available?[6]

The vast storage capacity of digital media would be of much less interest without a second and even more important advantage—*accessibility*. This quality derives both from the ability to condense the bits and bytes encoded in digital media into small spaces but even more from the emergence of ubiquitous computer networks that can almost instantly send those bits around the world. Historians have multiple audiences; digital networks mean that we can reach those audiences—students, other scholars and teachers, the general public—much more easily and cheaply than ever before. The distribution of history projects electronically approaches what the economists call "zero marginal cost"; once the initial expenses are met, reaching an additional person costs almost nothing (unlike, say, a print book where costs decline after the initial investment but still remain substantial). Our web server at the Center for History and New Media (CHNM) gets about three-quarters of a million hits a day, but on September 11, 2002 (when people looking to commemorate the attacks of the previous year descended in droves on the September 11 Digital Archive that we organized in collaboration with the American Social History Project), we handled eight million hits—a more than tenfold increase with no additional costs.[7]

Online accessibility means, moreover, that the documentary record of the past is open to people who rarely had entrée before. The analog Library of Congress has never welcomed high school students—its reading rooms, no less its special collections, routinely turn them away. Now the library's American Memory website allows high school students to enter the virtual archive on the same terms of access as the most senior historian or member of Congress. To those who previously had no easy access, online archives open locked doors. Nonacademic users of the University of North Carolina's archival website, Documenting the American South, reports university librarian Joe Hewitt, speak eloquently of how they "felt privileged to have access to these primary sources as if they had entered an inner sanctum where they did not fully belong."[8] But even for well-credentialed historians, such online archives put millions of historical documents at hand twenty-four hours a day and without the cost of a plane ticket or the delay of travel to Washington, D.C., or Chapel Hill, North Carolina. The instantaneous access to primary and secondary sources—the ability to very quickly make and test out intellectual connections—will likely alter historical research and writing in ways that we haven't yet imagined.

The accessibility and publicness of the web has consequences for history projects much less extensive than those mounted by the Library of

Congress or major university libraries. High school teachers can devise community programs in which students present the results of their historical research to an online audience of local residents. Historical societies based in small and declining towns on the Great Plains can keep in touch with—and gather historical information from—former residents.[9] A genealogical web page can bring together the descendants of a family who started out in County Cork, Ireland, but later scattered to London, Toronto, San Francisco, Cape Town, and Melbourne. The Internet allows historians to speak to vastly more people in widely dispersed places without really spending more money—an extraordinary development.

The past that is suddenly more accessible is also much richer because of a third characteristic of digital media—what we might call *flexibility*. Because digital media are expressed in a basic language of 1s and 0s, they can take multiple forms, and that means we can arrange those bits into text, images, sounds, and moving pictures. Thus we can more easily preserve, study, and present the past in the multiple media that expressed and recorded it. Online digital archives can contain images, sounds, and moving pictures as well as text. And you can present the past in multiple media that *combine* sounds, images, and moving pictures with words.

But the flexibility of digital data lies not just in the ability to encompass different media. It also resides in the ability of the same data to assume multiple guises instantaneously. Although language translation software is still primitive, we are moving toward a time when words in one tongue can be automatically translated into another—perhaps not perfectly but effectively enough. More generally, digital information organized into databases or marked up in structured languages like XML (see Chapter 2 and the appendix) can be instantly reordered or combined into new forms. Acting on the pieces in a database or XML document, small but powerful computer programs can pull together disparate materials in a way that compares, contrasts, and enhances them. For example, a scholar of ancient Greece simultaneously can see an image of a vase, commentaries from several other historians about that vase, and suggestions of similar artifacts from a database. As new media theorist Lev Manovich points out, the "numerical coding of media" and the "modular structure of a data object" means "a new media object is not something fixed once and for all, but something that can exist in different, potentially infinite versions." Thus Manovich sees the database—with its infinitely rearrangeable data—as one of the fundamental forms found in new media.[10]

Flexibility transforms the experience of consuming history, but digital media—because of their openness and *diversity*—also alters the conditions and circumstances of producing history. The computer networks that have come together in the World Wide Web are not only more open to a global audience of history readers than any other previous medium, they are also more open to history authors. A 2004 study found that almost half of the Internet users in the United States have created online content by building websites, creating blogs, and posting and sharing files. An astonishing 13 percent maintain their own websites, and one recent census counts more than seven million blogs.[11] No publishing medium has ever had such a low barrier to entry. At virtually no cost, millions have access to their own printing press. Already, the number of authors of history web pages is likely greater than the number of authors of history books. But the even more dramatic contrast is in the social composition of the two sets of authors—web history authors are significantly more diverse and significantly less likely to have formal credentials. Their strong presence online unsettles existing hierarchies, thus producing Himmelfarb's jeremiad and the laments of other techno-skeptics.

The web, as a result, has given a much louder and more public voice to amateur historians. If you searched for "Abraham Lincoln" in Google in 2004, the top site listed was the *Abraham Lincoln Research Site*, which features the writing of Roger Norton, who says of himself "I am not an author or an historian; rather I am a former American history teacher who enjoys researching Abraham Lincoln's life and accomplishments."[12] Through Google's eye, which is how an increasing number of people view the web, Roger Norton was a more influential Lincoln historian than the Pulitzer-Prize-winning Harvard professor David Donald.

For the most part, these first four qualities of digital media provide what we might call quantitative advantages—we can do more, reach more people, store more data, give readers more varied sources; we can get more historical materials into classrooms, give students more access to formerly cloistered documents, hear from more perspectives. But does digital history do anything differently? Literary critic Janet Murray raises this issue in *Hamlet on the Holodeck*, her book on the future of narrative in cyberspace. There, she distinguishes between "additive" and "expressive" features of new media. She makes the useful analogy to early films, which were initially called "photoplays," and thus thought of as "a merely additive art form (photography plus theatre)." Only when filmmakers learned to use montage, close-ups, zooms, and the like as part of storytelling did photoplays give way to the new expressive form of movies.[13]

To consider these "expressive" qualities we need to think, for example, about the *manipulability* of digital media—the possibility of manipulating historical data with electronic tools as a way of finding things that were not previously evident. At the moment, the most powerful of those tools for historians is the simplest—the ability to search through vast quantities of text for particular strings of words. The word-search capabilities of JSTOR, the online database of 460 scholarly periodicals, makes possible a kind of intellectual history that cannot be done as readily in print sources. Say you want to trace the changing reputation of Richard Hofstadter in the historical profession; the 667 articles in JSTOR that mention Hofstadter provide an invaluable starting point. Historians of language are already having a field day playing with such massive databases. The librarian and lexicographer Fred Shapiro, for example, has uncovered uses of such phrases as "double standard" (1912) and "Native American" (for American Indian, 1931) that predate citations in the *Oxford English Dictionary* by decades. Similarly, CHNM's Syllabus Finder makes it possible to discover—by searching through thousands of online history syllabi—patterns in history teaching (the popularity of different courses, texts, or types of assignments) that were once invisible.[14]

But text searching is only one very simple technique, albeit a powerful one when leveraged through Boolean searches and the use of advanced pattern-matching techniques such as the "regular expressions" used by computer scientists. Even more tantalizing are the prospects of being able to search automatically through vast quantities of images, sounds, and moving pictures. And, at some point, we may be able to dynamically map (temporally and geographically) historical events drawn from tens of thousands of historical sources. Or we may be able to see new things in historical images through digital close-ups or manipulation. Jerome McGann, for example, talks about using software tools to "deform" images and see in them elements previously missed.[15]

Digital media also differ from many other older media in their *interactivity*—a product of the web being, unlike broadcast television, a two-way medium, in which every point of consumption can also be a point of production. This interactivity enables multiple forms of historical dialogue—among professionals, between professionals and nonprofessionals, between teachers and students, among students, among people reminiscing about the past—that were possible before but which are not only simpler but potentially richer and more intensive in the digital medium. Many history websites offer opportunities for dialogue and feedback. The level of response has varied widely, but the experience so far suggests how we might transform historical practice—the web becomes a place for new forms of collaboration, new modes of debate, and new modes of collecting evidence about the past. At least potentially, digital media transform the traditional, one-way reader/writer, producer/consumer relationship. Public historians, in particular, have long sought for ways to "share authority" with their audiences; the web offers an ideal medium for that sharing and collaboration.[16]

Finally, we note the *hypertextuality,* or *nonlinearity,* of digital media—the ease of moving through narratives or data in undirected and multiple ways. Hypertext, as is well known, is a constitutional principle of the World Wide Web; its original designer, Tim Berners-Lee, called its most basic protocol the "HyperText Transfer Protocol"—the "http" that begins every web address. For postmodernists, hypertextuality fractures and decenters traditional master narratives in beneficial ways. "Hypertext," writes literary critic George Landow, "emphasizes that the marginal has as much to offer as the central by refusing to grant centrality to anything . . . for more than the time a gaze rests upon it. In hypertext, centrality, like beauty and relevance, resides in the eye of the beholder." For Landow, hypertext reconfigures texts, authors, writing, and narrative. In this fundamental "paradigm shift" (what he calls "a revolution in human thought"), conceptual systems "founded upon ideas of center, margin, hierarchy, and linearity" are overturned by "ones of multi-linearity, nodes, links, and networks."[17]

To talk about revolutions in human thought starts to make us sound like one of the cyber-enthusiasts with whom we began. Are we, in fact, on the verge of a new, richer, and rewarding era of cyber-historical work—a digital history revolution? Although we would not disavow the profound advantages and features of digital history, we would quickly offer some caveats. Some equally profound barriers and difficulties keep all of us from reaching this rosy digital future. Moreover, some of the positive goods that online history is bringing to our desktops are accompanied by serious hazards and dangers—many of them are, in turn, the flip side of advantages we discussed earlier.

For example, the problems of *quality* and authenticity emerge, in part, out of the vast capacity of digital media. Often cyber-skeptics summarize this view in the simple phrase "it's mostly junk." "Internet search engines," writes Gertrude Himmelfarb, "will produce a comic strip or advertising slogan as readily as a quotation from the Bible or Shakespeare." Historian James William Brodman similarly worries that students will unfailingly grab the comic strip rather than Shakespeare: "Much of the material that students . . . unearth in cyberspace is of uneven character—juvenile, inaccurate, or sometimes simply wrong."[18]

And to be sure, we can find plenty of inaccurate history on the web. Take a look at the web pages of Citizens for a Sound Economy and the Federal Reserve Bank of Dallas and read a letter allegedly from Martin Van Buren to Andrew Jackson calling for government intervention to stop the threat to the railroads posed by the Erie Canal. A careful assessment of internal evidence (an important historical skill in all ages) readily betrays the twentieth-century origins of this "nineteenth-century" letter. But the forgery predates the web, and the web also offers crucial evidence about the origins of the counterfeit. Moreover, in general, the web is more likely to be right than wrong. A quick check of Google finds 613 web pages discussing the "Gettys*berg* Address" but 86,100 that correctly spell the locale for Lincoln's speech as "Gettys-*burg*." If the existence of misinformation on the web is no more of a problem than its existence in the rest of society, the web does actually pose some thornier problems of authenticity and authority. One is that both forgery and the movement of forgery into the "information stream" are considerably easier in the digital and networked world.[19]

Consider, for example, the famous "photograph" of Lee Harvey Oswald and Jack Ruby playing rock music together in a Dallas basement. Such fake photographs have a long history; Stalin's photo retouchers, for example, spent considerable time airbrushing Trotsky out of the historical record. But the transformation of the original Bob Jackson photo of Ruby shooting Oswald into "In-A-Gadda-Da-Oswald" did not require a skilled craftsman. George Mahlberg created it with Photoshop in forty minutes and it quickly spread across the World Wide Web, popping up in multiple contexts that erase the credit of the "original" counterfeiter.[20]

Himmelfarb implies a related problem in her horror that a comic strip could have the same authority as the Bible. In this new space, will traditional repositories of authority retain their stature and influence? In the heterogeneous space of the web, will the History Channel serve as a more influential authority than the History Cooperative, the online publisher of the *American Historical Review* and the *Journal of American History*? Anyone can gain admittance to the History Channel site, but the History Cooperative site is only open to journal subscribers.

Is there some way to police the boundaries of historical quality and authenticity on the web? Could we stop a thousand historical flowers—amateur, professional, commercial, crackpot—from blooming on the web? Would we want to? Of course, issues of quality, authenticity, and authority pre-date the Internet. But digital media undercut an existing structure of trust and authority and we, as historians and citizens, have yet to establish a new structure of historical legitimation and authority. When you move your history online, you are entering a less structured and controlled environment than the history monograph, the scholarly journal, the history museum, or the history classroom. That can have both positive and unsettling implications.

One vision of the digital future involves the preservation of everything—the dream of the complete historical record. The current reality, however, is closer to the reverse of that—we are rapidly losing the digital

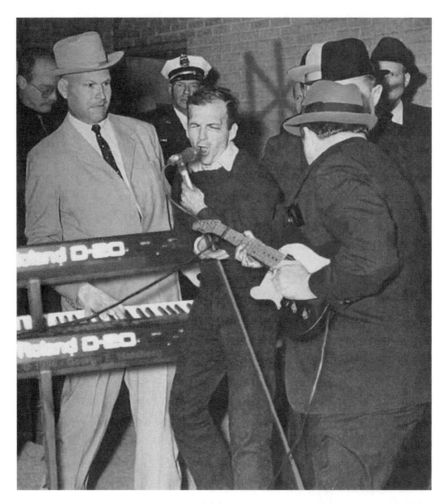

Figure 1. Fake photographs long predate the web, but digital tools have made them much easier to create and disseminate. Adobe Photoshop enabled George Mahlberg to produce "In-A-Gadda-Da-Oswald" in forty minutes. Copyright George Mahlberg and Bob Jackson.

present that is being created because no one has worked out a means of preserving it. The flipside of the flexibility of digital data is its seeming lack of *durability*—a second hazard on the road to digital history nirvana. The digital record of the federal government is being lost on a daily basis. Although most government agencies started using email and word processing software in the mid-1980s, the U.S. National Archives and Records Administration still does not require that digital records be stored in their original form.[21] Again, historical and archival preservation are hardly new problems, but the digital era has forced us to reconsider fundamental questions about what should be preserved and who should preserve it.

Prophets of hypertext have repeatedly promised a new, richer reading experience, but critics have instead seen the digital environment as engendering the death of reading as we know it. Sven Birkerts has expressed the most profound sense of loss in *Gutenberg Elegies: The Fate of Reading in an Electronic Age*. The more prosaic (and the most common) complaint centers on the difficulty of reading a screen, that is, the issue of poor legibility. But reading on screen may ultimately find a technological solution as high-resolution, high-contrast displays become cheaper to produce.[22]

The more profound problem of *readability* is figuring out what it means to be an author in this environment. Typically such experiments place large demands on the reader—they are, in Espen Aarseth's phrase, "ergodic" literature, in which "nontrivial effort is required to allow the reader to traverse the text." Historian Philip J. Ethington's online article on Los Angeles—the *American Historical Review*'s first all-electronic work—asks you to make your way through a relatively dense argument for a spatial theory of historical certainty as well as a vast set of videos, panoramas, maps, and essays on everything from photography to urban epistemology.[23]

Hypertext scholarship like this disrupts the conventions of the printed scholarly article. Yet although such conventions can be deadening, they can also make printed articles easy to read, at least by those who know the "codes." Most academics can rapidly find the thesis in the first few pages, the conclusions on the last two pages, and a sense of the sources used through a quick scan of the footnotes. Such strategies are worthless in confronting hypertext essays. Not only is the thesis often hard to find quickly, but it is not always clear that there *is* a thesis. Where is the beginning? The end? Reader expectations about the investment of time required to master an essay are entirely disrupted. In effect, those works undercut the unwritten social contract that exists between readers and writers of scholarly essays—a social contract in which the author agrees to follow conventions of argumentation, organization, and documentation, and the reader agrees to devote a certain amount of time to give the article a fair reading.[24]

Digital enthusiasts assume that the online environment is intrinsically more "interactive" than one-way, passive media like television. But digital technology could, in fact, foster a new couch potato–like *passivity*. Efforts to create nuanced interactive history projects sometimes become quixotic when the producers confront the fact that computers are good at yes and no and right and wrong, whereas historians prefer words like "maybe," "perhaps," and "it is more complicated than that." Thus the most common form of historical interactivity on the web is the multiple-choice test. But the high-budget version is little better. Take, for example, the History Channel's website *Modern Marvels Boys' Toys*, which is a combination of watching the cable channel and playing a video game. The true interactivity here comes when you click on the "shop" button. As legal scholar Lawrence Lessig has written pessimistically: "There are two futures in front of us, the one we are taking and the one we could have. The one we are taking is easy to describe. Take the Net, mix it with the fanciest TV, add a simple way to buy things, and that's pretty much it." At the same time, some wonder whether we really want to foster "interactivity" at all, arguing that it fails to provide the critical experience of understanding, of getting inside the thoughts and experiences of others. The literary critic Harold Bloom, for example, argues that whereas linear fiction allows us to experience more by granting us access to the lives and thoughts of those different from ourselves, interactivity only permits us to experience more of ourselves.[25]

A more serious threat in digital media, which runs counter to its great virtues of accessibility and diversity, is the real potential for *inaccessibility* and monopoly. The best-known danger—the digital divide in computer ownership and Internet use between rich and poor, white and non-white—has diminished somewhat, but it persists despite politically motivated claims to the contrary. And on a global basis, the divide is wide indeed; two-thirds of the people in the world have no access to telephones, let alone the Net. Moreover, even as more and more people acquire computers and Internet connections, they do not simultaneously acquire the skills for finding and making effective use of this new, free global resource.[26] Another concern stems more from the production than the consumption side. Will amateur and academic historians be able to compete with well-funded commercial operators—like the History Channel—for attention on the Net?

In any event, the most important commercial purveyors of the past are not, at the moment, the History Channel or the magazine-driven TheHistoryNet but global multibillion-dollar information conglomerates like ProQuest, Reed Elsevier, and the Thomson Corporation, which charge libraries high prices for the vast digital databases of journals, magazines, newspapers, books, and historical documents that they control.[27] Dividing cyberspace into a series of gated communities controlled by information conglomerates means that the dream of a globally interconnected scholarship is just that—a dream. The balkanization of the web into privately owned digital storehouses has been made worse by the scandalous Sonny Bono Copyright Extension Act of 1998, which extended already lengthy existing copyright terms by another twenty years (in part due to the aggressive lobbying of the Disney Corporation, whose Mickey Mouse was scurrying toward the public domain). Will "authority" and "authenticity" reside with the corporate purveyors of the past? Will these diverse, eclectic, and largely free online history resources survive the onslaught of these mega operations? Will access to the best historical resources be open or closed?

Such questions and concerns should not lead us to throw up our hands in despair. Rather—and this is a key message of this book—they should prod us to sit down in front of our computers and get to work. Historians need to confront these issues of quality, durability, readability, passivity, and inaccessibility rather than leave them to the technologists, legislators, and media companies, or even just to our colleagues in libraries and archives. We should put our energies into maintaining and enlarging the astonishingly rich public historical web that has emerged in the past decade. For some, that might involve joining "the international effort to make research articles in all academic fields freely available on the Internet," as embodied, for example, in the Budapest Open Access Initiative.[28] For others, that should mean joining in eclectic but widespread grass-roots efforts to put the past online—whether that involves posting a few documents online for your students or raising funds for more ambitious projects to create free public archives. Just as "open source" software has been the rallying cry of academic computer scientists, "open sources" should be the slogan of academic and popular historians. Academics and enthusiasts created the web; we should not quickly or quietly cede it to giant corporations and their pricy, gated materials. The most important weapon for building the digital future we want is to take an active hand in creating digital history in the present.

* * *

This book is intended to tell you how to do that. As our title indicates, this is meant to be a practical handbook rather than a theoretical manifesto. Our distinctive contribution, as we see it, is our focus on history and historians. The "History Web," as we call it here, has grown so large that it merits a separate introduction focused on the specific problems and possibilities faced by historians who want to enter it. Of course, historians are not so very different from other folks, and we hope that the book will also be of help and interest to a wider community of people, especially those in the humanities broadly defined.

Throughout we have tried to make the book accessible to the historian contemplating the web for the first time as well as to more experienced hands who might know a great deal about web design (and hence might skim over Chapter 4) but know little about copyright and preservation issues. Our goal is not to turn you into a master of all the matters covered in the book; that would be impossible, and frankly we can't claim expertise on all of them ourselves. Nor do we intend to teach you "how to build a web page," which is done better by other, generic volumes that sit on long shelves devoted to the subject. Similarly, we cannot cover in a short book all the dimensions of complex topics such as server infrastructure, scanning resolutions, web design, copyright, and preservation. Other volumes and web resources cover these topics in much greater detail, and we provide references to those works within these pages for those who want to develop their skills and knowledge further.

Rather, we want to get you to think about *why* you might build a history website and what challenges and opportunities that might pose. More generally, we want you to know enough to organize and lead an online history endeavor even if you are joined by collaborators (designers, programmers, lawyers, archivists, librarians) with more specialized knowledge of key aspects of your project. Our practical goals have a basis in a broader democratic aspiration to make the History Web a place where ordinary historians can practice their craft in new and innovative ways. We think that it is a mistake for historians to confine themselves purely to history (narrowly defined) and then turn their digital projects over to "experts." In this new medium, new and creative work will only come out of equal collaborations among partners with different perspectives and skills.

Chapter 1 (Exploring the History Web) provides a survey of the historical development (and current status) of the online history world. If you want to get involved with online history, you need to first get acquainted with the main genres of web-based history—the models that you will seek to emulate and exceed.

Before your first web pages are posted, you must consider a host of critical questions concerning your own and your users' wants and needs. Chapter 2 (Getting Started: The Nature of Websites, and What You Will Need to Create Yours) will walk you through the first steps in getting an online history project up and running. It then takes you "under the hood" of a history web project, outlining the operation of the "server-side"—that is, the setup and activities of the computer that historians will need to understand if they want to establish a website. Given that hardware and software options constantly change and multiply, we emphasize the basic principles of how you can structure and serve a site.

But what are you going to put on your website? That historians deal mostly in old stuff presents real hurdles to getting online. Current historians rarely rely on databases of materials created in digital form—"born digital" in the contemporary argot. Depending on the amount of material to be presented, its format, age, and condition, "becoming digital" can require a significant initial investment of time, energy, money, and technology. You need to understand these costs at the outset of any online history project. Chapter 3 (Becoming Digital: Preparing Historical Materials for the Web) discusses the costs and benefits of digitization, the digital formats to consider, ways of digitizing the past, and considerations about whether to do the work yourself or hire a commercial vendor.

In Chapter 4 (Designing for the History Web), we switch from behind the scenes to the most visible aspect of a history website. The historian's public role as a narrator and interpreter of the past requires clear and compelling expression. Although historians understand well the structural elements and composition of paper-based works such as books and essays, they generally know little about the principles and features that make for effective communication on the web. This chapter covers the basics of web design, including hypertext and multimedia, maximum access for different audiences, the use of fonts and typography, user-friendly page layouts and navigation, and the integration of images such as maps and diagrams.

A well-built, well-designed, and well-stocked history website is still like a tree falling in the digital forest if no one visits it. The Internet promises unmediated access to a potentially unlimited audience, yet this exciting possibility rarely lives up to its promise. Chapter 5 (Building an Audience) discusses strategies for attracting an audience as well as assessing its size and contours.

At least some historians will want to consider whether their audience can become co-creators of their site. Can you use the web not just to present the past but also to collect it? Chapter 6 (Collecting History Online) explores some of the ways in which the web has been used (and might be used) to build significant collections of born-digital historical materials such as first-person recollections, email, digital images, and video of events in recent memory.

Who, then, "owns" born-digital materials? And, more broadly, who owns the web pages you create or the documents that you want to present on your website? Historians who go online put themselves on both sides of the increasingly contested issues of copyright and fair use. They create intellectual property, which they may want to protect. And they very often use intellectual property—words, images, sounds, and films—owned by others. Chapter 7 (Owning the Past? The Digital Historian's Guide to Copyright and Intellectual Property) explores what every historian needs to know about copyright, fair use, intellectual property, and the collective "commons" of the web.

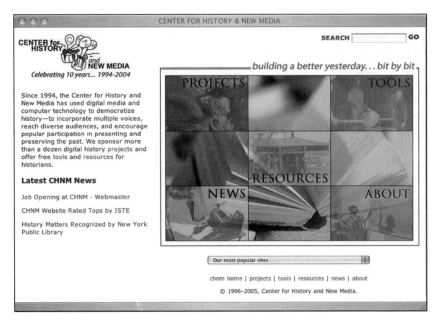

Figure 2. The Center for History and New Media at George Mason University was founded in 1994 with the goal of using digital media and computer technology to change the ways that people—scholars, students, and the general public—learn about and use the past. Many of its projects have been undertaken in collaboration with the American Social History Project at the City University of New York.

Given the central mission of their profession, surprisingly few digital historians have thought about ensuring that what has been created today in digital formats will survive into the future. Digital materials are notoriously fragile and require special attention to withstand changing technologies and user demands. In particular, projects that collect and present historical materials online assume a special responsibility for the long-term survival and availability of those materials. Online historians must therefore think prospectively, creatively, and strategically about issues of digital preservation and access. Chapter 8 (Preserving Digital History: What We Can Do Today to Help Tomorrow's Historians) will help you meet this challenge by offering simple, practical, and affordable advice.

In offering such advice, we realize that we are speaking to a diverse audience of historians—students and teachers, research scholars and museum curators, history enthusiasts and professional historians. Even more wide-ranging, no doubt, is your degree of familiarity with the subjects covered in this book. We have tried hard not to be too technical in our discussions, but we know that some readers will want more detail on audio sampling rates, and others will wonder what they are in the first place. In general, Chapters 2 and 4 are the most "technical" from the vantage point of hardware and software. To make things easier for novices, however, we have placed some more advanced topics such as databases and XML in an appendix.

We should also say something here about the authorial "we" behind the book. Most obviously, that reflects the two authors—Dan Cohen and Roy Rosenzweig. But the "we" also indicates some broader collaborations stretching over more than fifteen years. For Roy, they go back to his earliest work in new media done in collaboration with the American Social History Project (ASHP) at the Graduate Center of the City University of New York (and especially Steve Brier and Josh Brown) and the Voyager Company starting in 1990. And for Roy and Dan, they are rooted in the larger work of the Center for History and New Media at George Mason University, which Roy founded in 1994 and Dan joined in 2001. Not surprisingly, we regularly draw on our own experiences with ASHP and CHNM for examples. And for reasons of linguistic convenience, we talk about those as "our" projects, but readers should be aware those projects are the work of literally dozens of people—some of them thanked specifically in the acknowledgments and others who are credited on the web pages for those different projects.[29] Those projects have been our postgraduate education in the potentials and perils of digital history and the basis of our belief in its democratic possibilities. This book is an invitation to our fellow historians to join in exploring that potential.

Chapter 1
Exploring the History Web

In this chapter you will learn about:

- The genesis and development of historical websites
- How these sites have exploited the advantages of the web discussed in the introduction
- The ways historians have gone about translating their work to the web, through examples both large and small
- The genres of historical websites, with an eye toward defining yours

Only the brashest among us would set about composing a work of history without reading some comparable historical works first. Writing history requires that you first immerse yourself in the styles, conventions, and methods of historical writing and that you understand the different *genres* of history books, whether scholarly monograph, popular narrative, textbook, or reference work. The same holds for those who want to create history museum exhibits, make history films, and teach history classes. History website authors, however, have not always followed this simple rule, especially in the World Wide Web's first decade. Before you begin creating online history resources, you need to take a good look around the aggregate of history-related websites that we are calling the History Web. This chapter will get you started, pointing out some highlights to spark your imagination. But like any guidebook, it can only tell you where to begin your own explorations; armchair readers of a Paris Baedeker don't know the city like those who walk along its streets. (For that reason, this chapter is probably best read with a computer in front of you; links to the sites mentioned in this book are listed at http://chnm.gmu.edu/digitalhistory/links.)

When the Web Was Young

As historians, we begin with a little history. The first web pages emerged in that faraway era of the early 1990s. Email and the Internet were already becoming well known, but the web, which like email uses the

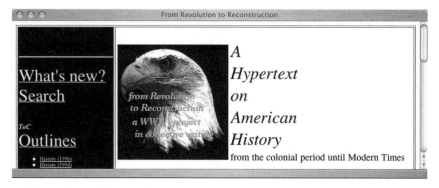

Figure 3. George Welling of the University of Groningen (Netherlands) created one of the earliest history websites in 1994. Here is how it looked in February 1999.

Internet's global computer network to share information in commonly agreed-upon ways, had its start among physicists only in 1991. It moved into the mainstream in 1993 when the National Center for Supercomputing Applications (NCSA) at the University of Illinois released Mosaic, an easy-to-use graphical web browser that ran on most standard computers. Between mid-1993 and mid-1995, the number of web servers—the computers that house websites—jumped from 130 to 22,000.

Even with the user-friendly Mosaic encouraging a major expansion of this new medium, only a few historians ventured out on the web frontier. Many of the pioneers already had some technical interests or background. In November 1994, Morris Pierce, an engineer who had recently earned a history Ph.D., created one of the first departmental websites for the University of Rochester. It "seemed like a natural thing to do," he recalls. George Welling already worked in a department of humanities computing, which the University of Groningen (Netherlands) had created in 1986. In the fall of 1994, Welling developed a course in computer skills for American history students and asked them to construct an American Revolution website. Welling's site, From Revolution to Reconstruction, quickly became one of the first popular history websites, although he observes, "it took quite some time before my colleagues accepted this as an academic venture."[1]

Other History Web pioneers came to the medium out of experience with earlier Internet applications, particularly email. In the late 1980s, Joni Makivirta, a student at the University of Jyvaskyla, Finland, started an online history discussion list because he noticed lists on other topics and thought a history list would allow him "to get ideas from professional historians around the world" for his master's thesis. The participants included George Welling; Thomas Zielke, who later took over the list; Richard Jensen, who went on to found H-Net in 1993; Donald Mabry, a Latin American historian at Mississippi State University; and Lynn Nelson, a medievalist at the University of Kansas. In 1991, Mabry—responding to the difficulty of circulating large documents via email—began to make available primary sources and other materials of interest to historians via "anonymous FTP"—a "file transfer protocol" that allows anyone with an Internet connection to download the files to his or her own computer. Nelson created his own site and then had the idea of linking the emerging set of history FTP sites into HNSource using Gopher, a hierarchical, menu-driven system for navigating the Internet that was much more popular than the web in the early 1990s. In September 1993, just after Mosaic was released, Nelson made HNSource available through the new web protocols, and it became one of the first historical sites on the web—perhaps the *very* first.[2]

In the 1980s and early 1990s, the most intense energy in digital history centered not on the possibilities of online networks but rather on fixed-media products like laserdiscs and CD-ROMs. In 1982, the Library of Congress began its Optical Disk Pilot Project, which placed text and images from its massive collections on laserdiscs and later CD-ROMs. With a large amount of material already in digital form, the library could quickly take advantage of the newly emerging web. In 1992, it started to offer its exhibits through FTP sites. Two years later, the library posted its first web-based collection, Selected Civil War Photographs.[3]

Around the time that these early settlers carved out primitive digital history homesteads, the first signs emerged that this new frontier might feature more than noncommercial exchange of documents and information. In October 1994, Marc Andreessen and some of his colleagues who had developed Mosaic at the government-funded NCSA released the first version of a commercially funded browser they called Netscape. Within months, Mosaic was, as they say, history, and Netscape was king of the World Wide Web. The Netscape era (from 1995 to 1998, after which Microsoft's Internet Explorer browser began to displace Netscape) saw the History Web come into its own.[4] In mid-1995, when one of us co-wrote the first published guide to the web for historians in the American Historical Association's (AHA) *Perspectives*, it announced, "the explosion in Web sites has brought with it an explosion in materials relevant to historians."[5] Earlier that year, the Center for History and New Media (CHNM) had helped the venerable AHA launch its website; by that summer, forty-five history departments had posted home pages.

The online presence of the AHA and the Library of Congress provided an imprimatur to the History Web. But in those early years, amateurs, not professional historical organizations, provided the crucial

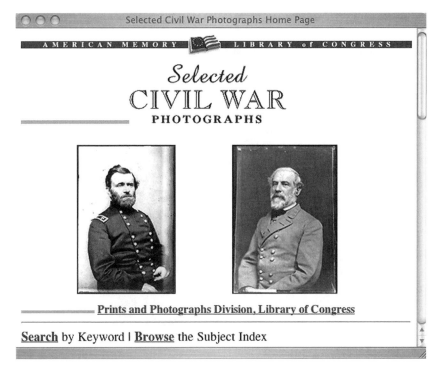

Figure 4. The Library of Congress's first web-based collection was *Selected Civil War Photographs.*

energy for much of its growth. Starting in 1995, for example, Larry Stevens, a telephone company worker from Newark, Ohio, established a series of websites on Ohio in the Civil War. The sites combined his two hobbies of history and computers, and, he explained, he "decided to carve a niche into the net before the big boys, a.k.a. the Ohio Historical Society, Ohio State University, etc., entered the field." Like Stevens, many early web history enthusiasts had some technical background. In 1994, Nicolas Pioch, a computer science instructor at the École Nationale Supérieure des Télécommunications in Paris, launched the Web Museum, which soon became an online archive of several thousand works of art. Political commitments—from Marxism to libertarianism— also motivated early web historians.[6]

Since the mid-1990s, the History Web has spun its threads with astonishing speed. We thought that we would impress readers in 1995 by telling them that a search on "FDR" brought up forty-nine "hits" in a commonly used search engine. In 2005, the same search yields 950,000 hits. In the fall of 1996, we did some additional history searches with what we thought were even more remarkable results—200 hits for the Civil War General George B. McClellan and 300 for the Socialist Eugene V. Debs. Eight years later, those same searches would overwhelm the web researcher with 97,000 and 18,000 hits, respectively. Even by 1996, the "walking city" that was the History Web a year earlier had become a sprawling megalopolis that no one person could fully explore. Yahoo counted 873 U.S. history websites in an incomplete census that fall. But seven years later, an even less complete tally returned almost ten times as many American history websites. These results reveal a deep and wide fascination with history among the web-browsing public.

Mapping the History Web

Despite the enormity of Yahoo's current history web directory, a cursory glance reveals its incompleteness. For example, it only lists 218 of the more than 1,200 history department web pages. Just thirteen online courses and syllabi make their way into the Yahoo directory; yet probably more than 15,000 history syllabi are publicly available on the web. Yahoo catalogs 888 Civil War websites, whereas the United States Civil War Center has 8,000 links in its directory.[7] Of late, Yahoo's web directory is becoming something of a historical artifact. In the first five years of the web, Yahoo was one of the dominant websites because it added the librarian's touch of classification and order to a confusing hodgepodge of sites. Now Google's rapid search of the raw mass of disorganized, heterogeneous web pages has replaced, by a tremendous margin, Yahoo's tidy directory as the leading referrer of web visitors. The brute force of computer algorithms has proven far more useful than any human cataloging.

But neither the human-created directories nor the machine-based search engine capture all of the History Web. Much of the web has moved into databases (the "deep web") that search engines have trouble accessing because they require some input from the visitor—a word or phrase—to call up their contents. Google searches on "George McClellan" don't turn up the five hundred references, including letters, photos, speeches, and sheet music, within the eight-million-item American Memory collections at the Library of Congress. In addition, only paying customers can access vast precincts of the History Web, especially those containing secondary sources and even major collections of primary sources. The most careful Google searcher will not locate the 170 references to McClellan in scholarly articles provided online through JSTOR, a subscription database gated off from the public web. And although MIT leads the charge for "OpenCourseWare," many universities keep their syllabi locked behind the doors of commercial programs like WebCT and Blackboard, thus making their educational materials unavailable to the broader world.[8]

The History Web has become so sprawling that some history websites concentrate solely on steering perplexed ramblers through the thicket. The World Wide Web Virtual Library's History Index, begun by Lynn Nelson in 1993, has evolved into a network of two hundred different gateways and more than ten thousand links with volunteers taking responsibility for developing lists on particular topics (e.g., historical journals or ancient Greece). Others have developed more specialized gateways focusing on particular topics (e.g., librarian Ken Middleton's American Women's History: A Research Guide) or audiences (e.g., retired teacher Dennis Boals's History/Social Studies for K-12 Teachers). Many of the gateways have struggled with the problems of keeping up with the proliferating numbers of sites and sorting the wheat from the chaff. Six of the nine gateways to U.S. history listed on the Virtual Library's History Index are dead or out of date, perhaps reflecting the Sisyphean task taken on by their editors. In response, some sites have emerged that emphasize qualitative filtering such as our own History Matters: The U.S. Survey Course on the Web and World History Matters, or Best of History Web Sites organized by Thomas Daccord, a high school history teacher.[9]

Comprehensive and clear categorization of the History Web has proven elusive. Yahoo and many other directories take the most conventional approach, dividing listings by region, topic, and time period. Such divisions make clear that the History Web's composition, in part, follows obvious patterns of economic and political dominance. For example, Yahoo counts 1,352 sites in British history but only 7 on Uganda. Popular history preferences clearly take precedence over professional concerns. Yahoo lists almost 3,000 genealogy sites and 900 on the American Civil War but lacks separate categories for cultural, social, and intellectual history, three of the largest areas of interest among members of the AHA. After having placed most history websites in geographic, topical, or temporal categories, Yahoo's cataloguers—many of them trained as librarians—then throw up their hands at the eclecticism of the History Web and dump the remains under a catchall heading of "Additional History Categories," which includes everything from "Archives and Bibliographies" to "Shopping and Services."

The History Web is both more and less than a good historical library. It has spotty coverage in some areas that have well-developed historical literatures. But it provides rich information on topics—African American heritage tours and popular appropriations of historical figures like FDR among them—that most libraries don't touch upon.

If conventional library categories are inadequate for mapping the History Web, are there other ways of classifying websites that provide further insight? One obvious division involves the types of authors. Because the web allows everyone to be a publisher at a remarkably low cost, amateurs and enthusiasts have a much more prominent place online than they do in print. Not only has the web called into existence a new group of grassroots historians but those nonacademic authors have acquired a much more public voice than they had before the rise of this new medium. Nevertheless, Larry Stevens's fear about the "big guys" muscling in has proven prescient. Although the number of amateur sites remains larger than those coming from professional historians or historical organizations (museums, libraries, archives), the weight of web traffic has swung in the direction of such establishments. The sites ranked as most popular by Yahoo generally come from universities, government agencies (e.g., the Library of Congress or the National Park Service), or corporations (e.g., the History Channel).

The entry of large corporations into the History Web creates two further distinctions—between commercial and noncommercial sites and between gated sites and those with open access. So far, the presence of commercial history websites within the public web has been less prominent than many assumed in the era of the Internet gold rush that began shortly after Netscape's stock price went through the roof. Discovery Communications sank more than $10 million into a site that prominently featured history. Today, it presents only historical material closely related to its cable programs. Even the original content that it expensively created in 1996 has disappeared.[10]

After the dot-com boom fizzled, the companies presenting history online were primarily those selling history as adjuncts of more traditional "bricks and mortar" businesses. Most prominent are the History Channel website (an affiliate of the cable television outlet) and TheHistoryNet (owned by Primedia, which publishes a stable of such popular history magazines as *Civil War Times* and owns About.com's online guides to a variety of subjects, including history). Both sites reflect the advantages and disadvantages of most popular history—solid writing and production values, but a tendency to avoid controversy or strong interpretations and to focus on topics like war, technology, and entertainment. This is not surprising because these sites largely support businesses (cable TV, videos, magazines) that emphasize these topics.

The greater corporate presence on the History Web is behind closed doors—the "gates" erected by vendors who sell resources to libraries, especially university libraries, who then dispense them to their customers. Global information conglomerates like ProQuest and the Thomson Corporation have developed vast online databases of newspapers, documents, and books that they license to libraries for large fees and are, hence, available only to the patrons of those libraries able to afford the stiff price.

From the perspective of those who are thinking about creating their own website, probably the most helpful way to classify history websites is by the types of materials they provide and the functions and audiences they serve. The past decade has seen the emergence of five main genres of history websites that follow preexisting patterns and categories: archives (containing primary sources); exhibits, films, scholarship, and essays (that is, secondary sources); teaching (directed at students and teachers); discussion (focused on online dialogue); and organizational (providing information about a historical group). Yet these categories are often loosely followed and frequently blurred. Almost every exhibit site has primary source documents, as do many teaching sites. Few archival sites totally abstain from historical interpretation. And a large number of sites seem to defiantly reject the categorizations neatly laid out above. This is particularly true of topical sites that are intent on covering every possible facet of a given topic rather than trying to provide a certain kind of resource or serve a specific audience.

If categorizing sites is so difficult, why bother? One good reason is that it forces the incipient History Web creator to think about genres themselves, what Phil Agre calls the "expectable form that materials in a given medium might take." Genres imply, in Agre's words, "a particular sort of audience and a particular sort of activity" and are "the meeting-point between the process of producing media materials and the process of using them." To pay attention to genres is to think about how what you are doing relates to the audience you are hoping to reach— something less necessary "in the old days, when media were few and their uses evolved slowly," or when they evolved in an ad hoc, organic way.[11] The newness of the web requires historians to be much more deliberate about what we are doing and why we are doing it. Moreover, thinking about genres focuses your attention on possible models. You may well aspire to break through categories and surpass what has been done previously—ambitions we applaud—but first you need to be familiar with what has been done before and why it was done that way.

Archival Websites

Professional archivists complain that many archival websites are not archives at all because they lack "provenance," that is, a firm history of the custody of a coherent body of materials since their origin.[12] Instead, their creators have assembled them, sometimes carefully and other times haphazardly, from diverse sources. But even archivists would consider most (though not all) of the one hundred collections in the

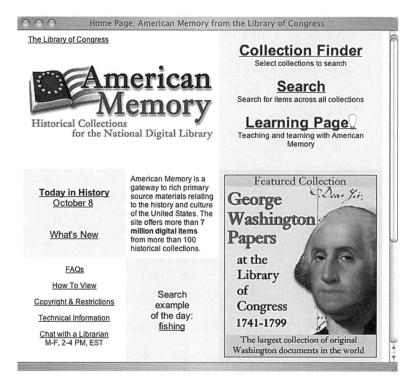

Figure 5. In a surprising bit of understatement for the usually hyperbolic web, American Memory boasts of "7 million digital items from more than 100 historical collections." The current count is more than 8 million items.

Library of Congress's American Memory website (a central component of its National Digital Library Program) "true" archives. Whatever you call them, taken together these sites are one of the History Web's greatest achievements and one of its most popular destinations.

In the early 1990s, the library distributed optical discs of major collections to test locations around the country and discovered to its surprise that K-12 teachers and students eagerly embraced the digital gifts.[13] In 1994, the library began moving these collections to the web. Less than a decade and more than $60 million later, American Memory had posted more than 8 million items. The collections cover every period of American history and almost every type of historical document in the library's collections, including books and other printed texts, manuscripts, sheet music, maps, motion pictures, photographs and prints, and sound recordings.

American Memory succeeds because it exploits two intrinsic advantages of the digital medium: accessibility and searchability (despite a cumbersome interface). Using the online version of the Washington papers, the historian Peter R. Henriques undercut the claims of those who insist on Washington's religiosity by showing not only that Washington never referred to "Jesus" or "Christ" in his personal correspondence but also that his references to death were invariably "gloomy and pessimistic" with no evidence of "Christian images of judgment, redemption through the sacrifice of Christ, and eternal life for the faithful."[14] Historians around the globe, not just those with physical access to the Library of Congress, may now conduct such investigations, and with a speed impossible when searching entailed months of manual turning of pages.

The early success of American Memory and other pioneering web archives sent hundreds of other libraries and archives to work on getting their own collections online. In 1997, for example, the Bibliothèque Nationale de France began the Gallica project to put documents in various media from the Middle Ages to the early twentieth century online. Dozens of similar projects have given the History Web a global reach: PictureAustralia presents 600,000 images from twenty-one cultural agencies, the Digital Imaging Project of South Africa offers the text of 38 anti-apartheid periodicals, the International Dunhuang Project serves up 20,000 digitized images of Silk Road artifacts, and the Nagasaki University Library displays more than 5,000 hand-tinted photographs from the second half of the nineteenth century.[15]

Beyond its own collections, the Library of Congress played an important early role in spreading digital archives in the United States. With a $2 million grant from the midwestern telephone company Ameritech (now SBC), the library sponsored a competition from 1996 through 1999 to enable museums, historical societies, archives, and other libraries to create digital collections of primary resources. Twenty-two funded collections on such topics as Chicago anarchists, the Chinese in California, the Northern Great Plains, and the Florida Everglades now reside within American Memory.

Soon other funding sources as well as the sweat equity of individuals brought dozens of other major collections online. The Academic Affairs Library at the University of North Carolina at Chapel Hill—with support from Ameritech, the National Endowment for the Humanities (NEH), the Institute of Museum and Library Services, and the university itself—created Documenting the American South, which includes six digitization projects drawn primarily from the library's Southern Collections, including massive holdings of first-person narratives and Southern literature. As with the Library of Congress, greatly expanded access to primary sources has proven to be the most significant contribution of

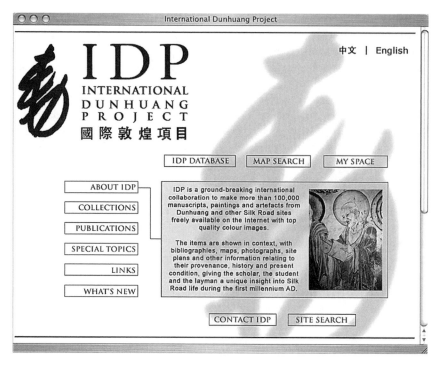

Figure 6. Over the past century, artifacts initially found in the Dunhuang caves and other ancient Silk Road sites have been dispersed among museums and private collections around the world. The International Dunhuang Project has begun to reunite—virtually—tens of thousands of these artifacts on its website. The Chinese and English interfaces reflect the international character of the project.

Documenting the American South. Although the Academic Affairs Library conceived the project as a service to Southern studies scholars at the University of North Carolina and other colleges and universities, three-quarters of the users have turned out to be nonacademics.[16]

Though American Memory and Documenting the American South have found a worthy mission in giving general and student audiences access to materials previously limited to the scholarly community, other archival projects have focused more squarely on scholars, particularly because special collections, archives, and major research libraries have been at the forefront of some of the most important and largest digitization projects. For example, the Digital Library Production Service at the University of Michigan defines K-12 and community colleges as "low priority" audiences and instead focuses on research universities and their graduate schools. Making of America, which the library developed in collaboration with Cornell University with funding from the Mellon Foundation, provides a digital library of printed materials published between 1850 and 1876. The University of Michigan portion of the collection alone encompasses more than 11,000 volumes and more than three million pages. Like scholars using American Memory, those taking advantage of Making of America for their studies can find information formerly available in principle but not necessarily in practice due to the hindrance of flipping through reams of paper. Historian Steven M. Gelber reports that he located "a treasure trove of data in a matter of a couple of days" for his research on the origins of hobbies.[17]

The ability of digital searching to turn up previously hidden riches applies particularly to records that contain large amounts of detailed information with no easy way to find specific pieces of data. Genealogists, for example, have spent days and weeks pouring over censuses and similar records seeking information on family members. Putting those records into digital form means not only saving the trek to distant archives but also gaining the chance to locate individual names with a quick word search. In April 2001, the Statue of Liberty–Ellis Island Foundation placed online a computer database of the passenger arrival records of more than twenty-two million immigrants who entered through the Port of New York and Ellis Island between 1892 and 1924. Web surfers immediately clogged the site, which was soon the number one destination from the Lycos search engine. In its first year of operation, the site received almost two million visitors. Similarly, volunteers working for the Church of Jesus Christ of Latter-day Saints digitized the records of the fifty-five million people listed in the 1880 United States Census and the 1881 Canadian Census and made them available for free at the church's FamilySearch Internet Genealogy Service, which averages 3.4 million page views per day.[18] Genealogy has long been a grassroots pursuit, but now it has become a cooperative effort whose results are shared among an international community.

The fever to bring the primary sources of the past online that began in the mid-1990s has infected many people—especially scholars and teachers, but also students and amateur enthusiasts—who think differently about documents than librarians and archivists. Their passion generally focuses on a particular historical topic, and they want to make documents related to that topic available online—even if those artifacts don't necessarily have a shared "provenance" and common association in the manner of a traditional archive. Instead, these website producers create their own virtual collections, often mixing published and unpublished materials in ways that "official" archives avoid.

One of the first and still one of the most impressive of this new genre of "invented archives" is Valley of the Shadow. Like most of the early

Figure 7. The ability to look for ancestors in online immigration records instantly made the American Family Immigration History Center a popular stop on the History Web.

work coming out of the University of Virginia's Institute for Advanced Technology in the Humanities (IATH), Valley of the Shadow had its origins in a scholarly project. In 1991, Edward Ayers, a leading Southern historian, began work on a book that would compare the experience of two communities on either side of the Mason-Dixon Line during the Civil War, Augusta County in central Virginia and Franklin County in southern Pennsylvania. In 1992, Ayers and literary critic Jerome McGann, who created a massive site about the Pre-Raphaelite poet and painter Dante Gabriel Rossetti, became the institute's first two fellows. With the aid of a large team of collaborators and several grants, Ayers began digitizing the collections that would underlie his book. Initially Ayers and McGann planned to put their new media archives on standalone computers or local networks, but when they saw Mosaic in the fall of 1993, they knew "everything had changed for our digital projects."[19]

Valley of the Shadow has since developed into a massive compendium of documents about the two communities before, during, and after the Civil War, including tens of thousands of newspaper articles, 1,400 letters and diaries, full census records from 1860, 45 Geographic Information Systems (GIS) maps, and more than 700 photographs and images.

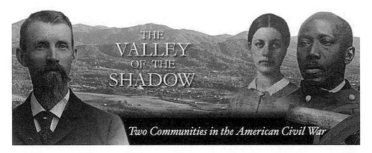

Figure 8. The Valley of the Shadow was one of the earliest sites the History Web. The copyright notice time span indicates both its pioneering status and the many years it took to complete the project.

The site offers at least an implicit interpretation of these materials rather than taking the hands-off approach of most archives, and this blurring between archive and historical argument perhaps makes Valley of the Shadow and similar sites more like edited collections of documents than traditional archives.

Jim Zwick, another early pioneer in "inventing" an online archive, brought an even more distinctive authorial voice to his efforts. In early 1995, as a Syracuse University graduate student, he began digitizing and posting a few documents on anti-imperialism, the subject of his dissertation. Like most historians, Zwick had assembled his own personal collection of sources, and he realized that these materials he had gathered for scholarly research could be made public through the web. Over time, Zwick's efforts have expanded well beyond anti-imperialism to encompass 10,500 pages of historical documents that he personally digitized.[20]

Zwick's Anti-Imperialism in the United States, 1898–1935, illustrates not only what a single scholar can accomplish with energy, passion, and

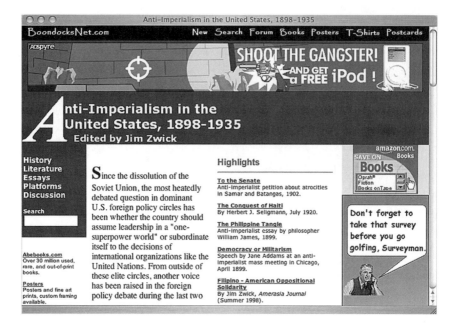

Figure 9. Jim Zwick began his Anti-Imperialism website in 1995 and has kept it going for a decade without any major grants or institutional supports. In recent years advertising revenues have helped to defray some of the expenses.

a good scanner, but also how "invented archives" can shape popular historical understanding. Zwick combines the scholar's enthusiasm for his subject with a commitment to the cause espoused by his historical subjects, and that perspective has shaped his assiduous digitizing of documents, such as his remarkable collection of more than fifty anti-imperialist responses to Rudyard Kipling's poetic apologia for imperialism, "The White Man's Burden." As a result, the researcher who types the title of Kipling's poem into Google gets Zwick's compendium of critiques as the first hit rather than a site organized by a Kipling acolyte. Similarly, despite the current popular antipathy to Marxism, the first hit on a Google search on "Marx" is the Marxists Internet Archive, a site that seeks "to show the value of Marxism."[21]

Ayers and Zwick approached the web as scholars. They created sites that grew out of their own research interests. But they quickly encountered a large student audience, eager to touch some pieces of the past, even if only virtually. This should tell us something about the latent interests and curiosity of a vast Internet audience and the potential good service that can be done as online historians.

Many others began their websites with pedagogy front and center. In

1995, Doug Lindner, a professor at the University of Missouri–Kansas City Law School, began to post some background materials for students enrolled in his course on famous trials. Lindner's Famous Trials website gradually grew to thousands of documents (maps, trial transcripts, chronologies, appeals, newspaper accounts, etc.) on thirty-five trials, from Socrates in 399 B.C.E. to O. J. Simpson in 1995. The audience has also blossomed, now including high school, college, and law school students around the world. Despite the impressive scope of the site, Lindner disavows any intention to offer a traditional archive. Such an archive would run counter to his "basic goal of providing a clear, concise, and reasonably balanced understanding of the trials." He responds to critics with a sentence that summarizes the advantages of low-cost self-publishing on the web: "I'm not getting paid a penny for this—I put up the trials that I, with all of my idiosyncrasies, find interesting or compelling in some way."[22] An even larger but still homegrown and self-financed teaching archive is Paul Halsall's Internet History Sourcebooks Project, which presents hundreds of public domain and copy-permitted historical texts for teaching organized into a family of sites, including the Internet Ancient History Sourcebook, the Internet Medieval Sourcebook, and the Internet Modern History Sourcebook.[23]

Most grassroots web archivists lack Zwick, Lindner, and Halsall's dedication, but they generally start with a similar teaching need or historical passion. Peter Bakewell and two colleagues at Emory University have posted a modest selection of primary sources on Colonial Latin America to "provide expanded access to limited documentary resources" for students in their courses. Eyler Robert Coates, Sr., a self-employed investor and consultant, wanted to publish a volume called *Quotations from Chairman Jefferson* that he saw as "freedom's alternative to 'Quotations from Chairman Mao Tse-Tung'" and began assembling quotations on more than two thousand handwritten cards. Then he learned to use a computer and in December 1995 launched Thomas Jefferson on Politics and Government: Quotations from the Writings of Thomas Jefferson, which became one of the best known and most visited Jefferson sites on the web, ranked number six by Google among sites related to the third president. Stefan Landsberger's online archive of hundreds of Chinese propaganda posters grew out of his doctoral dissertation and his desire to share his own passionate collecting. In 1995, software consultant Omar Khan started Harappa: The Indus Valley and the Raj in India and Pakistan because it was the "cheapest way" to bring his "hobby" to "the widest possible audience." It has turned into a major scholarly and teaching resource for those interested in South Asia.[24]

Not all the work of energetic, grassroots web archivists has remained noncommercial. In 1972, businessman John Adler, a history buff since his college days at Dartmouth, acquired a full run of *Harper's Weekly* (1857–1916) for $10,000. Adler decided that indexing the popular illustrated weekly would make a nice retirement project. Ultimately his efforts turned into a commercial web-based archive, HarpWeek. Despite the high price (purchasers pay $9,900 for a five-year segment), Adler has only recouped about 40 percent of the $10 million he has invested in the project.[25]

Other for-profit projects, especially from large information companies like Canada's Thomson Corporation and Michigan-based ProQuest, have made even more massive investments in digitizing the past. For example, Thomson, a "global e-information and solutions company" with close to $8 billion in annual revenues, offers Eighteenth Century Collections Online, which includes "every significant English-language and foreign-language title printed in Great Britain" in the eighteenth century—thirty-three million text-searchable pages and nearly 150,000 titles. Thomson Gale, a subsidiary of the Thomson Corporation, calls it "the most ambitious single digitization project ever undertaken" and boasts, "we own the 18th century." Those who want their own share must pay handsomely. A university with 18,000 students can spend more than half a million dollars to acquire the full collection—a hefty price, albeit less than the cost of acquiring the original books.[26]

ProQuest, formerly the camera company Bell & Howell, goes head to head with Thomson in the fight to own the past. The half-billion-dollar corporation has launched a Digital Vault Initiative to convert more than 5.5 billion pages into "the world's largest digital archival collection of printed works." Already, its ProQuest Historical Newspapers offers almost eight million online pages containing the full runs of the *New York Times, Los Angeles Times, Wall Street Journal, Christian Science Monitor,* and *Washington Post.* Plans for an even more massive digitization project have emerged recently from search engine giant Google, which intends to digitize 15 million books and make them available for free online, possibly using advertising to underwrite the costs. If they succeed, Thomson's boasts about "owning" the eighteenth century will look petty. Google will "own" the library.[27]

Massive corporate funding (and Google's soaring stock price) gives the commercial digitizers a key advantage over public sector institutions like the Library of Congress and grassroots archivists like Zwick. They can easily bear the upfront costs of converting paper into marketable bits. Moreover, in addition to the costs of scanning and indexing, the copyright ownership of most of the intellectual products of the twentieth century means that only an entity that can sell access to the past can also afford to purchase the rights to it. Under the Copyright Term

Extension Act of 1998 (see Chapter 7), almost everything published after 1923 remains covered by copyright in the United States until at least 2018. As a result, only companies with gated archives like ProQuest can offer the *Times* of London or the *New York Times* (and other newspapers) for most of the twentieth century. (Even Google faces sharp constraints on the display of copyrighted works; current plans call for them to display just limited passages and links to libraries, where the book can be borrowed, and Amazon, where it can be purchased.) Not until the twenty-*second* century will most of the history of the twentieth century find its way into free online archives.

Exhibits, Films, Scholarship, and Essays

The web offers a vast new canvas on which historians can depict and interpret the past, as we have formerly done in scholarly monographs, popular histories, museum exhibits, documentary films, high school classrooms, or family gatherings. Hundreds of thousands of secondary sources have materialized on the web in its short history. Yet although the medium is new, the interpretations are not. Most digital interpretive historical materials simply translate analog materials like museum exhibits, scholarly articles, and popular essays to the new medium. The much smaller corpus of born-digital historical sites more often originate from the computers of amateur rather than professional historians and offer few historiographic innovations. But although such digital history— whether created for the web or not—rarely departs from historiographic conventions, it vastly expands the traditionally limited audience for historical presentations and sometimes offers features not possible in print.

Online museum exhibits, for example, transcend the barriers of time (most exhibits are temporary installations), distance (museum visitors must be area residents or tourists), and space (gallery space is a scarce resource) that have often frustrated museum curators. Physical exhibits also translate naturally to the web because of their combination of text and images. After a $20 million gift allowed the Smithsonian's National Portrait Gallery to acquire Gilbert Stuart's 1796 portrait of George Washington, the museum sent the famous portrait on an eight-city tour. But even that ambitious nationwide tour left most people unable to see the exhibit. Through the web, anyone with a computer can visit the full exhibit, although not share the experience of seeing the original painting. Even Metropolitan Lives: The Ashcan Artists and Their New York, which the Smithsonian American Art Museum closed in August 1996, continues to have a virtual life. Virtual exhibits also overcome the space limitations of their analog counterparts. The online version of the New Jersey Historical Society's exhibit What Exit? New Jersey and Its Turnpike includes many full-length documents that the physical exhibit represented only through brief excerpts.[28]

Some online exhibits have incorporated additional features that physical exhibits cannot offer, or at least not as well. The San Francisco Exploratorium's Remembering Nagasaki (on exhibit in the museum in 1995) combines a straightforward presentation of twenty-five photographs taken by Yosuke Yamahata with an invitation (unconventional a decade ago) to website visitors to "share their recollections of learning about the bombing of Hiroshima and Nagasaki" and "their ideas and opinions . . . about the nuclear age in general." The curators then posted 150 of the responses on the site, where they offer a public memory space about the nuclear age. As one of the curators later commented, "The extraordinary discussion that developed during the months that this exhibit was online far exceeded any of our expectations of community dialog." Writing in the still early days of the web, he concluded, "this new tool of the Web provide[s] museums with a new way of interacting with its public."[29]

Although most online exhibits have not fulfilled this promise, some web exhibits on resonant or emotional subjects have evoked strong responses from online visitors. The site Without Sanctuary: Photographs and Postcards of Lynching in America features little more than a movie narrated by the man who collected these disturbing images. But hundreds of visitors to the site have offered deep and heartfelt responses.[30] The online version of the Smithsonian's September 11: Bearing Witness to History has led more than 6,000 people to contribute personal reminiscences about their experiences on that date. Bearing Witness has also attracted more traffic and kept visitors on the site longer than any other Smithsonian website.[31] (Chapter 6 explores in greater detail ways of turning sites into receivers, as well as exhibiters, of historical recollections and materials.)

Personal reflections on websites such as Bearing Witness and Without Sanctuary testify to the web's ability to permit and promote interactivity. Some exhibits have allowed visitors to interact with artifacts from the past. The Getty Research Institute's exhibit Devices of Wonder: From the World in a Box to Images on a Screen enables you to turn the crank of an 1870 choreutoscope (a magic lantern slide device) or watch a dancing skeleton displayed by it. Many other exhibits make use of Apple's QuickTime VR technology or Macromedia Flash to allow visitors to virtually rotate historical objects they might not be able to touch (e.g., African masks, antique motorcycles) or explore places that are difficult to reach or that no longer exist (from the Chetro Ketl Great Kiva to Julia Child's kitchen). Others engage visitors by having them solve historical puzzles or click or rollover images for more information on an artifact.

The Smithsonian's The Star-Spangled Banner: The Flag that Inspired the National Anthem asks visitors to explore a group of primary sources to "solve mysteries" such as "why the flag was altered" and "who made the flag." Rolling your mouse over the evidence reveals hidden clues that help you in solving the mystery. Then, you can compare your answer to what a Smithsonian historian says about the same primary sources.[32]

Done poorly, of course, such interactivity can border on mere gimmickry. But done well (as at the Smithsonian), these additional web features can engage users in interrogating historical evidence closely. Increasingly, major history museums such as the Smithsonian have turned their website design over to professional firms like Second Story, which gives their exhibits a much more professional feel than most history websites. Smaller museums and historic sites generally have the homemade look of less well-off relations.

Whereas most online exhibits have relatively directly translated gallery installations, some originate in a digital form. One of the earliest and most impressive examples is The Great Chicago Fire and the Web of Memory, mounted in 1996 by the Chicago Historical Society and Northwestern University under the leadership of the historian Carl Smith. It mixes extensive archival materials (maps, photographs, lithographs, letters, newspapers, and pamphlets) with interpretive essays by Smith, making the site into a combination archive, museum exhibit, and historical narrative. Some virtual exhibits have involved even more wide-ranging collaborations. For example, Voices of the Colorado Plateau brings together eight libraries and museums to present oral histories and historic photographs documenting life in the Four Corners region.[33]

At its most venturesome, the web therefore undercuts the most basic features of museums (their location in specific places, their possession or borrowing of specific objects, and the fixity and "sacredness" of those objects) and museum going (the tendency to share the experience with others). Whether or not online visitors find this virtuality as appealing as an actual museum visit remains an open question, and one that is still asked—with skepticism—by numerous museum curators.

Despite the web's ability to incorporate film footage, producers of historical documentaries have been even less inclined than curators to use the web to do something fundamentally new. Almost every major historical film has its companion site, but these web pages generally just advertise or supplement the video. Their connection to projects with extensive resources, including large advertising and marketing budgets, gives these websites some of the best production values on the History Web. American Experience, the PBS series that has broadcast more than 150 programs on U.S. history since 1988, offers sixty websites covering such diverse program topics as Abraham and Mary Lincoln, Coney Island, and Marcus Garvey. The sites generally offer timelines, images, primary sources, program transcripts, and teaching materials as well as "special features" such as games, interviews done for the programs, online forums with historians, and QuickTime VR explorations of historical places.

Not surprisingly, websites that supplement films and videos tend to be shaped by the interpretive stance of the original production. Historian Donald Ritchie observes that the website for the PBS series *The American President* reflects the focus on the character and personality of the presidents that characterized the television production. "Students using the site," he notes, "will find as much or more information about presidents' homes, spouses, and children as about their dealings with the cabinet, the Congress, and the courts." Similarly, Western historian John Mack Faragher complains that the companion website to the documentary *The Oregon Trail* does "little to suggest new historical perspectives on the trail experience—the history of gender roles, epidemic disease, or environmental impact"—and primarily promotes the film and related products.[34]

Historical scholarship translated into the online environment has been even less daring in format than museum or film efforts—a reflection of the formal conservatism of most scholars, the power of conventions in scholarly writing, and the heavily textual nature of most scholarship. Although vast quantities of scholarly work appear online, the mold of that scholarship is overwhelmingly traditional. Indeed, in some cases, online work is merely an electronic reproduction of an existing print format, with some of the major advantages of the digital form, such as searchability, tacked on. This conventionality has not, however, limited interest in these websites. JSTOR, which presents page images of the full runs of more than forty historical journals (with the exception of the most recent issues), attracts 8,500 visitors per day to its history publications despite the highly specialized content and the hefty licensing fee libraries must pay. Project MUSE, which offers the current and recent issues of almost forty historical journals in searchable text, and the History Cooperative, which offers seventeen journals, similarly attract substantial readership.[35] Quicker access than a trip to the library and the ability to search the journals by any word, as opposed to flashy multimedia or interactivity, attracts these users.

Most major online history journals open themselves only to paying customers, but some scholarly historical publications have created open-access, electronic-only journals. Not surprisingly, given their focus, the *Journal of Multimedia History* and the *Journal of the Association for History and Computing* have taken this e-route, as have more than 400 other history journals. *Common-Place: The Interactive Journal of Early American Life* seeks to transcend the narrow confines of the conventional historical publication by being "a bit friendlier than a scholarly journal, a bit more scholarly than a popular magazine." *Common-Place* also seeks to exploit the web's potential to bring "people together to discuss ideas," although it has only had modest success in providing the space for online discussion. History News Network (HNN), a more avowedly popular publication that combines history and journalism, has been more successful in sparking conversation and debate on the web. In the first six months of 2003, readers posted more than 6,000 comments.[36]

Another hybrid approach combines the article with its underlying cache of historical documents and artifacts. Virtually every scholar who writes an article or book assembles an archive of sorts. Previously they could not readily share that archive given the expense of print publications. But web-based versions of journals have begun to offer supplements of primary sources. For example, Robert Darnton's 1999 presidential address to the American Historical Association on news and the media in eighteenth-century Paris, the first article with an electronic supplement published by the *American Historical Review*, includes a map of Paris, links to police reports, illustrations, and even songs.[37]

The emerging experiments in electronic book publication such as the Gutenberg-e project sponsored by the American Historical Association and Columbia University Press, and the American Council of Learned Societies History e-book project, have also followed this practice. For example, Michael Katten's e-book *Colonial Lists/Indian Power: Identity Formation in Nineteenth-Century Telugu-Speaking India* includes photographs, sketches, maps, petitions, manuscripts, videos, statues, and palm leaf verses. The e-book version of Joshua Brown's *Beyond the Lines: Pictorial Reporting, Everyday Life, and the Crisis of Gilded Age America*, which the University of California Press published in hardcover, has more than 180 illustrations, including four slideshows comprising twenty-six images—much more visual evidence than could be encompassed in the print edition.[38]

Scholars have made only very tentative steps toward employing the digital medium to break free from the scholarly forms of the book, article, and conference paper, to reconsider such basic matters as the form of narrative, the role of illustrations and multimedia, and the writer's authority. In 1999, *American Quarterly* published four online articles on such topics as films and the Spanish-American War and photographs as legal evidence that looked very different from the standard journal fare. The most unconventional was Louise Krasniewicz and Michael Blitz's "Dreaming Arnold Schwarzenegger," which includes descriptions of more than 170 dreams about the actor (now governor), totaling more

Figure 10. Not your ordinary scholarly article: Louise Krasniewicz and Michael Blitz created the hypertext "Dreaming Arnold Schwarzenegger" because they believed it was the only way to represent the fullness of their work on the actor-turned-politician.

than 31,000 words of text, brief comments on at least eighteen of his films and detailed essays on two, fifteen magazine covers of Schwarzenegger, and dozens of 1995 emails between Krasniewicz and Blitz discussing love, life, and Arnold. Krasniewicz and Blitz embraced hypertext because the usual scholarly forms did not seem to meet the needs of their subject and their analysis. "We needed a medium, a forum," they write, "that would allow us to incorporate not just the more formal components of investigative research, but also the kinds of discoveries and reflections that are more traditionally relegated to the margins of qualitative research." For Krasniewicz and Blitz, hypertext doesn't merely do a better job of representing the fullness of their work on Schwarzenegger; it is the only way of representing it.[39]

Two online articles from the *American Historical Review* hew more closely to conventionality while still pressing the scholarly boundaries.

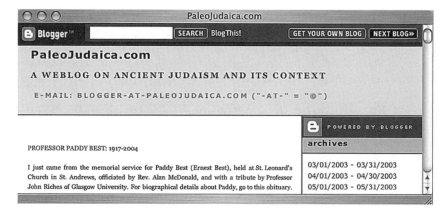

Figure 11. Like millions of other Americans, historians have taken up blogging. James R. Davila, a Lecturer in Early Jewish Studies at the University of St. Andrews in Scotland, mixes together commentaries on the *Comprehensive Aramaic Lexicon* and Mel Gibson's *The Passion of the Christ* with reports on the state of the field, including here the death of an esteemed colleague.

Philip J. Ethington's "Los Angeles and the Problem of Urban Historical Knowledge" combines a massive historical archive with a theoretical discussion of issues of historical certainty. William G. Thomas III and Edward Ayers offer their hypertext article "The Difference Slavery Made: A Close Analysis of Two American Communities" using digital media and a highly structured presentation "to give readers full access to a scholarly argument, the historiography about it, and the evidence for it."[40]

An even more experimental form that has begun to attract some academic historians is the blog. Jorn Barger, the proprietor of the *Robot Wisdom Weblog*, first coined the term in December 1997. Originally, weblogs (in Barger's definition) were simply web pages "where a weblogger . . . 'logs' all the other webpages she finds interesting." But rapidly blogs (the truncation of the word quickly took hold) became something closer to personal journals, especially popular among twenty-somethings working in dot-coms. Starting in 1999, blogs spread rapidly across the net, fueled, in particular, by the availability of easy-to-use software packages like Blogger that simplified the task of creating and maintaining a blog.[41]

In the next few years, some historians began joining in. By 2004, HNN, which sponsors eight blogs of its own, could list another twenty-three history blogs, most of them coming from academics of one sort or another. Taken as a group, the history blogs appear more about historians than history, particularly historians' takes on life and politics. Thus HNN editor Rick Shenkman's own blog, Potus, compares Bill Clinton's memoirs to other presidential memoirs and ruminates on how Ronald Reagan should be ranked compared to other presidents. The Invisible Adjunct chronicled a year in the life of a young history Ph.D. teaching without any employment security. Josh Greenberg's Epistemographer offers reflections on life, leisure, teaching, and progress on his dissertation.

But some history bloggers stick more closely to scholarship itself. In PaleoJudaica.com, James R. Davila, a Lecturer in Early Jewish Studies at the University of St. Andrews in Scotland, "chronicle[s] and comment[s] on current developments (mainly as recorded in Internet sources) in the academic field of ancient Judaism and its historical and literary context." He mixes together commentaries on the *Comprehensive Aramaic Lexicon* and Mel Gibson's *The Passion of the Christ*. It may be that history blogs will succeed where scholarly journals have failed so far and will be the basis of a new form of historical writing that challenges existing forms like the journal article. At the very least, the format represents a way to break down long-standing barriers separating academics and the public, text and image, research notes and finished narratives, and past and present. Another even more radical departure from professional norms and conventional notions of historical authority is the wiki—a piece of collaborative software that allows people to edit web pages directly through any browser. This makes it possible for history to be written and then re-written in an iterative and participatory—and some would say troublingly anarchical—process. The most dramatic example so far is the Wikipedia, a free online encyclopedia with more than a half million articles, hundreds of them on historical topics and most written by enthusiasts rather than professional historians.[42]

Web-based commercial history writing has generally not taken such an experimental approach and has moved from print to screen with few changes. The online articles at TheHistoryNet: Where History Lives on the Web—the offshoot of such popular history magazines as *Civil War Times* and *Aviation History*—are actually *less* interesting than the print originals. The web versions display mostly text and steer clear of the lavish illustrations of the print magazines—presumably to avoid the expense of picture permissions.[43]

Enthusiasts and amateurs have put the greatest energy into posting new forms of secondary literature online. Unlike the professional scholars and commercial popularizers, these amateurs traditionally have not had access to the print medium. They do not see the web as merely a new way to disseminate what has long been offered in print. Rather, it represents in many cases their first opportunity to be published. Thus the web features a new genre of popular history writing that formerly only had limited representation on library shelves—the passionate commentaries of those with a deep personal, but not professional, commitment to a historical topic. As William Thomas notes in his survey of Civil War websites, most "are not the product of universities or libraries" but rather "the work of dedicated individuals without financial reward or scholarly credit." These individuals generally display an unswerving commitment to a particular point of view rather than the detachment to which most professional historians (ostensibly) aspire. Sites devoted to such Civil War military leaders as Patrick R. Cleburne, James Longstreet, and George B. McClellan come from what Thomas and his colleague Alice Carter describe as "fans" and "partisans."[44]

The historical "fanzine"—sites created by people who are devoted to a particular topic, e.g., jazz aficionado Scott Alexander's wide-ranging Red Hot Jazz Archive—has become a major feature of the History Web. Many such sites originate out of a particular passion; others come from a strong personal connection. For example, descendants of veterans have developed many Civil War and World War II sites. Historical fanzines find an outlet on the web because the authors lack the professional credentials to find a commercial or scholarly publisher or they have a historical enthusiasm that is too narrow to merit publication. Still others emerge out of a strong connection to a particular locality. On the web, Kevin Roe's Brainerd, Kansas: Time, Place and Memory on the Prairie Plains tells the story of a community that is now virtually abandoned but even in its heyday had only 500 people, hardly the basis of a successful commercial market. Nonetheless the site has found a small, but engaged, audience among a few dozen former town residents and their relatives, who have created a virtual historical society for a community that has largely disappeared.[45]

Professional historians appreciate the ways that such enthusiasts have brought large quantities of primary sources online. Thomas praises entomologist Thomas Fasulo's "vast archive on the Battle of Olustee," with its official records and letters from participants. But historians often view the interpretations offered at these sites with more skepticism. Thomas notes that many Civil War websites "broadcast old prejudices, ancient theories, and long-disproved arguments about the Civil War" such as the "idea that the Civil War was fought not over slavery but over economic differences having to do with the tariff."[46] The amateurs may have leapt ahead of the professionals in using the web as a vehicle for original publication, but their interpretations often look backward rather than forward. The amateurs could learn some historiographic lessons from the professionals while in turn teaching those who practice history as a vocation to think beyond traditional forms of publication.

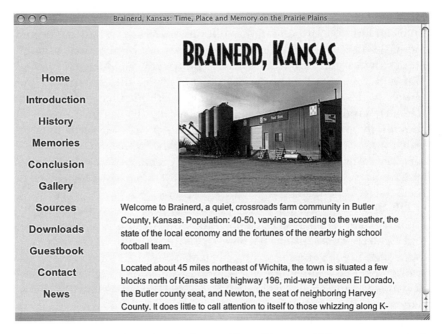

Figure 12. Kevin Roe's Brainerd, Kansas: Time, Place, and Memory was created initially to fulfill a course requirement but has been sustained by the author's passion for the now almost abandoned town where his grandmother once lived. It has become a virtual historical society for former residents and their relatives who have deposited a rich collection of memoirs in the site's guestbook.

Teaching and Learning

Scholarly, public, and popular historians who have gone online have repeatedly confirmed the Library of Congress's early discovery that the web reaches unprecedented numbers of K-12 students and teachers. As a result, a very large percentage of websites, regardless of their primary focus, have incorporated teaching materials and advice. Although traditionally archives and libraries have eschewed a direct teaching function, on the web they have often embraced it. American Memory's Learning Page offers many resources for teachers, including lesson plans, tips on searching the collections, and links to other websites. The National Archives and Record Administration's Digital Classroom offers a similar array of resources. Online lesson plans have become so ubiquitous that no one has yet cataloged them.[47]

Many museum sites offer extensive teaching resources. The Smithsonian's online version of the exhibit The American Presidency: A Glorious Burden includes lesson plans, advice on using the site with students, and an annotated bibliography. Linked to the virtual exhibition George Catlin and His Indian mounted by the Smithsonian American Art Museum (Renwick Gallery) is an extensive "Catlin Classroom" organized around Campfire Stories with George Catlin: An Encounter with Two Cultures. It includes four multimedia exhibitions featuring artworks by Catlin, a searchable database of Catlin's writings and hundreds of his artworks, fourteen lesson plans, and an online discussion board. The openness of the web to multiple audiences has even led some scholarly journals to think about teaching, a subject rarely broached within their covers. For example, the *Journal of American History* has created a site called Teaching the *JAH*, which focuses on an article from each issue and offers teaching suggestions and related primary sources.

Although teaching enters at some level into many archival, museum, and even scholarly websites, many sites relate primarily to teaching and learning. The most ubiquitous and numerous of these are syllabi— surely the most common history websites. Perhaps 30,000 history syllabi are posted on the web, with about half of those gated behind passwords through university sites and commercial courseware like WebCT and Blackboard. But even just the publicly available syllabi provide a remarkable snapshot of the state of history teaching: How are courses conceptualized and structured? What books are being assigned? They also sadly reflect on the limited design skills of most historians, a topic that we consider in Chapter 3.[48]

Most online syllabi reduce logistic hassles endemic to college courses, such as frequently needing to hand out lost assignments. Some, however, aim much higher. The online syllabus for Stanley Schultz's University of Wisconsin telecourse on the United States since the Civil War includes lecture notes, biographical sketches, exams and review sheets, a photographic gallery, and a directory of history websites. Our GMU colleague Michael O'Malley has mounted several online syllabi that are notable for their clear interfaces and creative design. His most elaborate effort supplements an inventive course, "Magic, Illusion, and Detection at the Turn of the Last Century." The website not only provides a syllabus and an extensive collection of primary sources (including books, posters, images, and early movies) but also a mystery about turn-of-the-century identity that students are asked to solve. Along the way, it expresses an original historical thesis in nonnarrative, multimedia terms.[49]

Course websites are almost always individual efforts. As a result, they reflect a personal vision, even one that is embodied only in the structure of course assignments, owing to limited design skills and time constraints. Particularly energetic and creative instructors like O'Malley, however, transcend these obstacles. The most extensive teaching sites

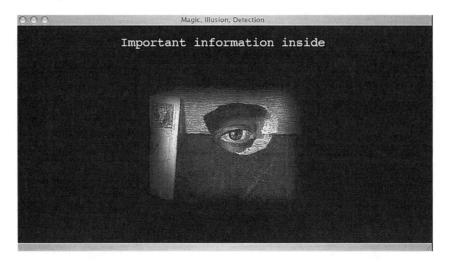

Figure 13. The home page for Michael O'Malley's course on "Magic, Illusion, and Detection at the Turn of the Last Century" beckons students to join in an online investigation of the past.

generally reflect the efforts of a group or institution and external funding support from an agency like NEH, which has underwritten many online teaching projects.

Some of these large-scale projects have developed portals or resource centers for teachers in particular areas. For example, historians Thomas Dublin and Kathryn Kish Sklar at Binghamton University have, with support from NEH, created Women and Social Movements in the United States, 1775–2000. The site contains more than forty mini-monographs designed to be used in teaching; each one poses an interpretive question and offers a set of primary documents related to that question. Similarly, TeacherServe at the National Humanities Center offers extensive online materials for teaching about religion and the environment in American history.[50]

Still other projects strive to offer resource centers for even broader swaths of history. History Matters: The U.S. Survey Course on the Web, developed by CHNM in collaboration with the American Social History Project (ASHP) at the CUNY Graduate Center, presents a range of materials for teachers of U.S. history, including 1,000 primary documents in text, image, and audio; an annotated guide to more than 800 websites; model teaching assignments; sample syllabi; and moderated discussions about teaching with leading scholars. A companion site, World History Matters, makes available some similar materials across an even broader canvas. Both sites also seek to give students the skills and tools needed to analyze the enormous number of primary sources that have become available online. As Randy Bass has pointed out, the web has put the "novice in the archive," but it has not taught him or her what to do there. Thus History Matters and World History Matters provide guides and interactive exercises showing students how "expert learners" make sense of primary source evidence like films, music, maps, and travelers' accounts and demonstrating how historical insights are formed.[51]

Most teaching websites offer resources (especially primary sources) and advice (for teachers on how to teach, for students on how to work with evidence). What has been talked about endlessly but has been much harder to achieve is interactive learning exercises. A significant challenge with computer feedback is the difficulty of portraying the subtlety and ambiguity of real history through the either/or, yes/no choices encouraged by the binary nature of digital logic. One approach that two innovative sites offer is to provide exercises—in both cases, mysteries—that have no right answer and where the learning comes through the exploration. ASHP's The Lost Museum, centered around a three-dimensional re-creation of P. T. Barnum's American Museum as well as a searchable archive of primary documents and a set of teaching activities and background essays, asks students to solve the mystery of who burned down the museum in 1865—a mystery with no answer but one that requires an exploration of antebellum life and culture to offer a plausible solution. Who Killed William Robinson? Race, Justice and Settling the Land similarly presents students with the problem of solving the murder of William Robinson, an African American who was killed on Salt Spring Island in British Columbia in 1868.[52]

Discussion and Organizational Sites

Email appeared on the Internet almost twenty years before the web, and it remains the most important channel of online historical communication and debate. H-Net, established in 1993, dominates the world of online historical discussion with more than 150 lists on everything from African expressive culture to utopian studies. Another very early Internet form—the newsgroup—also remains an arena for popular discussion of the past with fourteen history groups available through Usenet discussion forums.[53] Although the web, like email and newsgroups, is fundamentally a communication medium, it has not yet proven to be a primary location for historical discussion. Most successful have been commercial websites that provide spaces for people with shared interests or experiences to engage in online debate and conversation.

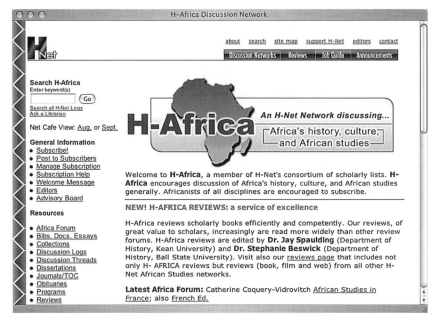

Figure 14. H-Net, established in 1993, "creates and coordinates Internet networks with the common objective of advancing teaching and research in the arts, humanities, and social sciences." It sponsors more than 150 lists on topics ranging from narrow specialties such as architectural stained glass to broad topics such as world history that reach more than 100,000 subscribers in more than ninety countries.

For example, the History Channel has active discussion boards on wars, religion, and sports that have attracted thousands of comments.

The liveliest of those discussion groups are those like the one on the Vietnam War in which participants share reminiscences and experiences. Similarly, SeniorNet has found a large following for online discussions of World War II about veterans and those who lived through the war on the home front. Though the goal in SeniorNet is more recreational and therapeutic than historical, some other sites have focused more directly on using the Internet to collect the past. For example, our own Echo project and some other websites supported by the Alfred P. Sloan Foundation have gathered online reminiscences on such diverse topics as women in science and engineering, the New York City blackouts of the 1960s and 1970s, the information theorist Claude Shannon, and electric cars. (Chapter 6 discusses these and similar sites in more detail.)

Now that the web has displaced the library and perhaps the phone book as the first place most people go to find information, it has become necessary for every historical organization to stake out a home on the web so that people can find them and learn about their activities. Every major and minor historical organization, whether professional or popular—from the American Historical Association to the Wisconsin Historical Society to the Third Regiment Infantry, Maryland Volunteers (a group of reenactors)—has its website. More than 1,200 college and university history departments use the web to inform current and prospective students about faculty, course offerings, and other resources.[54]

Historical societies, historic sites, and historic houses that want to attract visitors find the web the perfect way to let those visitors know about hours and directions. Some historic places and museum sites go considerably beyond such barebones information. The extensive Monticello website not only tells you how to plan your visit; it also provides detailed narratives about Thomas Jefferson and his house as well as virtual reality panoramas of all the house's public rooms, teaching resources, and research materials on controversial subjects like Jefferson's relationship with Sally Hemings. The National Park Service's Links to the Past, which connects web surfers to the two hundred NPS history locations as well as a wealth of other resources, attracts heavy web traffic.[55]

The slipperiness of these web history categories seems to be one of the web's characteristics; its heterogeneity almost inevitably blurs genres. Many archive sites offer historical interpretations and some museum sites provide teaching materials in addition to archives. Still, most of these sites fit predominantly in one category or another. At the same time the web has also given birth to a set of sites that aspire to provide everything or almost everything on a particular topic—primary sources, interpretive commentary, teaching materials, and discussion. Such a topical approach does not have obvious counterparts in the analog world where historical work is more clearly defined by relatively discrete audiences—researchers, scholars, students, or museum-goers, for example.

Some of the most impressive history sites on the web are massive topical sites, which provide a kind of one-stop shopping on a particular historical topic—such as University of Virginia American literature professor Stephen Railton's two websites Mark Twain in His Times and Uncle Tom's Cabin & American Culture, or DoHistory, an exploration of the diary of the eighteenth-century midwife Martha Ballard and Laurel Thatcher Ulrich's Pulitzer-Prize-winning study of it.[56] Yet topical sites are also among the weakest history websites because they sometimes lack focus and wind up being a hodgepodge of materials centered on a particular theme. Often, it makes more sense to try to excel at one

thing—at providing access to a rich archive, offering an intriguing interpretive exhibit, or supplying effective classroom tools or resources—
rather than straining to cover areas and reach audiences that go beyond
your talents or resources.

Even such a quick tour of the History Web reveals its potential and its
problems. For those who are seeking to get themselves started online, it
also suggests two basic steps that you should take before you put pixel to
screen. First, become familiar with what has already been done. The ten-
year record of the History Web has provided an abundant corpus of sites
that you can explore in detail and get ideas and inspirations—about
content, about design, about infrastructure—for your own efforts. Our
hurried excursion has no doubt emphasized well-known and conventional sites at the expense of the quirky and out-of-the-way corners of the
History Web. But we have done so with the conviction that a thorough
knowledge of standard practices is the starting point for building unconventional history websites that combine a personal voice and inventive
design with unusual primary sources and startling new historical interpretations.

Second, think hard about the "genre" of site you are creating. Is this
meant to be an archive of primary sources, a presentation of a historical
interpretation (whether done visually or in text), a resource for teaching, a place for discussion, an advertisement for a historical organization, or a combination of some or all of the above? To answer such
questions forces you to think about your audience—the community of
people you want to reach—as well as your most basic goals in doing digital history. Before you begin the more practical steps in the journey outlined in the next seven chapters you need to know why you are taking
that journey, who you hope will join you, and where you hope to go.

Chapter 2
Getting Started
The Nature of Websites, and What You Will Need to Create Yours

In this chapter you will learn about:

- The basic technologies behind the web
- Additional technologies that different genres of historical websites use
- How to match appropriate and properly scaled technologies to your particular project
- How to produce and serve digital text, images, and multimedia
- When to use databases and markup languages like XML
- What domain names are and whether you need one
- Hosts for your website
- Whether you might need to pursue funding for your site and how to do so

The wide variety of historical websites is accompanied by an almost equally varied set of methods for producing them. This should come as no surprise; in the equally diverse world of paper, authors, publishers, and printers produce the *Dictionary of National Biography*, a textbook on world history, a scholarly monograph on the Carolingian dynasty, and a popular biography of Susan B. Anthony in significantly different ways. Even the casual reader notices variations among bindings, paper, front and back matter, and other clues about the nature of such works. In their area of specialty, historians often can detect how a work was produced, when, and for what reason from characteristic nuances in the composition and material of printed sources. We can all gauge the size and length of a printed work through a cursory glance.

On the web, the seemingly clear window of the browser obscures many of these helpful clues. Type in an address (also known as a uniform resource locator, or URL, in the acronymic terminology of the Internet that will dot this chapter but we hope not spoil it), and the browser magically fishes a "web page" out of the wide sea of the

Internet. Although sometimes colorful, these web pages do not come in all shapes and sizes. The relatively small set of universally available fonts on computers and the low resolution (compared to print) of a web browser window restrict, somewhat, the potential for visual distinction. Moreover, you cannot easily assess from a web page the size of the website to which it belongs, in the way you do instantly and unconsciously when picking a book from a shelf. A web page is a web page is a web page.

Or so it appears. The truth about these "pages" is that they involve just as much human input as a papyrus or pamphlet, even if they can be reproduced virtually without limit or cost once created. Indeed, web pages probably require more shepherding than such physical manifestations of human expression. After a book page is printed or diary entry recorded, it is "fixed" (to use the U.S. Copyright Office's favorite word) in a form that will likely survive for generations.

A web page, on the other hand, can fall prey to unique electronic fates: it can be deleted, altered, or corrupted, or become technologically obsolete. Moreover, authors of web pages can produce them in a variety of ways, ranging from simple computer files similar to those produced by word processors to highly dynamic compositions that involve complex programming, databases, and the efforts of multiple computers. Visitors searching for information about the history of Douglas County, Kansas, via Google, the popular web search engine, and through the home page of the Douglas County Historical Society, for instance, proceed through two useful "pages" in their browser. Both pages are written in the HyperText Markup Language (HTML) that is the programming lingua franca of the web, and both include some text, an image in the upper left, and the links that are part of most web pages. In this sense, these pages do not seem that different, yet the Google results page is the nearly instantaneous creation of roughly 100,000 computers working in tandem, whereas the Douglas County Historical Society uses 99,999 fewer machines to satisfy web surfers interested in the same topic.[1]

This comparison is not meant to belittle the Douglas County Historical Society nor their website. Much the opposite. It points to a fundamental rule that all historians looking to move onto the web should follow: The technology used to produce a website should be appropriate for the website's content and purpose. The Douglas County Historical Society doesn't need 100,000 computers. Surely it could use this number if it wanted to (having first attained record levels of funding for a local historical society), but it would be more trouble than it would be worth. The number of visitors, type of information being presented, and extent of its site make such a purchase unreasonable. This may seem an obvious point, but new website creators often try to use too much technology for a project, or too little. For example, an archive of 20,000 documents like the New Deal Network could consist of 20,000 individually authored web pages, but it would be much better for it to consist—as it does—of a small computer program that creates those 20,000 pages automatically from a database.[2] Among other advantages, when the creators of the site want to change the look of every page, they only have to make a single change to the program rather than manually edit thousands of pages.

The teacher who wants to supplement a course syllabus with online student interactions could achieve this goal in several ways, from an email list to a web-based bulletin board to instant messaging to a blog to a wiki to commercial course management software. Each has its advantages and disadvantages, and level of required technical proficiency, and you need to understand these differences before committing too many or too few resources to this addition. Guides to creating websites often begin with stern warnings to plan ahead. This strikes us as a case of the cart coming before the horse. How can you plan your website when you are not sure whether you need a database or not, or even what a database is and what it can and cannot do? By looking "under the hood" of the History Web, this chapter provides background information to help historians make good decisions about which technologies and methods they will need for their particular digital project. This exploration, in turn, leads to further considerations about funding, staffing, and hardware and software purchases.

The Web, Websites, and Web Pages

A basic but useful question to think about before pondering more sophisticated technologies such as databases is: What is a website? Despite a certain amount of variation, historians have a good idea of what a book is and how it is produced. An author, editor, publisher, and printing mechanism are involved in a rough order and with roughly the same results, independent of the topic. Once produced, the book sits on a shelf awaiting readers. It has a firm existence. The comparison between the Google results page and the Douglas County Historical Society home page, however, gives the potential website producer the slightly unsettling feeling that websites lack any fixed characteristics, and that the answer to the question of what a website is depends on what the definition of "is" is.

In the case of the Douglas County Historical Society, the home page file was already sitting on a designated computer, waiting to be requested like a book on a specific shelf in a particular library. In the case of the Google web page describing the results of the user's search for information about Douglas County, the swift, combined efforts of thousands of computers created this file. Like the proverbial tree falling in the forest, the Google page came into existence only when a user wanted to view it, and it vanished once the viewer moved on. Google search results, thus, lack the reassuringly fixed quality of cards in an old-fashioned library catalog.

Most historians don't need to worry about the ontological status of expansive websites like Google, which seemingly contain everything and nothing at once, like Jorge Luis Borges's imagined "Library of Babel," which holds seemingly infinite volumes with every possible combination of letters.[3] (We do outline the technologies for producing fairly complex sites later in this chapter, and in greater depth in the appendix, for those who need to build them.) Although you can produce a website in many ways, beginners should recognize that a *website* is basically a collection of web pages, and a *web page* is simply a file produced or stored on one computer in a particular format that is sent to another computer that has requested it. The producing computer, generally turned on twenty-four hours a day and constantly connected to the Internet, is called a *server*, and the computer requesting a file from the server is called a *client*. The server computer must be running special software to send a file, and the client must have special software (a web browser) to receive and display the file. Beginning with first principles therefore reveals that you need very little to become involved in web production. If you have access to a server and can create one or more files to put there for others to request, you can have a website.

Moreover, the decentralized structure of the Internet—designed as a highly distributed network of machines (unlike the centralized telephone switching system of a prior era)—means that the locations of the server and client are essentially irrelevant. Your web browser software (such as Internet Explorer, Firefox, or Safari) cares not about the physical whereabouts or types of servers involved, nor about the path a file takes to it, as long as it receives that file promptly and in a language it can understand, namely, HTML. An open standard associated with HTML, called the HyperText Transfer Protocol, transmits web pages from one computer to another, but historians need not worry about this except perhaps to recognize its abbreviation, HTTP, which begins every web address.

The file that the server sends generally consists of regular text surrounded by HTML passages that tell a browser how to format the regular text, point to other web pages (through links), as well as request additional materials (e.g., images) from the server to complete the page. (More complicated pages may also have additional instructions, in non-HTML languages, telling the web browser software to take special actions in response to the activities of the user.) The simple but elegant idea behind HTML is thus to "wrap" passages of text with text markers, or tags, that identify the passage's contents, much like the front and back cover help to identify the contents of a book. For example, a web author might surround a book title with <i> and </i> tags, which turn the contents between them into italics when displayed by a web browser. The angle brackets signal the tag format, and the backslash symbol / indicates the end of that format. Those who are curious may look at the "source code" of a web page by selecting that option from their browser's menu. A typical HTML preamble looks something like this:

```
<html>
<head>
<title>My History Site</title>
</head>
<body bgcolor = "#FFFFFF" text = "#000000" link = "#0000CC"
vlink = "#800080">
<p>The history of . . .
```

As you can see, unlike the incomprehensible ones and zeros of the programming code that runs your computer or software applications like a word processor, the World Wide Web code is largely readable text—and new authors of websites should not be afraid to take a peek at it.

Indeed, a significant feature of the web is that anyone who writes a web page also exposes to the world the code used to create it. Historians should find this nicely matches our discipline's emphasis on the open dissemination of knowledge. Whatever the future brings, the web will likely remain a place built on freely viewable text code, and if some historians feel uncomfortable with the technology, they should still feel an affinity toward its underlying principles.

Thinking About Your Website's Genre and Features

Newcomers to the web (as well as many old-timers) are often tempted to focus, sometimes obsessively, on the technology. After all, technology is what most obviously distinguishes the web from our former primary realm of expression—paper—and despite our best efforts, we could not get through even the introduction to this chapter without delving into several technical computer terms. Individuals who are used to the world of books and journals often find themselves overwhelmed by the web's technological otherness, and its myriad terms and concepts—HTML, servers, design and graphics software, and a host of other acronyms like FTP and ISP.

After more than a decade of experience with web production, we feel that this temptation to focus primarily on technology is misplaced. Not only can it be daunting, it can be distracting. If you were thinking about building a house, how much time would you spend concentrating on the type of plumbing you would like to use or the amperage of the electrical service? How long would you spend thinking about the types of wrenches you would use to install the hot water heater? These elements are important—indeed, critical to the construction of a modern house (especially the indoor plumbing)—but few would say that they define a house and make it what it is.

Although both are honorable professions, we encourage historians to think of themselves more like architects than plumbers. What kind of house are you building? What is the general area that it will be in? How will its design reflect or differ from the other houses in the neighborhood? Are you building a mansion or a cabin? In the same way that you would plan a book with a clear sense of purpose, content, and audience—is it a reference work, a monograph for specialists, a popular introduction to a subject?—you should ask yourself some preliminary questions about the genre and scale of the website you are planning to build, and about the key features it will have. These sorts of questions are very different from technical questions such as, "What kind of server should I put my site on—Windows or Linux?" or "Which software is better for website development—Dreamweaver or FrontPage?" or "Which is a better database—Oracle or MySQL?" These questions should be secondary, not primary. For instance, if you are just posting a syllabus to a website, you don't even need to use a dedicated web development software program like Dreamweaver. Microsoft Word may be just fine.[4] The answers to the primary questions lead to answers to many of the secondary, technological questions, such as whether you need a database at all.

In the spirit of beginning with first principles, we might also pose a question you should answer even before thinking about your website's genre and features: Do you really need to spend the time to build a website at all? Although this book is a guide to the History *Web*, and we believe that the web has many virtues to recommend it (as we noted in the introduction), not all historical endeavors require a website. Some historical projects would be better off remaining on paper or in personal computer files, such as research notes that you don't want exposed to the world. Compared to graphically sophisticated productions such as a full-color, large-format art history book, the web still pales. Other projects might function better by using nonweb computer technologies, such as email. Email remains the most frequently used application on the Internet, and historians should not be embarrassed to stick with that simpler method. Ongoing communications about a historical subject, such as the Sixties-L discussion group (on the turbulent 1960s) or the wide variety of H-Net topics, are often carried out better via email.[5] Soberly assessing the web's advantages and disadvantages and how they apply to your project will mean a clear-eyed entry into the digital world.

If you still desire a website, you should then consider what you will need to build it. Again, focusing on the genre of website you plan to build will help you answer secondary questions such as technological requirements. Begin by investigating other websites on your topic, and websites that have a similar mission to yours. For instance, if you are planning a website on the American photographer Weegee, look at other sites on the man and his images, and other historical photography websites. Do you envision a site that functions like a large gallery of Weegee's photographs that visitors can wander virtually through (an "exhibit" as we categorized it in Chapter 1), or a site that is more like an online essay, with a smaller set of images chosen to illustrate a scholarly thesis?

Furthermore, assess what you like and dislike about the comparable sites you visit. How will your site differ from them, in scale, features, or content? Contact the creators of the best sites to ask them about their site-building experience. Did they have unforeseen problems that they could help you avoid? Did they discover some shortcuts to getting this kind of material onto the web? Which technologies or assistance did they find most useful—a good scanner, a web design company, a server host? If you can roughly match your website's ambitions to an existing site—allowing for Chapter 1's caveat that sites are hard to categorize and compare perfectly—you will begin to understand what you will need for your own creation.

Focus next on the features that will distinguish your site. What do you want, and what will you need? For a site on the Alhambra, you may want an interactive "zoomable" map that visitors can click on to explore different areas; to serve a diverse audience, including many nonspecialists, you may need a glossary of Arabic terms. Once you have a list of features, arrange them in order of priority. Which features do you absolutely need to launch the site to the public? Which features could wait? Perhaps some could be implemented later—or not at all if you run out of time or resources. Inherent in this analysis, of course, is some sense of how much effort (including technological complexity, staffing, cost, and time) each feature will require, to which we now turn.

Text and Images

Luckily the most prevalent genres of historical websites are also the easiest to produce. Most teaching websites, such as online syllabi and course materials, as well as text-heavy scholarship such as essays, require little technology beyond rudimentary website software. You can safely put your site into this category if you plan on having only text and static images, and a reasonably limited number of pages. As we have already noted, the web is set up to handle text seamlessly (it is, in a sense, text with embellishments), and images can be added to web pages relatively simply.

Many computer programs can help you create the files that make up such basic websites. These programs require varying levels of HTML or other technical knowledge. HTML "translators" exist for those who would rather not learn the web argot, but other website creators may choose to struggle through their pages in the "original" language. In a beneficial and relatively recent development, many programs that were not designed for web production now allow users to save files as web pages, without knowledge of HTML at all. For instance, Microsoft added this feature in the 2000 edition of Word, and Excel and PowerPoint can now do the same. Undoubtedly the "save as web page" feature will become even more prevalent, and more useful, for those who do not have the time to learn more complicated programs. Although they may be less sophisticated than web pages designed from the ground up with dedicated web development software, such pages will be viewable on the web with little fuss.[6]

Like Word, software designed specifically to produce a website runs on your personal computer and allows you to build pages before upload-ing them to a server. Currently Macromedia's Dreamweaver ($399; $99 with the educational discount) is by far the most widely used website development software, and for good reason: it has a visual "what you see is what you get" (often abbreviated WYSIWYG and pronounced WIZ-e-wig) interface that both novices and more advanced designers appreci-ate, and the ability to automate often onerous tasks in HTML like defin-ing tags and their attributes properly. Microsoft's FrontPage ($199; $99 with the educational discount) has most of the rest of the WYSIWYG market. FrontPage has fewer total features than Dreamweaver, and those new to web design may find that a blessing—indeed, most users of Front-Page are novices or nonprofessionals—but the program does a poorer job than Dreamweaver at complying with web standards, which may make sites developed with Microsoft's program look somewhat different on various computers and browsers, and harder to maintain in the future (see Chapter 8 on the usefulness of conforming to web standards such as XHTML). Free programs for creating basic websites with text and images also exist; they are generally usable, though not fantastic. First Netscape and now its free descendant Mozilla include the Com-poser HTML editor as part of a free web browser package.[7]

Although programs such as Dreamweaver and FrontPage do a good job at layout and design, and are more than adequate for most historical websites, they may not allow for pinpoint precision and control of every aspect of every web page. At the high end of the learning curve are programs that work directly in HTML without a graphical representation of what that text will look like when rendered by a web browser. Although they provide the greatest control of the final product, such programs (often just text editors pressed into service for web production) are the most daunting for novices because they require a comprehensive understanding of HTML. Historians with little background in web production should therefore think twice before using one of these editors. It would be nice to read Dante's *Inferno* in Italian, but you have to decide if the benefits outweigh the hassle of learning Italian (though surely that has other rewards), and whether you might just pick up a translation instead. If you do require the level of precision these programs allow, or if you already know HTML and feel comfortable looking at plain text without a graphical interface, you should look into programs such as EditPlus ($30), UltraEdit ($35), or BBEdit (for the Macintosh; $179).[8]

If you are at a college or university, your institution probably also has web-based software to help you build an online syllabus or course website. Common instances of this "server-side" software (as opposed to software like FrontPage or Dreamweaver that runs on your personal computer) are WebCT and Blackboard. These software packages have much to recommend them. First, they save you from having to install a program on your own computer. Second, they generally have templates for syllabi, saving you the time it takes to design your online course materials. Third, after you finish typing in the text and adding images, the page is already where it can be visible to other people, such as students (you can also hide the site from nonstudents if you want). And because of licensing agreements, this software is generally free to historians— though it costs universities roughly the equivalent of an assistant professor's salary to install and license Blackboard or WebCT for a single year. (The expense of the commercial packages and worries about course materials being in the hands of corporations has led recently to the development of an open source competitor to these programs known as Sakai.) Blogging software, which also runs on servers rather than clients and is discussed in greater detail in Chapter 6, also makes it easy to move text and images onto the web for courses or other simple history sites.[9]

Server-side software like WebCT, Blackboard, and blogging programs can have significant disadvantages, however. As in the political philosophy of Thomas Hobbes, you trade the ability to do whatever you like for the security of a controlled environment. The templates save time, but they also severely restrict your creativity in building a course website. A distinctive look or layout may be impossible, and video and other forms of multimedia are sometimes difficult to add. Depending on the installation of the software by your institution or blog company, other restrictions may hinder you in a way that you could avoid by using your own software or personal server space (see below for the pros and cons of different web "hosts"). In addition, either intentionally (based on the default settings of the system) or unintentionally (by the choice of their creators) syllabi and course materials within these commercial programs are often difficult to access by outsiders, a questionable segregation opposed to the ethos of open access championed by laudable projects like MIT's OpenCourseWare.

None of the server or client programs for creating websites provides a powerful way to compose, resize, or modify the images you will use. This task requires a dedicated graphics program, which you generally have to install on your personal computer. After you create (or modify) images in this program, you upload them into your web folder on your server, where they can be attached to specific web pages. By far the most venerable and capable of these image manipulation programs is Adobe Photoshop, which has an enormous following among professional web designers because it can generate, alter, and enhance not just photographs but also line drawings and more complex graphics. (It can also doctor photographs easily and with almost no trace, which in the future will give historians fits like Stalin's airbrushers.) Unfortunately Photoshop costs $649 (about half that with the educational discount) and runs better on the most powerful (and thus most expensive) computers. Luckily, Adobe also produces a slimmed-down image editing package called Photoshop Elements that includes many of the important features of its more robust sibling for a mere $99 ($59 with educational discount). Photoshop Elements should be an easy choice for most historians who need to do a fairly circumscribed set of tasks like resizing, cropping, and compressing images for their website (more on this in Chapter 3).

In addition to Adobe's offerings, Macromedia's Fireworks has more features than Photoshop Elements but fewer than the senior Photoshop (Fireworks sells for $299, $99 with the educational discount). Some historians may prefer to use Fireworks rather than Photoshop or Photoshop Elements because they can buy Fireworks as part of an integrated suite of web design programs (including the leading authoring software Dreamweaver) for $899 ($199 with the educational discount). You can find many other image editing software packages (including some free utilities that come with Windows), but Fireworks and the two Photoshops are the most capable programs on the market, and their special features help make images truly web-worthy.[10]

Multimedia

Once you move beyond the text and images associated with most basic history websites into the multimedia found on many exhibition and archive sites, as well as most sites on the history of music and film, you face additional hurdles. Although the web can handle audio and video, it often doesn't do a very good job compared to dedicated platforms (such as a CD or DVD player), and such multimedia adds a layer of complexity to any website. Two reasons for this complexity exist. First, moving from static elements like text and images to audio and video involves a quantum leap in the heft of a web page, or more accurately the file size of its multimedia components. Second, audio, video, animation, and other multimedia formats unfold over time, and thus raise the question of *streaming* versus *downloading*. If a video is 100 megabytes, do you really want to make a viewer wait for the entire file to download before beginning its display—about two hours on a 56K modem or fifteen minutes on a high-speed connection? (In 2004, the number of Americans accessing the Internet with a fast broadband connection finally surpassed the number of slow modem users, but that still leaves tens of millions of potential viewers in a poor position to receive large video files.) The alternative, streaming, downloads only the first bit of the movie and continues to download segments in the background as the viewer begins to watch the film immediately. Impatient viewers clearly prefer this method—yet it means that the website producer has to deal with additional, complicated software on the server.

Unlike the standards that undergird the web, such as HTML, commercial products that use proprietary technology to structure and serve audio and video dominate streaming media. At the current time, three main formats predominate, each with more or less a third of the market, depending on who you ask: RealMedia from RealNetworks, one of the pioneers in online multimedia during the dot-com boom and still a market leader (though possibly fading); Windows Media from Microsoft; and QuickTime from Apple. RealNetworks, Microsoft, and Apple have each pursued a similar strategy to profit from audio and video, a strategy that luckily benefits consumers but unluckily affects producers of web content: they all distribute free programs for playing audio and video streamed in their format, but charge producers for the means to stream that content. Fortunately the three large companies have also seen the benefit of giving away (or licensing at little cost) restricted versions of their media servers so that small website creators (including virtually all historians) can start to use these products for free. If you do not plan on having more than a few people access your audio or video at one time nor need to display extremely high-quality formats (e.g., full-screen video), these restricted versions will do.[11]

Each of the three major formats has its advantages and disadvantages, making it difficult to choose one format over the others. To nonaudiophiles, audio sounds roughly the same on all three; more substantial differences occasionally show up in video playback, which is far more taxing on both the server and client computers. (Indeed, though decent audio can be transmitted over a dialup modem, acceptable video requires much higher speeds.) High-volume sites have often chosen the RealNetworks product line because their server software is extremely sophisticated about the way it pushes audio and video out to a variety of users (it can discern how fast each user's connection is and compensate), and it can handle thousands of streams at the same time. Most viewers and listeners, however, consider RealMedia files to have the lowest (though still acceptable) audio and video quality of the three major formats. Microsoft also has server technology that helps to smooth out playback to large numbers of people and can also handle far more streams than will likely occur on any but the most popular websites. But probably its greatest advantage is Microsoft's preinstallation of the Windows Media Player on 95 percent of the world's computers. PC users have to actively seek out the RealMedia and QuickTime players (of course, Mac users have to seek out the Mac version of the Windows Media Player). For this reason alone, Dan Arthurs of StreamingCulture, a site that serves multimedia for numerous arts and humanities organizations, recommends Windows Media for any historian who has to choose a single streaming format. (With a high-capacity server and an audience that includes many artistic Mac users, StreamingCulture streams audio and video in both Windows Media and QuickTime.) If you do choose Windows Media, you need not have a Windows server; the server software runs on other platforms too.[12]

Apple's QuickTime (which in turn runs on Windows servers) has traditionally been the choice for websites looking to serve the highest quality video, but its slightly less robust server software (compared to RealMedia and Windows Media) means that it cannot handle huge numbers of visitors as elegantly (again, we are talking about hundreds of simultaneous users or more), and video has been known to be choppier than the other two formats during streaming playback.[13] On the other hand, because it uses an open encoding standard, unlike the proprietary "codecs" of RealMedia and Windows Media, the QuickTime format may survive for a longer period of time, and achieve a wider adoption across many devices and platforms, than its rivals. None of the three formats is truly adequate for long-term preservation because they compress multimedia so substantially as to lose considerable information from the original. Arthurs strongly recommends saving both the physical media (if any) on which the audio or video was recorded (e.g., Digital Beta or consumer DV) and a high-quality transfer to your computer (more on this in Chapter 3), in addition to whichever streaming format (or formats) you select.[14]

Interestingly, the three companies have recently begun to partially support some common and even rival formats. All support the extremely popular MP3 audio standard—a good neutral choice for serving (but not archiving) digitized audio—and some server and player software from RealNetworks supports (perhaps oddly) QuickTime and Windows Media formats. Because most people have more than one of the three main players (and sometimes all three) on their computers, it is difficult to go wrong—inevitably some of your audience will have to download the free player before viewing your content, and you should always include a link to the specific streaming media company's site for these downloads. Choosing a specific format for your multimedia does entail a commitment, however; switching to another format later on can be difficult.

Done well, the addition of audio and video to a site can be affecting. The Sonic Memorial Project, an audio history of the World Trade Center and its collapse on September 11, 2001, has an immediacy that pure transcripts lack. In addition to hearing the voices of hundreds of survivors, visitors can listen to longer segments from the Mohawk iron workers who helped to build the twin towers in the 1970s, and now-lost sounds of people on the observatory deck, in the neighborhood below, and at work in the skyscrapers. The sheer size of its collection of audio files and the creative way that the website allows for visitors to hear audio clips from a wide variety of people in its archive requires (unsurprisingly) a fairly complicated infrastructure, including server software from RealNetworks and extensive programming by Sonic Memorial's web developer Julian Bleecker.[15]

Few historical projects that require audio will need to reproduce such an effort. Either a "wait until download is complete" system for audio or video files or an installation of the basic (and free) versions of RealMedia, Windows Media, or QuickTime server software will likely suffice for almost all small- to medium-sized sites that are not receiving thousands of daily hits. Regardless, audio or video on the web must be digital rather than analog, which may involve substantial conversion issues, one of the subjects of Chapter 3.

Another popular option for moving beyond static text and images on your website is a commercial product for animation and multimedia called Flash, produced by the Macromedia Corporation, the creators of Dreamweaver. The great technological advantage of Flash versus streaming media software is that it permits files that are small relative to video files (but still not tiny, particularly for those viewing the web through a

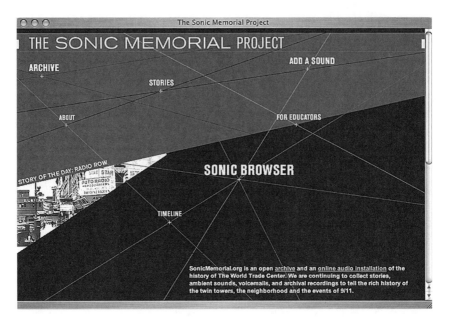

Figure 15. The Sonic Memorial Project captures the history of the World Trade Center from its planning and construction to the aftermath of September 11, 2001, through hundreds of audio clips, artfully accessed through a "sonic browser" that masks a fairly complex technical infrastructure.

slow modem connection) to seem like highly advanced graphical experiences. Moreover, Flash allows for interactivity with this content. To do its magic, however, Flash requires special software that plugs into your web browser and that takes over the display when it encounters a Flash file; luckily most computers now come with Flash preinstalled. More significant disadvantages of Flash include its poor accessibility to those with visual disabilities (see Chapter 4) and the difficulty search engines like Google have had finding information within sites heavily reliant on the technology—making it harder for your potential audience to find your online project. Also, like streaming media, Flash's costs are borne by the producers rather than the users. Creators of Flash content must buy special production software from Macromedia, and they also must spend the time to learn how to create Flash files, which differ substantially from the files created with an image editing program like Photoshop.[16]

Many of the best historical sites that use Flash combine its potential for interactivity with compelling graphics that help the viewer understand an event or place that would be difficult to describe with mere words. For example, National Geographic's Remembering Pearl Harbor

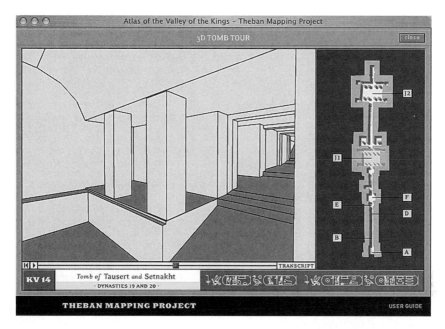

Figure 16. The extensive archaeological resources of the Theban Mapping Project include 3-D renderings of the tombs of Egyptian pharaohs, accomplished through the use of Macromedia's Flash technology.

places its archival photographs, video footage, and first-hand narratives into a timeline and map that the user can click on to go directly to key moments, such as the first sighting of an aircraft off Oahu. Using Flash technology, the user can then zoom into the map and choose related historical documents to study further. Just as impressive as Remembering Pearl Harbor in its use of Flash to convey visually the complexity of the past is the Theban Mapping Project, which provides interactive, highly detailed birds-eye maps of the Theban Necropolis and especially the Valley of the Kings, the location of so much important Egyptian archaeology. A 3-D re-creation of one Pharaoh's tomb, over 250 zoomable and pannable maps, and links from these interactive maps to over 2,000 images, provide a rich historical panorama of the era of the Rameses and their complex funerary constructions that easily rivals any book on the subject.[17]

Databases and XML

For archival or gallery sites that have hundreds or thousands of artifacts or documents to display, for sites gathering history online, or for running online discussions, historians will likely need at least one of two advanced technologies, the database or XML, and one of several non-HTML programming languages that often accompany these technologies. Both the database and XML are storage systems for materials arranged in a formal manner, and thus help deal with caches of documents or other materials that exhibit elements of repetition (a set of notecards or letters, a series of comments about a topic, or a slate of encyclopedia entries). XML and databases have structures for containing critical bits of information about historical objects, such as the author of a document or the dates of a battle. Researchers using sites that employ these technologies can examine the highlighted information in extremely useful ways. For instance, a database or XML archive of a thousand letters to and from Ralph Waldo Emerson could enable very precise searches by a range of dates, correspondents, keywords such as "wonder" or "slavery," or a combination of all three—thus allowing for more penetrating historical analysis by providing responses to questions such as, "To whom did Emerson write about abolitionism in the 1850s?" A thousand normal web pages with these same letters wouldn't be nearly as useful because there would be no way of combing through it with such specificity.

In some respects, databases and XML are similar technologies. Each allows you to define information such as "author" or "date" and then encode historical materials using those definitions. Yet they do this task in very different ways. XML is much like an HTML document: pure text with tags surrounding words or passages, in this case, representing the definitions such as author or date. Databases generally store their information in less readable files (that require a database program, not a simple text editor, to access them), and mandate that the bits of information one wants to highlight get separated from the main document into distinct "columns" or "fields." For example, the date of one of Emerson's letters would remain at the top of the full text of that letter in XML—though wrapped by informational tags—whereas the same letter in a database version would have the main text of the letter in one column and the date in another. The advantage of XML for archival websites is therefore that it permits in situ definitions. If you want to number the paragraphs of Shakespeare's plays and note where he fashioned new words, XML works extremely well. In short, XML works particularly well with sites that focus on historical texts.

The advantages of databases include the ease of updating entries (e.g., changing the dates of a hundred documents without editing each one), logging transactions (e.g., when did the visitor last view a document), and perhaps most important the native ability to search for matching records in a variety of ways (and with a sophisticated language called SQL). Such features make it a natural technology for history sites that involve forums, the gathering and editing of historical materials, or the membership rolls of a historical society, as well as many online archives. Because of these innate, robust features and long history of use (even before the web), sites using databases are far more prevalent than sites using XML, although recently the plain text simplicity of XML has led to an accelerating use of the technology for the easy sharing of information between websites. Because both technologies require more specialized knowledge that would be somewhat out of place in this introduction to the mainstream web, including an understanding of more complicated, non-HTML web programming languages that are necessary to transfer stored documents onto web pages, we have included a longer discussion of databases and XML in the appendix. We also cover how they work in greater depth in subsequent chapters.

Serving Your Website

The unique character of the Internet means that the production, hosting, and distribution of a website can be geographically dispersed with essentially no impact on the experience of the visitor. A web page can be written in one place, uploaded onto a server in another place, and accessed virtually anywhere else. The companion website to Not For Ourselves Alone, the historical documentary about Elizabeth Cady Stanton, Susan B. Anthony, and the women's suffrage movement made by Ken Burns (who lives in New Hampshire) and Paul Barnes (who lives in Vermont), was designed and "built" in Portland, Oregon, and is hosted on a server in Arlington, Virginia.[18] The options for where to put your website are therefore nearly limitless. The type of "hosting" situation may not be, however, depending on the genre of your website and its associated technical needs.

Almost any server will suffice for those who are building a relatively small site (say, under a hundred pages) that won't change frequently and doesn't involve databases or multimedia. Academic institutions sometimes provide a small area of their web server (or servers), generally around 5–100 megabytes, for affiliated students, faculty, and staff. If you are associated with such an institution, you should explore this possibility since academic web space is almost always free, the server software is already set up (and often includes at least a modicum of technical support), and is likely to be highly reliable because the institution's functioning depends on it. In most cases, the allotment provided is more than enough for a lifetime of course syllabi, a personal website for your work and family, and even another small site or two. If your marquee project ends up being much larger than you expected, the institution may be willing to allocate you more disk space (a cheap commodity).

A second possibility for hosting your website is your ISP, or Internet service provider. If you access the Internet from your home, your ISP may offer space for you on one of its web servers. As with institutional hosting, this space tends to be somewhat limited but still adequate for most uses (again, excepting websites that require a database or multimedia). The amount of technical support provided varies widely by the ISP, but is generally less than in an institutional setting where you can walk into someone's office if something goes wrong. (You can probably walk into the technical support office of an ISP too, but if you live in the United States it will probably require a very long journey because ISPs tend to outsource their technical support overseas.)

A third possibility is a commercial web host. This option usually involves a monthly cost ranging from around $5 for an amount of hard drive space comparable to that provided by an institution or ISP, to hundreds of dollars for enormous amounts of storage for extremely large sites. ("Free" web hosts, such as Yahoo's GeoCities, exist as well, though they will surround your material with advertisements.) Hundreds of companies offer this service; you can locate them through services like the Web Host Directory, but word of mouth from people you know is obviously better than trusting online reviews. The amount of data you *transfer* to visitors each month—rather than the amount you *store* on the web server—is generally the more important factor in your site's monthly cost on a commercial server. (One of the nice things about university servers is that they often do not restrict this data flow.) If you have a site heavy in multimedia files or are planning on thousands of visitors per day, you could end up owing hundreds of dollars per month in additional "bandwidth" costs if you don't plan ahead. But only the largest, most visited history sites will probably encounter such costs. Commercial hosts offer around 25–50 GB of data transfer a month for about $10, far more than most historical websites will require. (Data transfer of 50 GB in a single month is roughly equivalent to a twenty-page site with small images and no multimedia being thoroughly examined by 50,000 visitors.)[19]

If you are confident that you will receive a high volume of traffic to your site (tens of thousands of visitors per day or more), you should investigate the possibility of a commercial service with just a few sites on one server, or in extreme cases, only one site per server. The latter option is called "dedicated" hosting, and obviously is the most expensive option. You have the advantage of total control of a server—all of its hard drive space, every tick of its processor, the entirety of its wire out to the network. Unfortunately even the most inexpensive plans for high-

Figure 17. The advertising inserted at the top of every page by this site's free web host, Netfirms, detracts significantly from its serious historical tone. An inexpensive web plan from another Internet service provider (for less than $10 per month) would remove these "banner" ads.

quality dedicated hosting begin at around $200 per month, and go up sharply from there for faster machines and a faster connection to the Internet. For a major site with extensive databases, lots of multimedia, and significant traffic, this cost could easily top $1,000 per month, including technical support. For instance, at the Center for History and New Media (CHNM) we transfer about 300 GB of information per month to visitors, and need about 150 GB of hard drive space to hold our various websites and associated content. Although we currently run our own server, we have explored the possibility of outsourcing it to a commercial host; unfortunately it would cost us at least $15,000 per year for the same type of server and amount of bandwidth.

Once you begin to consider a dedicated server through a commercial host, you should (like us) probably contemplate the ultimate step of running your own server. For even $200 per month, you could buy a decent server of your own in less than a year. Relatively few historical operations, however, have taken this step. Running your own server entails tremendous advantages and disadvantages. For large sites, a number of hardware and software pieces need to come together, and owning a server gives you full control over this configuration. You can install the exact database, programming language, web server software, hard drive storage, backup scheme, and other elements precisely as you want. You can upgrade any of these pieces when you want, or choose not to if you are worried about the effects an upgrade will have on your existing web pages or other software on the server. You can give out accounts and space to collaborators in other organizations. You can add storage to your server at a relatively low cost.

You can also wake up every day (or fail to sleep through the night) with fear about computer crashes, glitches, patches, upgrades gone wrong, hackers, and power outages. Owning your own server is much like owning a house—you can paint the walls garish colors if you like, but you're also responsible for the lawn, the roof, and the crumbling staircase that may collapse at any minute. Operators of some large sites need to have such responsibility and have the great resources to accept it. For instance, the exceedingly popular Ellis Island website, which includes the manifest records of ships full of immigrants, is held on Hewlett-Packard servers running Oracle database software and connected to the Internet on high-traffic wires—all top-dollar options. For most small- and medium-sized sites, as well as many large sites that do not have advanced features requiring extensive programming, robust databases, or a high volume of traffic, it is better to outsource the server to someone else. Let a commercial or institutional host worry about all of the headaches so you can focus on the history.

Although the nature of the Internet collapses space and obscures the distinctions between web servers, each of these four possibilities for web hosting (institutional, ISP, commercial, do-it-yourself), as well as particular hosts of each type, has its advantages and disadvantages, which you should assess before making a choice. Technical support, as we've already mentioned, can vary widely, though none of the three out-sourced host types is uniformly best. Even though you are paying them monthly fees, some commercial web hosts only answer questions via email, and many take a long time to respond (for certain hosts, up to seventy-two hours). On the other hand, commercial services may provide web interfaces that greatly facilitate the uploading and management of your site (versus the file transfer program you generally have to use in an institutional hosting setting), as well as additional services such as a traffic monitor and special site-related email addresses. If you want to know how popular your site is, or to have a distinct email address for queries relating to your history site, those additional services can be worth the price (for more on assessing and communicating with your audience, see Chapter 5). All hosting possibilities other than dedicated hosting and running your own server involve sharing your server with a number of other websites. The computer owned by the commercial hosting company, your ISP, or your institution splits its hard drive space among the many people who are using it as their host. The number of these subdivisions and the volume of traffic to the other sites on the shared server can sometimes affect the speed and responsiveness of your site.[20]

Naming Your Site and Presenting It to the World

A noticeable difference among the four main types of web hosting that may matter more than the snappiness of your site is the way each type of hosting appears to the end user in the address for your website, or URL. Although most historical websites, as we noted at the beginning of this chapter, are merely a set of files that can be located on virtually any server, the address to locate those files varies depending on where you host it, and in what manner. To understand why web addresses can vary so much, we must look at the anatomy of a URL, the unique location in cyberspace every web page has, and how it relates to the structure of the Internet and the servers connected to that network of computers.

One of the great innovations of the web is the way in which it has made computer technology and networking more accessible, and among the techniques for doing so was a new system that named computers with letters and words rather than the numbers preferred by computer scientists. Each server (not website) on the Internet has a unique Internet Protocol address, or IP address, so that other computers can find it. Currently that address is four one- to three-digit numbers separated by periods. (Because the world is running out of these numbers, there are plans to move to longer designations, just like when the phone company moved from four-digit dialing to seven-digit, and from seven-digit dialing to ten-digit.)[21] For example, the IP address for the Smithsonian Institution's National Museum of American History is 160.111.76.139. Shrewdly divining that average human beings have enough trouble remembering the phone numbers of their family members, the creators of the web laid an alphabetical layer on top of this infrastructure of numerical IP addresses. This layer of technology, called the Domain Name System (DNS), translates (or "resolves" in computer-speak) addresses written in a more readable format of characters and words into underlying numerical addresses, which the requesting computer then seeks out. When someone types "http://www.nmah.si.edu" into their web browser, a request is sent to a special computer called a domain name server (alas, also abbreviated as DNS), which sends back a numerical IP address that matches those letters and the client computer then requests a web page from the computer that goes by the name of 160.111.76.139.

Without a doubt, the DNS is a fantastic innovation that has greatly advanced the use of the web because it allows regular people like historians to choose a name that they would like associated with their website. (Regular people like historians cannot assign themselves a numerical IP address.) Like Hebrew or Arabic, "domain names" should be read backward to be understood properly. Let's return to our example of the Douglas County Historical Society. The URL for the organization is www.watkinsmuseum.org. The string of letters to the far right, "org," is called the top-level domain (TLD). Common TLDs are "com," "org," "net," "edu," and "gov," in addition to the 242 two-letter country codes, such as "uk" for the United Kingdom and "fr" for France. More recently, the powers that govern the Internet have added the .museum TLD, which may hold attraction for some readers of this book, although most museums already use .org instead; to qualify for this new TLD, you must show the appropriate institutional bona fides.

Large companies and organizations called "registries" own and manage the TLDs. For all intents and purposes, you cannot make up your own. The real action is in the *second*-level domain (SLD). The Douglas County Historical Society based their second-level domain on an abridged version of their physical home, the Watkins Community Museum of History. Together with the TLD "org" (which stands, appropriately enough in this case, for nonprofit organization), watkinsmuseum.org is commonly referred to as the "domain name" (even though technically it consists of a SLD and a TLD).

Like the Douglas County Historical Society, you can register a domain name with a "registrar." Your registrar should be accredited by the international body responsible for managing domain names and the DNS, the Internet Corporation for Assigned Names and Numbers (ICANN).[22] Nonaccredited registrars often promise things they can't really deliver except through technological trickery or a suspect business model, like your own TLD or a "free" domain name. Only ICANN can approve new TLDs (and they have done so very slowly), and registrars must pay registries around $5–6 per year for each domain they register. If you are being offered a domain name for less than $6 per year, something funny is probably going on. Having said that, with hundreds of ICANN-accredited registrars, the domain registration business has rapidly become competitive and so you can find decent registrars for around $10 per year, and even less for multiyear registrations. Though the once-monopolistic Network Solutions remains the leading domain registrar, lower prices and equivalent service can be found at Dotster and the oddly named but very cheap GoDaddy.com (the third and fourth most popular registrars).[23] Given the low cost of registering a domain name, you might also want to consider buying other domains that are similar to your main name to prevent confusion among possible visitors. For instance, the Douglas County Historical Society could also purchase watkinsmuseum.com (and watkinsmuseum.net, etc.) if they wanted to be sure that web surfers looking for their site didn't instead end up by accident at another, nonhistorical website. (Traffic to these extra domains can be redirected automatically by domain registrars to your primary domain.)

Do you need a domain name? This is partly a question of user ease and aesthetics, and partly a question related to your preferred web host. In general, your site can only use its own domain name if you go with a commercial hosting service or run your own server, or in unusual cases where an institution or ISP allows you to "point" a registered domain to their server. In order for a domain name to work properly and cause a website to appear in a browser, not only does the domain name server have to list a relationship between a domain and a numerical IP address, but the computer that goes by that IP address also has to be "listening" for requests for that domain name. In other words, you cannot merely register a domain name and then point it to any old computer. (Some registrars have a feature called domain masking that seems to allow you to do just that, but they are really just inserting all of your web pages in an artificial frame with your URL at the top, and this method can be confusing as visitors go to different pages on your website without the URL changing.)

If you are using a host that can accept your own domain, and if you choose it carefully, a domain name can facilitate the ease with which people find your website and associate it with a specific historical topic. Which would you rather type into your browser, www.institution.org/~username/topicname/home.html—a typical address on an institutional server—or www.topicname.org? This comparison becomes even more stark as you move from the home page of a site into internal pages. For instance, you could place a timeline at yourdomain.org/timeline.html (easy to hand out to others and cite in written materials) rather than www.yourispdomain.net/users/username/topicname/time line.html. M. M. Eskandari-Qajar's site on the history of the Qajars in Persia previously sat on his ISP's web server, at home1.gte.net/eskandar/qajtoc.html. After registering a domain name, Eskandari-Qajar, a professor at Santa Barbara City College, moved the whole site to www.qajarpages.org. He is now able to hand out easy-to-remember URLs for sections of his site such as the events calendar and the FAQ (frequently asked questions) page.

The American Historical Association ended up with their current domain, www.historians.org, through a more circuitous route. Initially, the association occupied a subdomain within CHNM's server with the address http://chnm.gmu.edu/aha. By the time they had decided to register their own domain, the early-bird American Hospital Association had already taken the obvious aha.org. So the historians' AHA had to add "the" to the domain. Unfortunately people had trouble remembering or guessing the somewhat inelegant theaha.org, and so more recently they purchased secondhand the simpler historians.org. This domain is more memorable and also has an appropriate keyword in the domain name, which may help when people are trying to find the association using a search engine (as we will see in Chapter 5). Other less obvious advantages to having your own domain name rather than using the domain of your web host includes the ability to keep your site at the same URL if you change ISPs or move from one institution to another, and the potential to group multiple projects under a single domain.

With institutional web hosting, the URL instantly conveys the affiliation of the web author. For example, Paul Halsall, who built the extensive Internet Sourcebook we mentioned in Chapter 1, taught a course at Brooklyn College on Chinese culture, materials for which resided within his personal space on one of CUNY's servers, namely, one of several Sun servers in the Atrium Computer Lab. Observant people can see Halsall's username in the URL for the site (academic.brooklyn.cuny.edu/core9/phalsall/), everyone who comes to the course website can identify its association with Brooklyn College and CUNY by glancing at the URL. Even though the site has almost one hundred images and a lot of text, it is still relatively modest in extent, and Halsall did not need a lot of space to contain it. The Brooklyn College server made a great deal of sense, and to the college's credit the files have not been purged from their server even though Halsall left the campus in 1999 to go to the University of North Florida. Today he continues to maintain his course websites in a simple but effective way on the UNF servers (www.unf.edu/~phalsall/).

Hosting your website on your ISP's server may appear less desirable than an institutional home, but it provides the independence of having your own space without the cost of a commercial host and the yearly domain registration fee. For example, David E. Brown uses personal space on the web server of his ISP, Comcast, for his site on the Fifth Regiment of the U.S. Colored Cavalry, as the URL (mywebpages.comcast.net/5thuscc/) shows. The modest-sized site (about thirty pages) fits easily within the space the cable company allots. Brown could have registered 5thuscc.org as his domain name for this project and contracted with a commercial hosting service, but the Comcast arrangement works

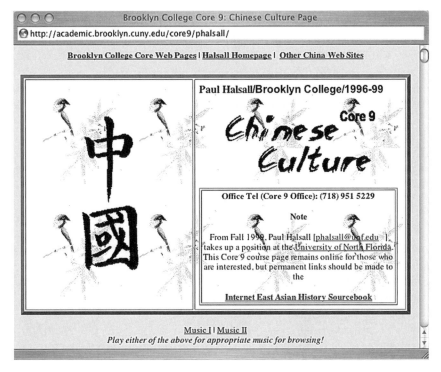

Figure 18. Paul Halsall has made good use of institutional servers to house his websites for courses and historical resources. His course site from the late 1990s on Chinese culture remains on a Brooklyn College server even though Halsall has long since moved to the University of North Florida.

just fine. Of course, should he change Internet service providers, he would have to change his site's URL.

Eskandari-Qajar's, Halsall's, and Brown's websites are on very different topics and are hosted in three different ways, but all represent personal historical sites with little need for complicated technology. The nature of web hosting can change significantly as additional technologies we discussed in this chapter (and in more detail in the appendix)—audio, video, databases, XML—become important to your site. Also, if a site grows to gargantuan proportions or receives an extremely high number of visitors, you may have to explore new hosts for your website. The Internet is perfectly structured for such transitions, thankfully; you can transfer your site's files directly from your old host to your new, often in mere minutes.

Funding

We hope you now have a better sense of whether you will be able to build your website on a shoestring budget or need to seek additional resources, and whether you will be able to create all the parts of your site yourself. Looking once again at your prioritized list of website features, you should understand which elements—that zoomable map, the introductory video—may seem less desirable, or simply more complicated to implement. Other features, such as the creation of a large database, will clearly require a lot of work (in both data entry and the technology to serve that information), and in such cases you will naturally begin to think about additional help and resources.

Funding can be difficult to come by, but is a necessity for complex or large sites, or sites with unique features. The Sonic Memorial Project, with its extensive multimedia capabilities, storage requirements, and programming, needed significant funding from multiple sources. National Public Radio's Lost & Found Sound, which archives recordings of everyday life from the past and present, received support from the Corporation for Public Broadcasting, the National Endowment for the Arts, the New York State Council on the Arts, the Third Wave Foundation, Creative Capital, and others. They also received in-kind support from another well-funded (by the Alfred P. Sloan Foundation) September 11 web history project, the September 11 Digital Archive (run by CHNM and the American Social History Project). Special arrangements were made to host the site on a powerful and highly specialized server at George Mason University, and the maintenance of that site and the software it runs on will be a concern—and cost—for years to come. Stephen Railton's Mark Twain in His Times website received similar nonmonetary support from within the University of Virginia (UVA), including designated graduate research assistants to update it. Railton's Uncle Tom's Cabin & American Culture site received a $7,000 grant from the National Endowment for the Arts and a matching amount from UVA's Institute for Advanced Technology in the Humanities (IATH), but still required significant generosity and in-kind support from within his university, including the library's Special Collections division, the E-Text Center, the Digital Media Center, and the English Department where Railton teaches. This sort of cobbling together of resources—frequently nonmonetary—is commonplace for historical websites.[24]

Finding resources is difficult, and you should assess potential funding from all available venues before a project begins. You should start with what you know best. Think about funders who might be interested in what you are trying to do—e.g., trying to improve teaching in your own course, enhance student learning in your school district, or make people aware of the history of your local community—rather than the more diffuse areas of "history" or "technology." Many colleges and universities offer seed grants or technical support for projects proposed by faculty. The Valley of the Shadow (see Chapter 1) started with a seed grant and support from IATH before it went on to win major national funding. For our own project on the French Revolution (Liberty, Equality, Fraternity), we obtained startup money from the Gould Foundation, a small foundation with no particular interest in new technology but with a passionate devotion to promoting French history. The Alfred P. Sloan Foundation has generously supported our work on the Echo project, in part because of their strong commitment to the history of science, technology, and industry. Many cities and towns have local foundations that care deeply about that community and would support a local history project. Every state and U.S. territory has a humanities council, which receives funds from the National Endowment for the Humanities (NEH) and often raises other funds as well. Their rules vary widely, but they often support local history projects.

A few, larger, national foundations have provided significant support for digital history projects. But you need to keep in mind that applications to such foundations are complex and difficult, often requiring weeks of work. NEH, for example, uses a rigorous process of peer review in which the required full documentation can run hundreds of pages. But they have given crucial support to dozens of digital history projects, including a number of our own. If you are interested in NEH support, you need to closely read their guidelines and also think carefully about the "genre" of your project. NEH is not interested in supporting digital history as an abstract category but rather in digital history projects that further its goals of disseminating the humanities to multiple audiences. Hence, the largest number of projects it has supported have been educational projects, although it has also provided funds for some— DoHistory, for example—through its public programs division. The National Science Foundation (NSF) has also given millions of dollars to digital history projects such as the Perseus Digital Library at Tufts University and the National Gallery of the Spoken Word at Michigan State University (with other partners).[25] But NSF's goals (and hence the requirements for receiving funding) are quite different from NEH; they seek (as part of their larger interest in computer science and information technology) to support research work in "digital libraries." That your project will transform our understanding of the Civil War will make little headway at NSF; that it will develop a new method for efficiently searching a million Civil War documents might get them very excited.

Thus the starting point for seeking money is very similar to the one

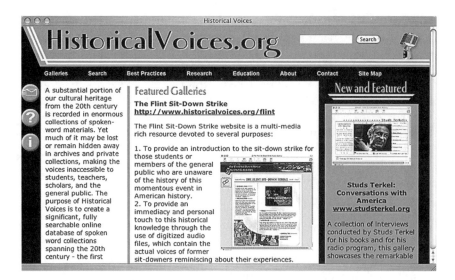

Figure 19. A major digital project with significant technical demands and the human resources that go along with such demands, such as the National Gallery of the Spoken Word's HistoricalVoices.org website, requires significant funding, in this case from the National Science Foundation.

we have emphasized in Chapter 1—first, be clear on the goals for your project. Then, figure out a funder who shares those goals. The Institute for Museum and Library Services, another federal agency, offers grants to groups providing "national leadership" for the museum and library fields through a variety of projects, including digital ones. The Mellon Foundation's Program in Scholarly Communication has provided tens of millions of dollars to "the applications of technology in the development of scholarly resources," including, for example, two projects to foster online publication in history, the Gutenberg-e Project of the American Historical Association and Columbia University Press and the American Council of Learned Societies History E-Book project. But a project that enhances K-12 education, however worthy or innovative, is of no interest to them.[26] Just as you need to seek appropriate technology, you also need to seek appropriate funders.

Although multimillion-dollar grants are alluring, many of the most successful digital history projects have begun with no resources but the passion of their creators. Especially in the early days of the History Web, that initial dedication won these sites equally dedicated audiences, which in some cases then won the hearts of funders. Other sites have remained labors of love. Even on modest (or nonexistent) budgets, such sites have contributed significantly to the public understanding of the past. Regardless of your funding needs—and whether you are able to meet them—most historical websites can begin simply, with the choice of a web host, a careful assessment of what you'll need, perhaps the creation of a few web pages outlining your project to the world, and a plan for constructing the site in full. Once you've taken care of these basic elements, you can begin the hard work of putting together primary and secondary sources for your website. In many cases, because so much of what we study remains in nonelectronic forms, this means bringing artifacts and documents to the web through digitization.

Chapter 3

Becoming Digital
Preparing Historical Materials for the Web

In this chapter you will learn about:

- The pros and cons of digitization
- The different ways that text can be digitized
- The benefits and costs of marking up text
- How to make text machine readable
- The ways to make images digital
- How to digitize sound and moving images
- Whether you should do all this work yourself

The past was analog. The future is digital. Tomorrow's historians will glory in a largely digital historical record, which will transform the way they research, present, and even preserve the past. But what can today's historians do with the massive analog historical record of the past millennia? This chapter provides some answers, offering advice on how to make the past—in the form of written records, photographs, oral history tapes, films, material culture, or other analog documents and artifacts—into digital files. In doing so, we can allow these resources to gain the significant advantages we outlined in the introduction, such as accessibility, flexibility, and manipulability.

An astonishing amount of the analog historical record has already become digital in the past decade. As we mentioned in Chapter 1, the Library of Congress's American Memory project presents more than eight million historical documents. ProQuest's Historical Newspapers offers the full text of five major newspapers including full runs of the *New York Times* and the *Los Angeles Times*. The Thomson Corporation's 33-million-page Eighteenth Century Collections Online contains every significant English-language and foreign-language title printed in Great Britain in that period. Most dramatically, the search engine behemoth Google has announced plans to digitize at least 15 million books.[1] Hundreds of millions in federal, foundation, and corporate dollars have gone into digitizing a startlingly large proportion of our cultural heritage.

This treasure of digital history presents an incredible boon to historians, offering possibilities for online research and teaching that would have been unimaginable just a few years ago. For the aspiring digital historian, it also imparts another benefit: the experience of the first generation of digitizers provides a set of benchmarks and approaches that will help you convert historical documents for your own site with greater efficiency, better reproductions, and, we would hope, a lower cost than the pioneers. But, as historians know all too well, the lessons of the past are never simple and straightforward. "There are no absolute rules," observes a report from the Digital Library Forum. "Every project is unique."[2] This caution applies particularly to historians with small projects because the advice literature focuses on large-scale, library- or archive-based projects. Your own goals and budget for organizing an exhibit for your local historical society or posting some documents for your students may be much more modest.

This chapter won't turn you into an expert on scanning resolutions for photographs or sampling procedures for audio; rather, we want to give you enough information to plan intelligently and to oversee a digital history project. To do that, we offer you an overview of the basic whys, whats, hows, and whos in digitization: why it is useful (and when it isn't), what digital formats you should consider producing, how it is actually done, and who should do it (you, your organization if you have one, or another person or company).

Why Digitize the Past? Costs and Benefits

The aura of excitement that surrounds the new has created an implicit bias that favors digitization over a more conservative maintenance of analog historical artifacts. This was particularly true in the dot-com boom years of the mid- to late 1990s. An advertisement on the web in those heady days captured the prevalent mixture of opportunity and anxiety. Three little red schoolhouses stand together in a field. A pulsing green line or wire lights up one of the schools with a pulse of energy and excitement, casting the others into shadow. "Intraschool is Coming to a District Near You," a sign flashes. "Don't Be Left Behind!" That same fear of being "left behind" pushed many historians, librarians, and archivists into the digitizing game. But some leading figures in library circles like Abby Smith warned about getting swept away in the enthusiasm. "We should be cautious about letting the radiance of the bright future blind us to [the] limitations" of "this new technology," she admonished other stewards of archival resources in 1999.[3]

For Smith and others, one of the most important of those limitations is intrinsic to the technology. Whereas analog data is a varying and continuous stream, digital data is only a *sampling* of the original data that is then encoded into the 1s and 0s that a computer understands. The continuous sweep of the second hand on a wristwatch compared to a digital alarm clock that changes its display in discrete units aptly illustrates the difference. As Smith nicely observes, "analog information can range from the subtle tones and gradations of the chiaroscuro in a Berenice Abbott photograph of Manhattan in the early morning light, to the changes in the volume, tone, and pitch recorded on a tape that might, when played back on equipment, turn out to be the basement tapes of Bob Dylan." But digitization turns the "gradations that carry meaning in analog forms" into precise numerical values that lose at least a little bit of that meaning.[4]

But how much of that meaning is lost depends, in large part, on how much information you gather when you digitize. One dimension of this, as the excellent *NINCH Guide to Good Practice in the Digital Representation and Management of Cultural Heritage Resources* explains, is the "density of data" captured—how much or how frequently the original is being sampled, a calculation that is reflected in the sampling rate for audio or the resolution for images. A second dimension is the breadth or depth of information gathered in each sample.[5] For example, if you gathered just one "bit" of information—the smallest unit of computer memory or storage—about a tiny section of a painting, you would be able to represent that detail only as black or white, which would be highly distorting for a work by Monet. But with 24 bits, you would have millions of colors at your disposal and could thus better approximate, though never fully match, the rich rainbow hues of Monet's *Water Lilies.*

Capturing more information and sampling more frequently makes digitizing more expensive. It takes longer to gather and transmit more complete information, and it costs more to store it. Fortunately the stunning rise in computer power, the equally stunning drop in the cost of digital storage, and the significant (but less stunning) increase in the speed of computer networks have made these costs much less daunting than before. But even in the best of circumstances, the move from analog to digital generally entails a loss of information, although the significance of that loss is the subject of continuing and sometimes acrimonious debate. For example, partisans of (digital) music CDs played with solid-state (digital) amplifiers tout their quality and reliability, with the thousandth playback as crisp and unblemished as the first, whereas devotees of (analog) vinyl records amplified by (analog) tube amplifiers enthuse about their "authentic," "warmer" sound, despite the occasional scratchiness of an old platter. "Taking an analog recording of a live concert," writes one analogista, "and reducing it to 0s and 1s is not unlike a root canal: by extracting the nerves, the tooth is killed in order to save it."[6]

At first glance, the analog versus digital debate would seem to apply to sound and images and not to text, which has the same precise quality in print as digital data. A letter is an s or a t; it can't fall on a spectrum between them. But some comparable issues in the digitization of text point us to the largest concerns about the digitization process. Text digitizers also need to worry about the "density of data" collected. For example, should a digitized text capture just the letters and words or also information about paragraphs, headings, centering, spacing, indentations, and pagination? What about handwritten notes? Novelist Nicholson Baker blasted libraries for digitizing (and then disposing of) their card catalogs, thereby losing valuable information in the knowing marginalia scribbled over the years.[7]

Faithful digital representation is even more difficult with manuscripts. Take a look at the Library of Congress's online versions of the Works Progress Administration (WPA) Life Histories, which require some complex notation just to represent a small handwritten correction:

*{Begin deleted text}*Nosy*{End deleted text} {Begin inserted text} {Begin handwritten}*Noisy*{End handwritten} {End inserted text}*

And this is a mostly typed, twentieth-century text; medieval manuscripts present much thornier difficulties, including different forms of the same letters and a plethora of superscripting, subscripting, and other hard-to-reproduce written formats.[8]

It may be impossible (or at least very difficult) to move from analog to digital with *no* loss of information; what you really need to ask is the cost of representing the original as closely as possible. In other words, not only does digitization mean a *loss* (albeit in some cases a very modest one), it also incurs a *cost*. Technological advances have gone much further in improving our ability to make faithful digital surrogates than they have in reducing the costs of doing so. If you are contemplating a digitization project, you need to consider those costs soberly and what they might mean for you or your organization.[9]

The need for such an assessment is great because the costs are not always obvious. We naturally tend to focus on the literal costs of moving documents into digital form—paying someone to type a handwritten document or employing a student to operate a scanner. But this neglects other crucial and expensive parts of the process, especially preparing and selecting the materials to be digitized and assembling information about the materials—what the librarians call "metadata." Steve Puglia of the U.S. National Archives and Records Administration calculates that only one-third of the costs in digitization projects stem from actual digital conversion; an equal third goes for cataloging and descriptive metadata and the final third is spent on administrative costs, overhead, and quality control.[10]

First-time digitizers typically overestimate the production costs and underestimate the intellectual costs such as those associated with making the right selections and providing the most helpful metadata. Even a sophisticated library team at the University of Virginia reports that they "dramatically underestimated the labor and time" in preparing the documents for a digitizing project on Walter Reed and yellow fever.[11] An equally important, but even less often considered, cost is maintaining the digital data, as Chapter 8 covers in greater depth.

This recitation of the costs and difficulties of digitization might sound prohibitively gloomy. If digitization is imperfect, difficult, and expensive, why bother? Because digitization offers stunning advantages. We don't want to talk you out of digitizing the past, but rather encourage you to carefully weigh the problems and expenses against the benefits.

Among the many benefits of digital history we outlined in this book's introduction, digitization particularly highlights the advantages of access, in a number of senses. It can mean new access, for example, to historical sources that are otherwise unavailable because of their fragility. Pierre-Charles L'Enfant's original 1791 plan for the city of Washington is so brittle and deteriorated that the Library of Congress no longer allows researchers to examine it. But now millions can view the digital reproduction on the library's website. Most Library of Congress documents are not quite this delicate, but like many other primary source collections, they cannot be browsed easily in analog form. Traditionally, researchers faced the painstaking process of ordering up boxes of items in order to find what they were seeking. Sometimes you could not study the archival documents (e.g., glass plate and film negatives) without prior conversions into readable or viewable media (e.g., prints). Digitization, by contrast, permits quick and easy browsing of large volumes of material.[12]

Even more remarkable is how remote access to documents and archives that digitization (and global computer networks) makes possible has dramatically broadened the number of people who can research the past. Just two decades ago, research in the Library of Congress's collection of early Edison motion pictures required an expensive trip to Washington, D.C. Now, high school students from Bangor, Maine, to Baja California, have instant access. The library reports that in 2003 approximately 15 million people visited American Memory, more people than have worked in the library's reading rooms in its 200-year history and 1,500 times the number who annually use the manuscript reading room.[13]

This exciting prospect of universal, democratic access to our cultural heritage should always be tempered by a clear-headed analysis of whether the audience for the historical materials is real rather than hypothetical. Local historians would ecstatically greet a fully digitized and searchable version of their small-town newspaper, but it would not justify hundreds of thousands of dollars in digitizing costs. Nor would it make much sense to digitize a collection of personal papers that attracts one or two researchers per year. The archive that holds these papers could spend the money more effectively on travel grants to prospective researchers. "The mere potential for increased access," the Society of American Archivists warns, "does not add value to an underutilized collection." Of course, digitization can dramatically increase the use of previously neglected collections by making inaccessible materials easily discoverable. The Making of America collection largely draws from books from the University of Michigan's remote storage facility that had rarely been borrowed in more than thirty years. Yet researchers now access the same "obscure" books 40,000 times a month.[14]

Digital searching most dramatically transforms access to collections. This finer grained access will revolutionize the way historians do research. Most obviously, digital word searching is orders of magnitude faster and more accurate than skimming through printed or handwritten texts. Even Thomas Jefferson scholars who have devoted their lives to studying the third president appreciate the ability to quickly find a quotation they remember reading in a letter years earlier. But the emergence of vast digital corpora—for example, the full texts of major newspapers—opens up possible investigations that could not have been considered before because of the human limits on scanning reams of paper or rolls of microfilm. Such quantitative digital additions may lead to qualitative changes in the way historical research is done.

As yet, the benefits of digital searching have not been brought to images or audio, although computer scientists are struggling to make that possible. If they succeed, they will transform research in these sources, too. But, even now, these other media also benefit from a new level of accessibility. Consider, for example, images that the naked eye cannot readily decipher. The digitization of the L'Enfant plan has made it possible to discern Thomas Jefferson's handwritten editorial annotations, which had become illegible on the original. Similarly, users of the Anglo-Saxon *Beowulf* manuscript in the British Library could not see letters on the edges of each page because of a protective paper frame added to the manuscript in the mid-nineteenth century. Digitization with a high-end digital camera and fiber-optic lighting revealed the missing letters. Some of those missing letters offer the only extant record of certain Old English words. Art historians may eventually use computer programs like the University of Maastricht's Authentic software, which can find patterns in digitized paintings to help with dating and attribution.[15]

Digitizing Text: What Do You Want to Provide?

Let's say your cost-benefit analysis has convinced you that digitization makes sense. The audience, you conclude, is relatively large, scattered around the nation or globe, and eager to get their hands (or rather mice) on the materials you have. What does it actually mean to place a digital text online? Digitized text is any kind of text that can be read on a computer, but that text can take many forms. Decisions about which form you should choose depend on the state of the original, the audience for the digitized version, and your budget.

The simplest format is a "page image" produced by scanning a printed page or a roll of microfilm. These digital photocopies have three major advantages and an equal number of serious drawbacks. First, you can create them quickly and easily. Second, good page images closely represent the original. The page image of the WPA life interview mentioned earlier not only shows you the handwritten insert of the editor but also indicates precisely where he inserted it. Third, page images give a "feel" for the original. Students can read the printed text of Harry Truman's diary entry for 25 July 1945, in which he contemplates the dropping of the atomic bomb. But the impact grows when they see the words "the Japs are savages, ruthless, merciless and fanatic" written in his own hand.

So, why not just stick to page images? As mere visual representations of text, page images cannot be searched or manipulated in the same ways as machine-readable text. A student looking for Truman's views on the Japanese and the atomic bomb in a series of page images from his diary would need to read every page, just as with the analog originals. In addition, image files are much larger than text, which makes them much slower to download to your audience's browsers and slower to print as well. The files that the Universal Library at Carnegie Mellon University uses to present individual page images of the *New York Times* are about 1 megabyte in size. By contrast, that amount of plain (machine-readable) text would take up about 30 kilobytes, a mere 3 percent of the image. As a result, even with a fast computer and a high-speed connection, it takes about twenty seconds to turn a page on the Carnegie Mellon site. Page images of detailed folios of text can also be difficult to examine on most computer monitors with their limited size and resolution (although some software programs might allow you to segment the image into smaller chunks). With unaided eyes, you can browse an entire page of a printed newspaper easily; it is possible but more difficult to do that with microfilm; it is impossible on a standard computer monitor.

Finally, providing more detailed metadata, which some digitizing projects do to help users find content within page images, erases some of this format's inherent savings. Even without metadata, machine-readable texts come ready to be searched. You can find your way through them by using a simple word search, as with the "Find" command in Microsoft Word. Large collections of page images, however, usually need additional information and tools so that readers can locate their desired topic or folio.

This discussion of page images points to the obvious advantages and disadvantages of machine-readable texts—they are searchable and easy to work with (you can readily copy and paste passages of text, for example) but more expensive to produce and less likely to faithfully represent the original. Not surprisingly, a variety of hybrid approaches have developed to mitigate these two disadvantages. Some websites link page images with uncorrected transcripts automatically produced by software (more on this in a moment)—the approach taken by JSTOR, the massive online database of 460 scholarly journals. A related approach, which does not, however, offer any cost savings, links page images with machine-readable text proofread by humans. For example, the Franklin D. Roosevelt Presidential Library and Museum website combines images of important presidential records with fully corrected and formatted text.[16]

To Mark Up, Or Not To Mark Up

Still another approach to maintaining fidelity to the original—but often a costly one—is to create marked-up text, which has the advantages of complete machine readability but without much of the loss of information that often accompanies the move from analog to digital. Text mark-up can take many forms, but all of them involve classifying the components of the document according to format, logical structure, or context. As we discussed in Chapter 2, HTML uses mark-up for presentational purposes. For example, the tag <i> indicates that the text that follows should be displayed in italics—perhaps indicating the title of a book, a foreign name, the name of a ship, or a point to be emphasized. But more sophisticated encoding schemes also capture structural and descriptive aspects of the text. They might, for example, identify all dates and names; indicate whether something is a footnote, a chapter title, or a caption; precisely specify indentations, margins, and poetry line breaks, or even designate the title (e.g., Senator, Governor) of a speaker.

Lou Burnard, Assistant Director of the Oxford University Computing Services, explains that mark-up makes "explicit (to a machine) what is implicit (to a person)," adds "value by supplying multiple annotations," and facilitates "re-use of the same material in different formats, in different contexts and for different users."[17] Not only can you reproduce the text with greater visual fidelity, you can also examine it in much more complex ways. You could, for example, search only the footnotes or captions for a particular word. Even more powerful are the ways that multiple texts could be manipulated. You could automatically generate a list of all books cited in the Voltaire papers, or you could create a timeline of all events mentioned in the papers of Dwight Eisenhower.

Of course, more expansive and exciting possibilities emerge only when a large number of people or small projects follow a single mark-up scheme, or a large online collection thoroughly and consistently implements such a scheme. HTML works because everyone agrees that <b>, not <bold>, means bold face. Achieving agreement is a social, cultural, and political process and is thus a much harder problem than surmounting the technical difficulty of, say, getting a computer monitor to display the slanting characters that indicate italics. Because the theory and practice of text mark-up is so complicated (and because mark-up nirvana has not yet been achieved), we urge those who plan to go down this road to consult the many technical works available on the subject.[18] Instead, we offer you a brief overview of the main approaches that have emerged so far.

Document mark-up predates the Internet or even computers. Traditionally, copy editors manually marked up manuscripts for typesetters, telling them, for example, to set the chapter title in "24 Times Roman." Computerized typesetting meant that mark-up had to be computer readable, but the specific codes differed depending on the software program. In 1967, an engineer named William Tunnicliffe proposed that the solution to this Babel of codes lay in separating the information content of documents from their format. Two years later, Charles Goldfarb, Edward Mosher, and Raymond Lorie created the Generalized Markup Language for IBM by drawing on the generic coding ideas of Tunnicliffe and New York book designer Stanley Rice. IBM, the dominant computer company of the 1960s and 1970s, made extensive use of GML (an acronym for both Generalized Markup Language and Goldfarb, Mosher, and Lorie), which emerged in 1986 after a long process as the international standard SGML (Standardized Generalized Markup Language).[19]

SGML—unlike HTML, which is a specific language derived from SGML—does not provide predefined classifications, or mark-up tags.

Instead, it is a "meta-language" with a grammar and vocabulary that makes it possible to define any set of tags. This great flexibility means that different groups, from the Department of Defense to the automobile industry to humanists, can define their own specialized mark-up languages. SGML requires first creating a Document Type Definition (DTD). You need, in effect, to develop a specialized language based on the meta-language of SGML or adopt one that has already been created. This great openness and flexibility is also the Achilles heel of SGML because it makes it difficult, intimidating, time-consuming, and expensive—a particular problem for nontechnical and poorly funded historians. Insiders joke that SGML stands for "Sounds Good, Maybe Later."[20]

But at least some humanists decided to plunge immediately into the deep end of the SGML pool. In 1987, more than thirty electronic text experts began developing a common text-encoding scheme based on SGML for humanities documents. Three years later, this "Text Encoding Initiative" (TEI) published a first draft of their mark-up guidelines, a DTD for humanists working with electronic texts. Not until 1994, however, did the first "official" guidelines emerge. The goal of TEI was not to visually represent authentic texts, a task for which it is not that well adapted, but rather to offer them in a machine-readable form that allows automated tools to process and analyze them far more deftly than plain, unmarked-up text. The advantages of automatic processing increase exponentially with the size of the corpus of material—say, all Shakespeare plays or even all early modern drama—and when this corpus has been marked up in a common scheme.[21] Historians with properly marked-up texts could ask when the term "McCarthyism" became widespread in the speeches and writings of Senators (as compared to governors and Congressmen) or when Southern (versus Northern) women diarists started talking about "love" and "passion."

Thus the benefits of encoding for historians reside not simply in the adherence to a particular encoding standard, which may enable the scanning of diverse texts at once by a computer—all diaries on the web, for example. They rest even more, perhaps, in how the structuring of digital texts and the careful human indexing of the contents of those texts allow for new historical questions to be asked and answered. Stephen Rhind-Tutt, the president of Alexander Street Press, a company that focuses on creating digital texts and databases that are highly structured and indexed to enable powerful searching, argues strongly that the considerable investment required to mark up texts pays off by enabling "new ways of exploring, analyzing, and discovering information" and permitting researchers "to examine hypotheses much more quickly than before." He notes, for example, that his company's structured databases on early American encounters allow users to answer such questions as "Were the encounters between the Jesuits and the Huron more violent than those between the Franciscans and the Huron?"[22]

TEI made SGML a viable standard for humanities texts but not an easy one to follow. "There is no doubt," acknowledges one guide to creating electronic texts, "that the TEI's DTD and Guidelines can appear rather daunting at first, especially if one is unfamiliar with the descriptive mark-up, text encoding issues, or SGML/XML applications." In other words, historians without a strong technical background or a considerable amount of time and (monk-like) patience should be cautious before diving into this more robust form of digitization, despite its apparent advantages. They should also consider alliances with partners—perhaps a university library or press—who have already developed the necessary technical expertise. Learning to collaborate is an essential skill for any digital historian, and this is one area where collaboration may be unavoidable. The greatest benefits of mark-up come with its most careful and detailed implementations, but the more careful and detailed the mark-up, the greater the expense. The first exercise in a course taught by Lou Burnard is to decide what you are going to mark up in several thousand pages of text, and then to halve your budget and repeat the exercise.[23]

Some humanists and technologists question whether the benefits of complex mark-up justify the time and effort. They argue that more automated methods can achieve "good enough" results. Exhibit A for them is Google, which manages in a fraction of a second to come up with surprisingly good search results on the heterogeneous, often poorly formatted text of the World Wide Web. "Doing things really well makes them too expensive for many institutions," argues computer scientist Michael Lesk, who favors providing more material at lower costs even if it means lower quality.[24]

Fortunately two related developments have eased the pain of complex mark-up of electronic texts. The first was the development in the mid-1990s of a much simpler set of TEI tags—known as "TEI Lite"—to support "90 percent of the needs of 90 percent of the TEI user community." It has quickly become the most widely implemented version of TEI. The learning curve was further eased by the emergence of XML, a significantly easier to use subset of SGML—sometimes called "SGML Lite."[25]

TEI and especially TEI Lite have increasingly become standards for projects that mount scholarly editions of online texts, especially literary texts. Those who are considering applying for resources for text digitization projects from major funders like the National Endowment for the Humanities or the Institute of Museum and Library Services will likely need to follow these standards. Although many historians use TEI-marked-up resources, surprisingly few have organized such projects. The TEI website lists 115 projects using TEI but puts only 24 in the category of "historical materials." And more than half of these—for example, the "Miguel de Cervantes Digital Library"—are largely literary. Most of the other projects fall into categories like "language corpora," "literary texts," and "classical and medieval literature and language," in part perhaps a reflection of the greater applicability and utility of mark-up for highly structured literary forms like poetry rather than the more heterogeneous texts studied by the majority of historians.[26]

Most historians and historical projects continue to present their texts in plain old HTML—a reflection of both their lack of technical sophistication and their greater interest in the "meaning" of a text than its structural and linguistic features. This is not to say that they wouldn't benefit from closer attention to the structure of texts, but they have not made this a priority. Text marked up with a standard scheme like TEI or indexed precisely in a database is superior to unformatted and unstructured words on a screen (especially for large projects and ones that expect to grow over time), but the journey to achieving that format can be long, treacherous, and expensive.[27]

How to Make Texts Digital: Scanning, OCR, and Typing

Whether you envision simple page images or elaborately marked-up text, you will begin the transformation from analog to digital by scanning or digitally photographing the original text. For many digital projects, scanning will turn out to be one of the easiest tasks that you do. Operating a flatbed scanner is not much harder than using a photocopier. Put down the document, press a button (on your computer or your scanner), and you're done. (At least with that one page; the instructions from there become more like shampooing: Lather, Rinse, Repeat.) Moreover, for a modest-sized text-based project, you can get by with a low-end scanner of the sort that currently sells for less than $100. (Consumer digital cameras that capture at least three megapixels of data can work equally well, although they tend to be slower to set up and harder to frame precisely over a page or book.)[28]

Measures of scanning quality such as resolution (the density of information that the scanner samples, generally expressed in dots per inch, dpi) and bit depth (the amount of information gathered from one dot, which generally ranges from 1 bit per dot for black and white images to 24 bits per dot for high-quality color) matter more for scans of images than texts—and thus we explain them in greater depth in the next section. Nevertheless, there are some general rules for scanning texts. If you plan to lift the text off the page using optical character recognition (OCR) software (more on that shortly) rather than displaying the scans as page images, you need only 1-bit black-and-white scans, although you should probably scan at a fairly high resolution of 300 to 600 dpi. If you plan to display page images, most experts recommend high-resolution, high-quality (perhaps 300 dpi and 24-bit color) files for archiving purposes. But you can get even this quality with an entry-level scanner.[29]

Nevertheless, you might want to spend more for a faster scanner or a model that includes an automatic sheet feeder. Automatic sheet feeders greatly expedite and simplify scanning because they can reach speeds of twenty-five pages per minute compared to two to three pages per minute for manual page swapping, or flipping the pages of a book and returning the text to the surface of the scanner. Of course, you can't use them with rare or fragile materials. But projects that don't care about saving the originals "disbind" or "guillotine" the books for auto-feeding, vastly accelerating the process while making book lovers like Nicholson Baker cringe.[30]

In general, as one handbook puts it, "scale matters—a lot" for digitizing projects.[31] If your project is small, it doesn't matter that much if you scan in a time-consuming way. It will still only be a relatively insignificant factor in your overall project. But if you are scanning thousands of pages, you need to carefully consider your equipment choices, plan your workflow, and contemplate whether a professional service might be more economical.

Some more specialized projects require considerably more expensive equipment, and as a result, it is often more economical to outsource such work (discussed later in the chapter). Projects that start with microfilm rather than texts, for example, need expensive microfilm scanners. Many rare books cannot be opened more than 120 degrees and would be damaged by being placed on a flatbed scanner. The University of Virginia's Early American Fiction Project, for example, has digitized 583 volumes of rare first editions using overhead digital cameras and book cradles specially designed for rare books. The Beowulf project required a high-end digital camera manufactured for medical imaging.[32] Such approaches are common only in well-funded and specialized projects. What is more remarkable is how very inexpensive equipment can produce very high-quality results for most ordinary projects.

So far, however, we have only discussed digital "photocopies." How do we create machine-readable text that is used either separately or in conjunction with these page images? Those who like computers and technology will find the process known as optical character recognition (OCR)—through which a piece of software converts the picture of letters and words created by the scanner into machine-readable text—

particularly appealing because of the way it promises to take care of matters quickly, cheaply, and, above all, automatically. Unfortunately technology is rarely quite so magical. Even the best OCR software programs have limitations. They don't, for example, do well with non-Latin characters, small print, certain fonts, complex page layouts or tables, mathematical or chemical symbols, or most texts from before the nineteenth century. Forget handwritten manuscripts.[33] And even without these problems, the best OCR programs will still make mistakes.

But when the initial texts are modern and in reasonably good shape, OCR does surprisingly well. JSTOR, the scholarly journal repository, claims an overall accuracy of 97 percent to 99.95 percent for some journals. A study based on the Making of America project at Michigan found that about nine out of ten OCRed pages had 99 percent or higher character accuracy without any manual correction. A Harvard project that measured search accuracy instead of character accuracy concluded that uncorrected OCR resulted in successful searches 96.6 percent of the time with the rate for twentieth-century texts (96.9 percent) only slightly higher than that for nineteenth-century works (95.1 percent). To be sure, both of these projects used PrimeOCR, the most expensive OCR package on the market. Jim Zwick, who has personally scanned and OCRed tens of thousands of pages for his Anti-Imperialism website, reports good success with the less-pricey OmniPage. PrimeOCR claims that it makes only 3 errors in every 420 characters scanned, an accuracy rate of 99.3 percent. But the conventional (and very inexpensive) OCR packages like OmniPage claim to achieve 98–99 percent accuracy, although that depends a great deal on the quality of the original; 95–99 percent seems like a more conservative range for automated processing. Even with the most sophisticated software, it is hard to get better than 80 to 90 percent accuracy on texts with small fonts and complex layouts, like newspapers. Keep in mind, as well, that the programs generally measure character accuracy but not errors in typography or layout; hence you could have 100 percent character accuracy but have a title that has lost its italics and footnotes that merge ungracefully into the text.[34]

Moreover, you will spend a lot of time and money finding and correcting those little errors (whether 3 or 8 out of 400 characters), even though good programs offer some automated methods for locating and snuffing out what they euphemistically (and somewhat comically) call "suspicious characters." After all, a three-hundred-page book OCRed at 99 percent accuracy would have about 600 errors. We would very roughly estimate that it increases digitization costs eight to ten times to move from uncorrected OCR to 99.995 percent accuracy (the statistical equivalent of perfection). From an outside vendor, it might cost 20 cents (half for the page image and half for the OCR) to machine digitize a relatively clean book page of text; getting 99.995 percent might cost you $1.50–2.00 per page.[35]

Given that uncorrected OCR is so good and making it better costs so much more, why not just leave it in its "raw" form? Actually, many projects like JSTOR do just that. Because JSTOR believes that the "appearance of typographical and other errors could undermine the perception of quality that publishers have worked long and hard to establish," they display the scanned page image and then use the uncorrected OCR only as an invisible search file. This means that if you search for "Mary Beard," you will be shown all the pages where her name appears, but you will have to scan the page images to find the specific spot on the page. Visually impaired and learning disabled users complain that the absence of machine-readable text makes it harder for them to use devices that read articles aloud.[36] Making of America, which is less shy about showing its warts, allows you to also display the uncorrected OCR, which not only helps those with limited vision but also makes it possible to copy and paste text, find a specific word quickly, and assess the quality of the OCR.

For some projects, uncorrected OCR—even when 99 percent accurate—is not good enough. In important literary or historical texts, a single word makes a great deal of difference. It would not do for an online version of Franklin D. Roosevelt's request for a declaration of war to begin "Yesterday, December 1, 1941—a date which will live in infamy—the United States of American was suddenly and deliberately attacked by naval and air forces of the Empire of Japan," even though we could proudly describe that sentence as having a 99.3 percent character accuracy. One solution is to check the text manually. We have done that ourselves on many projects, but it adds significantly to the expense (and requires checking on the person who did the checking). A skilled worker can generally correct only six to ten pages per hour.[37]

Although it seems counterintuitive, studies have concluded that the time spent correcting a small number of OCR errors can wind up exceeding the cost of typing the document from scratch. Alexander Street Press, which puts a premium on accuracy and insists on carefully tagged data, has all of its documents "rekeyed"—that is, manually typed in without the help of OCR software. They (and most others working with historical and literary materials) particularly favor the triple keying procedure used by many overseas digital conversion outfits. Two people type the same document; then a third person reviews the discrepancies identified by a computer. Calculations of the relative cost of OCR versus rekeying will vary greatly depending on the quality of the original document, the level of accuracy sought, and especially what the typist gets paid. Still, for projects that need documents with close to 100 percent accuracy, typing is probably best.[38] This can be true on even relatively small projects. We wound up hiring a local typist on some of our projects when we realized how much time we were spending on scanning, OCR, and making corrections, especially for documents with poor originals. Manually correcting OCR probably makes sense only on relatively small-scale projects and especially texts that yield particularly clean OCR. You should also keep in mind that if you use a typist, you don't need to invest in hardware or software or spend time learning new equipment and programs. Despite our occasional euphoria over futuristic technologies like OCR, sometimes tried-and-true methods like typing are more effective and less costly.

Digital Images

As with text, turning analog visual materials into digital objects can be as easy as operating a photocopier. You can digitize many images with the same inexpensive scanners or cameras as you might use with text. But some visual materials—slides, transparencies, large format documents like maps, or fine linear illustrations (such as engravings in the nineteenth-century press)—require more specialized equipment, photographic expertise, or scanning techniques. In addition, you will often face the question of whether to work from an original or a surrogate like a slide. Although the original yields a higher quality digital reproduction, it also often increases costs because large or fragile originals require complex, special handling.

Also, as with text, the goals of your website, your intended audience, and your budget will shape your digitizing plan. You might, for example, be creating a website for your course and want a few images for purely illustrative purposes. In that case, you can do some quick scans from books on an inexpensive scanner; the standard should be whether it is large and detailed enough to convey the information you want your students to see. At the other end of the spectrum, you might be creating an online archive of color lithographs from the early twentieth century. In that case, you need to focus on a wide range of issues, ranging from fidelity to the original to long-term preservation. As with many of the more technical subjects we discuss in this book, image capture and management is a much larger and more complex topic than we can discuss in detail here, and those contemplating a major project will want to consult more specialized guides.[39]

In digitizing images, as with all digitizing, the quality of the digital image rests on the quality of the original, the digitizing method employed, the skill of the person doing the digitizing, and the degree to which the digital copy has adequately "sampled" the analog original.

For images, as with scanned texts, the two key measures of digital sampling are bit depth and resolution. Close up, a digital image looks as if the pointillist painter Georges Seurat decided to use graph paper instead of a blank canvas, carefully dabbing a single dot of color into each box of the grid. The breadth of the color palette is called the bit depth, ranging, as already noted, from 1 for simple black and white to 24 (or higher) for a virtually limitless palette of colors that Seurat and his Impressionist friends would have envied. Digital image size is expressed by two numbers, the width in dots times the height in dots (otherwise known as pixels on a computer screen). For instance, 900 × 1,500 would be the image size of a 3″ × 5″ photograph scanned at 300 dots per inch (3 times 300 by 5 times 300).

Note that digitization disassociates an image from its real-world size. With different settings on our scanner, we could digitize that same 3″ × 5″ photograph at 100 dpi and arrive at a much "smaller" image size of 300 × 500. Of course, the second digital image would still represent the original in its totality; it would just be less fine-grained than the first, as if Seurat used a thicker brush to make his dots. But when displayed side by side on the same computer monitor—"painted" onto the screen using identically sized pixels—the first image would look much larger than the second. (In contrast, if you blow up the second to be as large as the first and compare a detail, you will see that it begins to break up, or "pixelate.") To make matters slightly more confusing, monitors have not one but two characteristics that are sometimes called "resolution": the number of pixels per inch of screen (often referred to as ppi and roughly equivalent to dpi) and the total number of pixels on the screen horizontally and vertically. Generally the first "resolution" is a single number between 72 and 96 ppi, and it denotes the density (and thus clarity and detail) of a monitor; the second "resolution" ranges from 640 × 480 to 1,920 × 1,440 or more, and it is a measure of how much fits on the screen at one time. Our 100-dpi scanned photograph would fit perfectly well on a monitor with an 800 × 600 setting (because 300 × 500 is less in each direction), whereas our 300-dpi version would overflow the sides, thus forcing us to scroll to see it all, as we might do with a long essay in Microsoft Word. Thus the physical size of your image on the screen depends on how your monitor is set. If you change your screen resolution from 640 × 480 to 1,024 × 768, your image will appear smaller because its constituent pixels are smaller (more of them now having to cram onto the same size display).

The three most common formats for digital images are TIFF, JPEG, and GIF. (Almost everyone uses their acronyms rather than full names, and pronounces them tiff, JAY-peg, and jiff or giff, but in case you are curious, they stand for Tagged Image File Format, Joint Photographic

Figure 20. At a small size, both of these close-ups—the left scanned at 72 dpi and the right at 300 dpi—would look identical on a computer screen. But if you wanted to examine the eyes of Dorothea Lange's famous "Migrant Mother" more closely, the version scanned at a higher resolution would be a far better choice.

Experts Group, and Graphics Interchange Format.) Uncompressed TIFFs are the highest quality of the three and have become, as one guide suggests, "a de facto industry standard."[40] Unfortunately you pay for that quality with very large file sizes, which means increased storage costs and very slow downloads for your visitors. The Library of Congress's uncompressed TIFF version of Dorothea Lange's famous 1936 "Migrant Mother" photo is 55 megabytes, which could leave even a visitor with a high-speed connection waiting impatiently. Moreover, because this archival TIFF is 6,849 × 8,539 pixels in size, it cannot be viewed easily on a standard computer monitor without a great deal of scrolling back and forth.

Computer scientists have developed clever file compression formulas to deal with this problem of huge file sizes. For example, you can compress TIFF files by as much as one-third without throwing away any needed information—what is called "lossless" compression. Even so, they are still much too big for a typical website. JPEGs, which use a "lossy" compression algorithm (meaning that they throw away information—albeit much of it information that the human eye doesn't notice), are significantly smaller. How much you save in file size between TIFF and JPEG depends on the quality settings you use in the JPEG compression and the overall resolution of the image. But the savings can be quite dramatic. For example, the Library of Congress's high-resolution JPEG of Lange's "Migrant Mother" is only 163 kilobytes—hundreds of times smaller than the archival TIFF. Of course, much of the savings comes from the smaller pixel dimensions, which are 821 × 1,024 for the JPEG, and additional savings come from an almost imperceptible reduction in the color palette and some fancy mathematics used to condense the information that remains. An even lower resolution (513 × 640) version, less than half that file size, appears lickety-split even on the screen of a modem-bound web surfer and still provides a very nice rendering of the famous photograph. Not surprisingly, JPEGs have emerged as the most common delivery format for photographs on the web.

The main web-based alternatives to JPEGs are GIFs. Ostensibly, GIFs do not work as well for large photos or other images with subtle changes in shade and color, but they render more effectively simple graphics, cartoons, or line drawings with large areas of solid color and high contrast. On the web, this distinction is partly apparent; for example, most logos you see on websites are GIFs, whereas most photos are JPEGs. But a quick check in an image processing tool like Adobe Photoshop or Macromedia Fireworks shows you that the difference in how most photographs look in JPEG and GIF is not as dramatic as conventional wisdom suggests, and many photographs and complex images on the web are indeed GIFs, not JPEGs. [41]

If you can get very good looking images with low or medium resolution GIFs or JPEGs, why bother with bulky, high-resolution TIFFs? Perhaps the most important reason is to create a high-quality archival master copy that can be used for a variety of purposes. For example, if tomorrow's computer scientists develop a nifty new compression scheme to replace JPEG, you will be able to go back to the TIFF and recompress it. Trying to do so from the JPEG will only result in further degradation of the image—another round of "lossy" sampling on top of the first round used to create the JPEG. Or, if inexpensive 21-inch monitors start to become standard and thus the audience for larger sized images expands significantly, you will want to resize your JPEGs working from the original TIFFs. Similarly, if you wanted to "clean up" the image (a controversial move when dealing with famous works like the Lange photo), you would want the best possible "original" to start with, and you could allow people to go back to the master to compare your changes. A high-resolution image also lets you to single out a particular detail—Migrant Mother's eyes, for example—and study it closely. The higher quality (and especially higher resolution) images are also important to people who are going to use them in print, rather than on the web. If you provide a digital image for a print publication, the publisher will likely request something at 300 dpi or higher because print can render much finer detail than a monitor. A 100-dpi JPEG or GIF printed in a newspaper, magazine, or book generally looks horrible. But if you are only displaying the image on a computer monitor, you will have to shrink down a 600-dpi image and at the same dimensions it will look no better than a 100-dpi version.

These advantages of high-quality TIFFs may be disadvantages from the perspective of some institutions. Many art museums (or artists for that matter) don't want people "fooling around" with their images, and altering images is much harder to do if you are starting with a low-resolution JPEG. Many museums also earn significant revenues by charging fees for the use of their images in publications. Thus many sites will present images online at only 72 ppi and then provide higher quality images to those who pay a fee, which allows them to control usage. (Those sites that are particularly vigilant about protecting rights—like the commercial Corbis image library—display their images with visible watermarks and sell them with invisible digital signatures to dissuade unauthorized reproduction.) But sites like the Library of Congress that generally provide copyright-free images and are not concerned about earning licensing fees from their collections generously offer high-quality, uncompressed TIFFs.[42]

As this discussion suggests, the methods by which you digitize images and the formats in which you present them depend on your budget and the goals of your site, but guides uniformly recommend that you create the highest quality digital masters you can afford at the time of the initial scan, and then make other, lesser, derivatives (e.g., JPEGs) appropriate to particular circumstances. Typically your digital masters should be uncompressed TIFFs with a spatial resolution of a minimum of 3,000 lines across the longest dimension of the image, a dynamic range of at least 8 bits for grayscale images and at least 24 bits for color images, and scanned at 300 to 600 dpi. Scan your images at the highest possible quality, but keep in mind that an image scanned at 3,000 × 3,000 lines and 24 bits (in other words a 10″ × 10″ image scanned at 300 dpi) produces a 27 MB file. The William Blake Archive at the University of Virginia reports that some of its digital masters are as large as 100 MB.[43] As such, the quality of your digital masters necessarily depends on the amount of storage and staff time available.

These digital masters, then, provide a resource from which to produce files for other uses. For example, for the web you will want to compress your large TIFFs into JPEGs or GIFs to allow for quicker load times and to fit standard computer displays. You will likely also want to create a small "thumbnail" version of each image in either GIF or JPEG format, which will load very quickly and make it possible to browse multiple images on a single page, as we suggest as a design principle in Chapter 4.[44]

Although text digitization can be laborious, it is generally straightforward—you have either correctly rendered a word or not. But image digitization can require much more human judgment. After your initial scan, you need to make sure your images are as close to the original as possible. The Blake Archive, which lavishes great care on getting "true" images, reports that the "correction" process can take as much as several hours for a single image and even thirty minutes for a typical image. But for them, it is "a key step in establishing the scholarly integrity" of the project. Among the many things the Blake Archive and most other digital imaging projects correct for are image sharpness, completeness, orientation, artifacts, tone, color palette, detail, and noise. Photoshop or its less expensive and complex sibling, Photoshop Elements, is generally an essential tool in the correction process. Most guides, moreover, recommend in the interest of archival integrity that these corrections not be done to digital masters, but rather to derivative files, even if they are high-quality exact replicas of the masters. Even this small extra step, intended to ensure that the original remains uncorrupted, can add considerable storage costs to your project, as you are essentially doubling your storage needs right at the start if you follow this tenet. Some projects also "enhance" digitized images, but others worry about maintaining "authenticity" and whether bright white tones should be restored to yellowed photographs.[45]

The other laborious manual process in image digitizing is the provision of metadata, identifying data about the image. Metadata becomes very important when the files themselves are not text-searchable. If the images are just going to be used on your website, it might be enough simply to provide descriptive "alt" tags in your HTML code (see Chapter 4), both so you can remember what they are and so they can be read by the audio browsers used by the blind. On the other hand, if you are creating a larger reference collection, you will probably want to use a more elaborate metadata standard such as Dublin Core or METS (see Chapter 8) that will provide descriptive information about the content and creation of the original image; technical information about the digitized file such as resolution, compression, and scanning process; structural information about the file's relationship to derivative or associated files; and administrative information about rights management and preservation.[46]

Audio and Moving Images

Digitizing audio and moving image sources involves even more specialized technical issues, and our treatment of these questions must be necessarily more truncated. Even after twenty pages of detail, the NINCH guide concludes that "practice and technology are still evolving" and "it is difficult to draw general conclusions or to make firm recommendations on ideal storage, delivery and management of digitized audio and moving image materials."[47] As these are the most complex historical artifacts to digitize—film, for instance, is a rapid series of photographs with sound attached—this uncertainty should come as no surprise.

The hesitation of the NINCH guide highlights that audio/visual (A/V) digitizing presents some particular challenges that go well beyond those faced in most text and image projects. First, you need a device that can play back the original recordings, which are sometimes in obsolete formats—from wax cylinders to 8 track tapes.[48] Second, you need a lot of digital storage space. One hour of uncompressed video can take up 146 gigabytes—as much space as 146,000 digitized books, or almost twice the size of the average public library. Third, you may have to do serious editing to make the digital objects usable for your audience. That could range from editing out background noises in an audio clip to making a two-hour oral history more manageable for a hurried listener. Fourth, you are likely to spend more time creating metadata for audio and moving images than for text or images. For the foreseeable future, we are unlikely to be able to search automatically through sound or moving images as we can with text. (New video searches from Google and Yahoo do not actually scan the video itself, but instead search the closed captioning text and other transcripts.) Unless you provide some descriptive metadata, your users will have no way of knowing what they will find in your online A/V collection except by spending hours listening or watching. Of course, a full transcript provides an excellent finding aid, but it can be very expensive to prepare.

How do you get audio or moving images into digital form? The simplest procedure is to connect your playback device (e.g., the turntable or VCR) through its "A/V Out" port (or ports) to a digital audio or video capture device (e.g., a stand-alone CD or DVD burner). If you want more control over sound quality and more flexibility, however, you should place a computer workstation with a digital audio or video input card between the playback mechanism and the capture device. Sound editing programs improve and condense the sound file (e.g., by deleting unneeded parts of the audio spectrum) and help you to break the file into manageable pieces. The Library of Congress and MATRIX at Michigan State University, both of which have done extensive work with historical sound, strongly advise that you use professional quality equipment and avoid consumer multimedia sound cards, which are notorious for their poor reproduction of audio.[49] A single weak link in the digitizing chain can have a deleterious effect on sound or video quality.

As in other areas of digitizing and digital preservation, experts lament the absence of agreed-upon standards, but audio digitizers seem to be settling on a sampling rate (the number of times per second that the unbroken analog sound wave is digitally captured, usually expressed in kHz) of 96 kHz, a bit depth (the measurement of how much data you have in each sample) of 24 bits, and the WAV (waveform audio) file format. Most commonly, as noted in Chapter 2, audio is compressed (using a program like Autodesk cleaner) and then streamed (in Windows Media, RealMedia, or QuickTime formats) to make it possible for web surfers to begin listening while the clip is downloaded. But some sites provide direct downloads of MP3s (a powerful and widely accepted format for compressed audio) or WAV files.[50]

Digitizing moving images is an even less settled practice than audio. The EVIA (Ethnomusicological Video for Instruction and Analysis) Digital Archive at Indiana University and the University of Michigan, which is undertaking a major digitization project, explains that "digital video is an arena in which no ready solutions or models exist." They are first archiving existing videos on DigiBeta tapes—an approach also being followed by the Library of Congress, the SHOAH Visual History Foundation, and New York University's Hemispheric Institute of Performance and Politics. Then, EVIA uses a high-end digital video encoder to compress the tapes in an MPEG-2 format that still consumes 27 gigabytes per hour, or 4 terabytes for the entire project. They acknowledge that, from a strictly archival point of view, no compression would be better, but that would require 146 gigabytes of storage space for an hour of video—an expensive proposition even in these days of cheap storage. Even Internet2 (an experimental higher speed version of the Internet) cannot effectively deliver the compressed files to users, and so EVIA will create additional versions, for example, a version at one-seventh the size for classroom projection or research, and a dramatically smaller streaming version in RealMedia, QuickTime, or Windows Media.

As these complex specifications indicate, a large-scale video digitization project is not for faint hearts or shallow pockets.[51] But that does not mean that you cannot relatively easily digitize some old video-taped interviews, using a video capture card on your computer and standard video software like Apple's easy-to-learn iMovie, and then stream the results in one of the major streaming formats. It is even easier to incorporate interviews done with your digital camcorder into your website because no conversion from analog to digital is required. You won't be in compliance with the most rigorous archival standards, but it can be a nice addition to your site.

Who Does the Digitizing? Should You Do It Yourself?

Whether you set out to digitize video, sound, images, or text, you still need to ask whether you should do the conversion in-house or "outsource" it to a commercial vendor. As with much in the digital world, experts give the ambiguous answer that "it depends." In the fall of 2000 and the spring of 2001, researchers from Glasgow University's Humanities Advanced Technology and Information Institute interviewed people involved in thirty-six major cultural heritage digitization projects. More than half reported that they both digitized in-house and used commercial vendors. Most of the rest did all the work on their own premises; only two relied exclusively on outside companies.[52]

The project directors cited a range of reasons for their choices. The most common explanation they offered for doing projects onsite was that the original materials were rare or fragile. For example, the Oriental Institute of the University of Chicago cited "the cost and risk of transporting the original materials." Often, fragile materials are visual (e.g., the maps in the Library of Congress's vast cartographic collection) and local digitizing offers the further advantage of precise control over image quality—a serious concern, as we have seen. "The primary argument for digitizing in-house," Janet Gertz of Columbia University Libraries writes in an overview of the subject, "is that it gives the institution close control over all procedures, handling of materials, and quality of products." Sometimes, projects have chosen to do the work themselves in order to develop digitizing expertise. Gertz notes that "working in-house is a good way to learn the technical side of digitization," which may prove useful "even when most work in the future will be sent to vendors."[53]

Although a few projects cited savings from digitizing in-house, project directors much more often pointed to expenses as the reason to hire outside vendors. Many major projects such as those at Cornell University also favor outsourcing because the preset prices insulate them from any unexpected increases in costs. And though some projects want to develop local digitizing capabilities, others seek to avoid the considerable investment in staff training and equipment that in-house digitizing requires. That software, hardware, and technical standards continue to change rapidly means that such investments are not a one-time matter. Thus the National Monuments Record's Images of England project, which is creating a snapshot of English heritage through photos of 370,000 buildings of architectural or historic interest, has outsourced all its digitizing because "there were no resources in-house and they did not want to invest in the type of equipment and specialized staff that . . . this project required."[54] As the commercial digitization business grows, vendors are more likely than even well-funded large libraries to have specialized staffs and the latest technology.

For these reasons, outsourcing has become increasingly common for large digitizing projects. Even as early as 2000, Paula De Stefano, head of the Preservation Department at NYU, observed "the trend . . . to use outside contractors" after the initial wave of "demonstration projects." As David Seaman, the head of the Digital Library Federation, notes, outsourcing has become a "less mysterious" and more appealing option for those who work in cultural heritage projects, as large commercial vendors have begun to court their business, as the prices have dropped, and as vendors have become more willing to take on smaller jobs. At the same time, the prospect of setting up an in-house digitization lab has become more daunting and increasingly requires a multiyear commitment to expensive hardware, software, and especially staff. Dan Pence, the head of the Systems Integration Group, estimates, for example, that the equipment simply to capture page images from eleven volumes of fragile nineteenth-century scientific volumes would total about $60,000. Often commercial vendors have an advantage in dealing with both generic materials (e.g., thousands of ordinary book pages) because of the scale of their operations and nonstandard materials (e.g., large-format maps) because they own expensive specialized equipment.[55]

Of course, outsourcing also entails costs that go beyond the bill that arrives at the end of the project. These include the staff time to solicit bids, select a vendor, and monitor a contract. Gertz lists more than thirty items you should include in a request for proposal (RFP) from a vendor and more than twenty criteria for assessing bids from contractors. A close study of the digital conversion costs in University of Michigan's Making of America project notes that preparing the RFP for scanning vendors "consumed several days of the project manager's time," and that was for a relatively simple contract that involved only page images and not OCR or typing. Yet the investment in a carefully prepared RFP can reap substantial savings; Michigan received fourteen bids on their contract, with prices ranging from ten cents to four dollars per page.[56]

Those considering outsourcing will also want to talk to colleagues about their experiences with particular vendors before they sign on the dotted line. Some organizations like the Research Libraries Group provide online lists of data conversion service bureaus about which it has received "positive reports."[57] Even with a signed contract in hand, you still need to select and prepare the materials for scanning and check on the quality of the work produced by the vendor, preferably before a major portion of the digital conversion has been done.

One topic not emphasized in official guides on outsourcing digitization, but known and discussed by everyone involved, is that outsourcing generally means sending the work to the Philippines, India, or China, and that the most important cost savings come from the considerably lower wages that prevail in those countries—sometimes as little as one-eighth or one-tenth what the same jobs pay in the United States. A medical transcriptionist (a position probably comparable to many jobs in data conversion) earns between $1.50 and $2.00 per hour in India and $13 per hour in the United States. Not surprisingly, in the current political climate of concern over the outsourcing of American jobs, most cultural institutions would rather avoid talking about where their digitizing is being done. (Offshore vendors point out that the same skittishness does not extend to the purchase of the computers and scanners for in-house digitization; little, if any, of this equipment is manufactured in the United States.) Interviewed by *Computerworld* for an article describing how Innodata Isogen (probably the largest digitizer of cultural heritage materials) had digitized in the Philippines the records of the U.S. Exploring Expedition of 1838–1842, Martin Kalfatovic, head of the Smithsonian Institution Libraries' New Media Office, explained perhaps a tad defensively that "in terms of the marketplace, there aren't onshore options."[58]

Some commercial digitizing work is still done in the United States, but it is much more likely to involve preliminary scanning of rare and fragile objects—for example, setting up a local image scanning operation and then sending the images overseas for further processing. In addition, work that requires relatively little labor—running automatic OCR on standard texts—can be done at competitive prices here. Quite commonly, projects employ a hybrid approach—doing parts locally that are either more economical or that are dictated by the condition of the materials. Sometimes that means creating page images of rare or fragile materials that can't leave the premises, although even in this case, some vendors—Luna Imaging, for example—will set up shop at your location and do the work for you.

If you are not worried about the materials, it may be cheaper to send them off for scanning, as the Million Book project at Carnegie Mellon University is doing by crating up books and shipping them to India. The University of Michigan sent the volumes in their Making of America project to Mexico for the scanning of page images (an expensive proposition because someone had to place fragile, but not necessarily rare, pages individually on a scanner) but did the automatic OCR in their own facility. In fact, the University of Michigan offers data conversion services to external clients. But for large-scale and labor-intensive historical projects (e.g., those requiring careful setup, proofing, coding, or rekeying), the offshore vendors dominate. In-country "capability has essentially disappeared," says a leading museum consultant.[59]

The advice to seriously consider commercial vendors applies most clearly to large-scale projects, especially those subject to bulk processing, those that require substantial manual work (keying, correcting, or mark-up), and those that don't involve rare or fragile materials. By contrast, you should handle small batches of documents with your own scanner and OCR software or by sending them to a local typist. But it is hard to know where to draw the line between "large" and "small." Most large commercial vendors would probably disdain projects involving fewer than 5,000 pages of text, fewer than ten books, or a price tag of less than $10,000 unless they saw it as a pilot project that might lead to a larger contract later. Moreover, because commercial vendors charge set-up costs running into the thousands of dollars, you will wind up paying much more per page for a small job than a large one. Not surprisingly, vendors give their lowest prices to giant corporations like Thomson, Pro-Quest, and EBSCO, whose digitizing projects can run into the millions of dollars. If your project seems too small for a commercial vendor but not something you want to do yourself, you might investigate whether other groups within your institution or even at other institutions with whom you have alliances may be interested in bundling together a project with yours. Or, you might find a local vendor who digitizes smaller batches of materials, although they will generally lack the ability to deal with specialized materials or mark-up.

Considerations about whether outsourcing or in-house work is less expensive are essentially irrelevant for the very large number of history digitization projects carried out with very small budgets or no budget at all. If you have more time (or staff) than money, you are likely to do the work yourself. We happily note that the "do-it-yourself" spirit has driven some of the most exciting and pioneering history web efforts. Those contemplating that path should take inspiration from those who have digitized large corpuses of historical materials without the aid of grants or even research assistants. Jim Zwick, for example, has personally digitized—mostly with an ordinary flatbed scanner and OmniPage OCR software—the tens of thousands of pages of documents that make up the 1,250 web pages in his widely used Anti-Imperialism website. Although he reports that he has devoted "thousands of hours" to the effort, he also notes that he is "satisfied with the time it took" because "the site has received far more use and been far more influential than I originally expected."[60] Building your own website and digitizing your own documents may not be the quickest or the most cost-effective route to getting on the History Web, but like building your own house, it can be the most satisfying. The same goes for designing your site, to which we now turn.

Chapter 4

Designing for the History Web

In this chapter you will learn about

- General principles for designing a historical website
- How web design differs from print design
- The formatting of text for different genres of sites
- Methods for sizing and laying out images
- The presentation of audio and video
- Proper site structure and navigation
- Issues related to accessibility, and how they apply to your project

Even before you have finished digitizing the material you will need for your website, you will need to begin thinking about the site's design. At this point most historians once again face unfamiliar territory. But if historians typically have few preconceived notions about server set up or audio sampling rates, many hold firm opinions about web design. Users of the web encounter attractive and functional sites, and awkward and unfriendly pages, all the time, and each of us is confident we know the difference between good and bad design and that everyone else is wrong about such things. People who would rarely venture precise aesthetic commentaries about paintings in a museum nevertheless tend to have strong opinions about the layout, colors, fonts, and other design elements of a website—and of all websites. In no other medium has David Hume's dictum perhaps rung truer, that "Beauty is no quality in things themselves: It exists merely in the mind which contemplates them; and each mind perceives a different beauty."[1]

With these myriad viewpoints, web design has become highly contested and occasionally belligerent. Because the Internet is still in its infancy compared to other media that historians use, few conventions have arisen, yet everyone seems to know where true perfection lies. In addition, the pull of commercial designers has been strong across the web. Few books discuss academic web design, as opposed to commercial web design, and some would even say that separate guides are unnecessary. In light of this situation, we should remember that the self-declared gurus have been working in a medium that is barely a decade old and that has constantly changed in this incredibly brief time span. It seems a little unreasonable for a science (or a philosophy or an art) of web aesthetics to arise in such a short period of time.

This, of course, has not stopped anyone from making sure proclamations, and sometimes good business, out of web design. Listening to various schools of thought and companies involved with web design is important, if only momentarily and if only to gain some insight into what might be relevant to *historical* work on the web. Proponents of usability have provided web designers with a better sense of how actual human beings (instead of the human beings we envision—who are, naturally, all like ourselves) use the web. Like the economists who have approached their discipline's notion of "rational choice" (that human beings always make sane, calculated choices about money, prices, and major life decisions) with skepticism, usability consultants such as Jakob Nielsen and Steve Krug have made important discoveries about the quite odd ways people approach a web page that historians looking to use the web without frustrating their audience should note and consider. As these consultants highlight, most visitors to most websites do not take the time to look at every part of a web page with the same attention that their authors took in designing them. Hand constantly on the mouse, with an itchy trigger finger, the average web surfer often clicks on decent rather than optimal links to see if they will find what they are looking for. Sometimes coming to a web page directly from another site (rather than the parent site's home page), the surfer engages in disoriented stumbling rather than rational, linear touring. Words that seem clear to the web designer can be confusing to most web visitors. If a website is a tool, Nielsen and Krug tell us, then we want it to be as usable as possible, and good design helps to achieve that important goal. Surely there is nothing wrong with—and much to be appreciated in—the clear construction and function of your web pages.[2]

The problem with this sort of thinking, which has been developed in large part to make it more likely that web surfers check out and pay for items in their electronic shopping carts, is that it encourages oversimplification. As the title of Steve Krug's usability book declares, with scarcely a trace of cynicism, *Don't Make Me Think*. This can be a frightening title to show to a historian, whose very mission involves trying to make others think about the past. Don't make me think about what? Why not? And isn't commercial exchange a poor model for academic interaction? The usability camp, of course, would say that their writings and consulting fees are more about reducing the "friction" in use and obfuscation of information associated with bad design for any purpose, including academic ones. But sites that follow this method to an extreme often do end up with little to ponder and large buttons to press for obvious things. It *is*, after all, remarkably easy to check out with your books at Amazon.com, but are their editors' reviews as substantial as the *Times Literary Supplement*? Wouldn't more scholarly and nuanced reviews "clog" Amazon's web pages with lengthy digressions and footnotes to other works?

At the other end of the spectrum of web design are the aesthetes, who dangle the highly attractive possibility that every site, on any topic, can look beautiful and unique. We all want to be creative and, as we have already noted, we have definite notions of beauty on the web. Stuck with boring-looking texts and the confines of the book and essay for so long, why not revel in the freedom and artistic possibilities of the web? With the economically minded publisher out of the way and the world of color and graphics open to all, why not take advantage and make a lively, lush site? Surely any historical site that follows this path would be, at first glance, far more interesting than 99 percent of websites out there. The rub, of course, is whether such a focus would sacrifice historical understanding on the altar of the artistic muse, or instead enhance that understanding through novel, aesthetically pleasing design tailored to the material.

The South Korean poet and web designer Young-Hae Chang does a good job assessing and criticizing both the usability camp and the aesthetes, and the associated tension between beauty and utility in web design, in his Artist's Statement No. 45,730,944: The Perfect Artistic Web Site. "I've been thinking about it now for at least the last few minutes," Chang tells the viewer in the large-type style of the conceptual artist Jenny Holzer as Bud Powell's piano jazz plays in the background, "The newest multimedium: The web. The biggest art space: The web. The greatest chance to say something or to make something . . . dumb, or, better yet, boring. Breathtakingly boring. Deathly boring." As Chang's lighthearted musings about the nature of the web devolve into more serious concerns about the military ambitions of North Korea, the viewer quickly gets the idea that the web can be a powerful medium of expression in addition to a bazaar for one-click commerce, and it seems a shame to dumb it down, or design it down, to the point where it is simple to use but has lost its ability to convey profound thoughts and emotions. At the same time, however, Chang gently mocks the artistic aspirations of many using the web. "Yes, upload for a long time, for a long long time, for the time it takes to watch day turn into night, a fat, juicy file of web art. Waiting for reply . . . still waiting . . . and while waiting, isn't this the perfect moment to reflect on life and death?" he jokes, tongue firmly in cheek.[3] Does web art really aid expression, or is it as heavy-handed as the files are large? Is it worth the wait at the end

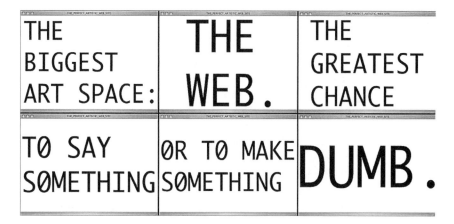

Figure 21. Through sequential screens of black words on a blank white background, Young-Hae Chang's Artist's Statement No. 45,730,944: The Perfect Artistic Web Site cleverly mocks the aspirations of both the "dumb it down" and "make everything art" schools of web design.

of a slow modem? Or is text, even the hyperbolic text of Chang's "Perfect Artistic Web Site" (ironically, one of rare "artistic" websites with absolutely no color or images) ultimately more interesting?

We believe historians can learn important lessons from both the usability camp and the creativity of the aesthetes, and that we can successfully navigate a middle way between these poles. Surely historians cannot blindly follow a design regime that relegates thinking to a secondary status; neither should we obscure historical materials and our ideas about the past in deference to pure artistic license. Clio is our muse, and she is the muse of history, not art (although some particularly creative individuals strive to crossbreed history and art). To follow her seems to imply that we refrain, in most cases, from hindering our website visitors' ability to use the materials and think for themselves about them, or from obscuring our historical interpretations—which most of the time we will still express in that most ancient of formats, text—in a swirling mist of colorful pixels. Yet done properly, graphical sophistication and occasionally even challenging design can help place historical materials and ideas in formats that solicit powerful responses from viewers. Put succinctly, our rallying cry on the web must therefore be: *enable and inspire me to think about and grasp the past*. Our colleague and fellow historian Michael O'Malley similarly argues that "the look and feel of a website . . . are part of its ideology, part of its thesis or argument," and he tries in his inventive course websites "to convey some of the philosophy of history informing the course" through their design.[4] Design in the service of historical understanding is easier said than done, however, and this chapter is intended to go through the specifics of what that means, and with different kinds of historical websites.

A final, and perhaps counterproductive, word about design before we begin this discussion. An honest appraisal would show that many historical websites have successfully answered our rallying cry without great or even decent design. For example, one of the best-known sites on the history of atomic bomb tests from the perspective of American servicemen is the Atomic Veterans History Project. Compared, for example, to the Korean War Educator site, which has similar memoirs from veterans, this site pales in a designer's eye. However, because of its early launch on the web (1997), wealth of information, constant updating, and a particularly active user base that contributes content via email (more about this process in Chapter 6), the Atomic Veterans site has received a large share of traffic and notice. Indeed, many of the links on the Korean War Educator's subsection on the atomic tests link to the more poorly designed Atomic Veterans site. This is a not uncommon situation across the History Web.[5]

If design appears to have little to do with the overall success of a site such as the Atomic Veterans History Project, some might question whether good design matters at all. That is the position of law professor Doug Lindner, who defends what he admits to be the "clunky" and "garish" design of his Famous Trials website by noting that "I'm not a web design expert and I can't afford to hire one." His goal, he writes, is not to display "all the capabilities of modern web-building technology" but "to lay out the materials in an obvious and understandable way."[6] We feel that the importance of good design depends, in part, on the expectations of visitors. Most visitors to amateur websites, such as Atomic Veterans and Famous Trials, will forgive design flaws as long as the information desired is placed within easy reach or the site has other virtues such as a unique point of view or documents found nowhere else on the Internet—as both of these sites have in abundance. Atomic Veterans devotees may actually find its imperfect design validating, since thematically the site sets itself in opposition to the slicker, official information sources on atomic testing from the government.

In contrast, visitors to websites constructed under the auspices of institutions known to pay more attention to design in the real world, especially museums and historical societies but also official college or university websites, demand much more. In fact, they may consciously or unconsciously register disappointment or skepticism about such sites if their design is thoughtless or underdeveloped. For this reason, more and more large institutions, such as the Wisconsin Historical Society, now hire professional web design firms to create their sites.[7] Even some individual historians and organizations with modest funding have handed off the web production so that they may focus on composing or digitizing the content of the site itself. We do not cast shame on those who had their dissertations typed and formatted for them; the same generosity should hold for the digital age.

Costs can be significant if you outsource your web design, but may be worth it if you need to meet high expectations among your audience. With web development rapidly becoming part of the curriculum of many undergraduate and graduate design programs, you may be lucky enough to find an enterprising art student who would be willing to help you for little or no fee, as a chance to try out and improve their new skills. Many capable individual web designers can be found locally or on online freelancing exchanges for hourly rates around $25–$75, and for a small, noninteractive site, design costs could be held to several thousand dollars—still a significant amount of money, of course. A modest site for a historical society with good-looking yet basic pages describing the organization and how to join generally falls into this range. High-end museum exhibit and television tie-in websites such as those produced by Second Story for PBS or the Smithsonian Institution cost tens of thousands of dollars. For example, the Smithsonian's National Museum of American History handed off the production of their site exhibiting artifacts from September 11, 2001 to Second Story for roughly $30,000, a reduced rate in deference to the subject matter. Sites that require extensive programming or databases can easily top $100,000 because hourly rates for software developers and database administrators are commensurately high. There may very well be a chasm between the high design of museum sites and the more stripped-down productions of dedicated (but cash-poor) individual historians or small historical societies, but we nevertheless believe that all creators of web content can benefit from solid principles of good design, navigation, and accessibility that this chapter lays out.[8]

General Principles of Design

We do not have to start such a discussion from scratch. Surely all historians, even those with no experience with the web, have encountered good design in other media, and without getting into any technical issues we can discuss what makes historical materials and the interpretations of them more accessible and thought provoking. Historians who are novices in web design would do well to look at other instances of design than just the web. The bookshelf, home to so much historical endeavor through the ages, is as good a place as any to start.

As Michael O'Malley reminds us, we take the book for granted, but it embodies literally centuries of thought about design and use.[9] Indeed, the book's familiarity masks many of the elements that make it such a rich and easy-to-use medium for ideas. Modern books have limited parameters, certain structures and conventions that have arisen through an evolutionary process akin to natural selection guided by the predilections of book buyers, readers, and publishers. You do not find many outrageously large books or many tiny ones. Indeed, aside from some large format coffee table and special purpose books, most come in an easily handled size between 6 and 12 inches high and 4 and 10 inches wide. The text within a book rarely goes to the edge of the page, instead nestling itself within roughly half-inch to inch-wide margins. Almost without exception there are numbers on the pages to tell you where you are. A title page, table of contents, and index are found far more often than not. In most history books footnotes or endnotes help to clarify the main text and refer to other books and documents. Chapters bring together more focused themes. Certain fonts are more prevalent than others. All of these elements are design choices, though by now so codified and commonplace as to seemingly disappear. Good design, in this case, does not necessarily mean *obvious* design, or design that attracts attention to itself rather than the content of a book.

Of course, books can also be beautiful. In an age when machine production triumphed over handcrafted goods, some Victorians actually became *more* interested in high quality design that augmented the beauty of books. Along with his work in the decorative arts and furniture, William Morris designed intricate cover illustrations, page borders, and bindings that lent Kelmscott Press books a rich look and feel. More recent designers of history books have used a mixture of graphics, maps, and text to create elegant works that also help readers come to a robust appreciation of the past. The study of the Peloponnesian War and ancient Greece is surely enhanced by the dynamic and beautiful design of Robert Strassler's *Landmark Thucydides*. Few historians would argue that this edition is inferior, say, to the flat, uninterrupted text of a cheap paperback edition. Diagrams explaining complex battlefield movements or photographs of archaeological finds from the era, such as coins and vases, are aptly placed adjacent to the relevant passages by Thucydides. One feels the reality of the war and the way of life in the fifth century B.C.E. far more than if the text (rich as it is with Thucydides' lucid depictions) was on an otherwise barren page.[10]

Graphical elements in books such as the *Landmark Thucydides*, including charts, small photographs, and other images, have achieved a certain formal design status in the same way the text of books has, though perhaps with less consistent success. As information designer Edward Tufte has shown with great skill in his books on information visualization, the

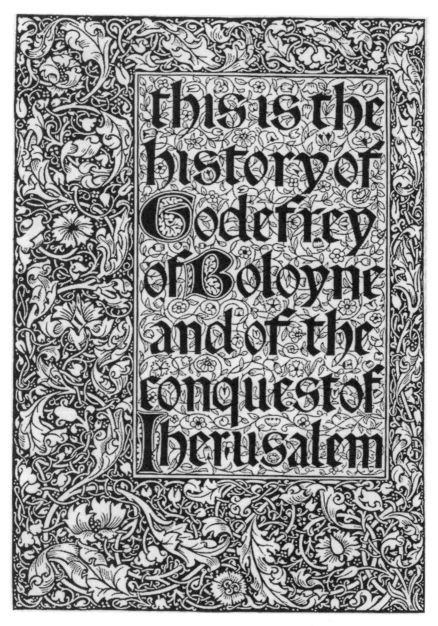

Figure 22. When information sources proliferate, design helps to distinguish them. The mass production of books in the Victorian age led some aesthetes, such as William Morris, to expend a greater effort on design, shown here in an elaborate title page to Kelmscott Press's *The History of Godefrey of Boloyne and of the Conquest of Jherusalem.*

presentation of graphics in print is often lacking compared to the presentation of text. Like text, visual information should be an effective means of communicating ideas from historians to their audiences, as well as allowing those audiences to draw their own conclusions, just as they do reading interpretive prose. But sometimes graphics that break up the text of history books and essays, such as bar graphs and pie charts, create unnecessary distractions rather than provide substantive information. Instead of helpful graphical additions, publishers and authors often treat readers to what Tufte derisively labels "chartjunk."[11]

To combat this tendency, Tufte provides some basic design rules that are as useful online as they are in print. He highlights the essential tension between getting lots of information across to a reader or viewer in a small amount of space and crowding the page with "ink." For Tufte, the elegance and impact of design comes in the resolution of this tension. How do you get your points across without presenting a dizzying array of text and graphics? How can you maximize expression without cluttering a page? How can you juxtapose elements in a way that allows readers to draw their own conclusions rather than bludgeoning them with the obvious?

One of Tufte's most celebrated examples of great design in historical texts is Charles Joseph Minard's map showing the disastrous expedition by Napoleon's army into Russia in 1812. As Tufte shows, the map (which he believes "may well be the best statistical graphic ever drawn") accomplishes all that a well-designed historical work should. First and foremost, it depicts a tremendous amount of historical knowledge in a way that illuminates an important conclusion about the Napoleonic Wars and the consequences of Napoleon's enormous hubris. On the two-dimensional space of the printed page (and similarly on a computer screen) there are actually six variables compared, the most telling of which are the rapidly shrinking size of the French army throughout the ill-fated campaign and the commensurate frigid temperatures of the Russian winter. Of the 422,000 men who leave Poland to conquer Moscow (the beige swath running from left to right), a mere 10,000 return (the black line just below the beige, running from right to left). The tragedy of this pivotal historical event comes through in the thin (and constantly thinning) graphical depiction of the retreating forces. An unconventional yet unmistakable beauty arises from an elegant font, careful proportions, and judicious use of white space and contrast. Minard's *carte figurative* is an ideal that one suspects can be emulated, although perhaps not matched, on the web.[12]

Larry Gales of the University of Washington Computing and Communications Department has done a good job translating Tufte's ideas to the web. Some of the key points Gales makes are worth adding here,

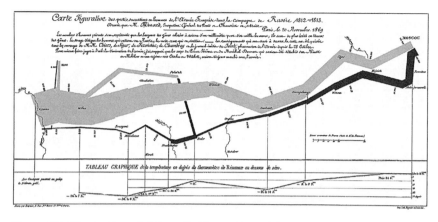

Figure 23. Charles Joseph Minard's illustration of the fate of Napoleon's army during a cold Russian winter conveys a tremendous amount of historical information in an economical, elegant, and persuasive way. (For a larger, color version, see ⇨ link 4.12.)

especially for historians who work with statistics, graphics, and images. The breadth and fine-grained quality of a printed page (or poster or work of art) can display a bird's eye view of a subject more easily than a computer screen, Gales notes. Thus the web implicitly encourages sequential "pages" of information rather than one giant creation in the style of Minard. In turn, this sequentiality and the ease with which you can jump around and between these pages (rather than move in a linear fashion through a book) means that good navigation is essential on the web to allow an audience to figure out where they are and where they might like to go next. At the same time, and in tension with this point, the more space on a web page taken up by navigation, controls, menus, and links, the less left for the content the audience wants. Finally, in the balance between text and graphics, the web (and the Internet in general) still favors text as the best method to disseminate complex information quickly.[13]

Underlying many of Tufte's and Gales's tenets is the technology of the web itself. Part of the problem with translating many of the best design elements of print to the web is that the web is in many respects a greatly inferior medium. Fully unfold a section of the *New York Times* and hold it up next to an average 15-inch computer screen. Not only is the total page size more than four times as large as the screen, but the much finer printing mechanism of a modern newspaper press (1,200 dots per inch for the *Times*) compared to a common screen (between 72 and 96 pixels per inch) means that in the former medium text and graphics can be scaled fairly small while still remaining legible. The stock tables and charts in the *Wall Street Journal* versus the same information on Yahoo Finance makes this abundantly clear—in a two-page spread the *Journal* can cover most listings on the New York Stock Exchange, whereas on a single screen Yahoo can barely show the chart for the Dow Jones Industrial index and the ten most active stocks for the day. This giant gap in resolution between the old medium and the new makes designers like Tufte despair about the prospects for displaying information elegantly and efficiently on the web.

Worse—and often not appreciated by those new to web design—is that we can't fully control the medium, even when we can dictate our site's underlying code. A publisher totally commands the production and display of a book, and once a book is printed it is fixed in its format and doesn't change (other than to acquire coffee spills, dog-ears, and other hazards of use). By contrast, the web producer may roughly control the design of a site through HTML, but the client computer has a large say in how this HTML renders on a user's screen. Each browser interprets HTML in its own fashion, which can cause headaches for those who want to be sure that every visitor sees exactly the same thing. Indeed, this consistency is essentially impossible on the web, unlike in print where each copy of a book is identical. Although Microsoft's virtual monopoly on computer operating systems and web browsers means that close to 85 percent of audiences for historical websites are using a Windows PC with Internet Explorer, there are many versions of both Windows and Internet Explorer, and some combinations render the same web pages slightly differently. In addition, the small minority of Macintosh users (though larger than 5 percent in academic institutions), and a smaller but growing minority of Linux users, will see minor differences in sites compared to the Windows masses. Moreover, screen sizes vary from 640 × 480 pixels on a small screen to over 2,000 x 1,500 pixels on the largest screens. And color can vary somewhat from screen to screen and platform to platform, so that a bright yellow on one computer may look slightly brownish on another.

Yet we must forge on in this uncertain environment where we do not have full control of what our site's visitors see. The web has more than enough flexibility and methods for laying out text and images to ensure that basic design principles from the past can be brought successfully into the future. In addition, those who hew closely to web standards will find that their sites render more consistently on different computers and in different browsers than they did in the 1990s, given that most recent browsers implement these standards effectively and in a similar way.[14]

In *The Non-Designer's Web Book* Robin Williams and John Tollett take their ultimate inspiration not from the new medium of the web (though

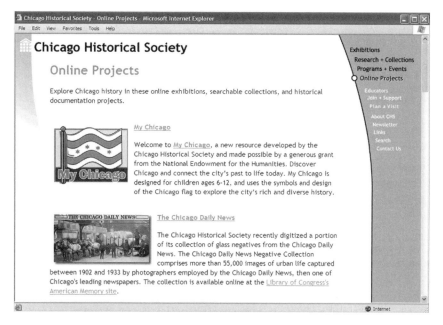

(a) A Windows PC with Internet Explorer.

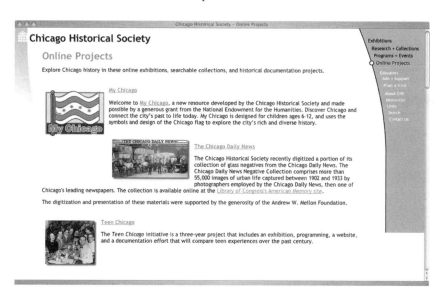

(b) A Macintosh with Safari.

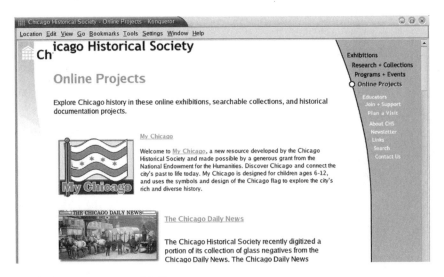

(c) A Linux computer with Konqueror.

Figures 24a–c. Comparing the Chicago Historical Society's online projects web page on (a) an average PC using the Internet Explorer web browser, (b) a Macintosh with a larger screen using the Safari web browser, and (c) a Linux computer using the Konqueror web browser shows how a site can appear slightly differently in different situations. With its bigger window, the Mac version stretches the paragraphs horizontally, while its browser mysteriously discontinues the vertical swath of color that runs down the right side of the page. The Linux version breaks apart the Society's name, and since the operating system does not have the Trebuchet font specified in the HTML for this page (as the Mac and PC do), the browser defaults to a plainer font that also renders in different sizes in each paragraph. Using web standards such as Cascading Style Sheets (CSS) would solve some of these inconsistencies across platforms, though not all of them.

they use many digital examples), but from design principles first perfected in the world of print. They highlight four helpful tenets of design. First, Williams and Tollett emphasize the importance of *contrast* on a page, as elements are set off against each other in a pattern that allows the eye to explore different features, draw conclusions, or simply appreciate the pattern itself. Similarly, they note how *proximity* implies a relationship between features on a page, so that a caption or a subtitle needs to be placed close enough to a photograph or a passage for a viewer to associate the two elements. Feeling the order (or disorder) from the *alignment* (or misalignment) of elements—vertically or horizontally on a page—is also a natural part of the way we look at visual creations. Finally, human beings tend to associate elements that are produced in the same way—the same font, the same color, the same size, the same texture—and so a web designer must be careful to *repeat* certain design elements appropriately to make a point, or to maintain consistency across the many web pages of a single website.[15]

The application of Williams and Tollett's four fundamental principles of design will raise a confusing eyesore to a legible, comprehensible, and aesthetically acceptable site. To go further, it is worth spending a little bit of time examining not the conventions of print but the conventions of art. Reacquaint yourself with artists who are masters of some of the formal techniques necessary for a well-designed website. For example, to get a sense of how light and dark elements can be placed on the page and made to contrast with one another and arrange themselves in telling and aesthetically pleasing ways, look at paintings by Joseph Wright of Derby or photographs by Ansel Adams. To see how text can look elegant in columns and rows, spaced properly, and laid out next to images, pick up a book on the Chinese painter and calligrapher Zhao Mengfu or a medieval European book of hours. Such works of art will add other principles—perhaps higher principles—to Williams and Tollett's fundamentals of alignment, proximity, repetition, and contrast. These include proportion and balance, the advanced use of color and geometry, and the elusive concept known as beauty.

As the saying goes, however, you must first learn to crawl before you can walk, or perhaps run. Good historical web design begins, as Williams and Tollett emphasize, when you place text and any images or multimedia into relationships with each other and the other essential elements of a web page—for example, navigation buttons or a logo—with each element taking its rightful place and garnering the appropriate amount of attention. Alignment, proximity, repetition, and contrast must be used intelligently for visitors to your site to view, read, and understand these elements. We first look at each of the basic features of a web page, and then examine some good examples (and a few less optimal ones) of placing these features together in ways that enable and inspire us to think about and grasp the past (or in the imperfect examples, to obscure it).

Text

Text, the largest part of most historical sites, has to be formatted properly on the web, just as in print. Centuries of experience with books has taught us that we cannot display the written word comfortably in a limitless variety of formats. The way the eye moves across the page mandates

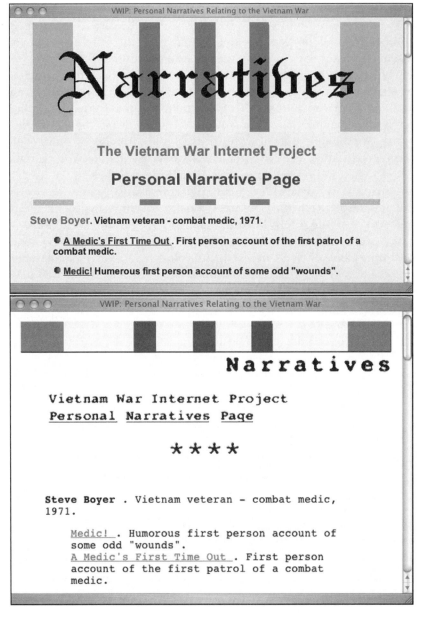

Figure 25. Michael O'Malley's redesign of this Vietnam history site shows how attention to the major principles of design, such as alignment and repetition, as well as some thought about the site's theme (why gothic fonts when there are more appropriate ones such as Courier, which suggests typewriting?), can transform a haphazard website into a more compelling form.

that the length of a line of characters be within a certain range—a parameter true for all languages, including those that are written from right to left, such as Arabic, Hebrew, and Urdu, or ideographic languages that are frequently written from the top of the page to the bottom, like Korean, Japanese, and Chinese. Carrying this important print design convention over to the web means that you should restrict a column of text to a width of between 300 and 600 pixels, for a total of between 8 and 16 words per line if you use an average-sized font such as 12 point Times. Obviously, narrower columns look (and read) more like a newspaper, whereas 500 to 600 pixel-wide columns appear more like a book. Regardless of the look you are going for, be sure to maintain white-space (or at least neutral-color) margins on either side of the text. If you plan to have images, illustrations, or charts next to the text, leave at least 10 pixels (and preferably between 30 and 50 pixels) of space between these graphical elements and the block of text.

Robin Walsh's Journeys in Time, 1809–1822: The Journals of Lachlan & Elizabeth Macquarie shows how historians can design text well on the web. In this case, the text consists of commentaries and historical background by Walsh, as well as featured transcripts from the subjects of the website, two Scots who moved to Australia during a period of great upheaval. Mostly casual journal entries rather than the formal prose found in a book, the text is appropriately set in a relatively slim column 340 pixels wide, nicely aligned vertically with other elements on the page, and with a separation of 40 pixels from the blue left-hand navigation bar. Legacies of the digitization and transcription process (the conversion of the journals from handwriting to machine-readable text), such as strike-throughs and superscript writing, are also handled well.[16]

The font you plan to use depends somewhat on your own taste, but a survey of sites (commercial and noncommercial) that have a lot of text shows a growing agreement that sans-serif fonts (those without little flourishes at the ends of the letters) are more readable than serif fonts online. Years of reading historical texts has predisposed us to the view that sans serif fonts are less serious than serif fonts, but long passages of text do look a little crisper on most screens in sans serif, and moreover they are easier to read at different sizes, particularly the smaller sizes used for notes. Sans-serif fonts found on most computers include Verdana, Arial, and Helvetica; common serif fonts include Times, Times Roman, and Bookman. Try to avoid monospaced fonts like Courier for main blocks of text (though Courier is nice for suggesting typewriting where you seek that effect). While the flexibility of the web permits any font to be of any color, only in rare circumstances should you make your fonts a color other than black (the default color on the web) or near-

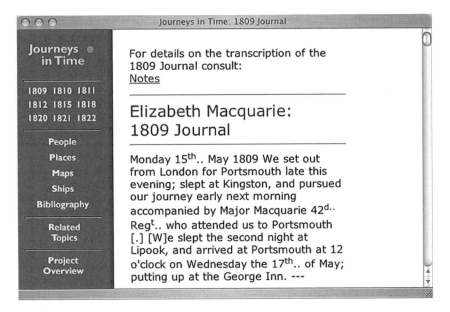

Figure 26. Robin Walsh's Journeys in Time, 1809–1822: The Journals of Lachlan & Elizabeth Macquarie formats its primary source texts extremely well, making them easy to read while retaining as much of the character of the original documents as possible, including super- and subscripted writing.

black, or white or near-white if the background of the text is black or very dark. High contrast is essential for legibility.

But what about the more important question of the text itself, once you have decided on a legible format with the proper specification of column widths, margins, fonts, and hues? Here we diverge from many in the web design community—both commercial and nonprofit designers—as part of our mission as historians. Not surprisingly, the usability school advocates placing only small, quickly scannable passages of text on the web, and far too many web designers have followed this lead. While acknowledging that long-form writing like the journal article can remain intact online, even Patrick Lynch and Sarah Horton, the university-based authors of the *Web Style Guide* and standard-bearers for academic web design, accept the need for a reduction or "chunking" of most text on the web for ease of use. Lynch and Horton talk about the "disorientation" that occurs when a poor web surfer is forced to read long passages, and they seem resigned to the notion that "most information on the World Wide Web is gathered in short reference documents that are intended to be read nonsequentially." This acquiescence strikes us as too close to the lowest-common-denominator thinking that historians have always fought against in favor of rich interpretation and the joy of the written word itself. As Jay Leno disparagingly remarked when *USA Today* began publication, "If you can't write, list." Must we condemn the web to a similar future?[17]

This skepticism toward long-form text on the web may turn out to be transient. More people are reading ever longer passages on a computer screen, and for better or worse that trend will continue because a greater and greater percentage of our lives involves digital media. Monitors have continued to improve, with flat-panel liquid crystal displays now comprising a large share of the market. While these newer technologies still fall short of the exemplary contrast and resolution of print on paper, they are a great improvement and surely the harbinger of even better screens to come. And we concur with Lynch and Horton that users can print out web pages when they want to read a lot of text without the eyestrain associated with screens. Making sure your web pages print easily, or having special pages just for printing, can be a good idea for a historical essay or exhibit site with a lot of text.[18]

Moreover, we believe in the simple proposition that good writing produces willing readers, regardless of the medium. After all, there are committed readers of websites such as the *Chronicle of Higher Education*'s Arts & Letters Daily and other sources of relatively highbrow and lengthy texts on the web.[19] Unchallenged, the widespread agreement about the chunking of text may produce even less tolerance for long passages on the web as time goes by. Historians must combat this trend aggressively if we are to claim this medium as our own. Instead of cultivating a style that seems suitable to a chronically short attention span, we should rather look for ways to make long passages of text acceptably quick-loading (dividing them if necessary into a sequence of reasonably sized pages, reducing the number and heft of graphics that accompany the text) and readable (by following the formatting rules above in addition to reducing distractions like bands of color and encroaching images). Most of all, we need to give as much attention to our writing on the web as we do to our writing in media that we know will be read, assessed, criticized, and responded to by our peers. Just because the web makes it easy to disseminate the written word doesn't mean that we should abandon our high standards for prose.

Images, Color, and Multimedia

Edward Tufte's conclusions about the often superfluous or distracting role of graphical elements in print media represent an equally good admonishment to historians who find themselves attracted by the ease with which one can place images and other nontext features on a web

Figure 27. The popularity of the text-heavy Arts & Letters Daily shows that many web surfers have longer attention spans than many web usability and design consultants believe.

page. Indeed, the mere availability of color and the possibility of using an unlimited number of images (or even video and audio) on a site present welcome opportunities for scholars who have had to content themselves with producing black-and-white books with at most a small number of gray-scale photographs or graphics. A publisher's concession of a handful of additional images, or a segment of a book with color reproductions, has been known to cause much rejoicing among historians who have signed a book contract. The fact that you can add as many full-color graphics as you would like and even change the color of the "paper" a web page is "written" on is enticing.

Although historians do not need to stoically ignore the magical temptation of color and graphics, they would be wise to remember what happened to the sailors who became entranced by the goddess Circe. No one wants a porcine website replete with ugly images and garish hues. Lynch and Horton make some sensible recommendations about the use of color that can help historians avoid this predicament. If you decide to use large areas of color on your website, either to differentiate sections of a page or as a background, choose an unobtrusive color such as beige, grey, or one of the pastels, or at the very least choose a color your text will read well against.[20] With a restrained baseline color, images and text will stand out, and the viewer's eyes will be attracted to what's important rather than the background or page margins. Although HTML makes it possible to have an image as a background (either singly, taking up the whole page, or "tiled," where it repeats across the page), avoid doing so. Background images distract readers and make any overlaid text less legible.

Follow the same principles of color that have proven successful in print. In *Envisioning Information*, Edward Tufte notes that color is the principal way the mind separates elements in space and chooses something to focus on. Thus you should use rich or bright colors like red and yellow sparingly, and generally only for items you really wish to emphasize. Use different colors rather than different shapes to distinguish features on a page. Beware of the negative effects of certain highly contrasting colors placed next to each other (such as green and red), as well as the off-putting optical illusions created, for instance, by a series of parallel lines. If navigational elements have color at all, make sure their hues don't distract viewers from focusing on the main content of the page.[21]

Web design publications often talk about using only "web-safe" or "browser-safe" colors, meaning a limited palette that will show up roughly the same in all browsers and operating systems. But, as the web designer Lynda Weinman has noted, very few computers still display only 256 colors, their capability when the web was young. Indeed, most people view the web in millions of colors now, and so historians just starting on the web may ignore the browser-safe palette and its often garish, overly bright colors chosen for their mathematical simplicity rather than aesthetic value. Those experienced with this palette can continue to use it with no harm, but others shouldn't bother. The possible exception to this rule is if many of your anticipated users will be using very old computers, in which case you should choose something from the web-safe palette for any major swath of color on your page, as well as any colored fonts.[22]

In Chapter 3 we discussed the differences among various digital image formats. Now is the time that you can show what you have learned by making sure that you predominantly use one of the slimmer formats, JPEG or GIF. You do not have to banish those larger TIFFs, however. If your site needs detailed images to illustrate historical points or if it is an archive that values the extra information only a "heavy," high-resolution format can provide, link to the larger image from a thumbnail version (a small version of the original) that is in JPEG or GIF format (and warn your visitors about a possible delay in downloading the bigger file). Fred

Lifton, Michael Hanrahan, and Reed College's Faculty Multimedia Lab's website on nineteenth-century Formosa reflects a good understanding of the technical aspects of image reproduction on the web—at least beyond its large-graphic home page, which takes too long to load over a dial-up modem. Starting with small thumbnails on introductory pages, they then provide internal pages that have not one but three higher resolution formats. You can easily find what you are looking for, and then zoom in to the level of detail you desire.[23]

Thumbnail images also present an excellent opportunity to use a fundamental design principle Tufte calls "small multiples." Small multiples empower the strong human ability to compare and contrast—an important element in historical reasoning and argument. On the web, placing a series of thumbnail images of between 75×75 and 300×300 pixel size close to each other creates the effect. Although they are a bit too small in our opinion, the dozens of black-and-white images of the Amiens Cathedral Project at Columbia University show the power of small multiples. Redone in a slightly larger size and released from their slender right-hand frame, these images could provide in a single glance an overview of the cathedral and smart navigation for the site. Harappa: The Indus Valley and the Raj in India and Pakistan also uses small multiples to display and annotate finds from archaeological digs. The thumbnails are again slightly too small but they are clear enough to give the novice viewer of this art history a fascinating overview of the field. Dana Leibsohn and Barbara Mundy's Vistas: Visual Culture in Spanish America, 1520–1820 gets almost everything right in their gallery of images. The multiple images are sized well and contrast nicely with the black background. No unnecessary borders or fake frames crowd the images. You feel as though you are in a museum, and yet the web experience means that you can zoom in on any of the thumbnails to examine them more closely. As Vistas shows, besides providing information in a potent and compact format while providing links to other pages and sections of a website, small multiples also tend to look good in a purely artistic way.[24]

The same principles hold true for multimedia: if you have many video, Flash, or animation files, you should try to use thumbnail stills from them as launch points. For audio, brief text excerpts transcribed from the best part of the recording or a short summary provide acceptable substitutes. Historical Voices's website Remembering the Flint Sit-Down Strike, 1936–1937, uses several methods to provide entrée into their recordings: in some cases they matched archival photographs with the audio segments, and in other cases they composed brief descriptions. For both audio and video, you should add a time stamp showing how long a segment is (in minutes and seconds) and the total size of the mul-

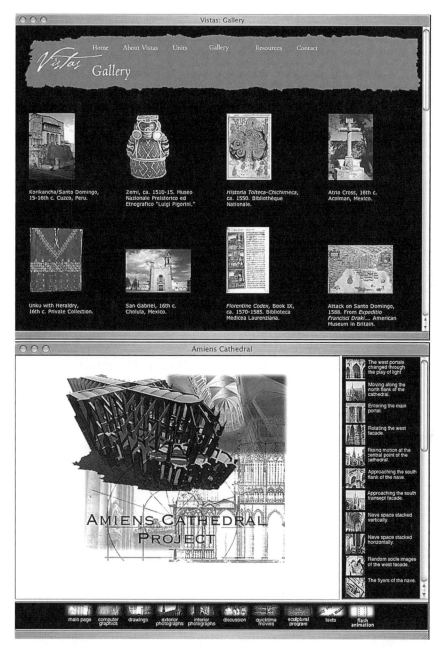

Figure 28. Vistas: Visual Culture in Spanish America, 1520–1820 and The Amiens Cathedral Project use small versions, or thumbnails, of their images to provide a helpful overview of what's inside.

timedia file in megabytes (if you are not using streaming software). The Flint website does not do this, and thus visitors are left to wonder how long the audio will last.[25]

Putting It All Together

Hypertext, which provides the ability to move in a nonlinear way from one place to another, is a foundational principle of the web, and in such a medium you need to include some basic navigation tools on most, if not all, of the pages on your site. Common to most websites is some way to get back to the home page (for instance, by clicking on the logo for a historical organization or project); links to other main sections of the site, if any; a link to an "about the site" or credits page; and links to pages for any copyright, privacy, usage, or other legal notices (see Chapter 7). For large historical sites or archives, it may also be useful—some would say necessary—to have links to a site map and especially a search page (or simply a search box right on each page).[26] Navigation should be an integral part of the design of your site and can help to unify the site's overall look across a multitude of individual pages.

When all of the pieces—text, images and multimedia (if any), and navigation—come together in a well laid-out and structured historical site, the results can be both visually appealing and informative. The Sport of Life and Death: The Mesoamerican Ballgame, for example, is a well-funded museum site geared mainly toward a K-12 audience that displays many elements of good design, particularly in navigation. In providing a basic history of Mesoamerican culture from 1500 B.C.E. to the encounter with the Spanish, and in allowing schoolchildren (and the young at heart) to show what they've learned by putting the appropriate ceremonial garb on the ballgame players and helping them on the field, the site maintains an outstanding graphical consistency. Fonts and the beautiful Mesoamerican icons used for navigation are repeated throughout. Flash graphics and animation are integrated well and supplement the basic navigation for the main sections of the site with helpful, clickable maps and other ways of accessing materials. You could question whether the site's ubiquitous reliance on Flash and heavy graphics is necessary, especially if you view it over a slow modem. Interactive features would have been difficult to do without Flash, but the site's creators could have made most of the other parts of the site in plain, faster loading HTML. This is the sort of richly illustrated site that wins web awards (indeed it won the Best Museum Web Site at the Museums and the Web 2002 Conference) because those who hand out such awards always have the latest, fanciest computers and high-speed Internet con-

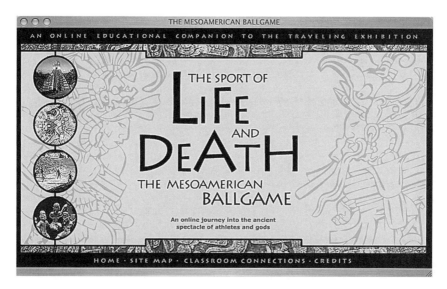

Figure 29. Like many other high-end museum websites, The Sport of Life and Death: The Mesoamerican Ballgame uses images and Flash technology extensively, serving the subject matter well through graphics and interactivity, though making the site less tolerable over a slow modem.

nections and thus care less about the time it takes to load a web page containing an engaging video clip or interactive map.[27]

Far less flashy (so to speak) but equally informative, and a good example of an important historical archive made accessible through unobtrusive design, is Gwendolyn Hall's Afro-Louisiana History and Genealogy, 1718–1820. An attractive grayscale opening page leads to simple, but also attractive (and more colorful), interior pages with information about the collection as well as essential search forms. (The jarring contrast between the home page and the interior pages is somewhat odd, and the designers probably should have chosen one theme or the other.) Throughout, Hall and her team keep things simple, with an emphasis on easily accessing the vast archive of slave records. In particular, the search form uses nicely shaded tables that allow first-time visitors to understand instantly the various fields they can search (such as name, gender, and location), and the search results page is exemplary in its Google-like crisp design. You can scan the results without graphical distractions. All of this would look equally as good on a small or large screen and would function properly on an old computer as well as a brand new one. The explanatory text of the other interior pages is well laid out, though the use of elastic column sizes for text (programmed to

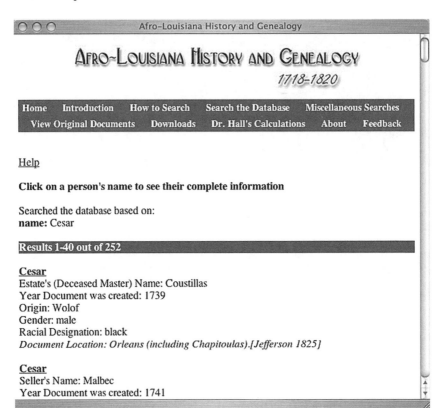

Figure 30. The spare, nicely laid out search results pages of Gwendolyn Hall's Afro-Louisiana History and Genealogy, 1718–1820 provide a clear window into its extensive archive of primary sources.

fill a certain percentage of the browser window rather a specific number of pixels) means that on a very large screen, some of the text stretches out to less-than-desirable line lengths. For the novice user, Hall could simplify and clarify the Afro-Louisiana History and Genealogy site even further by clarifying the distinctions between the normal search and the "miscellaneous" search, and between the "Introduction" and "About" pages. Combining these elements and using a slightly smaller font, the thick top navigation band could be reduced to a single line, thus freeing up more of the browser window for the site's important historical content.[28]

Rice University's Galileo Project, an engaging topical site on the Renaissance thinker and scientist, has a consistent and attractive light blue and gray design theme throughout, from the home page through

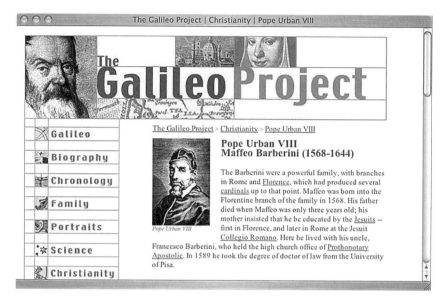

Figure 31. This page from Rice University's Galileo Project highlights the effectiveness of principles such as alignment and repetition. Unfortunately, some other pages on the site have poor contrast and hard-to-read right-justified text.

the most interior pages. This theme, however, works better for the similarly hued images than the text, which most visitors to the site will regard as more important. Take the first page of Galileo's biography, for instance. The serif typeface is blue with the underlined links in gray, both of which are difficult to read against the white background. Worse, the text is right justified to cozy up with the image of the Leaning Tower of Pisa, yet readers of English are used to text that is justified to the left margin and thus would find this page's legibility less than ideal. The creators of the site have constructed the more text-heavy pages, such as the biography of Pope Urban VIII, better, using a left-justified, 403-pixel-wide column that marshals the words into a book-like, readable format. Unfortunately, even here, the text remains blue and gray, poor choices for a historical website consisting predominantly of text.[29]

Site Structure and Good URLs

At the same time that you are creating all of those lucid and perhaps even attractive web pages, you must also figure out where all of them will "go" when you're finished, and how you will connect them. Although perhaps not as exciting as graphics and page layout, mapping a clear overall structure is critical to all well-designed websites. As Louis Rosenfeld and Peter Morville summarize in *Information Architecture for the World Wide Web*, such structure "clarifies the *mission* and *vision* for the site . . . [and] specifies how users will find information in the site by defining its *organization, navigation, labeling,* and *searching systems.*" Simply put, a properly structured site allows visitors to understand where they are, the location of the historical materials they want, and the site's underlying logic, just as chapter divisions and subtitles help to organize a book. An online historical essay will have a very different structure than an archive, and an archive will have a very different structure than a website for a historical organization.[30]

Recalling from Chapter 2 that a website is fundamentally a set of files, web producers add structure by placing these files into "directories," or distinct electronic folders on the web server, just as you place documents into specific folders on your personal computer. These directories become part of the URL of a web page, found between slashes to the right of a site's domain name. The British Library has placed its digitization of the Magna Carta, for instance, at http://www.bl.uk/collections/ treasures/magna.html, which nicely parses out to (reading from left to right), the web server of the British Library (in the U.K., of course), in their collections division directory, in the special "treasures" directory of the collections division (where the Magna Carta surely belongs), followed by the first word of the famous document and the ".html" that comes at the end of most web files. So that they will function properly on all types of computers, try to keep your directory and file names in lowercase, and eschew spaces or any symbols other than underscores and dashes.

Creators of history websites should strive to emulate the clarity of the British Library's site structure, using mostly words (where possible) rather than numbers or symbols for their directories, and naming directories in a sensible fashion that tells visitors—even without looking at the contents of the web page in the main window of the browser—where they are and what they can expect from a page. This process involves carefully grouping the materials you plan to put on your site. For example, a topical site might have some files that relate to teaching the subject matter, a set of interpretive essays, and a mass of raw archival documents. Although these materials could sit in a single directory, it makes sense both from the creator's and the user's perspective to divide the materials into three separate directories. Directories also can be nested, like babushka dolls, when a main section of a site has a set of subsections. Each URL slash indicates that the directory or file to the right of the slash resides inside of the directory named to the left of the slash. At

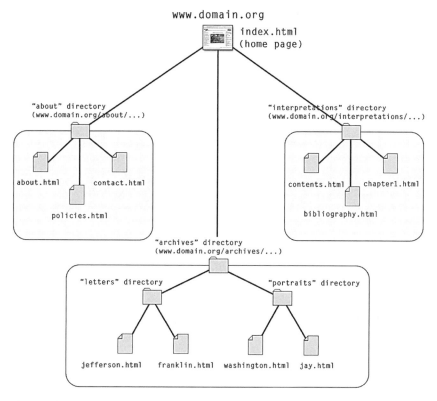

Figure 32. A rough diagram of the major sections of your website and their contents will help you to organize your materials into "directories" of files on your web server, which will, in turn, help to clarify your site's goals and structure for visitors.

the "top" of this hierarchy of directories and files, and providing an entrée to all of the others, is the home page, which is usually a file titled "index.html," and to which the web server software automatically sends a visitor who types in your domain name. A diagram of a basic website's structure can look like a genealogical tree, where a parent is a directory with children that are individual web pages.

Good sites sort themselves out and make their logical structure transparent through well-named directories and files. For instance, the African Studies Center at Boston University resides, aptly, at http://www.bu.edu/africa. Programs and courses underneath the umbrella of the center have their own directories, so the Environmental History of Africa course by James C. McCann can be found at http://www.bu.edu/africa/envr. This is a very easy URL to hand out to prospective students,

though McCann did not have to skimp on the digital ink; http://www
.bu.edu/africa/environmental would have been fine, too, and probably
easier to remember.[31] Beyond making it easier to hand out or email the
clear URLs that it creates, good site structure allows search engines, particularly Google, to pick up on keywords in URLs and use them to assess
how well a web page matches a search request (see Chapter 5).

Creating and displaying a lucid site structure is much easier for a simple history site like a small exhibit or a course website than for a complicated site like a museum collection with thousands of documents or
artifacts. More complex websites such as large archives, as we noted in
Chapter 2, tend to be database-driven and can have a relatively incomprehensible mix of letters and numbers following the domain name due
to the way they pull information out of the database using a set of variables inelegantly appended to the URL. For example, JSTOR, the indispensable online journal repository, has especially ungainly URLs. Edd
Wheeler's article "The Battle of Hastings: Math, Myth and Melee" in
Military Affairs, 52, No. 3 (July 1988), pp. 128–134, is found on the
JSTOR site at http://links.jstor.org/sici?sici=0026-3931%28198807%
2952%3A3%3C128%3ATBOHMM%3E2.0.CO%3B2-A, which is difficult to cite or type into a browser, much less remember. We would hope
these URLs will not be truly "permanent" or "stable," as they are so
declared by JSTOR's management. A more logical structure for JSTOR
would highlight the key components of the site: the journal itself, then
the year or volume number, then the number or month, then the pages
or author. Modern web server software makes it possible to hide the
numbers and variables for databases to produce more memorable URLs,
though this feature is rarely used. Our suggestion for JSTOR, which has
inadvertently out-Deweyed the Dewey Decimal System, would be to
recast poor Edd Wheeler's online article as http://links.jstor.org/
military_affairs/52/3/128-134.html, or better yet http://links.jstor.org/
military_affairs/1988/june/wheeler.html. Note how easy it would be to
go straight to another article under this revised system; if you knew the
journal name, date, and author, you could type them directly into the
location box in your browser without having to page through search
results or tables of contents.[32]

The importance of comprehensible web addresses should caution historians against using frames on their sites because these HTML elements
generally mask a site's true URLs and thus its structure. (Frames, or the
ability to split a web page into separately functioning windows, are a
poor idea in general because they tend to breed confusion, e.g., when
you click on a link to another site in one window and remnants of the
initial site stubbornly remain, hogging part of the screen and making
it unclear which site you are on.) For example, though attractive, the

Koninklijke Bibliotheek's Medieval Illuminated Manuscripts website suffers from a major flaw. How do you bookmark a specific folio, or more important, cite one of the remarkable folios the National Library of the Netherlands has spent the time and money to digitize? Unless you are a technically savvy user, all you get when you try to bookmark or cite a folio is the URL for the overall directory because the image of the folio resides in a secondary frame. This lack of specificity may upset scholars more than the general browsing public, but it shows how reliant—perhaps unconsciously—we are on good site structure and useful URLs.[33]

Accessibility

Many of the elements we have just discussed—formatting, images, color—may be irrelevant or a hindrance for those who "view" or use a page in a different way than we expect due to blindness, color blindness, or motor skill disabilities. For example, though you might find it aesthetically pleasing to use a detailed map as the sole form of navigation for your historical site, you should think how this choice affects those whose vision is less than perfect. As Tim Berners-Lee emphasizes on the World Wide Web Consortium (W3C) accessibility home page, "The power of the Web is in its universality. Access by everyone regardless of disability is an essential aspect." The W3C has issued a helpful series of white papers, guidelines, and techniques to make websites more accessible for a variety of people.[34]

Unsurprisingly, however, government regulations and laws, rather than moral suasion, have done the most to advance the cause of web accessibility. In 1998, President Clinton signed into law the Workforce Investment Act, which included the Rehabilitation Act Amendments, which in turn contained an important section, 508, relating to information technology like the web. Section 508 required that beginning in 2001, federal agencies had to make sure that individuals with disabilities could access their electronic documents and information. Because of the trillion-dollar purchasing power of the federal government, and because so many other companies, organizations, and local governments fall into line when Washington makes major regulatory decisions, Section 508 has had significant repercussions across the web. Many institutions, public and private, now demand that website designs be "508 compliant," and achieving such compliance has become a big business.[35]

The question for historians is how much Section 508 matters, or should matter, to you. With the exceptions of some Smithsonian museum employees and in-house historians in the Department of

Defense, the State Department, NASA, the Park Service, and other historically conscious parts of the government, most historians cannot be considered "employees of federal agencies" under the definition of the law. On the other hand, many historians work at public universities, and many states have added versions of Section 508 to their books. Adoption varies by state, however; the Rehabilitation Engineering and Assistive Technology Society of North America (RESNA) and the Georgia Institute of Technology's Information Technology and Technical Assistance Training Center maintain state-by-state lists of 508-related laws.[36] To make matters more confusing, many private universities, colleges, and schools accept some amount of federal funds, and thus in a very liberal definition of the law could be considered subject to Section 508. In addition, a lesser known but perhaps more broadly applicable and stronger provision in the federal law, Section 504 of the Rehabilitation Act, might also apply to the design of websites. This section "prohibits recipients of federal funds from discriminating on the basis of disability," and courts have interpreted "discrimination" to include failure to provide access to information as well as buildings.

Whether you are legally bound to comply with Sections 508 and 504 depends on your affiliation (if any) and the project you are working on (if it has federal funding). Most universities, colleges, and schools have taken the stance that despite receiving federal funds, they are not bound by Section 508. After all, the language of the law specifies "federal agencies"—not institutions receiving federal funds. Nevertheless, educational institutions that feel bound by a broad interpretation of Section 504—or that are worried about an Americans with Disabilities Act lawsuit, even if they feel that 504 does not apply to websites—might impose or request compliance with accessibility guidelines. Even so, history students or faculty members at these institutions could question whether compliance means *every* website on *every* university server, or just those that provide important information from the university to current and prospective students, faculty, and staff. For instance, it is probably more important that an online application to a history graduate program comply with the mandates of 508/504 than a specialized or experimental archive site. Kathy Cahill, the Lab Coordinator for Adaptive Technology for Information and Computing (ATIC) at the Massachusetts Institute of Technology, helpfully notes that although her university receives a tremendous amount of federal funding, they do not feel bound by Section 508 because they are a private university. "That being said, MIT takes accessibility seriously due to Sec. 504 of the Rehabilitation Act," she continues, and the ATIC program she works on educates and consults with the MIT community so that those with disabilities have the best chance to access MIT's extensive web resources.[37] We believe that with the exception of those who work for the federal government, historians—even those at public universities or educational institutions receiving federal grants or aid—are not legally bound to meet the strong accessibility requirements of Sections 508 or 504.

Ethically, however, historians—as chroniclers of the past who want to disseminate the truth as far and wide as possible—should try to make their sites accessible to the greatest number of people, regardless of ability. Done in a modest, sensible fashion, following accessibility guidelines on your website not only will serve a larger and more diverse audience, but it will also improve the experience of your site for everyone else. Many of the recommendations from the W3C and the mandates of Section 508 are relatively painless to follow and can (and should) be done as the site is being designed and developed.

Jim Thatcher, a retired IBM veteran who works with the Institute of Technology and Learning at the University of Texas at Austin, has produced a good summary of what 508 compliance means for the average web designer. First, you should have text equivalents for images and other multimedia. Consistently use the "alt" attribute in your image tags, which will appear as replacement captions for certain visitors. Although it may be difficult to provide synchronized subtitling for a video or audio file, try to produce a basic transcript if possible. Historical websites with maps and graphical navigation should have redundant text links. Blind web surfers using an audio or Braille web browser often find themselves suffering through seemingly interminable menus and navigation to get to the main content of a web page, so a link that gives these visitors the option to skip over the top part of a page is a welcome addition. These same surfers find most interactive or dynamic web design (through Flash, JavaScript, or Java applets) inaccessible. In deference to those with photosensitive epilepsy (or simply those with decent aesthetic sense) avoid graphics that flicker or pulse. More generally, all web designers should take the time to view their site in a variety of "alternative scenarios." For instance, use the monitor control panel on your computer to set the number of colors to sixteen or even fewer and the resolution to its lowest setting, and look at your site again. Turn off image loading in your browser to get a sense of what a blind person (who may use an audio browser to vocalize all of the text on a site) will "see." Are you as satisfied with your site in these stripped-down formats as you are with it in its full splendor? If so, disabled viewers of your site will likely be happy as well.[38]

As with good URLs, accessibility compliance has the secondary benefit of improving your site for everyone and making it more easily found. Transcripts of video and audio files will be picked up by search engines, which will drive more traffic to your site. The text in the "alt" attribute of the image tag will similarly be indexed by search engines for additional visibility. Although maps and graphical navigation are nice, many people, regardless of their vision, prefer to click on the clear links of a text equivalent. If a person with sight is viewing a graphically rich historical site over a slow modem, a web browser generally displays the contents of the "alt" attribute before the image shows up, thus giving them a sense of what's on the page and allowing them to decide whether they want to wait for the full page to load, or to click on a link to move to another page on the site. The anchor tags within a page that are helpful to skip large sections of navigation or text also provide all visitors the ability to jump around a page without scrolling. With such anchors in place, it is also possible to save a bookmark that goes directly to one part of a page—the part a visitor wants to read or cite.

*   *   *

As with the other principles of good design, sensible adherence to accessibility guidelines thus amply rewards both the users and the creators of historical websites. An accessible website means that more people can gain a better sense of the past through your digitized materials and commentaries, and also that researchers can locate these documents and artifacts in the first place. Yet good design does not guarantee a large audience for your project—or even a small one. Although search engines that index the text, "alt" attributes for images, and transcripts of audio and video may send some interested surfers your way, many others will never know your site exists unless they hear about it through alternative means, both digital and analog. In Chapter 5, we explore how to let your intended audience know that your site exists, and what it can offer them in the way of historical understanding.

Chapter 5

Building an Audience

In this chapter you will learn about:

- Defining and reaching your project's audience(s)
- Ways to market your site, from individual contacts to mass media
- How Google and other search engines rank your site and refer visitors
- Getting your visitors to come back to your site regularly and contribute suggestions for improvement
- What server logs are, and how they may help you understand the strengths and weaknesses of your site

We all wish we lived in a world where interest in history rivaled the popularity of Google, Amazon, and Yahoo, but interest—even modest interest—in your history website is not a given. To reach an audience, you will to have to think carefully about who it is you want to reach and how best to reach them. Although the web greatly facilitates the distribution of your work, it doesn't make it easy to ensure that it is being used widely, deeply, well—or at all.

As historians, we receive training in many helpful skills, such as the close reading of texts, the ability to read and speak foreign languages, the art of essay writing and historical argument, and the way to moderate discussions. No graduate history programs offer courses on marketing or public relations, however. Moreover, print, film, or museum historians can generally count on well-defined and well-established audiences assembled and organized through journal subscriptions, libraries' buying priorities, publishers' catalogs, newspaper listings of television programs and films, museum membership programs, and tourist patterns. But for the most part, comparable mechanisms have not yet emerged on the web.

Digital historians have typically spent much more time on the matters discussed in the previous three chapters (infrastructure, digitizing, and design) than on the subject of this chapter—reaching your desired audience, getting them excited about your site, improving your site over time to best serve your (hopefully growing number of) visitors, and closely tracking how well you are meeting your goals.[1] In part that reflects a distrust of topics like "marketing." But, as we argue here, to build an audience for your site is to serve the most fundamental democratic and intellectual goals that we share as historians.

In Chapter 4, we noted that some historians consider any special attention to design as an unnecessary frill. Many historians view the idea of "marketing" their site even more skeptically. Some argue that this "commercial" perspective is not in keeping with the professional work of historians and that any genuinely valuable site will already have an eager audience that will flock to it without any encouragement. Others question whether we should worry about numbers at all and insist that a few satisfied "customers" are more than adequate.

We agree that market size should not be the sole or even primary criterion for judging good historical work. After all, a small site detailing Akkadian myths will receive fewer visitors than a site detailing the battlefields of the American Civil War (at least in the United States) regardless of the respective quality of the sites or the intelligence and energy of their creators. Indeed, one of the advantages of the web is that it can reach small and targeted audiences cost effectively. The number of people interested in a book, film, or museum exhibit on the history of a small town in Montana might not be large enough to justify the expense of production and distribution. A self-published website, however, can reach at almost no cost the widely dispersed former residents of a Western ghost town—or geographically scattered Akkadian experts.

However small your audience, you still need to reach them, and in the increasingly crowded world of the web, quality is not enough to guarantee that your intended audience will find you by word of mouth. Moreover, reaching an intended audience online has become a matter of survival for historical organizations. The scholarly American Historical Association (AHA) may not appeal to a cross-section of the population, but its site still needs to connect with those committed to a scholarly and professional view of the past. Nine out of ten new members of the AHA now arrive through its website. Similarly, because visits to historic sites and museums often start with a stopover at their website, a hard-to-find or difficult-to-use site will result in fewer paying visitors. Of course, most historians measure success not by dollars but by looks of understanding from our students, nods of agreement from our colleagues, the prompting of further insights from others who work in our field, or even the reshaping of public debates. But without at least a modicum of usage, a historical website is unlikely to inspire any of those lofty and satisfying outcomes.

Two basic principles can help you create and maintain a *useful* and *used* website. First, think about community, not numbers of visitors. This is not so different from most nondigital work in history, where historians aspire to enter into and shape a community of discourse, whether scholars of medieval women's history or undergraduate students of world history. You should measure your website's success not just by how *many* people use it but even more by how *well* they use it. And the most important step in building an audience for your site is having a clear idea of its purposes, who precisely you want to speak to, and why.

Second, be simultaneously flexible and focused in your approach. If you notice that significant numbers of your site's visitors are not part of your intended audience, be ready to rethink your efforts. Perhaps you should redirect your efforts toward this unexpected audience. The Library of Congress, as we highlighted earlier, launched their project of digitizing vast quantities of their collections envisioning an audience similar to the one that walks in the door to their reading rooms—serious scholars and researchers. Early on, they learned to their surprise that high school students and teachers eagerly embraced the opportunity to connect with primary historical sources. As a result, they began to develop tools, resources, publicity, and especially programs directed specifically at that audience, an unconventional departure for an institution that had not previously served K–12 students.

Similarly, if you discover that your site is so broad in its subject matter that few visitors feel a sense of connection or allegiance to it, you should be ready to narrow your focus. Or if you learn that your website has attracted two distinct audiences using it for two distinct purposes, then relaunch different incarnations of your website for each purpose, or at least "segregate" elements of your site beyond the home page to serve each audience in a more targeted way. Naturally, you may need to adjust your voice as you speak to these different audiences, especially ones not accustomed to an academic writing style.

DoHistory, a site organized around the diary of eighteenth-century midwife Martha Ballard, uses a simple device to orient multiple audiences to its site. The home page features a drop-down menu that asks whether you are interested in any of seven diverse areas: Martha Ballard herself, midwifery and herbal medicine, genealogy, films about the past, diaries, the use of primary sources, or teaching with the site. If you choose "midwifery and herbal medicine," you are directed to a list of all the medicinal ingredients mentioned in Ballard's diary, an annotated bibliography on midwifery, and about twenty primary source documents related to these topics. If you instead click on the link for "genealogy," you are sent to the site's "History Toolkit," which offers advice on conducting oral histories and working with deeds, probate records, diaries, gravestones, and other sorts of primary records. "You can serve multiple audiences," notes Randy Rieland, who headed up Discovery.com's history efforts, "but don't try to serve them in the same way."[2]

Connecting with a Community

In Chapter 1, we urged you to think about the "genre" of history website that you want to create—for example, an archive, a teaching site, a museum exhibit, or an organizational hub. One of the chief reasons for such an approach, as social theorist Phil Agre explains, is that genres connect with particular communities, and if you don't understand the communities to which your site is directed and how you can help those communities, you are unlikely to be successful. But focusing on genres and communities does more than just bring visitors to your site. Agre argues that a key goal for design in new media should be supporting "the collective cognitive processes of particular communities" because "broad access to the means of collective cognition" is "a core democratic value."[3]

In other words, building your audience by supporting and connecting with communities is not only the least expensive and most effective way of promoting your site, it is also the one that most likely supports your larger social goals. If you create a site for teaching high school students about women's suffrage, you will only have accomplished your mission if you both reach those teachers and improve their teaching about women's rights (their collective cognition). Although you lack the resources of commercial web marketers, you also likely have the advantage of being part of, or at least being familiar with, the community you are trying to reach. Chances are that if you are creating a site on Akkadian myths, you are an Akkadian scholar and already know many other members of that scholarly community. You might even have access to a mailing list or an email discussion list of researchers of Mesopotamia.

To be sure, not all promotional efforts are that focused. In general, web audiences are less likely to be well defined than those in print and other media. Although most communities form around occupations and social locations (teachers, scholars, museum curators), substantial communities of interest also organize themselves around particular historical topics—notably the amateur enthusiasts who bring deep passion to subjects ranging from the Peloponnesian War to the American civil rights movement.

You therefore need to develop ways to reach the members of those communities. Where do these folks congregate—both offline and online? Which organizations do they join? What do they read? For our archival and teaching site on the French Revolution, entitled Liberty, Equality, Fraternity, our first target audience was teachers of French history at colleges and universities in the United States, a very manageable community of about one thousand. Many of them attend the annual meeting of the Society for French Historical Studies (SFHS), the U.S.-based group for historians of France, and smaller meetings of regional groups such as the Western Society for French History, where we demonstrated our site to colleagues. If we had a bigger promotional budget, we might have purchased the mailing list for the SFHS and sent out a postcard announcing the site. We employed that strategy in launching our site for U.S. history survey teachers called History Matters, spending about $1,500 to mail cards to 5,000 members of the Organization of American Historians. We could also have advertised in publications directed at American historians like the *Journal of American History*, a strategy used by the Abraham Lincoln Historical Digitization Project.[4] Email, of course, offers a cheaper (free) alternative. Almost every promotional plan for a history website should begin with an announcement on the relevant H-Net lists.

Unfortunately not every community is as easy to identify as college and university French historians or H-Net subscribers. High school, community, and college western civilization and world history instructors also teach about the French Revolution. How do we reach them? Some belong to groups like the American Historical Association, and so we made sure to make presentations at its annual meeting and to get Liberty, Equality, Fraternity noticed in *Perspectives*, its newsletter. (Almost every professional group sponsors a newsletter, and they will generally run free announcements. We promoted our Echo site on the history of science and technology extensively through these announcements.) High school teachers are one of the hardest audiences to reach. The National Council for Social Studies' 18,000 active members represent only a small fraction of the country's estimated 120,000 high school history and social studies teachers.[5] In any case, it would cost you about $1,700 to buy just the more limited mailing list, and then you would have to pay for postage and a flyer. A less costly approach is placing an article in *Social Education*, their national magazine, or getting on the program for their national meeting or one of their regional or state meetings. You can also rent exhibit space at one of these conferences. We spent about $1,000 for an exhibit booth to promote Liberty, Equality, Fraternity and History Matters, which gave us the opportunity to speak one on one with dozens of teachers.

Purchasing an exhibit booth at a conference is probably less effective than getting on the program. These formal presentations give you an opportunity to demonstrate the value of your site to colleagues. Matthew Nickerson of Southern Utah University notes that whenever he speaks about his site, Voices of the Colorado Plateau, at a conference, the server logs show a spike in visitors.[6]

Perhaps even more influential than your own enthusiasm is the recommendation of your site by trusted colleagues. You should try to get your site reviewed as widely as possible. The *Journal of American History* (in collaboration with History Matters) has been reviewing history websites since 2001, and other journals are beginning to do the same. The Scout Report, run by the University of Wisconsin, provides influential reviews on a wide range of topics. If you are proud of what you have accomplished, you should make sure your site is considered for prizes and other recognitions. The early days of the web brought a proliferation of largely meaningless "top website" laurels. But now more reputable organizations have begun to recognize digital history—for example, the "Best of the Web" awards given at the annual "Museums and the Web" conference as well as the American Association of Museums MUSE Awards. The National Endowment for the Humanities organizes regular panels to evaluate sites for listing in its EDSITEment directory.[7]

Although the most effective approach to publicity is to think about your target communities and then try to find out where they congregate and what they read, you will also want to do online research on related communities that might be brought to your site. What are similar sites to yours, and who is their audience? Look at history "gateway" sites such as History Matters, World History Matters, and Best of History Web Sites (see Chapter 1) and see what sites they list (and also try to get your site listed there).

Once you've identified those sites that have the most in common with your project, contact their operators to introduce yourself and ask for advice and reciprocal links. Not only do you need to court your fellow website operators, you need to join their communities of users. Participate in the bulletin board discussions and listserv exchanges that these sites host. Take a serious interest in your community—"make them feel like you're paying attention," as Rieland of Discovery.com puts it—and they will pay attention to you.[8]

Finally, if your site is connected to a museum exhibition or a book, try to come up with ways to create virtual communities from the actual communities that those offline productions attract. In fact, even if your site is not formally connected to a real-world installation, see if you can piggyback on related efforts by placing postcards with your URL in local or on-topic museum galleries or by meeting with teachers to explain the educational possibilities of your website. Given the virtual nature of the web, face-to-face meetings and physical objects retain considerable power—or perhaps acquire an even greater impact. Many history sites, including our own, have found that inexpensive novelty items—pens, bookmarks, mouse pads, and mugs—help to remind people to take a look at your site. (And while you are at it, include your URL on your business cards, stationery, and email signature.) Establishing and maintaining a real-world presence through partnerships with schools, museums, groups of enthusiasts, and professional organizations gives you a ready pool of potential visitors and access to networks of interested community members.

Mass Marketing, Online and Off

Although you should devote most of your resources to building your audience in a focused way that relies on identifiable communities, you should also try to reach visitors in much larger aggregates, including through the mass media of newspapers, radio, and television. If you succeed, it can dramatically expand your audience. For example, on August 19, 2002, the Associated Press ran a story on our September 11 Digital Archive that was picked up across the country and featured on the CNN .com home page. That day, the number of visitors to our site jumped almost ten-fold, from 3,700 to 36,000. Other history website operators have similarly reported that a story in the *New York Times* or on National Public Radio suddenly sent their web traffic through the roof. Timothy Messer-Kruse, a professor of history at the University of Toledo who created Toledo's Attic: A Virtual Museum of Toledo, Ohio, notes that whenever the local public television station plugs his site, traffic goes up so much that it threatens to crash their modestly powered server.[9]

Although we had spent months seeking publicity for our September 11 Digital Archive, only in the weeks leading up to the first anniversary of the attacks did we suddenly find ourselves the subject of stories in *USA Today*, the *Washington Post*, *Le Monde*, the BBC, and NPR. Few stories are that big, but connecting your site to current anniversaries can attract attention. So can other current events, sometimes unexpectedly. The Cuneiform Digital Library, an electronic database of ancient tablets, might normally only attract the interest of specialized scholars. But in the aftermath of the destruction of Iraqi historical treasures in 2003, its digital preservation of the record of Mesopotamian civilization became news. Similarly, reporters suddenly began calling University of Chicago history professor James Sparrow about his site on the New York City blackouts of 1965 and 1977 when a power outage plunged the Northeast into darkness in the summer of 2003. Traffic to the site jumped an astonishing 280-fold in two days.

Even if you are not the beneficiary of a catastrophe, you should still try to attract press attention to your site by thinking about it from the perspective of a reporter. What is the "news" in your site? Are you the first to make some body of historical materials available online? Have you developed an innovative way to teach history or present the past online? That news should be the headline in a press release that you write whenever you launch a site. In some cases, you may be part of an institution—a college or a museum—with a press office that will help you write the press release. If not, get some samples from colleagues and write it on your own. Send the release to newspapers, magazines, and broadcast outlets as well as friends and colleagues.

You should also pay attention to the new and increasingly influential world of blogs. These frequently updated sites often review or highlight new and useful websites and link to other blogs in their community. "Bloggers on History News Network link to other bloggers," notes editor Rick Shenkman about his site's eight blogs, "which helps drive up our numbers. In addition, each blogger includes a blog roll of favorite blogs. Other bloggers reciprocate and include our blogs in their blog lists, thereby using the power of networking to increase the number of readers who consult their sites and ours."[10]

Mass marketing online generally relies on search engines, which will likely provide the most important source of visitors to your site. Almost 60 percent of those who come to History Matters arrive via a search engine, especially the currently dominant search engine, Google, which gives us about three-fifths of that traffic. Thus you need to understand how your site gets listed and ranked in Google. Steer clear of people trying to sell you access or to "optimize" your site for the search engines; instead spend some of your own time learning the fundamentals of how they work.[11]

Unfortunately Google works in somewhat mysterious ways. It protects its formula for how it ranks sites on its search page as closely as Coca-Cola guards its secret recipe. A cottage industry has arisen to figure out how Google ranks websites, but it is more of an art than a science, and the formula undoubtedly changes from time to time as Google's engineers try to keep up with the web's changes (and the attempts of "search engine optimizers" to crack its formula for commercial gain). Yet some basic ingredients will likely remain strongly correlated with a high ranking in Google because they explain the rise of this search engine in the first place.

Indeed, perhaps the best way for historians to understand Google (and the efforts of major companies that are trying to catch up to it, including Yahoo and Microsoft) is to understand the short, tumultuous history of search engines. Unlike most of the top sites on the web, Google appeared quite late (1998), at a time when everyone thought that the search wars had ended and those with the biggest brand names (e.g., AltaVista, HotBot, and Excite) would forever be the first stops for web searchers. The founders of Google, Larry Page and Sergey Brin, had several clever insights about the web, however, that allowed them to develop far superior technology than these earlier search engines.

First, they noticed (as many users of AltaVista, HotBot, and Excite did) that machines are often terrible at finding the best sites through keywords. A poorly written site that mentions "Thomas Jefferson" twenty times might be mechanically ranked more "relevant" than an authoritative site from the Library of Congress that happens to mention his name only twice on its home page. Page and Brin also realized that the creators of the web were naïve to think that "meta" tags, or hidden tags describing the contents of a web page (and written by the page's author), would provide assistance to search engines; no one anticipated the deviousness of online pornography purveyors and other unsavory types who quickly added bogus keywords to their sites' meta tags so they would show up in a wide variety of more innocent searches. Finally, though meta tags seemed unreliable, Page and Brin noticed that certain other features of web pages provided better measures of which sites were most relevant to a specific search, including the presence of keywords in the title and URL. You can't fudge these one-liners as readily as the potentially endless contents of a web page or meta tag. But most important was an element unique to the medium of the web: links. Page and Brin envisioned the web as consisting of billions of "votes" for websites in the form of links from one page to another. A site on Jefferson with twenty links to it from other sites was probably better than one with two links to it, they surmised. If in turn some of those other sites were "authoritative" (i.e., they also had lots of links to them), so much the better for the first site's ranking. In short, Google found a way to measure *reputation* on the web through a recursive analysis of the interconnectedness of the medium itself.[12]

Although this brief recounting of Google's innovations likely ignores many smaller factors in its complicated ranking system, it does reveal some of the best ways to make your site more visible through the dominant search engine as well as others that follow its methodology. In an ideal world, a valuable and well-regarded site will naturally end up with numerous, authoritative links to it, but it cannot hurt to accelerate this process by asking related sites to add a link from their web outpost to yours. In particular, try to get links from respected or prominent sites. Your site's ranking will benefit much more from a link provided by the highly linked (and highly ranked) Library of Congress website than from your cousin's personal home page. Web directories are by nature highly linked, and it is worth trying to get your site into them. Google appears to put particular weight on listings in the directories from

Yahoo, Looksmart, and especially the Open Directory Project, which is the basis of Google's own web directory.

Make sure your web page title includes the keywords by which people would search for your site, avoiding vague labels such as "page one" or "home page." An additional benefit of this practice is that the title is what appears on the search results page as a clickable link, further attracting potential visitors who glance quickly at these highlighted words. The keywords important to your site should obviously also be in the page text, preferably near the top and not confined to a graphic. In addition, try to get keywords into the main URL for your site, as in www.mayanhistory.org or www.college.edu/~user/mayanhistory. Because Google's relentless spiders will probably find most sites with external links to them pretty quickly, submitting your site to the major search engines may be less useful than you imagine, though it can't hurt. On the other hand, don't waste a second creating meta tags for your website. The importance of Google and other search engines in attracting visitors means a successful website is one that is surrounded by and part of strong communities of interest, practically represented by links, and clearly marked with identifying keywords in several locations, not just in the bodies of the web pages.[13]

One obvious other avenue of online promotion is advertising. Most readers of this book will not have a budget that would cover the cost of banner ads on major portals such as Yahoo, where an ad campaign typically costs $10,000 or more per month. More recently, however, a form of highly targeted advertising—popularized again by Google—has emerged that might interest developers of history sites. Google sells "search words" and places an ad on the side of its results page linking to a site that has paid to be associated with that word or phrase. (Overture, a subsidiary of Yahoo, has a similar system.) For example, if you enter the word "historians" in Google's search, you get a "sponsored link" for History Associates Inc., which offers historical research, writing, and archival services. If you enter "American Civil War," you get a link for Ancestry.com, which sells access to enlistment rosters, regimental histories, and other genealogical records. What's appealing about this system is that you only pay when someone clicks on your link, and an auction involving others interested in buying the same search words sets the price. Not surprisingly, then, "French Revolution" (6 cents per click) costs considerably less than "sex" (45 cents) or "flowers" ($3.13). "Historians" (22 cents) can be had for much less than "dentists" ($2.33). But those clicks can add up, and so even advertising unsexy (or unflowery) history topics requires a hefty budget and should not be undertaken before you seriously consider whether it will bring you the audience you are seeking.[14] In most cases, your time and money will be better spent on community-building efforts and other forms of free publicity.

Encouraging Return Traffic

Unlike a book, film, or exhibition, the success of most websites relies on repeat usage, on becoming one of your users' favorite places on the web.[15] Most website creators launch their site with fanfare and then make the mistake of expecting these initial efforts will carry them forward. The most important strategy for encouraging return traffic is to keep your site "fresh" with continual updates to make your website look active and lived-in. For example, have a link on your home page that points to a changing "featured" page. When you make substantive changes to your website, advertise them with a publicity push similar to the one you undertook when you launched your site. This does not mean you should constantly redesign your site. On the contrary, you want to maintain a consistent look and feel to your website, allowing your visitors to feel comfortable and familiar with its contents. Probably the most important thing you can do is to begin to develop a regular relationship with those who visit your site. If possible, provide your community with some valuable service that will bring them back frequently—a continually updated bibliography, for example. The Center for History and New Media (CHNM) developed a searchable database of history department web pages, which many people found to be an easy way to locate historians.[16]

A simple way to connect with your audience is to create a guestbook that asks people to register for the site. Some sites make registration mandatory, but that approach will drive people away unless you have a very compelling site. Once you have a mailing list, you can establish a newsletter that can be a key mechanism for bringing visitors to your site. History News Network (HNN), where the site changes daily, sends out two newsletters per week to 11,000 subscribers and those newsletters are responsible for at least one-third of the traffic to the site. In these days of proliferating spam, however, you need to avoid sending your regular users more notices than they want to receive.

But you should encourage them to be in touch with you. Set up a "contact us" email address or web form, whereby visitors can send you technical or historical questions. This lets you know about common problems users encounter and helps make visitors feel that they have a connection to you. Save all inquiries and turn them into an FAQ (frequently asked questions) page. The National Park Service invites historical queries directed at their historians and gets about fifteen to twenty questions a day. Many questions only take one minute to answer, but others can take ten or fifteen minutes—a considerable amount of work but spread out among dozens of Park Service historians.[17]

Discussion boards can make people regular visitors to your site. The History Channel's very active forums, which focus heavily on military history, get thousands of postings. Discussion boards, however, run the risk of either getting little or no participation, which will give your site a neglected or abandoned feel, or attracting too intense a following, which could cause unseemly controversy. HNN's discussion feature, which allows for commentary on every article posted, has drawn thousands of respondents, but some have pushed the boundaries of civility, annoying others and driving them away from the site. HNN eventually had to limit participation to those who registered and insist that posters use their real names.

Games and quizzes can also attract a following, though they run the risk of seeming gimmicky. During the late 1990s, for instance, Discovery Communications' history website featured Someone In Time, in which participants guessed the identity of an unnamed historical figure from clues provided. Every two weeks, the game's creators revealed the identity of the historical figure and then introduced a new one. "People played the game religiously," explains Rieland of Discovery.com. "There was a message board, and people became friends with one another—they were all connected by the common experience of playing the game. They had reunions. Two participants died during the period of the game, and there were online wakes for them."[18] Despite Rieland's enthusiasm, games and puzzles require significant staff time to come up with new editions. Over time, we found it harder and harder to change our own History Matters puzzles regularly.

Tracking and Assessing Your Audience

Despite the high technology of the web, it can be surprisingly hard to know whether your site is reaching its intended audience and achieving its overall goals. Speculating about a website's audience can be similar to the fable of the six blind men who came to wildly different conclusions about an elephant they encountered, based solely on the part they touched. Nevertheless, some tools and techniques can help you better know your audience. Every time someone visits your server (or the server that houses your site), they leave a series of electronic traces that the computer might record cryptically as follows:

81.174.188.105— [02/Jun/2004:04:59:35 -0400] "GET /d/5148/ HTTP/1.1" 200 4905 "http://www.google.com/search?q = AIR + RAID + WARDEN&ie = UTF-8&oe = UT F-8" "Mozilla/5.0 (Macintosh; U; PPC Mac OS X; en-us) Apple-WebKit/125.2 (KHTML, like Gecko) Safari/125.7

Put into English, this "sentence" tells us that on June 2, 2004, at 4:59 A.M. Eastern Daylight Time, a computer connected to "Force 9," an Internet service provider in Sheffield, England (where it was a more sensible 9:59 A.M.) that owns the IP address 81.174.188.105, sent a request to CHNM's web server on the George Mason University campus for a web page that contains the words to the 1942 tune "Obey Your Air Raid Warden," a big band recording that doubled as a wartime public service announcement. (We know this because these are the logs for our Historymatters server, and the machine has requested—with a "get" command—the page http://historymatters.gmu.edu/d/5148.) The Google search engine kindly referred our British visitor after he or she entered the words "air raid warden"—a search for which Google ranks us first. Back in England, our visitor read our page on a Macintosh computer with the Mac OS X operating system (update 10.3.4) and the Safari browser.[19]

The server faithfully records each one of these connections and saves them into files, called "logs," that can run into millions of lines. None of us has the time to read through these massive logs, and so fortunately programmers have written log analysis software (with names like Net-Tracker, Absolute Log Analyzer, Web Trends, and Webalizer) that summarize them in easier to read charts and graphs. If you don't run your own server, you will be limited to the program your provider uses.[20]

Log analysis programs compile pages and pages of "hard" numbers about your visitors. But they turn out be squishy soft when you press on them. The most misleading and misused statistic—although one still frequently cited—is "hits." You will often hear people boasting about the millions of hits their site gets (and we must admit we have ourselves indulged in this conceit). But the number is largely meaningless. Hits merely count each one of the lines from the log files. If, however, you read further in the log file quoted above, you will see seven lines (hits) from our English visitor—most of them recording that his or her computer requested six different images embedded in a single web page. Thus, if we added two more graphics to that page, our number of hits would suddenly jump by almost one-third. Bad design—having too many images on your pages—would allow you to brag about more "traffic."[21]

Because most people really want to know about "visitors" rather than "hits," log analysis programs offer that statistic and it appears to be more reassuringly solid—a measure of how many people come to your site. But the problem is deciding what constitutes a "person" when we only know about one machine contacting another machine. Our English visitor departed after looking at the lyrics to "Obey Your Air Raid Warden" and appears no further in our logs for the next twenty-

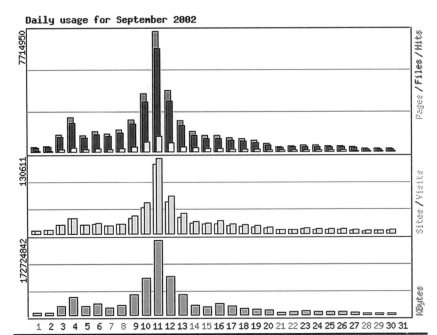

Daily usage for September 2002

Daily Statistics for September 2002												
Day	Hits		Files		Pages		Visits		Sites		KBytes	
3	1051946	2.82%	906368	2.92%	145970	2.69%	14292	2.66%	14478	3.05%	19600014	2.54%
4	2159985	5.79%	1820512	5.86%	245417	4.53%	26819	4.99%	25865	5.45%	40465557	5.25%
5	1028936	2.76%	872336	2.81%	136560	2.52%	14277	2.65%	14542	3.06%	19818683	2.57%
6	1309107	3.51%	1091386	3.51%	163317	3.01%	16403	3.05%	17969	3.78%	26353449	3.42%
7	1124040	3.01%	946660	3.05%	147072	2.71%	13046	2.43%	13235	2.79%	17018341	2.21%
8	1409026	3.78%	1193273	3.84%	198161	3.66%	16533	3.07%	16467	3.47%	22277674	2.89%
9	2037515	5.46%	1745893	5.62%	295689	5.46%	25837	4.80%	30082	6.33%	45668178	5.92%
10	3690428	9.90%	3190851	10.27%	606412	11.19%	45141	8.39%	53511	11.27%	85200278	11.05%
11	7714950	20.69%	6564852	21.13%	966874	17.85%	120195	22.35%	130611	27.50%	172724842	22.39%
12	3912191	10.49%	3252694	10.47%	532723	9.83%	54096	10.06%	64198	13.52%	88827261	11.52%
13	1978824	5.31%	1646458	5.30%	279383	5.16%	27974	5.20%	34316	7.23%	46993201	6.09%
14	1292189	3.47%	1027784	3.31%	214368	3.96%	17298	3.22%	20036	4.22%	22662088	2.94%
15	1042675	2.80%	814349	2.62%	186890	3.45%	15633	2.91%	17756	3.74%	18004938	2.33%

Figure 33. Raw numbers of hits and visits in web logs can be misleading, but they do clearly indicate trends in usage. Here, we see the huge jump in visits to the September 11 Digital Archive on the first anniversary of the attacks.

four hours. It seems easy to describe him/her as a single "visitor" to our site. But what about the person from 203.135.21.42, who shows up in the logs at 5:52 A.M. and is still looking around at 6:03 A.M. after stops at various different pages. Was that a single visitor? Probably. But what if 203.135.21.42 is the IP address of a computer in a university computer lab? A student comes in and takes a look at our site and then leaves. Five minutes later another student arrives and sits down at the same machine and also visits—perhaps they both have the same assignment. How do we know if that was really two "visitors" or whether it was simply the first student who had been interrupted by a friend and then returned to looking at the site? From the perspective of the server, they *are* the same—two requests from the same machine across the Internet.

Further complications arise because people can simultaneously (rather than sequentially as above) access your site from the same IP address. That is the case with many AOL users who are directed around the Internet from massive "proxy servers" (intermediate computers that group many web surfers under one IP address), or with some student labs (especially in high schools) that are behind a firewall and proxy server for reasons of security or student control. Thus fifty students from a class could access your site in an hour, but they would all appear to come from the same IP address. Another problem posed by Internet service providers like AOL is that its servers "cache" (save a copy of) frequently requested pages, which means their readers don't show up in the logs at all.[22]

To decide on your number of visitors, the log analysis program therefore makes a guess that any series of requests from a single IP address during a preset period (generally thirty minutes) counts as one "visitor." That can mean that it is under-counting your traffic, as in the example above, or over-counting it as when a single person spends two hours on your site and is counted as "four visitors." It is even more misleading to confuse "visitors" with "users." After all, a single person who quickly stops at your site three times a day would count for more than 1,000 of your annual visitors. (That person may very well be you, obsessively checking on your site.) And keep in mind that not all of these "visitors" are living, breathing people. A request to your machine from an automated program—most commonly a "bot" operated by a search engine company—counts just as much as one from a high school student in Iowa, unless you set your analysis program to exclude such visitors from its calculations.

The final aggregate statistic from logs—page views (a count of requests to load a single web page)—has the virtue of not being a statistical construct. Page views measure how many actual pages from your website your server has sent out—in effect, it counts "hits" without the graphics. Perhaps because it is less subject to manipulation, this figure has emerged as the most frequently cited number by websites. Even so, you can easily break your content into shorter "pages" and thereby up your page view count.

In any case, you should avoid confusing either "visitors" or "page views" with the active *use* of your site. After all, many web visitors depart with barely a glance at your pages, as with our English friend who was probably hoping to learn something about English, rather than American, air raid wardens. Commercial sites cast an even more skeptical eye on such statistics. One new media commentator points out that "traffic by itself is actually a burden" because it makes your website slower and less reliable, requires extra customer service and technical support, increases your web hosting charges, and "distracts you from your key goals." "Page views without corresponding sales," observes Marketing-terms.com, "may even be viewed as an expense."[23] (Of course, if you are selling advertising, then page views are precisely what you want to deliver.) You should try much harder to measure active users of your site—for example, by noting how many people write in your guestbook, ask to be added to your mailing list, or download files—than to count passive visitors.[24]

In the commercial world, no one trusts the self-reporting of hits, visitors, and page views. Instead, Nielsen/NetRatings (the same folks who bring you TV ratings) and comScore Media Metrix track web usage from a representative sample of users through monitoring devices installed on their computers. News reports that Yahoo, Microsoft, and Google are the most visited websites come from summaries these services provide. (The detailed reports, which offer demographic breakdowns sought by advertisers, circulate only to those who pay for high-priced subscriptions.) Although the sample sizes are vastly larger than for television (more than 100,000 for Nielsen and 1.5 million for comScore), the monitoring challenge is also much greater. Even with cable, TV viewers have only dozens of choices; web surfers can choose from millions of sites. In addition, TV ratings services can just focus on folks gathered before the home television hearth, but the web ratings services need to consider the vast amount of surfing done during the workday. As a result, the two rating services often report divergent numbers, and advertisers (the main audience for these studies) gnash their teeth in frustration over the "discrepancies and inconsistency" in the data.[25]

In the end, self-reported log numbers are largely about PR, about making your funders and supporters feel good about your efforts—hence, the temptation to brag about millions of hits rather than tens of thousands of visitors or the failure to report less edifying statistics such as the number of people who leave your site almost immediately. For the

Statue of Liberty–Ellis Island Foundation, for example, a listing of the visitors and hits at www.ellisisland.org occupies a parallel place in their Annual Report to physical visitors to Ellis Island and number of employees on the payroll.[26]

The more important use of logs is the internal analysis that you can do to help you understand how your site is being used and by whom. Unfortunately this can be a very time-consuming process. But here is a list of some of the information provided by a typical log program and how you might use it:

- *Requested Pages* tells you about your most popular pages, an essential tool for gauging what your audience wants. Angela O'Neal, the project manager for Ohio Memory, notes that they look at these figures to help them plan what projects they might do next. Harry Butowsky, the webmaster for the National Park Service, says that they sometimes move content with a lot of hits to a more prominent location on the site to make it easier to find.[27] Some related statistics—traffic by pages, entry pages, and requested downloads—provide similar clues as to what is popular on your site. By contrast, "exit pages" can sometimes offer hints about pages that are not keeping visitors within your site. Analysis programs can generally tell you which pages prove the "stickiest," the ones that visitors linger over the longest. But be prepared to be depressed by the large number of visitors who depart from your site in less than one minute.

- *Referrers* tells you about the sites that are providing important links as well as the search engines that drive traffic to your site. Such information helps to give you a better sense of your audience, what they are seeking on your site, and the kinds of relationships you should cultivate (and the kinds of materials you should provide) to increase your audience. A log analysis program can tell you what words and phrases people are most often entering into Google and then being directed to your site. For example, "Atlanta Compromise" is a popular search term that brings people to History Matters—probably because we include an audio clip from Booker T. Washington's famous "Atlanta Compromise" address of 1895. Knowing that might lead us to expand our coverage of the address and Washington.

- *Browsers and Operating Systems*: As you have learned in Chapter 4, getting your pages to display properly on multiple platforms and browsers can be frustrating. But if it turns out that only 0.3% of your visitors are browsing with Netscape Navigator 4.0, you should not devote major resources to getting your site to work well with it.

- *Traffic Patterns*: Log software can give you nicely arranged graphs of traffic at your site by the hour of the day and by day of the week. Commercial sites—concerned about bursts of traffic, interested in monitoring sales promotions, or staffing their shipping department—find this information enormously useful. But it can still help you to gauge some of your own promotional efforts. For example, Rick Shenkman, who emails his HNN newsletters on Wednesday and Friday, can tell that the Wednesday edition brings more traffic to the site.

Despite their limits, logs can provide a revealing window into how your site is being used. But serious analysis takes considerable time. Major commercial websites such as Discovery.com have research staffs that issue weekly reports on the traffic logs. For those of us who don't do this for a living, it is hard to carve out the time to study logs, but it is something you should examine quickly on a regular basis and more closely at least every six months. A very active history site like Colonial Williamsburg reviews log reports monthly.[28]

Still, even the most sophisticated log analysis will only tell you about aggregates and patterns rather than individuals. If you want to know how particular individuals use your site, you need to ask them first to register with you. If they are registered on your site, you can track their usage with "cookies"—small text files placed on their hard drive by your website's server. Usually this file contains a simple ID number, which allows the website page in question to know that you've visited there before. Cookies allow Amazon.com to greet you by name when you arrive on their site. Cookies would allow you to customize your home page for different visitors or to remember what photograph they were studying or which multimedia player they use to play streaming audio. But that requires some technical expertise and also runs the risk of alienating those who view these "foreign objects" with suspicion. We would advise you to think carefully before programming your website to place cookies on visitors' computers.[29] Providing respected and frequently used historical resources online involves cultivating trust, and hidden technologies like cookies—however innocent—can be counterproductive in an age of spam, viruses, and spyware.

A more open approach to learning about your audience is to seek out their views directly. As we have noted, mandatory registration can drive away visitors, but a voluntary guestbook that gathers names and addresses is generally a good idea. Even if you don't plan on issuing a newsletter, a mailing list of regular site users is invaluable. If you are planning an overhaul of your site, you can write and ask for feedback. If you are applying for grants, it could be the source of helpful letters of support. Surely the best way to learn about your audience is by talking to them in person, either one on one or in "focus groups." Arranging commercial focus groups is an expensive proposition, but historians with captive audiences of students or museum visitors can do this relatively inexpensively. Bruce Tognazzini, one of the creators of the Macintosh interface, encourages all creators of electronic designs to convene less formal focus groups (however unscientific) for helpful feedback.[30] In these settings, you get the richest information on what users find most and least useful, and most and least confusing or off-putting, about your site. Angela O'Neal notes that staff from Ohio Memory tries to meet with users at least once a year to ask them how they would like to see things evolve or change. She describes this as "the most helpful tactic," much more useful than studying server logs.[31]

* * *

This connection to "real" people is important not simply because face-to-face interactions offer rich and dense responses that are hard to capture online, but also because it breaks down the illusion that online communities are somehow fundamentally different and separate from those that exist offline. "The hidden assumption," observes Phil Agre, "is that the 'community' is bounded by the Internet. But . . . communities are analytically prior to the technologies that mediate them. People are joined into a community by a common interest or ideology, by a network of social ties, by a shared fate—by something that makes them want to associate with one another." You will be most successful as a history website operator if you understand that your goal is not to attract anonymous (and often meaningless) hits on your server but rather to "support the collective life of a community."[32] Chapter 6 describes another way to do that—by not just presenting the past but also by collecting it, by not just talking to your audience but also by listening to them and making their voices part of the historical record.

Chapter 6
Collecting History Online

In this chapter you will learn about

- Using the Internet to collect accounts and artifacts from the recent past
- Which projects are most amenable to this new method of building a digital archive
- How to add interactivity to your site so that visitors can contribute their memories and other historical materials
- Ways to encourage subjects to participate in history-making in this new medium
- Assessing and improving the validity and worth of what these subjects contribute
- The experience of various individuals and institutions in recording the history of September 11, 2001, online

The previous five chapters generally cast the Internet as a one-way street, delivering materials from historical practitioners to their audience. Yet, its very name—the *Inter*net—underscores how this advanced computer network exists to shuttle information *between* and *among* people. It does not, like print, merely deliver documents from point A (historians) to point B (audience). If we want to make full use of this two-way street, we must go beyond passive "texts" such as websites and web pages and also think about active processes such as communication and interaction.

To be sure, historians have already largely embraced such activity on the Internet. Almost all of us use email, and an increasing portion use instant messaging and other forms of online communication. Thousands of professional historians participate in the 150 discussion groups sponsored by H-Net.[1] Enthusiasts and amateurs are involved in dozens of discussion boards and forums sponsored by the History Channel and Yahoo. In contrast to paper media, the Internet seems ideally suited for this kind of vibrant, daily exchange.

Another form of interactivity on the web remains less developed but has the potential to create novel forms of history in the future: using the Internet to collect historical documents, images, and personal narratives, many of which would be lost if historians did not actively seek them out. For historians working on topics in the post–World War II era, the web can be a valuable yet inexpensive tool for reaching individuals across the globe who might have recollections or materials. Present investigations and future research could both benefit from this practice. Furthermore, a significant segment of the record of modern life exists in digital form. Historians will need to find ways to capture such documents, messages, images, audio, and video before they are deleted if our descendants are to understand the way we lived. This chapter explores using the new technology of the Internet in service of the ancient practice of collecting and preserving the past.

Why Collect History Online?

Think for a moment of the outpouring of thoughts and emotions in thousands of blogs on September 11, 2001, or the breaking news on the home pages of myriad newspaper websites. A large percentage of this initial set of historical sources, unlike paper diaries or print versions, will likely be gone if we look for them in ten years. Blogs disappear regularly as their owners lose interest or move their contents to other systems or sites. Similarly, unlike the pages of their physical editions, newspaper websites change very rapidly (almost minute by minute on September 11) and have no real fixity. Had "Dewey Defeats Truman" been splashed across Chicagotribune.com rather than the paper *Chicago Daily Tribune*, it would have taken just a few keystrokes by the newspaper's editors to erase the famous blunder instantly and forever. As we describe here, we felt an obligation to save the rich personal record of blogs in our September 11 Digital Archive so future historians could understand the perspectives of thousands of ordinary people from around the world. Through even swifter action, the Library of Congress, the Internet Archive, WebArchivist.org, and the Pew Internet and American Life Project were able to save thousands of online media portrayals of that day's events. Had they decided months later to save these web pages, instead of within mere hours, many already would have vanished into the digital ether. Collecting history online may not always be this urgent, but these examples show the critical need for historians to find the most effective ways of using this new technology to supplement the historical record on paper, as we did in the twentieth century with tape recorders and video cameras.

This is particularly true because we can use the Internet for more than just gathering the history that was made online, or "born digital." The

Figure 34. An important, but highly ephemeral, piece of digital history: the home page of the *New York Times* website at 4:43 P.M. on September 11, 2001. Stripped down to its bare essentials so as to reduce the stress an exponential growth in news seekers imposed on their server (note the basic, rather than gothic, font), and constantly changing as the day went on—with no paper trail of these many "editions"—had the Library of Congress and the Internet Archive not acted immediately to capture it, the page would be gone forever.

Internet also allows us to reach diverse audiences and to ask those audiences to send us historical materials that originated offline, or at least off the web. They can "upload" to us their digital or scanned photos, their sound recordings, or their lab notes. They can use a computer keyboard or microphone to transmit to us their recollections of earlier events and experiences, especially ones for which there are no or few records.

Unfortunately, using the web to gather historical materials is harder than using the web as a one-way distribution system. It can involve more technical hurdles than a simple history website; legal and ethical concerns, such as invasion of privacy and the ownership of contributed materials; and skills, like the marketing techniques we discussed in Chapter 5, that are unfamiliar to most historians. In addition, collecting online elicits concerns about the quality of submissions: given the slippery character of digital materials, how can we ensure that what we get is authentic, or that historical narratives we receive really are from the people they say they are? How can we ensure that a mischievous teenager isn't posing as an important historical subject? Moreover, some historians argue—not without merit—that online collecting excludes those older, less educated, or less well-to-do subjects who may not have access to the necessary technology. They also worry that the nature of such collections will inevitably be shallow, less useful for research, and harder to preserve.

Some of these worries are relatively easy to address. In our experience, for instance, teenagers are generally too busy downloading music to play games with historians and archivists online. But other concerns are not as easily answered. Collections created on the web through the submissions of scattered (and occasionally anonymous) contributors do have a very different character from traditional archives, for which provenance and selection criteria assume a greater role. Online collections tend to be less organized and more capricious in what they cover.

They also can be far larger, more diverse, and more inclusive than traditional archives. Indeed, perhaps the most profound benefit of online collecting is an unparalleled opportunity to allow more varied perspectives to be included in the historical record than ever before. Networked information technology can allow ordinary people and marginalized constituencies not only a larger presence in an online archive, but also a more important role in the dialogue of history. "There are about ten to fifteen million people's voices evident on the Web," Brewster Kahle, the founder of the Internet Archive, has said. "The Net is a people's medium: the good, the bad and the ugly. The interesting, the picayune, and the profane. It's all there."[2]

Furthermore, in contrast to traditional oral history, online collecting is a far more economical way to reach out to historical subjects. For example, because subjects write their own narratives, we avoid one of the most daunting costs of oral history, transcription. Consequently, although live individual interviews are often quite thorough and invaluable resources, online initiatives to collect personal histories can capture a far greater number of them at lower cost, while at the same time acquiring associated digital materials (such as photographs) just as cheaply. Of course, even if highly successful in the future, online collecting will not mean the end of traditional ways of gathering recent history, including what will surely remain the gold standard, oral history. As oral historian Linda Shopes observes, newer technological methods will have a hard time competing with many aspects of the oral historian's craft: "the cultivation of rapport and . . . lengthy, in-depth narratives through intense face to face contact; the use of subtle paralinguistic cues as an aid to moving the conversation along; the talent of responding to a particular comment, in the moment, with the breakthrough question, the probe that gets underneath a narrator's words."[3] Using the Internet will likely supplement or complement older, more time-consuming and costly methods such as this.

Despite the pitfalls and insecurities about online collecting, it has become a burgeoning practice. Recently, for example, the British Library, the Victoria and Albert Museum, the Museum of London, and several other British museums and archives have pooled their resources to display and collect stories of immigration to the U.K. in a project called Moving Here. Thus far, the project has posted almost 500 stories and artifacts—mainly digitized versions of existing archive records but also new materials acquired via the site—ranging from a documentary video on Caribbean life to the reflections of recent African immigrants. The British Broadcasting Corporation's two-year online project to gather the stories of Britain's World War II veterans and survivors of the London Blitz, entitled WW2 People's War, has been even more successful, with over a thousand narratives gathered through the BBC's website after only eight months, including dozens of harrowing accounts of D-Day.[4]

In the United States, the National Park Foundation, the National Park Service, and the Ford Motor Company are using the Internet to collect first-hand narratives of life during wartime for a planned Rosie the Riveter/World War II Home Front National Historical Park in Richmond, California. So far, more than six thousand former home front workers have contributed stories. National Geographic's Remembering Pearl Harbor site has received over a thousand entries in their "Memory Book." Over five hundred people have recorded their personal stories and artifacts of the civil rights movement on a site co-sponsored by the AARP, the Leadership Conference on Civil Rights, and the Library of Congress. The Alfred P. Sloan Foundation has taken a pioneering role in encouraging more than two dozen online collecting projects (including our own) in the recent history of science and technology, arguing that this history is growing much faster than our ability to gather it through more conventional means. Though there remains a healthy skepticism in the oral history community about the usefulness and reliability of narratives collected online, several new projects by major oral history centers (such as at Texas Tech University) show that they, too, are noticing the benefits of online collecting. Even Columbia University—the home of the nation's first oral history program—is encouraging alumni to join in writing "Columbia's history" by contributing stories online.[5]

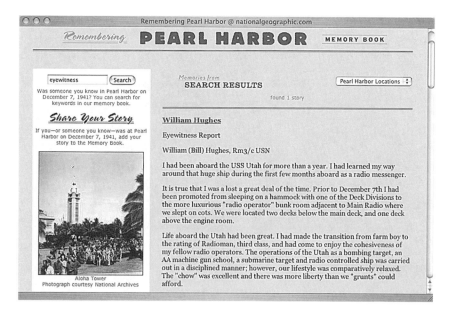

Figure 35. National Geographic's Remembering Pearl Harbor has a "Memory Book" that allows visitors to record first-hand accounts and other recollections about World War II.

Good Candidates for Online Collecting—and Poor Ones

Not every topic lends itself well to an online collecting project. Even with the global reach of the Internet and the world's most interesting subject matter (undoubtedly, whatever you as a historian study), you will need to connect with a fairly sizable body of contributors for your project to succeed. A website seeking personal narratives of the Roaring Twenties will fall flat (consider the average age of a person who can recall that era), as will most projects targeting topics before World War II. One website, on the history of Greenland ice drilling (co-sponsored by the American Meteorological Society, the American Geophysical Union, and the American Institute of Physics), attempted to capture memories from scientists who have gone to Greenland to study the environment by sampling tubes of ice drawn from millennia-old sheets, but it eventually faced a difficult reality: although the ice drilling projects in Greenland are tremendously important for ongoing debates about critical climate issues such as global warming, the number of climatologists and geologists who have set up and run such experiments is relatively small. There simply are not enough of them to populate the site with a highly active historical discussion.[6] Less obvious than the problems associated with a

Figure 36. Co-sponsored by the AARP, the Leadership Conference on Civil Rights, and the Library of Congress, the Voices of Civil Rights website uses narratives submitted by hundreds of people online to provide visitors with a rich sense of the experience and legacy of the 1950s and 1960s.

small pool of potential contributors is the opposite quandry: a topic so broad that it fails to excite any discernable cohort. A project directed at collecting the experience of "senior year in high school," in general, is much less likely to attract participants than one directed at the graduates of a particular high school.

Between too sparse and too diffuse pools of contributors, there are many large but discernable communities that will likely respond well to an online project that solicits, archives, and presents their stories and related images, audio, and video. A good candidate for a collecting website often revolves around a topic that already has an active, historically conscious online community. For example, Apple Computer's fanatical user base and committed employees have engendered numerous sites on the history of the Macintosh, including two major efforts to record the first-hand recollections of those who worked at Apple in the late 1970s and 1980s: the Computer History Museum's Apple Computer History Weblog and Apple software engineer Andy Hertzfeld's Folklore.org website. David Kirsch's electric vehicle history site appeals to a relatively small but committed, almost cult-like community of enthusiasts who were experimenting with zero-emission cars long before the major automobile manufacturers were. These hobbyists were used to exchanging

Figure 37. To capture the early history of Apple Computer from those who were there, Andy Hertzfeld, one of Apple's pioneering software engineers, set up the Folklore.org website.

helpful information with each other over the Internet. Before the much larger effort of the September 11 Digital Archive, we began our experiments in online collecting through similarly focused histories of recent science and technology in our Echo: Exploring and Collecting History Online—Science, Technology, and Industry project, funded, like the September 11 effort, by the Sloan Foundation as part of its program encouraging the use of the Internet to gather history.[7]

Online collection efforts tied to a real-world event, institution, or social network have a good chance of attracting and sustaining involvement. Many school and college alumni associations run discussion boards that recall the glory days. Flourishing sites related to actual communities, like one devoted to Brainerd, Kansas, or the Rowville-Lysterfield community center in Australia, craft online spaces where local people build their own historical record, contributing family histories, reminiscences, folklore, and personal artifacts such as photos and scanned documents. Sites connected to museum installations such as the powerful Atomic Memories site at San Francisco's Exploratorium use the shared experiences of visitors to their physical exhibitions to

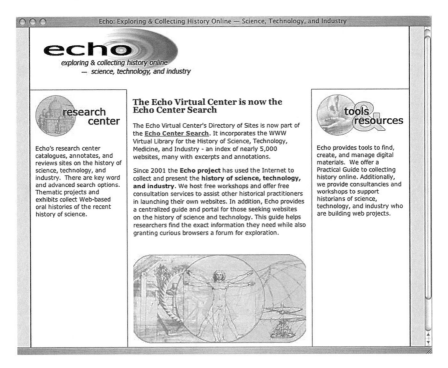

Figure 38. Our project entitled Echo: Exploring and Collecting History Online—Science, Technology, and Industry, funded by the Alfred P. Sloan Foundation, not only serves as a portal for those interested in researching the history of science, technology, medicine, and business, but has functioned as a laboratory for how to gather this history via the Internet.

encourage storytelling and historical reflection online. Established virtual communities for seniors, including SeniorNet's World War II Living Memorial and the History Channel's Veteran's Forum, host discussion "threads" with thousands of historical recollections and conversations about the past, and they allow veterans to reconnect to some of their most distant yet most significant life experiences and social networks. Indeed, perhaps the most active sites collecting history online today, for example, the World War II Living Memorial and the Veterans' Forum, exist primarily to enable personal connection among their membership. These sites simultaneously engage participants by bringing them into contact online with their cohort, while encouraging them to relate the details of their lives and the times through which they lived.[8]

Topics that do not match up with an existing online community or offline association still have the potential to succeed, but only if they are carefully framed to make them attractive to a discernable body of

contributors. Clearly delimited audiences make it easier to target potential contributors and for these potential contributors to feel comfortable
in the knowledge that they "belong" at a site. For example, Joshua
Greenberg's Video Store Project provided a space for the original owners and employees of video stores, before Blockbuster bankrupted or
bought out most of them in the 1990s, to discuss their history. An eclectic bunch, this "invented community"—more than nine hundred people—enjoyed the chance to recall the early years of the revolutionary
technology of the VHS and Betamax, and to read the recollections of
others. In turn, this online collection helped sharpen Greenberg's sense
of themes to highlight in his dissertation on the social uses of video technology, and provided him with a cache of primary sources that comple-
mented printed sources well.[9]

Tools for the Online Collector

Once you feel confident that your topic is a good candidate for an
online collection effort, you can begin to explore the technologies you
will need to do the actual collecting. As we emphasized in Chapter 2,
you should use the right level of technology for your project. Not everyone needs a Library of Congress–grade archival system or the capacity
to store millions of digital files. Regardless of the size of your project,
you should not overlook existing technologies that can make your job
easier. Much of the infrastructure and software required to do online
collecting has already been built and written, and you should take
advantage of these technologies, where possible, rather than reinventing
the wheel.

Choosing a contribution mechanism that is comfortable for your audience is critical. For example, if you are gathering young soldiers' experiences of the Iraq War, you may want to consider using instant messaging
as a collecting technology. By contrast, World War II veterans might prefer a more "traditional" email correspondence. The National Park
Foundation's Rosie the Riveter site has a web form for contributors to
enter their recollections, but it also has a prominent email link to Rosie-
theriveter@nationalparks.org. Though the BBC mandates that all contributions to their WW2 People's War collection come through the
Internet, they have joined forces with more than two thousand public
computer clusters (such as community centers and libraries) to help
seniors navigate the website and type in their entries.[10]

Similarly, you will need to think about what you would like to collect
from contributors, and plan accordingly. If you are doing a project on
the history of the Chicago Mercantile Exchange, you may want to consider collecting BlackBerry messages, a form of electronic communica-

tion very popular among traders; a project on tourism might do better focusing on digital photographs. In addition, you may want to change your collecting technology as the project gathers steam (and contributions), starting out with the simpler technologies we discuss at the beginning of this section and moving later on to more complex mechanisms.

Probably the oldest and still quite useful technology for online collecting is email—the choice of some of the most successful collecting projects. Almost all people who have Internet access have email and feel comfortable with it. Keith Whittle's Atomic Veterans History Project, devoted to the community of veterans who participated in nuclear testing during the Cold War, has collected and posted more than six hundred personal narratives from veterans, acquired solely through email. Furthermore, as Whittle discovered, emailers can send attachments such as digital photographs, many of which now grace the site alongside the narratives. Email also allows for long-term interactions, follow-up, and detailed exchanges. An online collecting project can get started right away with a simple, static web design that, like Whittle's, uses email links to encourage and accept submissions.[11]

Another possibly helpful collecting technology, closely related to email, is the listserv. If you work at a university or other large institution, you probably have access to listserv software, which essentially functions as a group email and newsletter distribution mechanism. In addition to personal narratives, primary documents, and exhibits, the Sixties-L discussion listserv, hosted by the University of Virginia, maintains an ongoing, active recollection (and scholarly discussion) of that decade of upheaval. Since its inception in 1997, there have been almost five thousand postings.[12]

Web-based collecting mechanisms need not be much more complicated than email. As we mentioned in Chapter 1, the explosion of online diaries, or blogs, has given millions of Internet users a taste of what it is like not just to read and view the web, but also to add their own perspectives to the medium. Without any knowledge of HTML or databases, historians can use a blog as a dynamic website for collecting and presenting the past. Many ways of maintaining a blog allow for more than one person to post there, thus enabling a community of historical participants to create an ever-expanding discussion about whatever topics interest them. Blogs may also allow for the exchange of images, other digital files, and more recently, audio, as well as links to other online materials. Through a modicum of additional web design, you can integrate a blog with a static site (or simply link to it from your main site and be satisfied with a clashing design) to have both an archive or gallery of historical materials and a way for visitors to post additional materials to the collection. Blogs generally have built-in search features and the ability to roll up what you collect for export to other locations (such as a different server or the desktop of your personal computer).

The two main types of blogging systems are those hosted on your server and those hosted on a blog company's server. Certain versions of both types are free, though there are also paid versions that have more features. Your decision about which type to use will probably come down to whether you want to spend the time to add more software to your server (or more likely, convince your webmaster to do this). Hosting your own blogging system allows you to customize how it looks and works, and gives you direct access to the "back end," or behind the scenes data, which permits finer control over submissions and the ability to transfer and backup individual files easily.

By far the three most prevalent hosted blogging systems are Blogger, owned by Google; LiveJournal, run by a small team of software developers and staff; and AOL Journals, owned by TimeWarner. Although it exists in a commercial version, LiveJournal can also be downloaded for free and installed on your server. LiveJournal and Six Apart's Movable Type are the predominant do-it-yourself blogging systems (Six Apart also runs a commercial hosting service for Movable Type blogs called TypePad.) Many other free and commercial blog sites and programs (including the open source WordPress) exist for those who find the dominant software and hosts too basic, or who demand other features like message encryption or the automatic resizing of images for web display.[13]

Contributors can submit to a blog-based collecting project in several ways. They can email their responses to you, and you can then post them to the site. Alternatively, you can share your blog's update mechanisms—the email address for automatic posts and the location of the web form you use to add entries to the site—and have others post directly, though this would not allow you to vet submissions first. More securely, most of the blog systems also allow you to set up a multiperson blog that permits anyone in a defined group to post materials to the site through individual accounts. This could work particularly well for small numbers of contributors who know each other—for instance, a group of professional colleagues or friends. Using the upload feature of blogging systems, you can also have members of the group send photographs to be archived on the blog. Other file formats are available, too; recently Google added the possibility of audio recordings, "uploaded" to a Blogger site using a telephone. The ease with which historians can set up blogs and have people add recollections and artifacts makes them an attractive possibility for a simple collecting site.

One disadvantage of blogs, however, is that they encourage stream-of-consciousness writing and are by nature somewhat disorganized.

Threaded discussion or forum software is generally better at creating distinct subtopical areas, so that you do not end up with an undifferentiated mass of rambling contributions. This technology is not new; millions of people have posted to the venerable and still quite active Usenet discussion groups that predate the web. In addition to imposing a higher level of order on contributions, discussion software packages, like more advanced multiperson blogs, allow you to keep better track of contributors because they can be set up to require users to log in and provide identifying information (such as email and other ways of reaching them). There are several easy-to-use forum programs and hosting services. (Like blogging software, these should be installed on your server by a webmaster or someone with technical knowledge of database software and programming languages.) PhpBB is an excellent free option, and you can purchase or lease the popular UBB or vBulletin for under $200. Host servers are available for all three, generally for a monthly fee starting at around $25.[14]

The most powerful and flexible way to receive collections is through an interactive website of your own design. Most of the blog and forum programs run on databases behind the scenes, and you (or your programmer) can create your own unique collection system from scratch using the same technology. The great advantage of this approach is that is allows you to set up customized web forms for visitors to enter information and files, as you find on web email systems like Yahoo Mail or Hotmail. Blog and forum programs normally have a single box for text entries and a rigid set of shorter questions about the contribution or contributor, making it difficult to ask historical subjects a series of questions about their experiences, or to ask more open-ended or evocative questions suitable for drawing out historical recollections. For instance, on its web form, Moving Here (the site that chronicles immigration to the U.K.) asks contributors to enter the *range* of years in which their historical narrative occurred—the single date box you commonly find on a blog would have been inadequate for this purpose.[15] Customized web applications allow greater flexibility in presenting contributions as well because you can continually adjust the way entries are pulled out of the database and arranged on the screen, instead of relying on the existing templates provided by a software package.

Although these features make do-it-yourself collection systems attractive, you should first explore simpler, preexisting programs like blogs or forums to see if one of them meets your needs. To offer a little self-advertising, we might suggest you also check out the Center for History and New Media's free database-driven Survey Builder application, which quickly and easily builds forms for acquiring historical files, images, and narratives. Because CHNM hosts the surveys, you don't need to have your own server or know anything about programming.[16] Unique systems may work well, but they often require ongoing maintenance, and if the original programmer leaves the project, they can be difficult to update or fix if there is a problem. If you decide to do it yourself, the learning curve for databases and web programming languages can be steep. But the technical appendix in this book provides some basic information on how to create a custom web application for your collecting project.

New forms of instantaneous communication on the Internet may further expand the toolkit for collecting history online. Millions are now using instant messaging (IM) software, which permits you to communicate in real time with individuals around the globe. Popular IM software such as AOL Instant Messenger, MSN Messenger, Yahoo Messenger, and Apple's iChat permit file transfers as well, so that contributors not only can recollect the past in online text interviews, but also can send you related digital materials as they converse. Although they do not have the tonal inflections of a spoken dialogue, these typed conversations do have the considerable advantage of being self-documenting, unlike oral history interviews, which require expensive transcriptions. More recent versions of these IM programs also allow rudimentary (but rapidly improving) audio and video chats as well, which opens up the possibility of a future that is much like the past of traditional oral history. But fast Internet connections are required on both sides of the line for these advanced multimedia features, which restricts the realm of potential contributors to those with high-speed connections. New services that accept voice recordings via a standard telephone line and convert those recordings into a digital format that you can receive via email or through a website offer another possibility for audio collections.[17]

Attracting Contributors to Your Site

Your choice of an appropriate collecting technology probably matters less to the overall success of your project than the content and design of your site and effective outreach to the potential contributors. Too many collecting projects have started with high hopes and ended with a frightfully low number of submissions. You should therefore spend more time thinking about how to excite your intended base of contributors than mastering every last detail of Internet communication.

One strategy for attracting contributors is to offer information or materials that will bring them to the site. What ultimately matters in choosing "magnet" content is not so much its exhaustiveness or the refinement of presentation, but rather its distinctiveness on the web. A small collection of compelling or provocative materials, carefully annotated or explicated in some fashion that appeals to the curiosity of your targeted audience, is far more effective than a vast but conceptually murky collection of materials or a set of documents that can be easily found elsewhere on the Internet. For example, the Atomic Veterans site provides its community with the information that it desires (e.g., an up-to-date collection of declassified documents on nuclear tests) and it presents it in a fashion that reflects the veterans' experiences (i.e., as it pertains to specific military operations and outfits). On effective collecting sites such as this one, the magnet content is seamlessly integrated with the contributions, leading to a historical collection that is greater than the sum of it parts. Atomic Veterans steward Keith Whittle has also recognized the importance of keeping a site current and fresh to maintain its attractiveness to visitors and contributors. Like Whittle, you should rotate featured items on your home page or highlight the most recent additions to the collection.

Probably the best magnet content on a collecting site is other contributions. This leads to a major paradox, however, and one that will be familiar to anyone who has ever taught a class: just as no one wants to be first to raise his or her hand, no one wants to be first to contribute to an Internet collection. Potential contributors of personal historical materials may be self-conscious, and even the most eager contributor can fall victim to the worry that his or her story or image will attract too much scrutiny as it sits alone on a featured web page. Visitors with historical recollections or materials to contribute may even visit the site several times, "lurking" as they try to overcome these worries, and many newly launched online collecting projects have enjoyed great peaks in traffic without seeing any corresponding increase in historical contributions. Thus the paradox: to build a collection, you first need a collection; often the only way to attract contributions is with other contributions. A second contribution is always easier to get than a first, and a third is even easier. Once you've collected a few items, it will become easier to collect more, and a kind of momentum will gradually build.

But how do you establish this momentum? You might ask a related online collecting project or physical archive if you can reprint some of their contributions on your website until you have established your project. The coalition of museums and archives behind Moving Here plumbed their rich physical collections for suitable materials that could serve as model "contributions," such as the Jewish Museum's transcripts of interviews with Jewish immigrants to London's East End.[18] If you do not have access to existing collections, try to seek out friends, family, and colleagues who are in the target audience for your site to have them "seed" the collection.

Unless you have such helpful contacts, however, you will likely be reaching out to a new community—one that may not know you—and you will have to convince that group of possible contributors that your project is worth their time. This will require marketing and publicity. As we noted in Chapter 5, historians usually have no training in such matters, but they are especially important for online collection projects. Successful projects devote much, if not most, of their resources to outreach. Potential contributors have to hear about a site, often repeatedly, before they become interested in contributing. Formulating a detailed outreach plan in advance will help you affirm that you can actually accomplish your collecting goals—after all, if you can't think of a way to reach possible contributors, you will likely face disappointment—and provide a quick jumpstart to your endeavor once the website is finished.

Probably the first step is contacting potential contributors directly through email, telephone, or postal mail. When Claude Shannon, the father of modern information theory and the mathematics behind key parts of the Internet such as modems, passed away in February 2001, we launched a modest project to collect his colleagues' reminiscences of him. Sending out approximately three hundred targeted emails pointing to our website, we collected more than thirty detailed accounts of Shannon's life and legacy from a variety of scientists and technologists, revealing new information about Shannon's work at Bell Labs and his enormous impact on such far-flung disciplines as computer science, computational biology, and genetics. We were also able to collect historical materials from people who would otherwise have been impossible to reach without the Internet. As our initial email was forwarded to listservs and online discussion groups, it ultimately reached a group of scientists working in Siberia who, it turns out, had been profoundly influenced by Shannon's work thousands of miles away.[19]

Indirect marketing focuses on reaching possible contributors through their social networks. You should spend some time identifying and contacting the key organizations and institutions most relevant to your historical subjects. Their assistance to you can range from a simple link on a home page to a feature story in their newsletter to a posting to their email list. If your project genuinely interests their members, they will likely help you. You should also spend some time in your contributors' communities, virtually or in the real world. Become a member of a web forum, newsgroup, or listserv related to your topic. You may want to attend a live meeting, where you can distribute literature about your project (along with its URL or a phone number to reach you). David Kirsch, director of the Electric Vehicle History Online Archive, spent hours posting on online discussion boards and days attending electric vehicle club meetings to become a trusted member of the electric vehicle hobbyist community and acquire the first set of contributions to his website.[20]

Although a direct, personalized email to a historical participant or a community newsletter article about your site may be more effective in building a pool of contributors than a colorful ad in a journal, magazine, or newspaper, you should not ignore the potential of a media campaign or a mass marketing approach. If you can tie your project in some way to current events, a well-placed press release can attract media attention and increase contributions. We experienced some success in this regard for a website we built with the National Institutes of Health called A Thin Blue Line, where we leveraged the thirtieth anniversary of the creation of the home pregnancy test to collect the popular history of that landmark reproductive technology. The *Washington Post* and other newspapers ran stories about the site because of its timeliness, which led to a spike in site traffic and a smaller bump in contributions.[21]

Combined with high-quality historical materials, a website that collects the history of the recent past can become a trusted center for information on the web and spark media coverage simply by its existence. As mentioned in Chapter 5, when the lights went out in the northeastern United States in August 2003, our colleague James Sparrow immediately received calls from the BBC, the *New York Times*, the *Boston Globe*, National Public Radio, and other major media outlets because he had created the definitive site on the history of the 1965 and 1977 New York City blackouts. With scanned primary documents and audio clips, as well as hundreds of stories gathered via the web, Sparrow's site shows how an Internet project, done well, can successfully collect history once it has achieved a status as the place to go for a particular historical topic. Following coverage in the mass media, the site gathered over a hundred new personal narratives for its archive.[22]

Encouraging Contributions and Building Trust

Most people will come to your site to view contributions or contribute themselves. You should therefore make it as easy as possible for visitors to contribute and to recognize the value of what you have already collected. You will also need to create trust about you, your site, and its mission. The design of your site and the ways in which you convince possible contributors that their submissions are worth saving for the future are at least as important as the technology. Image-heavy splash pages and Flash movies may be very attractive, but first and foremost you should have clear invitations to "Contribute," "Tell your story," "Read the stories of others," or "View donated images." Beyond these signposts, an attractive design, of course, does burnish the reputation of a website and makes it more likely to attract contributions.

When contributors find themselves on the correct web page to add their recollections or upload a digital file, they should face as few hurdles as possible. Even if you feel that the technology is self-explanatory, provide clear step-by-step instructions, and if possible test them ahead of time with potential contributors. Sites that require logins—usernames and passwords that you must register for in advance of your contribution—will almost always receive fewer submissions than those that allow all comers to proceed. This phenomenon is part of a larger tension between sound (and some would argue sane) archival practice and using the web to collect historical materials and narratives: the more you ask contributors to reveal about themselves, the less likely they will be to contribute. As we will see in Chapter 8, librarians and archivists relish "metadata"—that is, solid information about the who and what of an accessioned document, such as the name, address, and other contact information of the creator, and exact details about the provenance of what has been donated. Unfortunately, years of spam, online scams, and poor handling of private information by supposedly trustworthy institutions (such as banks) have made most web users extremely cautious about entering personal data.

This does not mean that you should accept only anonymous contributions. Instead, we recommend making only contributors' full names and an email address or phone number mandatory—some small bit of information necessary to reach a contributor later—and making other information (such as a mailing address) optional. Moreover, you should ask for this personal information *after* they have completed their submission. Many people will volunteer this information; others won't, but you can use the one piece of mandatory information to contact a contributor later to get further metadata for your collection. This flips the normal order of archival acquisition on its head, of course—get the materials first, then learn about the contributor—but it raises your chances of actually getting contributions in the first place. It also may be worthwhile to offer opportunities for contributors to keep their submissions "private," that is, saved in your collection but unavailable for a time to the public, or to offer to remove their names and other identifying information from any public display.

Likewise, it helps to link from your submission page to a reassuring policy statement that details how you will use the information provided. Specify in bold that all personal information will be closely guarded and not shared for any reason without the consent of the contributor. Online collecting projects should formulate these important policy pages early on and attempt to identify all potential legal and ethical

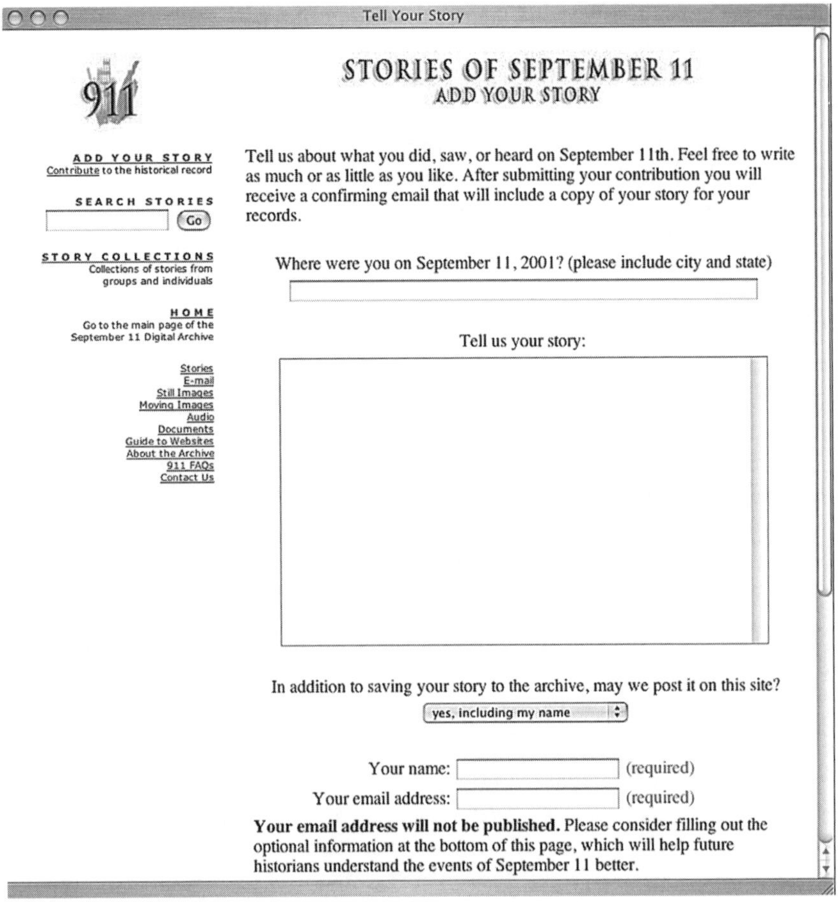

Figure 39. The stories submission page for the September 11 Digital Archive, which is co-sponsored by the Center for History and New Media and the American Social History Project, highlights some of the principles of online collecting forms, including a large upfront box for the first-person narrative, much smaller secondary metadata collection boxes (Zip code, age, gender, and so on), and the importance of building trust, in this case by highlighting our limited use of the contributor's email address.

problems. By accepting donations from your contributors, you are assuming responsibility for the information they provide you. It may become too easy to think of your contributors simply as subjects of your research, and for this reason you should always remember to treat them with humanity and respect.

If you are associated with a college or university, these concerns may have a legal import as well. Because of controversies surrounding medical and psychological experiments, all research involving "human subjects" has come under heightened scrutiny by institutional review boards (IRBs) that oversee university-based research. Whether or not oral history—to which this online collecting can be compared—should fall under the regulation of IRBs remains a controversial subject. Although we agree with those who believe it should be excluded (because it is very different from the kind of research that the federal regulations are directed at), many IRBs disagree and if that is the case at your university you will have to have your project reviewed for approval. If so, it will probably help your case if you describe it as "online oral history." Describing your work as a "survey" will place it in a category of social science research where it doesn't belong and where it will fall under closer official scrutiny. Whether or not you need to have your plans officially reviewed, you should always strive to follow the ethical guidelines provided by disciplinary organizations such as the Oral History Association.[23]

Regardless of your affiliation, a well-crafted policy page will help protect you and your contributors from ambiguities. The terms of attribution and ownership must be made completely clear, and participants should indicate their informed consent by acknowledging, either through a button click or a check box, their consent to a set of terms for every submission. These consent forms need not be overly detailed or legalistic. They merely should state in plain language what the rules of submission are, where the contribution is going, what may be done with it (such as transferring it to another institution or to other researchers), and whether there may be any further contact from the project staff following the submission. This last part of your policy statement is important because some people will consider further unsolicited entreaties as annoying spam. Although oriented toward companies, the online watchdog TRUSTe has a helpful guide to crafting such policies, including handling disclosures about personal information and related matters.[24]

The Moving Here site on immigration to the U.K. facilitates contributions and builds trust with contributors extremely well. It has a well-designed, simple entry form for stories, with boxes for the contributor's name and an email address or phone number. A clear note about the need to contact contributors and a reassuring link to their privacy policy, which is admirably less than two hundred words, sits adjacent to the short form. The policies on privacy and data protection are devoid of legal jargon, and they pop up when requested so the contributor doesn't need to leave the entry page. The Rosie the Riveter stories site requires only an email address to proceed, though it gently requests other information such as a contributor's name, phone number, and mailing

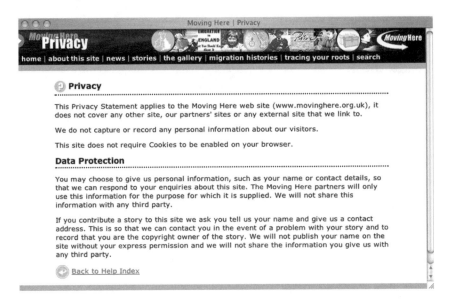

Figure 40. The coalition of British museums and libraries behind the Moving Here website chronicling immigration to the U.K. includes on their site a clear and concise policies page, devoid of legal argot.

address. Unfortunately the site puts some people off by mandating that they agree to a long, legalistic "Terms of Submission and Disclaimer" before beginning the submission process, though clearly this has not dissuaded the thousands of Rosie the Riveter contributors.[25]

We suspect that this acceptance is in part due to the reputation of the high-profile institutions behind Rosie the Riveter, prominently displayed with large logos on their website. Even if your site is not sponsored by a giant automobile company or government agency, it builds trust with contributors if you scrupulously reveal who you are and where they can find you. You should play up any affiliations because they give a website a feeling of being connected to the real world and provide a sense of where the contributions are going. Indeed, you may want to make an alliance with a local library, historical society, or university archive to sponsor your website and perhaps even house the final collection (in digital or printed form). Many people still consider the web an ephemeral medium; knowing that their donations have a nonvirtual home helps to overcome the hesitation engendered by this feeling of impermanency. Partnerships with brick-and-mortar institutions help add "weight" to an otherwise "weightless" online project.

Qualitative Concerns

Once you convince contributors to participate in your site, what do you actually want from them, and how can you ensure that what they submit is useful and authentic? Oral historians, ethnographers, and sociologists have carefully thought out sound and effective "instruments" (controlled and rigorous methods for collecting information).[26] Although consulting this literature is worthwhile, the limitations of web forms and other collection mechanisms such as email work against the strict replication of these standards online. For example, the common method of repeating an important question several times, using a different phrasing each time, to ensure an accurate answer from a respondent sounds good in the abstract. As we discussed in Chapter 4, however, the size and resolution of most computer screens permits only a fairly limited amount of text and response space, thus requiring a great deal of scrolling (and frustration) as the number of questions proliferate. Historical surveys on the Internet—in the interest of attracting a large group of contributors—probably should not match the density and complexity of offline versions. And, in any case, social scientists would not consider them true "surveys" in the sense of a scientifically valid form for collecting information.

In your web form, discussion board prompt, or email exchange, be wary of asking for too much. As Don Dillman, a sociologist who has studied the effectiveness of web surveys, notes, "Survey designers try to get too much detail from respondents. The result is survey abandonment, which the Internet makes relatively easy." Try to keep at least the initial entreaty short and as open-ended as possible—certainly fewer than ten questions, and probably better under five. We have found that some of the most effective online collection projects involve not much more than a call to "Share your story." (Yes, most people are narcissistic and like to talk primarily about themselves and their experiences.) In the narrative that results from such open-ended questions, you will often find the answers to more specific questions that would have been far down a long and off-putting survey form. One of the online collecting efforts related to September 11, 2001 (see below), simply asked "Where were you?" and yet was able to collect a vast archive of rich first-hand narratives—not just of where, but of when, with whom, and how their diverse set of contributors experienced that day. Historians new to survey design tend to be too specific. Although you may think a detailed survey will get you exactly what you want, it may in fact be confusing to visitors who do not know as much about the broad sweep of your subject as you. In addition, asking questions in the authorial voice of a scholarly essay or book repels most potential contributors. Write questions in a more casual prose style.[27]

Finally, be flexible. Remember that one of the advantages of the web is its ease of revision: you can change wordings and collection formats at any time if things are not working out the way you envisioned. (Do be sure to save earlier versions so that future researchers can properly understand older sets of responses.) You should also be prepared to accept things you had not intended to collect. Sometimes contributors will want to give you materials you did not ask for or tales that seem unrelated to your focus. Always consider accepting these donations. The public's generosity may surprise you, and it may enrich your project in ways you could not have anticipated.

Of course, along with great generosity sometimes comes undesired mischief. How can you be sure your contributors are who they say they are? How can you be sure their contributions aren't faked, or taken from other sources? Concern about the falsification of digital historical documents and materials, we believe, has mostly turned out to be a phantom problem. We are not alone in this assessment. Newspaper websites, which rely on the registration information given by surfers to make money off of targeted advertisements, have found (much to their surprise) that relatively few people enter fake information, even though there are sometimes no checks against such subterfuge. In one study, the *Philadelphia Inquirer* discovered that only about 10 to 15 percent of their 300,000 registered users had entered bad email addresses (and some of those were merely by accident or due to technical difficulties), even though a person's email address is among the most guarded possessions of the online world because a vast majority of people are worried about spam. Zip codes and other less problematic bits of personal information are falsified at an even lower rate.[28]

We think the nonprofit mission of online historical archives generally produces even higher rates of honesty. Most people who take the time to submit something to your project will share your goals and your interest in creating an accurate historical record. Rogues and hackers have more interesting things to do on the Internet than corrupt historical archives. But our best defenses against fraud are our traditional historical skills. Historians have always had to assess the reliability of their sources from internal and external clues. Not only have there been famous forgeries on paper, but written memoirs and traditional oral histories are filled with exaggerations and distortions. In the past as in the present, historians have had to look for evidence of internal consistency and weigh them against other sources. In any media, sound research is the basis of sound scholarship.

Nevertheless, some technical methods can help double-check online contributions. As we explained in Chapter 2, every computer connected to the web has an Internet Protocol (IP) address. A small bit of programming code can capture this address and attach it to the other metadata associated with a contribution. If you are skeptical that a contribution has come from a specific person or location, a WHOIS search, which translates the numbers of an IP address into a semi-readable format that often includes a contributor's Internet service provider and broad area of service, occasionally results in helpful information.[29] Less cloak-and-dagger is a simple email or telephone follow-up with the person to thank them for their contribution; if the email bounces back or the phone number is incorrect, you should be more skeptical of the submission. Following up in this way also presents an opportunity to ask contributors if they might have any other documents or recollections, and whether they might know of others who can supplement your archive.

A less obvious but perhaps more important measure of the "quality" of a historical collection created online becomes apparent when the collection is assessed as a whole rather than on the level of individual submissions. Like any collection, online or offline, a minority of striking contributions will stand out in a sea of dull or seemingly irrelevant entries. Historians who have browsed box after box in a paper archive trying to find key pieces of evidence for their research will know this principle well, and it should not come as a surprise that these grim percentages follow us into the digital realm. Yet as we also know, even a few well-written perspectives or telling archival images may form the basis of a new interpretation, or help to buttress an existing but partial understanding of a certain historical moment. At the same time, the greater size and diversity of online collections allow you more opportunities to look for common patterns. Why do certain types of stories reoccur? What does that tell you about both popular experience and the ways in which that experience gets transformed into memory?

Moreover, because of a digital collection's superior manipulability compared to a physical collection, historians can search electronic documents in revealing and novel ways. On the web, the speed with which one can do this sort of analysis can enable both quick assessments of historical collections as well as more substantive investigations. For instance, when historian Michael Kazin used search tools to scan our September 11 Digital Archive for the frequency of words such as "patriotic" and "freedom," he came to some important, if preliminary, conclusions about the American reaction to the terrorist attacks. Kazin discovered that fewer Americans than we might imagine saw September 11 in terms of nationalism, radical Islam versus the values of the West, or any other abstract framework. Instead, most saw the events in far more personal and local terms: the loss of a friend, the effect on a town or community, the impact on their family or job.[30] The ultimate quality of a digital collection may have more to do with the forest than the trees, so to speak.

Case Study: September 11, 2001

The most immediate, successful, and helpful examples of online collecting thus far indeed arose in response to those terrorist attacks of September 11, 2001. The date was a watershed moment in the short history of online collecting, a point at which the practice spread in a spontaneous response to historic events among amateur historians, as well as more deliberate responses from professional historians, museums, libraries, and historical societies. We participated in one of these projects, the September 11 Digital Archive, and as part of our project we cataloged hundreds of other sites that were accepting contributions in the form of stories, reflections, artwork, and photographs. To be sure, much of this activity took place in preexisting online locations, such as major media websites. For instance, the web portals of the *New York Times* and the BBC had extensive and quite active message boards recording responses to the events of that day and its aftermath. At the same time, however, many new outlets popped up to collect these feelings and perspectives in a vibrant example of what the Pew Internet and American Life Project has called "do-it-yourself journalism."[31] Starting with the clear conviction that momentous events were occurring around them, scholars, students, archivists, businesses, and members of the general public started online collecting projects in an effort to record the terrible events of September 11 and its aftermath.

Amateur collectors founded many of the earliest successful efforts to capture the history of September 11 online. Wherewereyou.org succeeded in collecting more than two thousand personal narratives of September 11 in the space of just a few weeks.[32] Working quickly and with admirable technical and design skill, the creators of the site developed a database-driven application that allowed people from around the globe to tell their story of September 11. Remarkably, the entire project was unfunded, and conceived and executed entirely by three undergraduate college students working in different cities in their spare time. Wherewereyou.org shows how the Internet can empower amateur historians who want to collect history.

In addition to scores of such amateur efforts, several large-scale professional and institutional efforts used the web to capture historical materials and narratives. Building on a partnership with the Internet Archive forged to collect web content during the preelection months and in the aftermath of the contested 2000 presidential contest, the

Library of Congress's Library Services Directorate moved immediately to capture web content related to the attacks. Their September 11 Web Archive officially launched on October 11, 2001, though the Internet Archive's computers began scanning the web just hours after the September 11 attacks. Led by the Library and funded with a grant from the Pew Charitable Trusts, this effort, like the project surrounding the 2000 presidential election before it, sought to "evaluate, select, collect, catalog, provide access to, and preserve digital materials for future generations of researchers." By the time the collecting wrapped up on December 1, 2001, the Library and the Internet Archive had collected the contents of nearly 30,000 websites and 5 terabytes (5,000 gigabytes) of information, representing an unprecedented snapshot of the world's real-time response to the tragic events.[33]

A second major online effort to document the history of 9/11 was our September 11 Digital Archive, a joint venture of the American Social History Project/Center for Media and Learning at the City University of New York's Graduate Center and CHNM.[34] Funded with a grant from the Sloan Foundation, the archive set out to collect, preserve, and present a range of primary sources, especially those born-digital materials that were not being collected by other projects like the September 11 Web Archive. Whereas the Web Archive aimed at collecting public web pages, our effort sought to collect—directly from their owners—those digital materials not available on the public Web: artifacts like email, digital photographs, word processing documents, and personal narratives. We also wanted to create a central place of deposit for the many and more fragile amateur efforts already under way. Now, more than three years into the project, the September 11 Digital Archive has collected more than 150,000 digital objects relating to the terrorist attacks, including more than 35,000 personal narratives and 20,000 digital images. In September 2003, the Library of Congress formally agreed to ensure the Digital Archive's long-term preservation.

Despite its large scale, the Digital Archive began fairly modestly. To get the site up extremely quickly, we ported over the basic database infrastructure and programming code from several earlier collecting projects on the history of science and technology (our Echo project). Funding from the Sloan Foundation arrived on January 1, 2002, and we launched the site on January 11, with the initial ability to collect digital images, email, and stories. As time went on, we added features as needed, including uploads for digital files other than images and fully automated voicemail contributions. To seed the contributions area, we first publicized the site to friends, family, colleagues, and the students and staff of our respective campuses. On the six-month anniversary of

September 11, on March 11, 2002, we had a full public launch, with press releases and some major media coverage.

With the technical concerns in the background, we focused heavily on outreach to both a wide audience and the communities near the crash sites in lower Manhattan; Arlington, Virginia; and Shanksville, Pennsylvania. Our marketing efforts paid off over many months as the number of contributions snowballed, and as we were able to forge alliances with the Smithsonian Institution's National Museum of American History as well as other museums and historical societies, which gave the site useful imprimaturs. Looking at just one section of the site, the one that accepted personal narratives, we had 28 submissions by the end of January 2002, 328 by the end of March, 693 by May, 948 by July, and 1,624 by August 2002. As media attention increased in the period just before the first anniversary of September 11, with major stories on the project on CNN, MSNBC, the Associated Press, as well as hundreds of newspapers, our numbers went exponentially higher. On September 11, 2002, alone we received more than 13,000 personal stories, including hundreds from direct witnesses of the events.

That last note raises a critical second point: These efforts and the growth of the archive led to both a broad response from around the country and the world, as well as from particular audiences we were especially trying to reach. Surely it is easier to garner a general public response via a website than to reach a small set of targeted contributors. But what we found happened as the project grew is that with the sheer number of contributions from the general public, it became much easier to gather materials from those directly involved with the events of September 11. Because of our prominence and partnerships with major institutions, we found that key constituencies had heard about us even before we contacted them and were very interested in contributing important historical materials to us, or if they had not heard of our project, were much more willing once they went to our site. We had achieved a sort of "presence" and "critical mass" that led to a greater and greater number of contributions and some valuable acquisitions, such as the real-time electronic communications of a group of co-workers evacuating lower Manhattan. Other groups, including Here Is New York, which gathered thousands of stunning photos of the city in the aftermath of September 11, asked us to serve as the repository of their own collections.[35]

The explosion of online collecting following September 11 was part of a larger change in Internet culture that the attacks precipitated. As the Pew Internet and American Life Project has shown, more and more people turned to the Internet as a "commons" after September 11; it became a place to communicate and comment rather than just surf for news. Although most Americans still got their news through traditional media outlets such as newspapers and television and overall Internet usage actually declined in the days immediately following the attacks, an unprecedented number of people used the Internet to share their feelings and perspectives on the tragedies. For example, nearly 20 million Americans used email to rekindle old friendships after September 11. Even more pertinent to the present discussion, 13 percent of Internet users participated in online discussions after the attacks. This interactivity represented an entirely new role for the Internet as a place for community-making and spontaneous documentation. "For the first time," wrote one electronic newsletter editor, "the nation and the world could talk with itself, doing what humans do when the innocent suffer: cry, inform, and most important, tell the story together." More specifically, people approached the Internet as a place to debate the United States government's response to terrorism (46 percent), to find or give consolation (22 percent), and to explore ways of dealing locally with the attacks and their aftermath (19 percent). Such usage of the Internet will only grow in the years to come.[36]

*   *   *

Surely not every collecting website will have the scale or results that the September 11 projects have had. Nor should they; not every historical project has a universe of possible contributors equivalent to that of the September 11 Digital Archive. Regardless of size, however, the payoff can be tremendous in a successful online collecting project. The massive capacity of the web means that historians can push beyond the selectivity of paper collections to create more comprehensive archives with multiple viewpoints and multiple formats (including audio and video as well as text). Given the open access of the web, it seems appropriate to cast the widest possible net (as it were) in projects like the September 11 Digital Archive, rather than focus on figures such as government leaders who will almost certainly dominate coverage in print. These archives, we hope, will partially make up for their lack of a curator's touch by their size, scope, and immediacy. The nature and extent of what you can gather, though clearly different from a traditional oral history project or museum effort, may be just as enlightening and important as a future historical resource, and likely will grow more so as an increasing percentage of our communications and expressions occur in digital media.

Upon reflection, it appears that these online collections of the future are not unlike the very first history of Herodotus, with the potential to promote an inclusive and wide-ranging view of the historical record. In his travels around the Mediterranean region, Herodotus recorded the sentiments of both Persians and Greeks, common people in addition to leading figures, competing accounts, legends as well as facts. He wanted to save all of these stories before they were forgotten so that the color of the past would not be lost. And as he told his audience, he was also cataloging and recounting it all because in the future people might have different notions of what or who is important: "I will go forward in my account, covering alike the small and great cities of mankind. For of those that were great in earlier times most have now become small, and those that were great in my time were small in the time before. Since, then, I know that man's good fortune never abides in the same place, I will make mention of both alike."[37] Using the Internet to collect history shares this vision: it is undoubtedly a more democratic form of history than found in selective physical archives or nicely smoothed historical narratives, and it shares democracy's messiness, contradictions, and disorganization—as well as its inclusiveness, myriad viewpoints, and vibrant popular spirit.

Chapter 7
Owning the Past?
The Digital Historian's Guide to Copyright
and Intellectual Property

In this chapter you will learn about:

- How copyright law is an ever-evolving set of principles, balancing the rights of producers and consumers, that must be actively engaged by historians
- The history of copyright law, and where it has left us today
- How the application of copyright can differ on the web from the print world
- Your legal rights—and ethical obligations—as both a producer and consumer of intellectual property
- Which written materials, images, audio, and video you can use on your website, and when

Once there was a real estate guide called "How to Buy and Sell a House." The author divided the book in two. From one end, he told you about purchasing a house. But if you flipped it over and began from the other side, the writer gave advice to sellers. The buying half warned you against the tricky devices that rapacious sellers might try. Simultaneously, he cautioned those reading the selling chapters about the underhanded behavior of shady buyers.

We could write a guide to copyright that similarly viewed the world as a Hobbesian marketplace of each person out for himself or herself. Those who create historical materials on the web are, indeed, likely to find themselves on both sides of the legal and ethical fence—creating intellectual property that they want to "protect" and "using" the intellectual property of others. Of course, some readers of this book will find themselves more often in one role than the other—museum curators, for example, probably worry more about protecting intellectual property than teachers mounting course websites.[1] But few people do digital history without both making a creative contribution of their own and benefiting from the creativity of others.

We prefer to view the web as a "commons," or a shared storehouse of human creations, rather than a "marketplace," and we align ourselves with the broad movement of lawyers and scholars, like Stanford University law professor Lawrence Lessig, who have promoted the notion of a "Creative Commons."[2] In this, we advocate a balance between the rights and needs of the "owners" and "users" of intellectual property, but a balance that favors the enlargement of the "public domain"—taken here to mean not just the formal realm of works with no legal copyright protection, but also more broadly the arena defined by fair use and the sharing and dissemination of ideas and creativity. To see intellectual work entirely as "property" undercuts the norms of sharing and collaboration that are integral to a field like history.

Such noble sentiments inevitably collide with the realities of the world. You may follow an ethic of community and sharing, but that doesn't help you if you come upon others guided by the impulses of Hobbes's state of nature. To prepare for that collision, you need to understand the regime of laws and courts, where such disputes sometimes get resolved. For historians, this encounter with the law often proves unsettling. They confront confusing rules and regulations that they seemingly must follow at the risk of lawsuits and fines. Historians, who know that pronouncements by fellow scholars are mere interpretations, sometimes mistakenly (and unwisely) treat copyright assertions by lawyers and other gatekeepers (e.g., the copyright officers of their universities or their journal and book publishers) as unvarnished truth. But copyright law, like history, is subject to conflicting interpretations as well as sharp contention between advocates of the rights of the owners of intellectual property and those seeking to enlarge the public domain.

To take a seemingly neutral position of deferential compliance with all copyright "rules" accepts one side in that argument and diminishes the intellectual commons. We believe that a more aggressive assertion of the rights and claims of that commons, when followed sensibly, does not entail excessive risk. In taking this stance, we depart from the conventional wisdom of dozens of copyright guides, whose favorite phrases are "do not," "ask permission," and "err on the side of caution."[3] Of course, we hasten to add (cautiously) that we are not lawyers, and we are not offering legal advice. Historians who go online will need to assess their own tolerance for risk and how they want to balance these competing claims. We encourage all historians, however, to explore how their actions, both online and off, might increase the common storehouse of documents and knowledge out of which much of our individual and collective work arises.

A Brief History of Copyright

The idea of a balance between the rights of the creators of intellectual property and the social and cultural claims of sharing and community finds support in the early history of American copyright law. Noah Webster, who was trying to protect the revenues flowing from his best-selling *American Spelling Book*, successfully lobbied the Connecticut State Legislature to pass the new nation's first copyright law in 1783. It gave authors control over the printing and publishing of their work for fourteen years with the option of a fourteen-year renewal—the same time period embodied in the Statute of Anne, the 1710 British law that set many of the terms for subsequent Anglo-American copyright legislation. The Connecticut law balanced the rights of authors with the claims of the public domain by requiring authors to "furnish the Public with sufficient Editions," which meant that those benefiting from the law could not restrict access to their work.[4]

Article 1, Section 8, of the U.S. Constitution most fully embodies this effort to balance public good and private reward. It grants Congress the power to give "authors and inventors the exclusive right to their respective writings and discoveries," while also specifying that such rights be granted only "for limited terms" and with the purpose of promoting "the progress of science and the useful arts." It is, indeed, the only section of the original Constitution that states a purpose behind the provision. The 1790 U.S. copyright law followed this by limiting copyright to two fourteen-year terms, requiring deposit of copies, and identifying its larger purpose with the title: "An Act for the encouragement of learning."[5]

The new law did not, however, satisfy Webster. Like the Disney Corporation two centuries later, he wanted to keep the healthy revenue stream flowing from his blue-backed speller as long as possible. He and his allies failed to win perpetual copyright (a clear breach of the U.S. Constitution) but did get a series of extensions—an indication that much of the subsequent history of American copyright would increase the rights of authors and owners and decrease the claims of the general public. An 1802 amendment extended the law to cover print illustrations. The 1831 law doubled the initial copyright period to twenty-eight years (with a total possible term now of forty-two years) and added a clause allowing the widows and children of authors to file for renewal—a provision in tension with the notion that copyrights (and patents) are an incentive to the creators of new work.[6]

Nineteenth-century court decisions vacillated between supporting and restricting the rights of authors. In the 1834 case *Wheaton v. Peters*, the U.S. Supreme Court embraced the Constitution's more limited view of copyright and rejected the idea that it could be a perpetual right. But seven years later, it ruled in *Folsom v. Marsh* that the Rev. Charles Upham, the author of a two-volume *Life of Washington,* had infringed the copyright of Jared Sparks's twelve-volume *The Writings of George Washington* by copying 255 pages of Washington letters from the longer work. Justice William Story ruled against Upham even though he had used only 3.8 percent of Sparks's work and the Washington papers were public, rather than private, property. In spite of Story's ruling, *Folsom* would later help to establish the concept of "fair use," the idea that limited borrowing from the work of others was acceptable when that borrowing produces something new and useful.[7] As we shall see, digital historians have many reasons to hold the principle of "fair use" close to their hearts.

Despite *Folsom,* American authors did not view the courts as their friend. Justice Robert Grier ruled against Harriet Beecher Stowe in her suit over an unauthorized German translation of *Uncle Tom's Cabin* in 1853. But seventeen years later, Congress revised the copyright law to give authors rights over translations and dramatic adaptations—a change that implicitly protected "ideas" and not just the specific expression of those ideas, as Grier had ruled and as copyright law formally insisted. Even more important was the passage in 1891 of the International Copyright Treaty. To the consternation of British writers like Charles Dickens, the absence of such a treaty had meant that American publishers routinely pirated English authors in cheap editions that paid them no royalties, and over time a growing number of American writers joined the campaign for international copyright.[8]

But, in the new century, the authors—now led by Mark Twain (who had become a fierce defender of authors' rights after his own works were pirated in Canada and Britain)—pressed for more. In 1906, Twain testified before Congress on behalf of a bill to increase the duration of copyright to the life of the author plus fifty years. The bill failed, but a compromise measure in 1909 broadened the scope of copyright to include all works of authorship and doubled the renewal period from fourteen to twenty-eight years. As the legal scholar Jessica Litman points out, the 1909 law emerged out of negotiations among "interested parties," especially "the beneficiaries of rights granted by existing copyright statutes." Missing from these negotiations was "the amorphous 'public,'" whose "interest in copyright and copyrighted works was too varied and complex to be amenable to interest-group championship" and the "push and shove among opposing industry representatives."[9] This dynamic of a vocal minority drowning out a voiceless majority would unfortunately persist for the remainder of the twentieth century.

Thus interest group lobbying also shaped the next major copyright law, which Congress passed in 1976 and went into effect two years later.

It extended copyright protection in precisely the way Twain had advocated seven decades earlier—protecting works for the life of the author plus fifty years and works for hire for seventy-five years. For historians, perhaps the most important change was that it extended the length of copyrights granted much earlier for an additional nineteen years. A book published in 1923, renewed in 1951, and scheduled to come into the public domain in 1979, now had its copyright extended until 1998. But the 1976 law did give the public something in return—an enumeration of the "fair use" doctrine, which is a crucial bulwark for your work as a digital historian.[10]

But the narrowing of the public domain through the copyright law continued in 1998. On October 27, President Bill Clinton signed into law the Sonny Bono Copyright Term Extension Act (CTEA), which gave an additional twenty years of copyright protection to works published before 1978. The 1923 works whose copyright life had been extended from 1979 to 1998 by the 1976 law were now given protection for a total of *ninety-five years*—until 2018. On January 1, 1998, such classic works as T. S. Eliot's *The Waste Land* and Sinclair Lewis's *Babbitt* entered the public domain where they could be shared freely, published online, and made the subject of derivative works like plays and films. But a set of equally important works—novels by F. Scott Fitzgerald, poems by Edna St. Vincent Millay, and films by Cecil B. DeMille—scheduled to enter the public domain the following New Year's Day will now remain outside of it until 2018.[11]

In addition, the copyright term of life plus fifty years that Twain had boldly sought in the early part of the century now became life plus seventy years. Twain believed that the law should protect an author's children, but Congress should "let the grandchildren take care of themselves." Under the CTEA, grandchildren—and likely a few more generations—will benefit financially from their ancestor's creativity. The copyright of Mark Twain's *Autobiography*, which was posthumously published in 1924, will outlive his own granddaughter (who died in 1966) by fifty-three years.[12]

The bad news for the public domain that began on October 27, 1998, continued the next day when President Clinton signed another sweeping revision of the copyright law, the Digital Millennium Copyright Act (DMCA). Among other provisions, the Act bans circumventing or tampering with the copyright protection and encryption devices commonplace in software, DVDs, and CDs. The DMCA thus remarkably grants corporations the right to limit how we use digital products even after we have purchased them. As a result, we can't read an electronic book purchased for a particular reading device on some other device; nor can we easily play a DVD we own on a Linux computer. The DMCA especially poses problems for historians who work with film. It will, for example, restrict their ability to play film clips as part of an in-person or online history course because they might need to circumvent the encryption on a DVD (emerging as the standard format for films) in order to get the clips. Similarly, they cannot copy a section of a borrowed DVD for later study in the same way that they can photocopy a chapter of a book. Ideally, copyright law establishes a balance between rights holders and rights users—a give-and-take that rewards authorship but that also fosters the dissemination of knowledge for educational and academic purposes. As with almost all of the copyright legislation of the past two centuries, the DMCA tips the legal balance toward rights holders, particularly corporate ones.[13]

The same is true of two key cases—*Basic Books, Inc. v. Kinko's Graphic Corp.* (1991) and *Princeton University Press v. Michigan Document Services* (1996)—that ruled against the once-common practice of commercial copy shops making course packs for students. In theory, the Kinko's case, as a U.S. District Court decision, is not binding on other courts. Similarly, the U.S. Supreme Court has not affirmed the Princeton decision and five of the Circuit Court judges dissented.[14] Moreover, the cases involve only commercial entities and not scholars and teachers working in an academic setting; it is not clear, for example, that a similar case could be won against a university copy shop selling copies at cost. Unfortunately, university copyright policies, which determine what you can put in your course packet and which tend to be shaped by university general counsels who are often not familiar with intellectual property law and are focused on risk to the university, generally follow these decisions closely. These decisions may not be *the* law, but they may still be the law in your university and, as most instructors know, they have significantly raised the price of the course packets we assign to our students.

In 1991, however, the U.S. Supreme Court ruled in a case that affirmed the principle that the copyright law protects the public domain. In *Feist Publications, Inc. v. Rural Telephone Co.*, it decreed that the white pages of the phone book lack the originality to merit copyright protection. The conclusion may seem self-evident. Few people choose the phone book for their leisure reading. But previously the courts had held that the "sweat of the brow" invested in such compilations made them eligible for copyright protection even though the contents were factual and organized in an obvious way and copyright doesn't protect facts.[15] This decision significantly affects those creating online historical databases—like the Ellis Island passenger lists. The facts revealed in the databases are not protected by copyright no matter how much sweat from however many brows went into compiling and organizing them.

The decision also affects other forms of historical work because history often involves considerable labor directed at uncovering facts. A film company that based a major motion picture on your scholarly monograph could argue that it doesn't need your permission because it worked from the "facts" that you uncovered.

A dozen years later, however, the U.S. Supreme Court ruled for copyright holders through a 7-2 decision in the case of *Eldred v. Ashcroft*. Eric Eldred, the lead plaintiff, was the organizer of the Eldritch Press website dedicated to providing free books by such authors as Nathaniel Hawthorne and Robert Frost. Eldred sued to overturn the CTEA on the grounds that the twenty-year extension subverted the constitutional provision of "limited" copyright terms and did nothing to promote new creativity. Writing for the majority, Justice Ruth Bader Ginsburg maintained, "the copyright clause empowers Congress to determine the intellectual property regimes that, over all, in that body's judgment, will serve the ends of the clause."[16] In other words, the vagueness of the original section of the Constitution on copyright—granting Congress the right to give authors a "limited term" of ownership over their work—has now subverted the explicit intent of that clause.

Nevertheless, even the majority conceded that the term extension could be seen as "arguably unwise." A new court could reverse it, and thus the future of the copyright law remains a matter of active contention. Historians therefore need to recognize that there is no fixed body of rules, but rather a shifting terrain of interpretations of the law. Even more, they need to be active participants in shaping the copyright landscape to make it more receptive to the sharing of ideas and expressions.

Copyright and the Online Historian: Is the Web Different?

Digital historians want to know whether it makes any difference that they are working online. Do they have more or fewer rights or liabilities? The simple answer is that the law is the law; there is not a different copyright law in cyberspace. Yet, in practice, the answer is not so simple. In large and small ways, the web has reconfigured the legal landscape for historians.

We can see this by returning to some of the intrinsic features of digital history we discussed in the Introduction. The vast *capacity* of digital media potentially increases the scale of the legal issues exponentially. A typical historian publishing a book might deal with a handful of picture permissions and perhaps one or two requests to quote from protected material. By contrast, the CD-ROM *Who Built America? From the Great War of 1914 to the Dawn of the Atomic Age in 1946* that the Center for History and New Media developed in collaboration with the American Social History Project required investigating or negotiating the rights to more than nine hundred pictures, texts, sounds, and motion pictures.[17] The cost of simply negotiating and tracking those rights—especially paying for the time of the person doing the work—may have exceeded the $36,000 we paid in actual permissions. But capacity affects rights issues in a second way; one of the tests for "fair use" involves the "extent" of protected work that is used. Given the ease with which "more" can be incorporated into a digital work, the digital historian risks crossing one of the fair use boundaries. If the Rev. Charles Upham had published a digital life of Washington, he likely would have used more than 3.8 percent of the documents in Sparks's work.

Another advantage of digital media—the *flexibility* that allows you to combine sound, moving pictures, and images with text—poses a major new challenge to digital historians. The rights for images, sound, and moving images are often more complex and more expensive than for text. For example, "quoting" a photo is much harder than quoting a paragraph from Hemingway; you pretty much need the whole thing to make any sense of most images. Multimedia historians will probably spend a great deal more time fretting about legal issues than their text-based counterparts. The *manipulability* of digital data creates another, less common legal issue. You can edit digital images, sounds, and moving pictures much more easily than their analog counterparts. But what if their creators or owners don't want them to be altered? Such concerns are further multiplied by the web's most obvious advantage—its global *accessibility*. Photocopying Allen Ginsberg's 1956 poem "Howl" and giving it to your students may violate the rights of the Allen Ginsberg Trust. But an attorney from the trust is unlikely to be sitting in your classroom. Post the poem on your course website and that attorney can find the violation in two seconds.[18]

If you mistakenly use "Howl" without permission in a print classroom anthology, the publisher is likely to have the happy responsibility of dealing with the lawyers (although you would have probably signed a contract in which you guaranteed that you did not infringe anyone's rights). The openness of the web—the ability of authors to publish themselves easily—means that you hold an even greater share of the legal responsibility. But self-publishing brings some advantages. Authors sometimes mistakenly assume that publishers share their same interests. But publishers don't want to get sued. And, as the owners of substantial intellectual property themselves, they generally identify with the holders of copyright rather than its users. When you publish yourself on the web, you have a publisher who identifies with you and understands your interests.

You also have a publisher who can respond quickly to any legal problems. Here it turns out that one of the key weaknesses of the web—its lack of *durability* or fixity—makes life easier for digital historians. Publishers avoid risk on copyright, in part because the remedies to copyright violations can be ruinous. Our colleague Lawrence Levine published a book with Oxford University Press, which neglected to get permission for the cover photo by Robert Frank. When the press belatedly contacted Frank's agent, he adamantly refused to grant permission and Oxford had to destroy the books and reprint them with a new cover photo.[19] If the photograph had simply graced your website's home page, it could have been removed in five minutes and with minimal expense. To be sure, this does not relieve you of all legal liability. But it might make a copyright owner willing to drop the matter rather than spend a lot of money on a lawsuit. The ease with which you can remedy inadvertent or questionable copyright violations on the web is the most important reason why historians should not worry excessively about many of the issues we discuss here.

Protecting Your Intellectual Property

For an entirely different set of reasons, we don't think historians should spend much time agonizing about how to protect their own intellectual property rights. Recent laws and court decisions have significantly increased the protection for creators of intellectual property. You do not have to do anything to make yourself eligible for the protection of the copyright law. Contrary to popular belief, you no longer (since 1989) need to place a copyright notice on your work.[20]

If so, why does anyone bother? Well, for one thing, placing a copyright notification on your website isn't much bother. You simply write "©Charles Beard 2003" on the bottom of your home page. (If you can't get your software to create the symbol, you could write "Copyright" or "Copr." but not "(c)".) And for this minimal effort, you remind readers that you care about the rights to your intellectual property.[21] We recommend including a copyright notice but not one of those overly broad warnings that proclaims, "no part of this work may be used or reproduced in any manner whatsoever without express permission." Such notices go well beyond the copyright law, offer no additional protection, and implicitly challenge the doctrine of "fair use" that digital historians should cherish. Good copyright citizens—cooperative residents of the digital commons—don't try to grab rights they don't have. (Some, as we will discuss, even avoid claiming all of the rights to which they are entitled.) Bill Gates's online digital image repository, Corbis, includes copyright notices on thousands of public domain images. "These claims,"

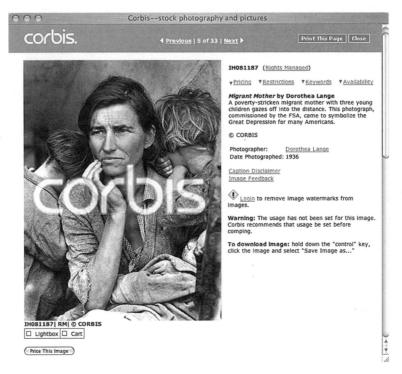

Figure 41. Corbis, a commercial digital image repository, puts copyright notices (and digital watermarks) on thousands of public domain images such as Dorothea Lange's famous Migrant Mother photo, which was taken as part of the government-sponsored FSA photography project and is available for free through the Library of Congress website.

says attorney Stephen Fishman, "are probably spurious where the digital copy is an exact or 'slavish' copy of the original photo." Some websites even slap copyright notices on famous public domain texts. At the bottom of a copy of Abraham Lincoln's Gettysburg Address, the *Atlantic Monthly* website adds the following: "Copyright © 1999 by The Atlantic Monthly Company. All rights reserved."[22]

Even the most carefully placed or most threateningly worded copyright notice does not protect you if the work does not meet the requirement enunciated in the *Feist* case that copyrightable works reflect a minimal degree of creativity and originality. You can spend thousands of hours scanning and digitizing public domain documents—say, the entire *New York Times* from 1865 or all of Charles Dickens's novels—but, according to most lawyers, you can't copyright the results. Even if you modernize the typeface, correct the spelling errors, and reformat the

spacing in a nineteenth-century novel, you have not met the law's standard of minimal creativity. The same—Corbis's copyright notices to the
contrary—applies to scanned images of public domain photos. And it
equally applies to the massive online historical databases—including the
fifty million records in the Church of Latter-day Saints online compilation of the 1880 U.S. Census. Some of the most time-consuming work
that digital historians are currently undertaking is not covered under
copyright law. But we hope that other good citizens of the digital commons will respect and credit your labor even while they take advantage
of the court's decision allowing them to make active and free use of it.[23]

If your work is, in fact, eligible for copyright, registering it (as well as
placing a notice) makes it easier for people to find you (not usually an
issue for online works) and gives you additional protection. You can't,
in fact, sue anyone in federal court for violating your copyright unless
you first register. You can, however, simply wait and register only if it
becomes necessary. But if you wait, you can't recover as much in a suit.
Only if you register your work within ninety days of publication are you
entitled to "statutory damages" and attorney fees rather than just actual
damages. Statutory damages send a sharp message against infringement
and can greatly exceed the financial harm suffered. Ocean Atlantic Tex-
tile Screen Printing found that out when it produced 2,500 t-shirts
adorned with a copyrighted photograph by Ruth Orkin. They made only
$1,900 from the shirts, but Orkin's daughter won $20,000 in statutory
damages and $3,000 in attorney fees. Even more dramatic is the case of
UMG Recordings v. MP3.com, in which the major recording companies
won $25,000 *per CD* uploaded on the MP3.com system in statutory dam-
ages. Potential damages could run as high as $250 million.[24]

Of course, few historians have much prospect of collecting millions in
statutory damages for violations of the copyright of their website. You
should weigh the potential gains of a lawsuit against the time and
expense in registering your website with the copyright office. Indeed,
you may be surprised to learn that it is even possible to register a website.
The cost is modest ($30), but the actual copyright deposit is complicated
because the office acknowledges that, as yet, "the deposit regulations of
the Copyright Office do not specifically address works transmitted
online." In the meantime, they will accept computer disks or print-
outs—neither of which is easy to produce for a major website.[25] We recommend that until the Copyright Office simplifies the registration
procedure (and perhaps not even then), you shouldn't waste your time
registering your site.

In any case, most historians worry more about someone stealing their
work for credit rather than for money. Historians considering putting
their work online commonly express the anxiety that "someone will

steal it." They fret more about the sin of plagiarism than the crime of copyright infringement. And plagiarism and copyright infringement are very different matters; Stephen Ambrose, who copied only short passages of text, could probably plead "fair use," even if we would not think of his use as "fair" in the moral sense we associate with eschewing plagiarism. To be sure, someone is more likely to steal your work if it is on the web than if it is in your desk drawer. But placing your work on the web actually gives you a better way of establishing that you are the original author than would be true of a paper that was delivered only orally at a conference. Moreover, historians are often most concerned about someone stealing their ideas, and the copyright law does nothing to protect ideas, only their formal and fixed expression. The most important goal for historians should be the circulation of ideas and expressions, and the web offers a wonderful new tool for such dissemination. We should focus more on getting others to pay attention to what we have to say rather than on ensuring that the proper individual gets the proper credit.

If you remain paranoid about wide and anonymous access to your work on the open web, you can restrict access through passwords or by Internet Protocol (IP) addresses (the unique numbers by which Internet connected machines are identified, the security approach used by many commercial and some nonprofit websites). A related form of noncopyright restriction is a license, which asks users to agree (in effect, contractually) to some conditions on their use of a website. These licenses have proliferated in recent years—in part as a response to the lack of copyright protection for electronic databases and more generally because, as librarian Mary Case points out, publishers believe they will be more successful in suing for breach of contract than copyright infringement. Such licenses can even try to restrict your use of public domain material. For example, HarpWeek presents public domain material from *Harper's Weekly,* but the license imposed on subscribers still limits access to and use of the site's content. Some attorneys question, however, whether licenses restricting access to public domain materials are legally enforceable.[26] Some historians—including the authors of this book—question whether such restrictions are in keeping with the original, open spirit of the web.

Our discussion here about *your* rights and responsibilities conceals a crucial ambiguity for many readers of this book. After all, digital history tends to be much more collaborative than traditional historical scholarship. You need to figure out upfront how to recognize everyone's contributions—including those of students and volunteers—adequately or risk facing later wrangles that can be much more unpleasant than disputes over copyright. In addition, many historians work for an institu-

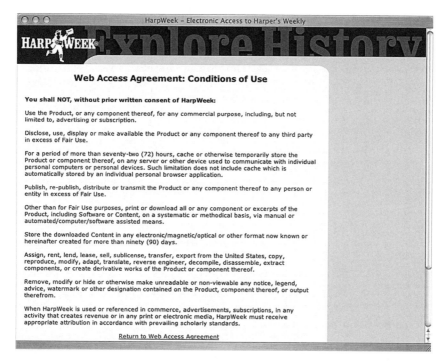

Figure 42. HarpWeek presents public domain material from the nineteenth-century periodical *Harper's Weekly*. But it asks users to click a button to signify their assent to "conditions of use" that restrict one's ability to use the material freely.

tion rather than themselves. Museum curators, librarians, and archivists who create websites know that under the "work for hire" doctrine, their employers own the copyright to their creations.

But what about college instructors? For much of the twentieth century, academics have operated under the "teacher exception," which says that instructors and not their employers own the intellectual fruits of their labor. But many lawyers see the 1976 Copyright Law as marking the demise of the teacher exception. At the moment, however, most university policies accept the spirit, if not the letter, of the teacher exception, at least for traditional academic writing. But those who are concerned about this issue need to follow historian-turned-lawyer Elizabeth Townsend's advice to "Read *All* [employer] IP [intellectual property] policies carefully." This is doubly true for those producing course materials and websites, which Townsend describes as "an area in flux." Universities are more likely to claim ownership of websites, especially course websites, created with significant university resources such as the help of research assistants and instructional resources offices.[27]

Others, however, argue that scholars shouldn't bother worrying about property rights in their work. Corynne McSherry, another academic-turned-lawyer, wonders whether academic work should be owned at all and argues that scholars should instead maintain their realm as a world of gift exchange, in which ideas circulate freely, rather than a world of commodities that are bought and sold. She argues that the very effort to maintain the teacher exception may be self-subverting. When teachers aggressively insist on intellectual property rights to course materials, they foster the idea that courses are just another commodity and instructors are just another kind of worker, which undercuts the basis of the "teacher exception" in the "idea that professors are special—that they're not like other kinds of knowledge workers."[28]

For those like McSherry, who view academic work as a matter of sharing, copyright law is more of a hindrance to the free circulation of historical ideas, interpretations, and sources. Those in this camp also see the insistence on property rights as conflicting with the ethos of sharing and cooperation that has been an attractive feature of the web and is embodied in the open source and free software movements, which generally oppose private ownership of software. Much of this software (like the operating system Linux and the software Apache, MySQL, and PHP, which run much of the Internet) has been released under the "General Public License" (GPL) or a license compatible with the GPL, which was developed by free software activist Richard Stallman to ensure that software licensed under it—and any derivatives—remain permanently in the public domain.[29]

Some have tried to take the ideas behind the GPL and open source and apply them to other forms of expression—for example, to the words of historians rather than the code of programmers. One effort, called Creative Commons, is "trying to transfer some of the lessons from . . . open source and free software to the content world," in the words of executive director Glenn Otis Brown. "Copyright is about balance," he observes. "We hope Creative Commons . . . helps put copyright balance back in vogue."[30]

So far, Creative Commons has primarily encouraged copyright balance by offering free legal advice to those who want to promote an ethic of sharing and mutuality. With the help of some high-priced legal talent, they have developed a series of licenses packaged under the rubric "Some Rights Reserved." For example, their "noncommercial license" permits free use and distribution of work only for noncommercial purposes. Other historians, who put a priority on getting their perspectives widely disseminated, might select the "attribution" license, which allows any site to display their work if it gives them credit. If you are even more firmly committed to the free circulation of historical work, you might simply deposit your work into the public domain with no strings attached. Short of this more drastic step, you might find the "Founders' Copyright" option appealing—especially because it has the particularly historical twist of mimicking the arrangements established in the 1790 copyright law and guaranteeing the entry of your work into the public domain after fourteen years (or twenty-eight years if you choose to renew the copyright once).[31] Copyright radicalism in the early twenty-first century has come to mean embracing an eighteenth-century law.

Sharing the Property of Others: Copyright and the Public Domain

Most online historians will probably conclude that more conventional copyright practices best serve their purposes. But familiarity with the principles behind the Creative Commons reminds us of the ethos of sharing and cooperation that should underlie work on the web and of the need for balance in matters of copyright. (And we should already know that *all* historical work relies on the open sharing of ideas and sources.) An even more forceful reminder comes when you begin to think about providing content on your own website. Very quickly, you start worrying more about "what am I allowed to include of the work of others" and less about "how can I protect what's mine." Even the most fervent defenders of copyright start to appreciate the need for balance when they start to assemble a website that includes historical resources or the work of other historians.

The copyright problems of the online historian are both easier and harder than those of others working in the digital realm. On the one hand, because historians focus on the past, they are less likely to get entangled in the realms where rights issues are mostly intensely focused and policing is most vigilant—the MP3 music files of hot new bands. On the other hand, working with the sources of the past, especially the twentieth-century past, puts you up against some of the thorniest copyright questions—and the most difficult issues to research. The good news is that vast swaths of documentary evidence of the past are in the public domain (the realm free of copyright restrictions), and you are free to post that evidence on your website with no questions asked. But how do you know what sits in the public domain?

Let's start with some easy cases and broad categories. The law puts works by employees of the U.S. government done as part of their jobs in the public domain. Twentieth-century historians benefit from this exemption because so many historical topics have in-depth coverage in

U.S. government records and documents. Even less obvious areas of cultural and social history find rich documentation in government records. For example, one of the most revealing collections in the Library of Congress's American Memory—the 160,000 photos from the Farm Security Administration and the Office of War Administration—is available online because a government project produced them. You can, for example, take any of those photos and use them on your own website. Interestingly, you can also purchase the "right" to use some of those same photos from Corbis—the digital equivalent of selling you the Brooklyn Bridge. Like your right to walk across the Brooklyn Bridge, you have the right to use these government-produced photographs however you choose. Always look first for a copyright- or royalty-free version before shelling out to Corbis or another stock footage company.

The same is true for everything published before 1923. Ironically, however, unpublished works from that same period have more protection, the same as works newly created today—the life of the author plus seventy years. Thus, only if the author has been dead seventy years or longer (since 1934 as we are writing this in 2005) is the work now in the public domain. If tomorrow you discover an unpublished song written by Irving Berlin in 1912, you will not be able publish it on your website (unless you have permission from his estate) until 2059 because Berlin died in 1989. On the other hand, you can do what you like with his *published* 1912 song "Alexander's Ragtime Band." If you don't know when the author died (or if the work is anonymous, pseudonymous, or written for hire), it gets even more protection—120 years from the date of creation (see chart).[32]

Some copyright guides, which often err on the side of caution, advise you to assume that everything published after 1923 is covered by copyright. Not true. First, some works were published without proper copyright notice. Remember those © notices that we told you not to worry about? Well, before 1989, you *did* have to worry about them and published works that failed to include the © before that date have, by definition, fallen into the public domain. Keep in mind that such absences were not always accidental. The young radicals in Students for a Democratic Society who mimeographed thousands of copies of the Port Huron Statement in 1962 did not bother with a copyright notice, and you can publish it freely on your website. By contrast, Martin Luther King, Jr., copyrighted all of his speeches, and his estate—to the consternation of many—claims copyright to his "I Have a Dream" speech delivered the following year.[33]

Other authors critical of the status quo have struggled with the ethics of deriving commercial benefit from the ownership of their words. In some drafts of his will, Leo Tolstoy dedicated his copyrights to the public

WHEN WORKS PASS INTO THE PUBLIC DOMAIN IN THE UNITED STATES

Unpublished Works

Type or Work	Copyright Term	What was in the public domain in the U.S. as of 1 January 2005
Unpublished work or unpublished works created before 1978 that were published after 31 December 2002	Life of author + 70 years	Works from authors who died before 1935
Unpublished anonymous and pseud-onymous works, and works made for hire (corporate authorship) or unpublished works when the death date of the author is not known	120 years from date of creation	Works created before 1885
Unpublished works created before 1978 that were published before 1 January 2003	Life of the author + 70 years or 31 December 2047, whichever is greater	Nothing will enter the public domain until at least 1 January 2048

Works Published in the United States

Date of Publication	Conditions	Copyright Term
Before 1923	None	In public domain
1923 through 1977	Published without copy-right notice	In public domain
1978 to 1 March 1989	Published without notice and without sub-sequent registration	In public domain
1978 to 1 March 1989	Published without notice but *with* subse-quent registration	70 years after the death of author, or if work of corporate authorship, the shorter of 95 years from publication, or 120 years from creation
1923 through 1963	Published with notice but copyright was not renewed	In public domain

Works Published in the United States (Continued)

Date of Publication	Conditions	Copyright Term
1923 through 1963	Published with notice but copyright was renewed	95 years after publication date
1964 through 1977	Published with notice	95 years after publication date
1978 to 1 March 1989	Published with notice	70 years after death of author, or if work of corporate authorship, the shorter of 95 years from publication, or 120 years from creation
After 1 March 1989	Notice no longer required	70 years after death of author, or if work of corporate authorship, the shorter of 95 years from publication, or 120 years from creation

Source: This chart is based directly on one first published in Peter B. Hirtle, "Recent Changes to the Copyright Law: Copyright Term Extension," *Archival Outlook,* January-February 1999 and the modified online version at http://www.copyright.cornell.edu/ training/Hirtle_Public_Domain.htm. Hirtle's chart is, in turn, based in part on Laura N. Gasaway's chart "When Works Pass Into the Public Domain," at http://www.unc.edu/ ~unclng/public-d.htm.

domain but then backed away in his final testament. In the late 1930s, according to Pete Seeger, Woody Guthrie distributed a mimeographed songbook that declared on one page, "This song is Copyrighted in U.S., under Seal of Copyright # 154085, for a period of twenty-eight years, and anybody caught singin it without our permission, will be mighty good friends of ourn, cause we don't give a dern. Publish it. Write it. Sing it. Swing to it. Yodel it. We wrote it, that's all we wanted to do." Yet by the late 1940s, Guthrie had hooked up with an aggressive young music publisher named Howie Richmond who copyrighted Guthrie's songs, which today generate substantial revenues for the Guthrie estate. Richmond, in fact, went well beyond securing the rights to new compositions; he also became very rich from his discovery that he could copyright traditional songs like "Greensleeves," if he made significant changes in the words or lyrics.[34]

The second exception—works that did not have their copyright renewed—is even more important and less recognized. Until the 1976 copyright act, authors were granted a twenty-eight-year copyright and the ability to renew that copyright for a second twenty-eight-year term. Thus a book copyright in 1930 fell into the public domain in 1958 unless renewed that year. Those authors (or heirs) who did renew their copyrights have had them continuously extended by subsequent revisions of the law. Most famously, the Disney Corporation copyrighted Mickey Mouse in 1928 and renewed the copyright in the 1950s, which should have protected the rodent's copyright until 1984. But the 1976 law gave him another nineteen years of copyright life (to 2003). Thanks to the Copyright Term Extension Act, Mickey can lounge profitably under the Disney corporate umbrella for another twenty years (until 2023). The Disney Corporation's copyright renewal in the 1950s was the exception rather than the rule. According to a 1961 copyright office study, fewer than 15 percent of all registered copyright holders renewed; for books and other texts, the percentage is half that.[35]

This very good news for historians of this period is tempered by the requirement that you must determine whether or not the copyright was renewed. You can do that by seeing if a later edition of the work includes a copyright renewal notice or by contacting the author or his or her estate and asking. But keep in mind that copyright holders—shockingly enough—have been known to lie about what they actually own. We once called *Atlantic Monthly* about permissions and were told that everything was renewed, but, in fact, they did not renew the copyright on anything from before July 1934. Finally, you can search the copyright records. Until recently, this required a trip to the Library of Congress or another major library for works copyrighted before 1978 or paying the Library $75 per hour to search for you. But computer scientist Michael Lesk and Carnegie Mellon University have recently created a searchable database of copyright renewal records for books published between 1923 and 1963. (After 1963, books were automatically renewed.)[36]

The situation gets murkier for works created and published outside the United States. Copyright terms within the European Union are generally similar to those of the United States (life of the author plus seventy years). Several other countries—for example, Canada, China, Japan, Russia, Australia, and Argentina—have terms of life plus fifty years. But numerous exceptions and qualifications exist. For example, works created by Americans during World War II get a 3,794-day extension in Japan.[37]

As if this isn't enough to drive you screaming from your computer, you need to figure out whether you should worry about the laws in countries where your website is accessed (i.e., the world), rather than located. Canadian attorney Christopher Hale maintains "the mere fact of accessibility may not constitute an infringement in the laws of other jurisdictions." Thus Project Gutenberg of Australia posts online copies of books like *The Great Gatsby* (1927) and George Orwell's *1984* (1949) that are still covered by copyright in the United States, although it (coyly) advises you not to read them if you are in a country where copyright remains in effect. But Columbia law professor June Besek cautiously warns (in a publication co-sponsored by the Library of Congress) that a digital archive "could be exposed to infringement suits if it were accessible outside the United States. Foreign copyright owners might be able to sue under the laws of a country where the presentation of the work was an infringement." On the one hand, the possibility of a nonprofit historical website being the subject of such a suit is remote. A French copyright owner would have trouble getting the Scranton Historical Society into a French court and would probably not bother, given that jurisdictional issues remain murky and that the historical society would not have any French assets that could be seized in a successful judgment. On the other hand, your university might react nervously to a threatening letter from a foreign rights holder, and you should try to respect foreign copyright laws as much you do your own.[38]

Another difference between U.S. laws related to intellectual property and those of many other countries is that those countries give authors "moral rights" that do not exist in American law. For example, authors, even if they have sold their work's economic rights, might have the right of "integrity," which prevents alterations of this work—for example, colorizing a film. In some countries, these rights continue beyond the end of copyright. If your project places you under non-U.S. law, you need to consult more specialized works on this topic or visit the UNESCO website, which contains the copyright laws of most countries.[39]

Even if you are working only in the United States, you need to be aware of one recent change that has affected the copyright status *within* the United States of many works originally published abroad. In 1994, the United States signed the General Agreement on Tariffs and Trade (GATT), and the implementing legislation restored copyright protection to foreign works that had fallen into the public domain in the United States because their owners had not complied with copyright "formalities" here or because the United States had no copyright relations with the other country at the time the work was published. For example, Jean Renoir's masterful anti-war film, *La Grande Illusion* (1937), which had fallen into the public domain in the United States because the copyright had not been renewed, had its copyright restored in 1996 through GATT. Because the United States had no copyright treaty with the Soviet Union until 1973, all works published there before that date were in the public domain in United States. Now they are covered by copyright. These changes have particularly vexed historians like

Paul Halsall who have developed extensive websites in world history and who, thus, want to include sources published outside the United States.[40]

Despite the vast quantity of material that has made it into the public domain, many historians will encounter materials for which copyright remains in effect. You will have two main options then: ask for permission, or consider whether you can make "fair use" of the copyrighted material. Asking for permission is the simpler of the two approaches to explain, although not necessarily simpler to carry out. But don't ask unless you are sure that you need permission. When people are asked, they often request a fee or impose restrictions—even if they don't have the right to do either. In the 1990s, when the Truman Presidential Library sought permission to include the *Chicago Daily Tribune*'s famous headline proclaiming "Dewey Defeats Truman" in an orientation video, the *Tribune* said "no." But, in fact, a three-word headline does not qualify for copyright protection, and the Library could have proceeded without asking.[41]

Of course, many copyright holders are more straightforward and generous than this, especially when the permission is for use by an educational project. The *Montgomery Advertiser* allowed us to publish a 1932 editorial at no charge in a history CD-ROM, even though the racist editorial did not portray the newspaper in the most favorable light. In the early days of the web, when much looser assumptions about copyright prevailed, Paul Halsall included in his online History Sourcebooks a number of older works that were still formally under copyright. After stricter adherence to copyrights became the web norm, Halsall wrote to the authors and offered to remove the texts. But he reports that most authors "have been most gracious" and allowed them to remain online.[42]

In other cases, the rights holder will ask you to pay a fee. Often they levy a modest charge for educational projects and nonprofit uses. Unfortunately, many publishers demand an annual payment for presenting something on the web, and that is a cost that is hard to cover in the long run even if you have a grant at the moment. For example, the *New York Times* charged us $150 to publish a 1927 interview with Charles Lindbergh on a CD-ROM. But when we later asked the cost to publish it on a public website, we were told that we would have to pay $300 *per year*, which they touted as a deep discount from their standard annual fee of $1,000.[43]

You may decide that your budget can't afford the *New York Times*, but at least you can track down the *Times* easily. Unfortunately, sometimes you will not find the rights holder so readily. You think that the text, image, music, or film might be under copyright, but you can't find anyone who claims to hold it. What do you do? Many publishers will tell you to forget about using it; historian David Kirsch got that response when he tried to publish a New York street scene in the *Business History Review* for which the rights holder could not be found. Kirsch had to settle for a much less revealing photograph. One of the most frustrating problems facing digital historians is dealing with what have been called "orphan works" whose copyrights have not expired but which are no longer available commercially and whose owners are, therefore, difficult to locate.[44]

On the web, however, you are the publisher. The buck (starts and) stops with you. Some history websites follow a strict policy of not posting anything without explicit permission. But the Constitution Society, a libertarian group devoted to "principles of constitutional republican government," which maintains an extensive website of historical documents, makes "a reasonable effort to find someone to grant permission" but "if none can be found," they publish the material anyway along with a disclaimer. Even if the rights holder later shows up, most reasonable people won't sue you if you offer at that point to remove the material or pay them a fee. Of course, we can't guarantee reasonable behavior. So carefully document the efforts you make to find a rights holder.[45]

Fair Use

The alternative to asking permission (or at least looking for someone to ask) is deciding you don't need to ask because your use is "fair." But what's "fair" is a philosophical, ethical, and legal question with no easy answer. Many people mistakenly assume that there is a "law" that tells you what constitutes "fair use." Unfortunately fair use is, in the words of library law consultant Mary Minow, the "grayest area of copyright law."[46] Section 107 of the 1976 Copyright Act explains that "fair use of a copyrighted work . . . for purposes such as criticism, comment, news reporting, teaching (including multiple copies for classroom use), scholarship, or research, is not an infringement of copyright" and then lists the following four nonexclusive factors to be used in determining fair use (our parenthetical comments are added):

1. "The purpose and character of the use, including whether such use is of a commercial nature or is for nonprofit educational purposes" (nonprofit educational uses are more likely to be fair as are those involving criticism, commentary, and parody);
2. "The nature of the copyrighted work" (uses of creative and unpublished works are less likely to be fair; uses of factual, published, and out-of-print works are more likely to be fair);
3. "The amount and substantiality of the portion used in relation to

the copyrighted work as a whole" (the smaller and less "central" the portion used, the more likely it is to be fair);

4. "The effect of the use upon the potential market for or value of the copyrighted work" (using out-of-print works and works for which there is no permissions market is more likely to be fair).

Unfortunately no magic formula balances these four factors. Minow notes that "courts often weigh" the market factor more heavily than the other three even though a 1994 U.S. Supreme Court decision says that it is no more important than the others. And recent trends give more weight to critical uses—an advantage to historians who discuss the works they are using as examples. The University of Georgia copyright guide notes that the four factors are not even exclusive; other facets (e.g., the ability to locate the copyright holder) can come into play and fair use determination needs to be made "on a case-by-case basis in order to protect the constitutional rights of users." Some guides, however, offer various benchmarks (e.g., only use a certain number of words), but the Georgia guide correctly rejects that approach as "without statutory authority" and insists that such guidelines "cannot legally mean that copying in excess of the guidelines is infringement." Even the *Chicago Manual of Style*, which previously offered some rough quantitative guidelines, now acknowledges that such "rules of thumb" have "no validity" and exist largely to ease the burdens on "an overworked permissions department."[47]

The biggest mistake that historians make is to apply only one of the four factors, and say, for example, "I am nonprofit and educational" and that makes my use fair. But if you placed online the history textbook that you assigned to your students, you could not argue that the use is "fair" because you are directly competing with the textbook company. Does that mean you cannot post any copyrighted material online? It is probably all right for you to post a chapter from a copyrighted book but only if you restrict access to the website to just the students in your class. If you open it to the entire web (and world), you are infringing the "copyright holder's right of public distribution."[48] The situation gets more complicated if you provided restricted access to the same book chapter every semester. In that case, the fairness of your use might depend on whether or not the book was in print and readily available.

A further set of complications arises for those who want to take advantage of the TEACH Act, which was passed in 2002 to deal with the use of copyright materials in distance education. On the one hand, it expands the range of copyrighted works that can be presented online (portions of films and songs are permitted, for example) and locations to which such works can be transmitted in an effort to give distance educators similar rights to those open to instructors in a face-to-face classroom. As such, the TEACH Act offers what one legal scholar calls "the best legislative solution to the barriers that copyright law imposes on online education that educators can hope to achieve in the near future." But on the other hand, the law subjects you to some significant and stringent limitations. For example, only accredited nonprofit institutions qualify, access must be limited to enrolled students in the context of "mediated instructional activities," and institutions must take steps to "reasonably prevent" the unauthorized retention and dissemination of copyrighted works presented online.[49]

Though it is dangerous and unethical to play fast and loose with fair use, it is equally a mistake to proceed too cautiously. As historian David Stowe points out in a perceptive article, those who unquestionably agree to every demand from rights holders "simply institutionalize a property right that doesn't exist." And their unquestioning compliance undercuts the ability of others to claim fair use rights. "Without being exercised," Stowe argues, "the right to fair use will simply atrophy." Even the more cautious *Chicago Manual* warns against seeking permission where there is only the slightest doubt because "the right of fair use is valuable to scholarship, and it should not be allowed to decay because scholars fail to employ it boldly."[50]

Images, Music, and Movies

The rules of fair use and copyright apply equally to nontextual materials like images, music, speeches, and moving pictures. But some distinctive issues arise. For images, the most complicated problem involves art and photographs that are in the public domain but are not publicly available. A photograph or work of art may have entered the public domain, but you can't copy it if you don't have access to the original. Because the original is often private property, the owner is not obligated to give you access to make a copy.[51] Thus you generally need to request a copy from the museum and they will often insist that you sign a license agreement that restricts how you can use the copy.

But can you use a reproduction obtained from a source other than the museum? Can you scan a copy of an artwork reproduced in a book and post it on your website? That turns out to be one of the most disputed, currently contentious issues in copyright. In the late 1990s, it became the subject of a court case that pitted the Bridgeman Art Library against the software company Corel. Bridgeman had paid for "exclusive rights" to license photographs of hundreds of public domain art works from major museums. Corel, however, took 150 images from the Bridgeman Collection and included them on a clip-art CD-ROM and made them available as inexpensive downloads from their website. Sounds like theft? In November 1998, U.S. District Court Judge Lewis A. Kaplan said "no." He ruled that the Bridgeman photos were not entitled to copyright protection. Bridgeman, he said, had sought "to create 'slavish copies' of public domain works of art. Though it may be assumed that this required both skill and effort, there was no spark of originality. . . . Copyright is not available in these circumstances." The Bridgeman photos were no more entitled to copyright than a photocopy.[52]

Some have concluded on the basis of Judge Kaplan's decision that any straightforward photos of public domain art can now be used freely, that you can, for example, scan them from art books and put them up on your website. Others advise caution. The decision does not apply to photos that go beyond "slavish" copies—ones that might highlight some particular feature. It also only applies to two-dimensional artworks because three-dimensional works like sculptures require many more decisions by the photographer. More important, Kaplan's decision reflects only one federal district court in New York; until a Court of Appeals or the U.S. Supreme Court decides a similar case, it will not be more widely binding. Yet even those like Stephen Fishman, who warn that "you could get sued for copyright infringement" for copying a reproduction of public domain art without permission, also concede that "you probably have a very good chance of winning."[53] Of course, you would probably prefer to do history than fight a lawsuit.

Some museums have responded to the Bridgeman case by having those who purchase permission to use their photos sign a "license agreement" limiting their use of it. But some lawyers wonder whether they can legally enforce these restrictions on those who obtain the images from a third party such as a college library.

Music poses significant difficulties both because the rights are more complicated and because the rights holders are often the most vigilant about enforcing copyrights and the greediest in seeking payments. Vanderbilt professor Cecelia Tichi spent $9,000 in permission fees just to quote lyrics in her book on country music. The $9,000 did not cover all of her costs because she also included a CD with her book, which required paying for the rights to use actual recordings.[54] These sound recording rights are entirely different from rights to the underlying words or composition. To make matters worse, the laws covering them are also different.

Copyright in words and music follow the same rules as copyright in books, articles, and photographs. But until February 15, 1972, federal copyright laws did not protect sound recordings. At first blush, this sounds great for those who want to set up a website that explores history through song. Doesn't this mean, for example, you can post any recording based on musical works published before 1923 or otherwise in the public domain? Unfortunately, no. Because there was no federal copyright law for recorded music before 1972, almost every state passed laws that criminalized the sale and distribution of sound recordings without permission. These laws did not have the expiration dates built into the federal copyright statutes. And, although federal law supersedes state law, the 1976 copyright act exempted pre-1972 sound recordings from the federal law for many decades. Until 2067 (thanks to this law and the subsequent CTEA), these earlier sound recordings will enjoy the protection they had won under state laws. Even one website that encourages aggressive use of the public domain offers the following "Rule of Thumb": "There are NO sound recordings in the Public Domain."[55]

As a result, history websites may not be able to make any significant use of the vast corpus of American recorded sound until late in the twenty-first century—a stunning loss to historical scholarship and teaching. There are a few ways around this, however. The first is a bit speculative and has to do with the difference between the earlier state laws and the current federal law and its impact on compositions published in 1922 or earlier. According to Georgia Harper from the University of Texas, "state law causes of action center on unfair competition for the most part. That is unlikely to affect archival and research activities." In other words, it may be that placing an early sound recording on an educational website would not be subject to any legal action.

If you are not willing to take a risk on this interpretation, you could still record the music yourself if the music (but not the recordings) is in the public domain. We did that with the music of the French Revolution for our website, Liberty, Equality, Fraternity: Exploring the French Revolution, producing our own version of "La Marseillaise" rather than paying to use an existing recording. Another safe strategy is to use U.S. government sound recordings. The Library of Congress, for example, has many recordings from 1930s-era arts projects as well as Edison company recordings, which have been dedicated to the public domain.

Finally, you can try to purchase rights to use a recording. But it may cost you dearly. For our CD-ROM on U.S. History from 1914 to 1946, we spent about $16,000 to use twenty-seven songs and that required time-consuming negotiations as well as dropping some songs because of the price. We also learned about the "most favored nation" clauses that most music companies put in their contracts. These provisions require you to pay them the highest price that anyone else gets. Thus, if you give in to one particularly greedy company, you have to pay everyone else the same rate of payment. In any case, most of these companies would not have agreed to making the songs available on the web at any price. And remember that even if you obtain rights to the sound recording, you still need to get the rights to the musical composition, which generally come from a different set of rights holders and itself can combine rights to both lyrics and the music itself. Further complicating matters, whether you stream the song or allow it to be downloaded will affect whether you need performance rights (streaming) or reproduction rights (download).

In addition, though many small and obscure book publishers have disappeared and hence can't claim rights and royalties, major corporations, which aggressively enforce their rights, have taken over many small music companies. Okeh Records, which pioneered the "race" record market with the first recordings by African American blues singers in the early 1920s, was later taken over by the Columbia Phonograph Company, which was, in turn, taken over by the American Record Corporation, and then the Columbia Broadcasting System, and most recently, Sony. Thus, if you want to make use of now obscure blues songs from the 1920s originally released by Okeh, you will find yourself negotiating with Sony Music Entertainment Inc. and sending your payments to a multinational conglomerate, not the heirs of the original bluesmen. Still, in terms of the recording (as opposed to the musical composition), you may find some protection in the more limited scope of the applicable state laws.[56]

Some music sites such as the Red Hot Jazz Archive take the position that they are broadcasting music rather than offering it for download by presenting it only in a streaming format like RealAudio. "I see the archive," writes Scott Alexander, the creator of Red Hot Jazz, "as a radio station of sorts, and that I am just broadcasting these works, not distributing them." So far, no one has challenged Alexander's "broadcasts," but he acknowledges that he is operating in a "gray area of law." "I've talked to lawyers about it and paid them lots of money, and they gave me no answers," he notes. But, according to industry lawyer Linda Tadic, the law is black and white, and what Alexander is doing involves "reproduction and distribution" and not just "public performance." But Alexander probably has avoided legal challenges because he is presenting old music, much of it out of active distribution, and because he maintains a relatively low profile and avoids publicizing his site.[57]

Another ambiguity about online multimedia involves fair use, especially the third factor in the fair use test—the amount of the work being used. Because scholars have long quoted from textual works by way of criticism and commentary, the right to do so is well established. Although the specific length of what is permissible is subject to dispute and individual interpretation, the broad parameters are clear. You can place a paragraph of a copyrighted novel online; you surely can't place an entire chapter (except on a site that is limited to students in your class). But the digital environment makes it much easier to "quote" images and allows you to quote sounds and moving pictures for the first time. But how much can you quote? Because most recorded songs are short, it is probably difficult to offer a short enough excerpt to qualify. But a case can be made for very brief selections.[58]

The problem is more vexing for film scholars who even before the emergence of the web had struggled over whether they could use film stills without permission. The major studios charge huge fees for these "rights." Historian Mark Carnes reports that permission charges exceeded $40,000 for the stills in his book *Past Imperfect: History According to the Movies*. Even worse, the studios may use permissions as a form of censorship. Warner Brothers refused permission to use stills because *Past Imperfect* "treated negatively" several Warner films. The Society for Cinema Studies (SCS) argues that Carnes should not even have asked for permission. Its ad hoc "Committee on Fair Usage Publication of Film Stills" concluded in 1993 that although "the legal situation concerning the reproduction of film frames and publicity stills remains undetermined, . . . a long-standing common practice has been established that could be drawn upon in arguing any case for the application of fair-use guidelines to cinematic images." Moreover, they argue that those like Carnes who seek and pay for permission to use stills undercut the fair use precedent. "I would urge my colleagues in the field of history to avoid paying unnecessary permission fees for film images," Kristin Thompson, the author of the SCS report, wrote in response to Carnes, "as it sets a precedent that endangers the ability of other scholars to use illustrations vital to their work."[59]

If you can include film stills on your website, what about film clips? Can online historians "quote" from the vast film record of the twentieth century? Film studios do not answer with one voice on this question. When we contacted Universal Studios about using a brief clip of *All Quiet on the Western Front* (1930) for an educational module about cinematic portrayals of World War I, the representative explained that the company charges a flat rate of $1,500 per fifteen seconds of footage. That rate does not vary based on the site's mission or purpose. Paramount, whom we asked about *Saving Private Ryan* (1998), said they would not license it for use on the web at any price. And Fox wanted us to pay $100 before it would tell us what a clip would cost. Warner Brothers, by contrast, said we could freely use three-minute clips from *The Dawn Patrol* (1938) and *Casablanca* (1942) as long as we used no more than two per film and streamed the clips rather than made them available for download because streaming limits the possibility of further circulation of the clips.[60]

We think that Warner Brothers' policy is good copyright citizenship, in accord with our understanding of fair use, and good for the legacies of their films. If you mounted a commercial website (that sold ads or required a fee to use) called "Great Moments in American Film" and included three-minute clips of five hundred American films, it would be difficult to meet the fair use standard. But let's say instead you developed a free, educational website on "Hollywood's View of American History" and included three-minute clips along with editorial commentary that showed how different films interpreted a key moment in U.S. history (e.g., Reconstruction in *Gone with the Wind* and the American Revolution in *Drums Along the Mohawk*). That would seem precisely in line with fair use. (Avoiding the most famous moments in a film also helps you meet the fair use test of "amount and substantiality.") A congressional report from the mid-1970s even acknowledges that fair use might apply to "the performance of a short excerpt from a motion picture for criticism or comment."[61]

The *Journal of American History* has embraced this perspective on fair use in its website Teaching the *JAH*, which explores how instructors can use scholarly articles from the journal in their classrooms. One section focuses on the 1943 film *Mission to Moscow*, a startlingly pro-Soviet film that served U.S. wartime diplomatic goals. The site includes a number of primary sources related to the film, including four short excerpts from the film itself. You could not readily teach about the film's impact without showing a few excerpts.

Is the *Journal of American History* engaging in fair use brinkmanship? The noncommercial and educational purposes of the site and the brevity of the clips work in their favor. Also weighing toward fair use is that the film is not currently marketed. But surely the most important reason why the *JAH* probably needn't worry about a lawsuit is the film's lack of economic value to its owner. *Mission to Moscow* did poorly even in its original run sixty years ago; a new release is unlikely. Would it be worth a lawsuit to defend such a "property"? On the other hand, the company might be much more likely to go to court against an identical use of *Gone with the Wind*, even though most of the same factors (except lack of current availability) would weigh in the *JAH*'s favor. The *JAH* did not formally request permission, and in our opinion they did not need to.

Will You Get Sued?

Not surprisingly, then, most of the active policing of the use of materials on the web focuses on materials that large corporations view as having great value. Most often, those efforts center on trademarks rather than copyrights. Firms like NameProtect, Cyveillance, and TrademarkBots troll the web looking for sites that violate their clients' trademarks. And "cease and desist" letters from lawyers about trademarks or other alleged infringements often have a very nasty, threatening tone. The website ChillingEffects.org calls this "Gorilla Chest Thumping" on the part of people who believe "that aggression is the best defense." Their advice is "take a deep breath" and "do not take it personally." In the case of trademarks, historians should know that scholarly and historical discussions involving trademarks will generally be considered "noncommercial" use and are fully protected by the First Amendment, although that will not stop a trademark attorney from sending you a threatening letter.[62]

The noncommercial nature of most historical projects generally protects you from several noncopyright legal hazards that other websites face. For example, in some states the "right of publicity" gives public figures, especially celebrities, the right to commercial gain in their own likeness, persona, and voice. Thus you can't create an advertisement incorporating Britney Spears without her permission. But because this right involves commercial gain, it is unlikely to concern most historians. Similarly, some websites have sued others for the practice of "deep linking," linking to interior information in their site in a way that bypasses home pages and other conventional entry pages that sites regard as important because they provide advertising revenue and establish their "brand." But this seems unlikely to apply to noncommercial history sites. We often receive requests for permission to link to portions of our site. We always say "yes," but in our view you don't need permission to link any more than you need permission to list a book in a bibliography. Two other areas of litigation—defamation and invasion of privacy—generally apply only to living people and are not of concern to historians who focus their attention on the dead past and dead people. But contemporary historians may need to consider whether they are portraying living people in a negative light. If you digitized a cache of letters from the 1960s that talked about contemporaries as "drunks" and "thieves," you could be liable for invasion of privacy or defamation—both of them likely to be more serious concerns than copyright infringement.[63]

The other particularly active area of policing of the web involves—as everyone knows since the advent of Napster—music. Major music companies have devoted large resources to tracking and prosecuting the trading of digital music files. Though such activity clearly exceeds fair use (if the music is not in the public domain), the fallout from the music company hysteria has spilled over to affect more legitimate uses of music online. For example, OLGA, the On-Line Guitar Archive, which allows guitar enthusiasts to share files that show how to play songs, has faced threatened lawsuits from recording industry giant EMI and the Harry Fox Agency, which represents more than 27,000 music publishers.[64] Its travails indicate the kinds of problems that a nonprofit history site would encounter if it ran afoul of a large corporation. We may be right in our public domain and fair use claims, but do we have the money to fight multinational bullies? A two-minute clip from Disney's 1995 film *Pocahontas* might both nicely teach something about popular understandings of the colonial period and be permissible under "fair use." But we would not advise going up against Disney's lawyers unless you have some top-notch pro-bono legal talent in your camp.[65]

Nevertheless, even the most rapacious corporations have better things to do than to prosecute nonprofit history websites—surely not the most popular stance to take. And though their pockets are considerably deeper than yours, they still have to weigh the costs of a suit, especially because *your* lack of deep pockets means that they are unlikely to recover much money. "You have to prioritize," says one attorney who enforces the online intellectual property rights of large corporations. The web-based publication *Education World*, which takes a generally cautious stance on the use of materials online, acknowledges that you have only a "slim" chance of winding up in court, especially if you promptly remove offending material upon notification by the copyright holder that your use is objectionable. Mary Minow reassuringly points out that a court can eliminate any damage award for copyright infringement if you "work for a nonprofit educational institution, library, or archives and are acting within the scope of your employment" and if you "believed and had reasonable grounds for believing that your use was Fair Use."[66]

*   *   *

The courts, alas, are a long way from the commons where we began— and where we would prefer to stay. And we believe that you will stay out of the courts. In our wide acquaintance, we know of no digital historians who have wound up in court. We can only think of a few who have received so much as a threatening letter from a lawyer. Your best defenses against finding yourself in court are, first, the promotion of learning, which has been the larger goal of copyright since the days of the Founding Fathers, and, second, your own efforts to nurture the creative commons—sharing generously in building a public "space" that is vital to our past and future.

Of course, if that virtual public space and creative contributions to it are to last into the future, you had better take steps to preserve it. That is the subject of our final chapter.

Chapter 8

Preserving Digital History
What We Can Do Today to Help Tomorrow's Historians

In this chapter you will learn about

- The perils of maintaining historical materials in digital formats
- What you can do right now to prevent the loss of your digital work
- Sound methods for constructing your website that will give it the best possible chance to survive inevitable technical changes over time
- What computer scientists, digital librarians, and archivists are doing to help preserve websites and other digital artifacts in the long run

At the end of 2002, My History Is America's History, an ambitious website aimed at promoting personal history among a popular audience and storing these narratives for others to read and reflect upon online, disappeared from the web with little fanfare. In the place of its hundreds of contributed stories, an essay contest on "The Idea of America," an interview with David McCullough about "the importance of history," and a guide to "saving your family's treasures," appeared a terse note informing visitors that "My History is America's History has closed its operations." Although it received significant financial support from the Internet company PSINet and Genealogy.com, and was created and managed by the National Endowment for the Humanities (NEH), the funding was for a limited time, and that period had drawn to a close. The dot-com bust (which brought down PSINet, among others, and led to ownership changes at Genealogy.com) hurt NEH's ability to raise private funds. In addition, My History was a "millennium project," established by Bill Clinton's White House Millennium Council in November 1999 to "honor the past" as the year 2000 approached. That year, of course, saw a heated election, and George W. Bush installed new leadership at NEH that may have found the populist design of the project less appealing than had the previous director, the folklorist William Ferris. Sadly, the Internet Archive only has copies of four of the stories from

My History Is America's History

A millennium project of the
NATIONAL ENDOWMENT FOR THE HUMANITIES

• **Home**

• **Kids' Corner**
• **In the Classroom**
• **In Your Community**

**Welcome to Our
Front Porch**
• About My History
• Guestbook
• Partners

**Exchange
Family Stories**
• Tell Your Favorite Family
Story
• Read America's Stories
• Create a Family Tree
• Find Your Family Online

Read America's Stories

B.B. King, Blues Musician

I was born in Mississippi in 1925, the son of a sharecropper. Like other young black men in Mississippi, I went to work on a plantation. It was a segregated society, and it was quite different from what you would know today. At the good gas stations--we used to call them filling stations--there would be a toilet for "White Men," "White Women," and another one that said "Colored." If it wasn't a very good station, they would have only two: "White Men" and "White Ladies," so they didn't have one for us. The same thing about water fountains in the city parks. If you were caught drinking out of the one that said "White," you were in trouble.

Figure 43. Now that the site is defunct we can only see a small portion of what was on the National Endowment of the Humanities' website My History Is America's History by entering its former URL in the "Wayback Machine" of the Internet Archive. Although the stories of B. B. King and a few other prominent names have been archived, the narratives of hundreds of lesser known individuals are gone because they were in a database that could not be accessed by the Internet Archive's computers.

My History, and those are from featured famous names such as B.B. King. Stories from the other, lesser known contributors were gated behind a search form and thus could not be archived by the Internet Archive's computers.

The loss of such a well-funded and popular site should give pause to any historian planning a digital project. Having read about planning, digitization, design, copyright, and building an audience of users and perhaps contributors, readers of this book now likely understand that digital history may require just as much work—and possibly much more—than projects involving paper and ink. Inevitably, any creative work that requires a significant amount of effort will elicit concern about how to ensure its ongoing existence. Although historians may not consider often short-lived materials such as exam study guides valuable, when planning a substantial online history project such as an archive or exhibit, it makes sense to think just as deeply about how to preserve such work for the long run as you do about how to undertake your digital project in the first place. Similarly, if you have spent a great deal of time collecting historical documents over the web, you should be concerned about being able to reproduce those documents for others in the years to come as well as upholding your ethical obligation to contributors to save their donations. It would be a shame to "print" your website on the digital equivalent of the acidic paper used by many Victorian publishers, which is now rapidly deteriorating in libraries around the world.

In this chapter we discuss why such losses are common in the digital realm, and how you can try to avoid such a fate. Although we touch on traditional archiving principles and cutting-edge digital preservation topics and software, as before, our aim is mostly pragmatic. We focus on basic ways that you can prepare your website for a long, if not perpetual, existence online.

The Fragility of Digital Materials

If only digital preservation were as easy as changing the quality of the paper we print on, as publishers and archivists have done by using high-grade acid-free paper for documents deemed sufficiently important for long-term preservation. Electronic resources are profoundly unstable, far more unstable than such paper records. On the simplest level, many of us have experienced the loss of a floppy's or hard drive's worth of scholarship. The foremost American authority on the longevity of various media, the National Institute of Standards and Technology (NIST), still cannot give a precise timeline for the deterioration of many of the formats we currently rely on to store precious digital records. A recent report by NIST researcher Fred R. Byers notes that estimates vary from 20 to 200 years for popular media such as the CD and DVD, and even the low end of these estimates may be possible only under ideal environmental conditions that few historians are likely to reproduce in their homes or offices. Anecdotal evidence shows that the imperfect way most people store digital media leads to much faster losses. For example, a significant fraction of collections from the 1980s of audio CDs, one of the first digital formats to become widely available to the public, may already be unplayable. The Library of Congress, which holds roughly 150,000 audio CDs in conditions almost certainly far better than those of personal collections, estimates that between 1 and 10 percent of the discs in their collection already contain serious data errors.[1]

Moreover, nondigital materials often remain intelligible following modest deterioration, whereas digital sources such as CDs frequently become unusable at the first sign of corruption. Most historians (perhaps unconsciously) know this. We have gleaned information from letters and photographs discolored by exposure to decades of sunlight, from hieroglyphs worn away by centuries of wind-blown sand, and from papyri partially eaten by ancient insects. In contrast, a stray static charge or wayward magnetic field can wreak havoc on the media used to store "digital objects" (a catchall term that refers to everything from an individual image file or Word document to a complex website) that we might want to look at in the future. Occasionally the accidental corruption of a few bits out of the millions or billions of bits that comprise a digital file renders that file unreadable or unusable. With some exceptions, digital formats tend to require an exceedingly high degree of integrity in order to function properly. In an odd way, their perfection is also their imperfection: they are encoded in a precise fashion that allows for unlimited perfect copies (unlike, say, photocopied paper documents), but any loss of their perfection can mean disaster.

Yet this already troubling characterization of digital materials only begins to scrape the surface of what we are up against in trying to save these bits. Historians—even those strongly committed to long-term preservation—can lose important digital resources in some very unsettling ways. The Ivar Aasen Centre of Language and Culture, a literary museum in Norway, lost the ability to use its large, expensive electronic catalog of holdings after the death of the one administrator who knew the two sequential passwords into the system. The catalog, an invaluable research tool stored in an encrypted database format, had taken four years to create and contained information about 11,000 titles. After desperately trying to break into the system themselves, the Centre sent out an open call for help to computer experts and less above-board types, the reward being a round-trip flight to a Norwegian festival of literature and music. Within five hours a twenty-five-year-old hacker, Joakim Eriksson of Växsjö, Sweden, figured out that the first password needed to access the system was the administrator's last name spelled backwards. (The second password, equally suspect security-wise, was his first name spelled forwards.)[2]

Beyond the frightening possibilities of data corruption and loss of access, all digital objects require a special set of eyes—often unique hardware and accompanying operating system and application software—to view or read them properly. The absence of these associated technologies can mean the effective loss of digital resources, even if those resources remain fully intact. In the 1980s, for instance, the British Broadcasting Corporation (BBC) had the wonderful idea of collecting fragments of life and culture from across the U.K. into a single collection to honor the 900th anniversary of William the Conqueror's *Domesday Book*, which housed the records of eleventh-century life from over 13,000 towns in England following William's invasion of the isle in 1066. Called the Domesday Project, the BBC endeavor eventually became the repository for the contributions of over a million Britons. Project planners made optimistic comparisons between the twentieth-century Domesday and its eleventh-century predecessor; in addition to dozens of statistical databases, there would be tens of thousands of digital photographs and interactive maps with the ability to zoom and pan. Access to this massive historical snapshot of the U.K. would take mere seconds compared to tedious leafing through the folios of the *Domesday Book*.

Such a gargantuan multimedia collection required a high-density, fully modern format to capture it all—so the BBC decided to encode the collection on two special videodiscs, accessible only on specially configured Philips LaserVision players with a BBC Master Microcomputer or a Research Machines Nimbus. By the late 1990s, of course, the Laser-Vision, the BBC line of computers, and the Nimbus had all gone the way of the dodo, and this rich historical collection faced the prospect of being unusable, except on a few barely functioning computers with the correct hardware and software translators. "The problems of software and hardware have now rendered the system obsolete," Loyd Grossman, chairman of the Domesday Project, fretted in February 2002. "With few working examples left, the information on this incredible historical object will soon disappear forever." One imagines that the *Domesday Book*'s modest scribes, who did their handiwork with quills on vellum that withstood nine centuries intact and perfectly readable, were enjoying a last laugh. Luckily some crafty programmers at the University of Michigan and the University of Leeds figured out how to reproduce the necessary computing environment on a standard PC in the following year, and so the Domesday videodiscs have gotten a reprieve, at least for a few more years or perhaps decades. But this solution came at considerable expense, a cost not likely to be borne for most digital resources that become inaccessible in the future. Though the U.S. Census Bureau can surmount a "major engineering challenge" to ensure continued access to the 1960 census, recorded on long-outdated computer tapes, an individual historian, local history society, or even a major research university will probably not foot similar bills for other historical sources.[3]

We could fill many more pages (of acid-free paper) with examples of such digital foibles, often begun with good intentions that in hindsight now seem foolish. Digital preservation is a very serious matter, with many facets—yet unfortunately no foolproof solutions. As Laura McLemore, an archivist at Austin College, concludes pragmatically, "With technology in such rapid flux, I do not think enough information is available about the shelf life . . . or future retrieval capabilities of current digital storage formats to commit to any particular plan at this time." The University of Michigan's Margaret Hedstrom, a leading expert on digital archiving, bluntly wrote in a recent report on the state of the art (co-sponsored by the National Science Foundation and the Library of Congress), "No acceptable methods exist today to preserve complex digital objects that contain combinations of text, data, images, audio, and video and that require specific software applications for reuse."[4]

It is telling that in our digital age—according to the University of California at Berkeley, ink-on-paper content represented an incredibly miniscule 0.01 percent of the world's information produced in 2003, with digital resources taking up over 90 percent of the nonprinted majority—the *New York Times* felt compelled to use an analog solution for their millennium time capsule, created in 1998-1999. The *Times* bought a special kind of disk, HD-Rosetta, pioneered at Los Alamos National Laboratory to withstand nuclear war. The disk, holding materials deemed worthy for thousand-year preservation by the editors of the *Times* magazine, was created by using an ion beam to carve letters and figures into a highly pure form of nickel. Etched nickel is unlikely to deteriorate for thousands, or even hundreds of thousands, of years, but just to be sure, the *Times* sealed the disk in a specially made container filled with the highly stable inert gas argon, and surrounded the container with thermal gel insulation.[5]

Even skimping a bit on the argon and thermal gel, this is an expensive solution to most historians' preservation needs. Indeed, we believe that any emphasis on technological solutions, whether they be pricy ones from Los Alamos or the more germane computer repository systems we explore at the end of this chapter, should come second to attention to more basic tenets of digital preservation that are helpful now and are generally (though not totally) independent of the murky digital future. Archivists who have studied the problem of constant technological change realized some time ago that the ultimate solution to digital preservation will come less from specific hardware and software than from methods and procedures related to the continual stewardship of these resources.[6] That does not mean that all technologies, file formats, and media are created equal; it is possible to make recommendations about such things, and where possible we do so below. But sticking to fundamentally sound operating principles in the construction and storage of the digital materials to be preserved is more important than searching for the elusive digital equivalent of acid-free paper.

What to Preserve?

Think for a moment about the preservation of another precious commodity: wine. Connoisseurs of wine might have cheap bottles standing upright in the heat of their kitchen—a poor way to store wine you want to keep around for a long time, but fine if you plan to drink it soon or don't care if it gets knocked over by a dog's wagging tail. But at the same time they almost certainly hold their bottles of Château Lafite Roths-child on their side at close to 55 degrees and 70 percent humidity in a dark cellar (ideal conditions for long-term storage of first-growth Bordeaux). Fine wine, of course, merits far more attention and care than everyday wine. Expense of replacement, rarity, quality, and related elements factor into how much cost and effort we expend on storing such objects for the future. Librarians and archivists have always considered such questions, storing some documents in the equivalent of the kitchen and others in the equivalent of a wine cellar, and historians interested in preserving digital materials should likely begin their analysis of their long-term preservation needs by asking similar questions about their web creations. What's worth preserving?

The U.S. National Archives and Records Administration (NARA), entrusted to preserve federal government materials such as the papers of presidents and U.S. Army correspondence, has a helpful set of appraisal guidelines they use in deciding what to classify as "perma-nent"—that is, documents and records that they will expend serious effort and money to preserve. (Although your archival mission will likely differ in nature and scope from NARA's ambitious mission to capture "essential evidence" related to the "rights of American citizens," the "actions of federal officials," and the "national experience," their basic principles still hold true regardless of an archive's scale.) Many of these straightforward guidelines will sound familiar to historians. For example, you should try to determine the long-term value of a document or set of documents by asking such questions as:

- Is the information (they hold) unique?
- How significant is the source and context of the records?
- How significant are the records for research (current and projected in the future)?

Other questions place the materials being considered into a wider perspective. For example, "Do these records serve as a finding aid to other permanent records?" and "Are the records related to other per-manent records?" In other words, by themselves some records have little value, but they may provide insight into other collections, without which those other collections may suffer. It therefore may be worth preserving materials that taken by themselves have little perceived value. Finally, for documents not clearly worth saving but also not obvious candidates for the trash bin, NARA's guidance is to ask questions related to the ease of preservation and access in the future: "How usable are the records?" (i.e., are they deteriorating to such an extent as to make them unreada-ble in the near future?); "What are the cost considerations for long-term maintenance of the records?" (e.g., are they on paper that may decay and thus require expensive preservation work?); "What is the volume of records?" (i.e., the more records there are, the more it will cost to store them).[7] This list of appraisal questions comes out of a well-established archival tradition in which objects such as the parchment of the Declaration of Independence and United States Constitution stand at the top of a preservation hierarchy and receive the greatest attention and resources (including expensive containers and argon gas), and less valuable records such as the casual letters of the lowest ranking bureaucrat receive the least amount of attention and resources. In NARA's physical world of preservation, this hierarchy is surely prudent and justified.

NARA's sensible archiving questions take on a wholly different character in the digital, nonphysical online world, however. Questions relating to deterioration—at least in the sense of light, water, fire, and insect damage—are irrelevant. The tenth copy of an email is as fresh and readable as the "original." "Volume" is an even odder question to ask about digital materials. What is "a lot" or perhaps even "too much," and when do we start worrying about that frightening amount? On one of its email servers, the White House generated roughly 40 million messages in Clinton's eight years in office. In 2000, at the end of his second term, the average email was 18.5 kilobytes. Assume for the sake of argument (and ease of calculation) that the policy wonks in Clinton's staff were as verbose as they were prolific, writing a higher-than-average 25 kilobytes per email throughout the 1990s. That would equal roughly a thousand million kilobytes, or a million million bytes—that is, 1 terabyte, or the equivalent of a thousand *Encyclopedia Britannicas*—of text that needs to be stored to preserve one key piece of the electronic record of the forty-second president of the United States. That certainly sounds like a preposterous amount of storage—or we should say that *sounded* like a preposterous amount of storage, because by the time this book is in print, there will almost certainly be computers for the home market shipping with that amount of space on the hard drive. At Clinton's 1993 inauguration, one terabyte of storage cost roughly $5 million; today you can purchase the same amount of digital space for $500.[8]

In the predigital age, it would have been impossible to think that a researcher could store copies of every letter to or from, say, Truman's White House, in a shoebox under his or her desk, but that is precisely where we are headed. The low cost of storage (getting radically less expensive every year, unlike paper) means that it very well may be possible or even desirable to save everything ever written in our digital age.[9] The selection criteria that form the core of almost all traditional archiving theories may fall away in the face of being able to save it all. This possibility is deeply troubling to many archivists and librarians because it destroys one of the pillars of archiving—that some things are worth saving due to a perceived importance, whereas other things can be lost to time with few repercussions. It also raises the specter that we may not be able to locate documents of value in a sea of undifferentiated digital files.

Surely this selection or appraisal process remains relevant to any discussion of preservation, including digital preservation, but the possibility of saving it all, or even saving most of it, presents opportunities for historians and archivists that should not be neglected. Archives can be far more democratic and inclusive in this new age. They may also satisfy many audiences at once, unlike traditional archives, by providing a less hierarchical way of approaching stored materials. Blaise Pascal famously said that "the heart has reasons that reason cannot understand"; we have found that in the world of digital preservation, researchers have reasons for using archives that their creators cannot understand.

Or predict. In 2003, most of the visitors to our September 11 Digital Archive came to the site via a search engine, having typed in (unsurprisingly) "September 11" or "9/11." But because of the breadth of our online archive (over 150,000 digital objects), 228 visitors found our site useful for exploring "teen slang," 421 were searching for information on the "USS *Comfort*" (one of the Navy's hospital ships), and 157 were simply looking for a "map of lower Manhattan." In other words, thousands of visitors came to our site for reasons that had absolutely nothing to do with September 11, 2001. Historians should take note of this very real possibility when considering what they may want to preserve. Brewster Kahle, the founder of the Internet Archive, likes to say that his archive may hold the early writings of a future president or other figure that historians will likely cherish information about in decades to come. Assessing which websites to save in order to capture that information in the present, however, is incredibly difficult—indeed, perhaps impossible.[10]

The NARA questions about the relationship between materials under consideration for archiving and those already preserved also take on different meanings in the digital era. One of the great strengths of the web is its interconnectedness—almost every site links to others. Such linkages make it difficult to answer the question of whether a set of digital documents under consideration for preservation is relevant to other preserved materials. Because of the interconnectedness of the web, the best archive of a specific historical site is probably one that stores the site embedded in a far larger archive of the web itself. But archiving a significant portion of the web to accompany your own site is practical only for the very few with tremendous resources, and the best course of action for most historians is to focus on the simpler preservation tactics we now explore.[11]

Documentation

The Commission on Preservation and Access (now merged into the Council on Library Information Resources, the group that has done the most to promote the need for digital preservation in the United States) and the Research Libraries Group issued a report entitled *Preserving Digital Information* in 1996, and its primary conclusion still holds true: "The first line of defense against loss of valuable digital information rests with the creators, providers and owners of digital information."[12] Historians can take some concrete steps in the process of creating content for the web that should increase the likelihood that this content will last into the future, and more important that it will still be readable, usable, or playable in the long term. In particular, they should make sure that their website's underlying code is easy to maintain through the use of documentation and technical conventions, and that it does not rely too heavily on specific technologies to run properly.

Historians are great documenters and in turn are great lovers of documentation. We adore seeing footnotes at the bottom of the page, even if we follow them only rarely. Indexes delight us with the prospect of a topic easily found. The only thing better than a cocksure preface to a new historical interpretation is a self-deprecating foreword to a second edition of that book decrying the author's earlier, rash hubris. This preference for documentation is not merely a pedantic predilection; good documentation allows current and future readers to understand where a text or object came from, who created it, what its constituent pieces are, and how it relates to other texts or objects. Like history itself, documentation contextualizes, relates, and records for posterity, and it helps to make a source more reliable.

The same values hold true for digital materials. Documentation, or little notes within the underlying code, provides guidance to current and future developers of your site so that they have the means to understand how your creations function, what the pieces are, and how to alter them with as little impact as possible on other parts of your website. The ease with which you can put web pages on the Internet will tempt you to spend all your time on that which everyone will see (the stuff visible on the screen), while ignoring the less flashy parts—the digital equivalents of the footnotes and preface. On many occasions we, too, have succumbed to this temptation. Documentation takes time and thus involves a trade-off: after all, you could spend that same time improving the site's design, digitizing more documents, or adding features that your audience might appreciate. Unsurprisingly, creators of websites often end up abandoning overly stringent or complex documentation regimes. We suspect that many scholars would go into print with incomplete footnotes if not for the stern hand of an editor. But websites go to press without those external prods to jar us out of our laziness.

Programmers, however, know that poorly documented code causes problems in the long term, and sometimes even in the short term, as others take over a project and scratch their heads at what the prior programmer has done, or an insufficiently caffeinated mind fails to comprehend what it did just a few days ago. Rigorous documentation provides a digital document like a web page with something akin to transparency, so that you and others can understand its pieces, structure, and functionality, now and in the future. So try to annotate your website as you create it, just as you would with a book or essay. Doing so in a thoughtful manner will allow you and others to modify and migrate the site in the future with less trouble, which in turn means that the site is more likely to live on when technological changes inevitably come.

The first step toward such website documentation is to use comment tags in HTML. Comment tags are fairly simple, involving greater-than and less-than signs, some dashes, and an exclamation point, like so:

<!—put your comments here—>

These comments are not visible on the web page, but those who are interested can see them by using an option in their browser to call up the page's code (generally by clicking on "source" under the "view" menu).

You might place an overall comment near the top of your web pages noting when it was created and who created and last modified the page, so they can be tracked down if there's a problem with the page in the future. (Alternatively, you could put the creation or last change date and the initials of the person responsible at the bottom of the visible page, i.e., without using the invisible comment tags.) Beyond this initial comment field at the top of the page, you may want to add comments at the top of any section of the file for which it is not utterly obvious what the ensuing code does. The official website of Thomas Jefferson's home, Monticello, has helpful comments for each section of their web pages, detailing in capital letters the purpose of that section. For instance, the comments note where the site navigation begins and ends, and where important images are loaded into the page.[13]

Comments on any "scripts," or small programs within web pages that handle the more complex or interactive features of advanced sites, are perhaps more important because these bits of programming in languages other than HTML tend to be more complicated and thus less transparent than the basic code of a page. The Monticello website provides an admirably brief explanatory comment above the JavaScript code that permits visitors to move easily between areas of the site. If you hand off the creation of this programming to others, be sure to tell them (or write into a contract if you are using a professional) that you expect clear and consistent documentation. Files are much easier to handle in the long run with these internal notes, and the notes make you less dependent on particular individuals (or your own long-term memory if you do it yourself).

In addition to these occasional intra-file comments, you should create an overall text file describing the contents of your website or its sections, often called a "README" file and frequently named README.txt. But feel free to use a filename that you deem appropriate, such as notes.txt or perhaps if_you_are_reading_this_file_I_am_long_gone.txt. Write in this brief document as a historian of your own work. Why did you create it and who else has worked on it? Has it changed significantly over time? Have new parts of the site arisen, and if so, when? Have other parts of the site withered away, and if so, why? For instance, a section of the README file for large changes to the overall look of the site might read like a terse diary, with the most recent changes at the top:

3 November 2004 – Added search engine
23 October 2003 – Two new features added
17 September 2002 – Initial release of the site

You can also note in this file where other important elements of the site reside, if not in the same directory as the README file. For instance, if your site uses a database, this critical piece of your site's content probably sits in a distant part of the web server, and it helps to point to that location in case someone needs to move your site to a new server. When we took on the hosting duties for the Film Study Center at Harvard University's DoHistory website, their README file, which included extremely useful information about the architecture of the site and the technologies used, simplified the transfer.[14]

In short, good documentation situates and chronicles your website. When Dollar Consulting helped the Smithsonian plan how to preserve its many web resources, they noted that the large institution had a "too many chefs in the kitchen" problem, with many different people altering and updating the same web pages. Because digital files show no signs of erasure or revision, Dollar suggested recording such changes over time—an "audit trail" similar to what we have suggested.[15] Experiment with this idea and our other commenting protocols; they are merely suggestions. The real key to good documentation is not a specific format or style but clarity and consistency.

We should acknowledge that our somewhat breezy approach to documentation would not sit well with some librarians who are deeply committed not just to internal consistency but to shared methods of documentation across all digital projects, to "interoperability" and "standards," in the widely used buzzwords. Indeed, a great deal of the effort by librarians and archivists focuses on developing standard ways of describing digital objects (whether individual files or entire websites) so that they may be cogently scanned and simply retrieved in the near or distant future. The technologies these parties propose revolve around metadata, or classifications of digital objects, either placed within those objects (e.g., as XML tags within text) or in association with those objects (i.e., as the digital equivalent of a card catalog). Created by a working group of experts in preservation and having found a home and advocate in the Library of Congress, the Metadata Encoding and Transmission Standard (METS) provides its users with a specific XML descriptive standard for structuring documents in a digital archive (unlike, though complementary with, the more abstract framework of the Reference Model for an Open Archival Information System, or OAIS). This includes information about the ownership and rights of these documents (author, intellectual property rights, provenance), as well as standard ways to structure, group, and move these documents across and within archival systems. Although METS can be used to encode digital content itself in addition to providing information about the content, the Metadata Object Description Schema (MODS), also promoted by the Library of Congress and developed in concert with archival experts, more narrowly provides a standardized method for referencing digital materials, as a card catalog entry references a book using its title, author, and subject. The Dublin Core Metadata Initiative promotes an even more restricted set of document references (fifteen main elements like title and author) that may prove to be helpful, like MODS, for electronic bibliographic references and digital archives. A broader schema from the Society of American Archivists and the Library of Congress, the Encoded Archival Description (EAD), uses XML to create finding aids for digital archives.[16]

Despite the considerable weight behind schemas such as METS, MODS, Dublin Core, and EAD, the quest to classify digital works with standardized, descriptive metadata and thus ostensibly to make them more accessible in the future has encountered substantial criticism from both technologists and humanists. Writer and Electronic Frontier Foundation evangelist Cory Doctorow, among others, has dismissed this pursuit of the standardization of digital object descriptions as an unachievable "meta-utopia." He skeptically catalogs some elements of human nature that mitigate against standardization and the implementation of reliable metadata schemas: people are "lazy" and "stupid," and they "lie," which makes it troubling to depend on their metadata for future retrieval. Other aspects of schemas may cause further trouble, such as the fact that "schemas aren't neutral," i.e., they are full of the biases of their creators and, more simply, that "there's more than one way to describe something." In other words, metadata schemas require such a high level of attention, compliance, and descriptive acuity as to be practically unattainable in the real world. What we are inevitably left with, Doctorow argues, are heterogeneous, somewhat confusing, partially described objects, and so in the end we have to muddle through anyway. (Or hope that a Google comes along to make decent sense of it all, despite the enormity of the corpus and the flaws within it.)[17]

To be sure, it would be difficult to get all or even most historians to agree on a set of rules for digital storage, even if uniformly following those rules would allow for a level of interoperability of our sites and retrievability of our work that we might all desire. But we should note that other groups of diverse people have been able to settle on common metadata standards, which have been mutually beneficial for their field or industry. For instance, the many scientists involved in the Human Genome Project decided on a standard to describe their voluminous data, thus enabling the combination of disparate gene studies. Similarly, competing manufacturers of musical equipment were able to agree on a standard for describing electronic music (Musical Instrument Digital Interface, or MIDI) so that various components would work together seamlessly. And we should not forget that whatever our views of librarians and archivists, historians have been able to do much of their research because of the helpful metadata found in card catalogs and classification schemas such as the MARC (MAchine-Readable Cataloging) format that came out of a Library of Congress–led initiative starting three decades ago. (MARC is now moving online, with Google and Yahoo having imported the library records for two million books so that links to them appear next to links for web content.) Without metadata that enables us to find documents easily and that allows various historical collections to be at least partially interoperable, we might find ourselves in a tomorrow with an obscured view of yesterday.[18]

Technical Considerations

But what about the code you are documenting? What can you do to decrease the likelihood that it will cease to function properly in years to come because of unforeseen changes to programming languages, software, or hardware, or because your site has to move from one web server to another? Without the benefit of a crystal ball, you can still implement simple technical conventions to make your website easier to maintain and transport. For example, use relative URLs, where references between files on your site are made using just the tail end of the URL that is different than the referring file's URL, rather than absolute URLs, which are the entire address, including the domain name, parent directories, and "http://". Relative URLs make it much simpler to move sections of your site around or transfer your entire site to a new domain without links breaking.

A more serious though perhaps more time-consuming approach to making your website's code future-friendly is to use XHTML, a sibling of XML, rather than HTML. In a web browser, XHTML renders in exactly the same way as HTML, and converting a site from HTML to XHTML does not affect its functioning at all. XHTML is a version of HTML written to the more stringent XML specifications—and therefore sites that use XHTML can take advantage of the strengths of XML. One of these potent traits is the capacity for XML to withstand the rapid changes of computer technology and its potential to be viewable on hardware and with software that do not even exist yet. Institutions cognizant of digital preservation, such as the Smithsonian, seem to be moving toward XHTML because of this flexibility. Along with Cascading Style Sheets (CSS) and a couple of more programmer-oriented technologies, XHTML is one of a handful of emerging "web standards" that professional web developers consider the basis for stable websites that will render well on different machines and that will have the greatest life expectancy.[19]

In general, it makes sense to rely as little as possible on specific hardware and software. Those concerned about the longevity of their site should therefore eschew marginal or unproven technologies. When flashy digital formats seem alluring consider whether they will be readable in five, ten, twenty-five years. We were once dazzled by the visual technology of a small software company called JT Imaging and ended up using it to display large maps on one of our websites. Unfortunately JT Imaging went out of business and their software vanished with them.

Consider future users of your site as important as current ones. It would be unwise to store archival documents that you spent a lot of money digitizing in a cutting-edge but unpopular format with uncertain prospects. For example, some in the technological cognoscenti do not use Adobe Corporation's popular PDF format, instead choosing a rival, far less popular format called DjVu, which is said to compress images of documents to a much smaller, yet still readable, size than PDF. At the time of this writing, however, Google shows over 150 million PDF and

PDF-related documents on the Web and fewer than a million DjVu documents and related materials. Common sense dictates that the much larger user base for PDF means a greater likelihood that documents in this format will remain readable in the distant future.

Similarly, at the same time that you avoid getting entangled in specific, possibly ephemeral digital technologies, you should be as neutral as possible with regard to hardware and software platforms. Dependence on a particular piece of hardware or software is foolish because, like most hardware and software through history, the computer technology you depend on today will eventually disappear, more likely sooner rather than later. The BBC's choice of the videodisc, specialized microcomputers, and a unique set of software instructions for its Domesday Project epitomizes this problem. This does not mean that you should avoid choosing specific hardware and software that meet your needs. Obviously you have to use some combination of hardware and software to create and serve your website, and it can be difficult to determine where the herd will go. When the Center for History and New Media (CHNM) decided five years ago that our old Macintosh server was no longer powerful enough to handle the volume of traffic we were receiving, we cautiously decided to buy a Linux server with Apache web server software. Apache now runs two-thirds of the world's websites, but this dominance was in no way assured, given Microsoft's aggressive push in the server market. But among other things, we liked how Apache could run on almost any computer with almost any operating system, making it easy to switch down the road if necessary. (Indeed, Apple now sells much more powerful servers—using the Apache program as its standard web server software.) We also chose the MySQL database program because its use of the Structured Query Language (SQL) standard for accessing information in databases meant that we would not have to recode our websites extensively if we changed to another database program later on. In general, try to use technologies that conform to open standards like SQL rather than proprietary standards. An international community of users is in charge of maintaining the open standard in a universal and transparent way, rather than a company whose profit motive is likely at odds with the principle of easily switching from one computer or program to another.

Backing Up

Once you've taken care of these initial steps to extend the life expectancy of your website, you can begin to think about what to do with your well-documented and structured files over time. Absolutely the first thing you should think about is safe storage. Questions about storage are similar to the questions we raise about a library or archive: Where should you keep your website's files? Who can access (and possibly alter) them? What happens if there's a fire or a flood? No matter how much attention you pay to documenting and standardizing your code, poorly thought out storage of your website can erase—quite literally—your entire effort. Having a robust storage plan provides further peace of mind that the digital materials you create about the past will have a future.

The fundamental rule of storage is that you should have copies, or "backups," of the files and data that make up your website. This may seem too obvious to mention. But the history of the interaction between historians and their computers is littered with tragic stories of papers, archival research, notes, data, dissertations, and manuscripts lost in countless ways. Some readers of this book will recognize themselves in these catastrophes, and we hope they have been chastened into a backup regime. Those who have not experienced the loss of computer-based work are merely victims waiting to meet their inevitable fate. For some reason, though lots of people talk about backing up, fewer people than you might imagine are actually doing it. We may curse the com-plexity of computer technology and feel annoyed that computer scien-tists haven't solved many of the problems that plague us, but with respect to backing up, we have seen the enemy, and it is us.

Backing up need not be convoluted or complex. First, store copies in more than one place, for example, at home and in your office, or in a safe-deposit box at your bank and your desk drawer. In addition to the Famous Trials files on his web server, Douglas Linder keeps a copy of his site on his personal computer and another copy on a tape backup stored at a different location.[20] Second, refresh, or re-create, these copies on a regular schedule, such as every Friday morning or on the first of every month (depending on your level of paranoia). Third, check to make sure, every so often, that these copies are readable. After all, your web server is not all that could fail; backups can fail as well. Fourth, institute social processes that support your backup plan. Tell others or record on paper (or in the README file) the location of backups so they are avail-able if you (or your site's steward) are not.

One of these backups should sit on a hard drive separate from the server's hard drive. Hard drives are generally the fastest way to shuttle information, and so in case of a problem, it is nice to have a hard drive backup around. Second (or third or fourth) copies may be on some kind of removable media, that is, a format that can be easily transferred from place to place. The candidates include tapes, which are very high-capacity digital versions of cassettes that look not unlike what we used to slide into a car stereo or VHS; removable magnetic media, other formats that store information on thin, revolving platters in a way that is essentially identical to hard drives but that can be separated from their readers and are thus more portable than hard drives; optical formats, which use lasers to scan and imprint single shiny platters—what most of us have known first as CDs (and CD-ROMs) and now DVDs (and DVD recordable formats for PCs); and most recently solid-state formats, which are essentially memory chips like the ones in your computer, encased in plastic, and which function as tiny drives when inserted in specially configured slots.

According to the Cornell University Library's somewhat chilling "Obsolete and Endangered Media Chamber of Horrors," no fewer than thirty-two distinct media formats for backing up digital information have emerged since the advent of modern computing. This includes (cue the funeral dirge) once revered technologies such as the 5 1/4 inch floppy, Sony's line of WORM disks, Syquest cartridges, and IBM's half-inch tapes (superseded, of course, by quarter-inch tapes). Even formats that seem to live forever, such as the 3 1/2 inch "floppy" (strangely, with a hard plastic shell) introduced with the first Macintosh computer twenty years ago, have declined in popularity and will soon join less celebrated formats in the dustbin of history; Dell Computer, the world's largest computer company, recently dropped the 3 1/2 inch floppy from its line of desktop and laptop computers.[21]

To be sure, all of today's formats work as advertised, providing copies of your files that can be moved easily and stored in secure, small places like a safe-deposit box given their slender form-factor. The costs for both the media and the drive to record and play that media vary widely. CD-ROMs and their optical successors generally have both cheap media (less than a dollar for each disc) and cheap drives (under $100). Not surprisingly, they dominate the low end of the storage market. The drives for magnetic media can also be inexpensive (often under $200) though the media themselves cost more (a Zip disk that holds the same amount of data as a CD-ROM costs roughly thirty times the price). Tape drives dominate the upper end of the market, with expensive drives (from several hundred to thousands of dollars) and media ($2–$50 per cartridge). With solid-state media like the popular "thumb" or "keychain" USB drives, the device is both the drive and the storage, so it is not expandable by plugging in additional discs or cartridges. When you need more storage, you have to buy another device. Many guides would advise you to run some calculations to figure out the cost per megabyte or gigabyte of storage (including the cost of the drive and the number of tapes, discs, or devices you will likely need), but most websites will fit easily on any of these media, with room to spare.

Those interested in long-term preservation still face two more significant considerations than cost when choosing a format. The first is the obvious question of the inherent longevity of the medium itself—that is, how long the bits on the volume can remain uncorrupted. As we noted at the beginning of this chapter, this question is quite difficult to answer, even with the best research tools at the disposal of the National Institute of Standards and Technology. Two hundred years, NIST's high-end estimate for optical media such as CDs and DVDs, sounds terrific, whereas their low-end estimate of twenty years seems barely adequate for "long-term" preservation. Given the additional problems of improper storage and the extreme variability of manufacturing quality that NIST outlines in their report on the archiving of digital information on these formats, some of these backups may become worthless in merely a few years.[22]

A second, perhaps equally important consideration can be called lightheartedly the "lemmings" question. What is everyone else using? As with web technologies, we recommend staying with formats that are popular because popularity alone is highly correlated with readability and usability over the long term. In the same way that Microsoft's effective monopoly on computer operating systems means that there is a far larger base of software developers for the Windows platform than for niche platforms such as Apple's Macintosh, strong market forces will increase the likelihood that information stored on the most popular formats will be readable in the distant future, though it may involve some cost in the outlying years. Currently the most popular storage format is the CD-R, and likely soon, one of the DVD recordable formats. Probably the best advice we can provide at this point is to choose one of these optical formats, and then follow NIST's one-page preservation guide for your chosen format. The Virginia Center for Digital History (VCDH) backs up their scans of nineteenth-century newspapers onto CDs.[23]

For sites that change frequently, such as a historical community site with a message board or a site that collects history online, as well as sites whose loss would affect many people, you need to consider a more rigorous backup scheme, including incremental backups (copies of what has changed since the previous backup) and full backups of the entire set of files. The number and timing of your incremental and full backups will vary depending on how frequently your site changes and how important it is to be able to "roll back" your site to prior versions in case of problems. You also need to keep full backups from prior weeks and months. Because a file can become corrupted without your knowledge (in some deep cul-de-sac of your site), if you merely have last week's full backup and the file was corrupted a month ago, that more recent backup will not help you retrieve the unblemished version of the file because the backed up copy itself will be corrupted. VCDH, which runs a number of popular history sites including Valley of the Shadow, backs up their entire server daily, on an incremental basis, onto magnetic tape that is stored at an off-site location.[24]

Mirroring, or the constant paralleling of data between two or more computers, is the most robust form of storage, but is probably only necessary for those sites that change so frequently that a failure of the main web server would result in the loss of significant amounts of information, or for sites that serve information that must be available constantly, even in the face of a computer crash. Under normal circumstances, the mirror provides a perfect, ongoing backup. In case of disaster, it can transfer data back to the original computer that has failed, or even be hooked up to the Internet, allowing your site to live on without visitors even noticing the swap. (Meanwhile, you will have to repair the main server and set it up to mirror your mirror.) Mirrors are the computer technology that allowed many Wall Street businesses to continue functioning with little interruption—or loss of critical financial data—in the aftermath of September 11.[25]

Commercial web hosts offer all of these backup options, though with increasing costs as the frequency of the backups increases. Most commercial hosts provide regular backups as part of a basic package, though "regular" can vary widely from once a month to once a day—a big difference for sites that change a lot. Be sure to check the fine print for your host's backup schedule. Universities tend to have once-a-week or once-a-day backups for their shared servers. (In all of these cases, we should note that backups tend to occur during the wee hours of the night when few people are accessing the server.) ISPs generally have the least reliable backup and restoration schemes. Regardless of who hosts your website, you should still make your own backups and keep them in safe places.

The Long-Term Fate of Your Site

Although you may enter a web project with great enthusiasm, no one can guarantee keeping their site up forever. Books have a natural preservation path: multiple copies get stored in libraries and personal collections. Websites, on the other hand, just disappear without proper and ongoing shepherding. In 2002, the History Department of the University of California, Riverside, took down its H-GIG website, a broad historical community site with more than 1,700 links to other history websites, after deciding that the department could no longer expend the energy to maintain it. They left a rueful and telling note behind: "It has been impossible for the History Department to keep H-GIG up-to-date. Most of the directories and pages have been deleted."[26] Unfortunately such bad news travels slowly on the web; two years after H-GIG's demise, more than fifty other sites continue to link to it.

Clearly you will need to consider how to maintain and update your site over time, or hand off those tasks to someone else. Virtually all sites, even relatively static ones, require such stewardship. There have already been several versions of HTML, enough to "break," or render partially unreadable, many of the pages created in the early 1990s. Who is going to "translate" your pages to the web languages of the future? Many of the scripting languages (like PHP, discussed in the appendix) also go through changes that alter the way that web pages must be written to function properly, and thus must be attended to over time. Even simpler elements of a web page, such as links to other pages on the web, must be checked periodically or a site may maintain internal integrity but appear out of touch with the wider world. For sites that have links to other sites, you need an ongoing process for checking those external links regularly so they do not break. Several low-cost programs will check links for you and highlight broken ones, and the World Wide Web Consortium provides a free link-checking service, but someone still has to correct these broken links or delete them.[27] Unlike books on library shelves, websites therefore require regular attention, and you need to plan accordingly.

Perhaps the best insurance for your website's existence is finding a permanent home for it in an institution that is in the business of long-term preservation. Libraries, archives, and historical and professional societies are in that business, and have the social systems—and funding—to maintain historical materials. Although some libraries do not have well-developed digital preservation plans or systems at the present time, and although plenty of web projects from such organizations and archives have disappeared over time, the fundamental nature of these institutions—focused on preserving resources and working for the public trust—should lead to such systems in the future. At the very least, these institutions have stable structures—they don't move, change email addresses, and lose things (like laptops) as much as you do. If you have built a site worth preserving, talk to someone at one of these institutions that might be interested in your topic. Douglas Linder has an arrangement with the University of Missouri-Kansas City Law School that they will maintain his site indefinitely should he leave the institution and decide not to take his site with him.[28] Some sites created through ad hoc institutional arrangements have found new homes with other organizations. For example, after DoHistory lost (through the death of the principal investigator, Richard P. Rogers) its active connection to the Harvard Film Study Center, they transferred custody of the site to

CHNM because we have a long-term commitment to work in digital history.

In addition to making such arrangements if possible, you should check with any institutions you are affiliated with or that might have an interest in your site to see if they have set up special repository software on their web server. Probably the best known and most widely implemented of these programs is MIT Libraries' and Hewlett-Packard's DSpace, which is currently in an early release (1.2 at this writing) that is being tested by dozens of universities and libraries. Although it involves complex technology behind the scenes, for end users like historians, DSpace looks more or less like a simple web interface through which you can search for documents stored in the system and into which you can upload your own documents or data. With its focus on single objects, such as articles, datasets, or images, DSpace currently seems less prepared to accept whole websites, however, because websites are interconnected sets of heterogeneous objects—some text, data, and images, pulled together with HTML and linked both internally and externally.[29]

Although it uses somewhat different technologies, Cornell University's and the University of Virginia's Fedora project has a similar repository mission to DSpace. Because it has a greater focus than DSpace on linking objects together and relies heavily on XML, the more sophisticated cousin of HTML, Fedora shows more promise as a system to store and preserve whole websites (in addition to articles, datasets, and images). But it, too, is in an early stage with some usability issues still to be resolved. Historians looking for a long-term home for their digital materials should keep an eye out for these two programs and other digital repositories as they become available. The best of such repositories are OAI compliant, meaning that they follow a highly regarded framework for digital archives that outlines standardized, rigorous methods for acquiring, maintaining, and disseminating digital materials.[30]

Although these advanced software solutions sound promising, we would be remiss without discussing—perhaps in hushed tones if technophiles are around—the idea of saving your digital materials in formats other than the ones they are currently in. For example, why not just print everything out on acid-free paper—the poor historian's version of the *New York Times* millennium capsule? For some websites, this method seems fine. For instance, text-heavy, noninteractive, relatively small sites are easy to print out and save in case of disaster—take your web essay and turn it into a traditional paper one. It would take a great deal of work, however, to retype even a modest site back into a computer format.

For websites that are large or have multimedia elements, the print-out solution seems less worthy. One of the major problems with printing out is that such analog backups lose much of the uniqueness of the digital realm that we highlighted in the introduction—for example, the ability of machines to scan digital materials rapidly for matches to searches, the ability to jump around digital text, the specific structure that can only be reproduced online. For instance, key features of DoHistory—the ability to search by keywords through Martha Ballard's Diary or the "Magic Lens" that helps you read eighteenth-century handwriting—have no print analog. These same issues hold true for preservation techniques that do the equivalent of printing out, but in a digital format—for instance, converting a website to static PDF files or turning interactive web pages into TIFF graphics files. Though such conversions maintain the fonts and overall look of a site (unlike many print-outs), they still lose much in the translation—too much, in our view.

You can, of course, do these things while simultaneously trying the other preservation methods we have discussed in this chapter. Indeed a basic principle of preservation is to keep the originals intact while exploring archival techniques with parallel copies. Because digital copies are so cheap, it does not hurt to have copies of digital documents and images in a variety of formats; if you are lucky, one or more will be readable in the distant future. For example, while keeping many files in Microsoft Word format, you could also use Word's "Save As . . ." menu function to convert these files (while keeping the originals) to basic text (ASCII or Unicode), as well as more complex, non-Microsoft formats, such as the Rich Text Format (RTF). If you have spent a lot of money digitizing photographs for a website in a high-quality TIFF format, why not buy another hard drive and store them as JPEGs and GIFs as well? Only the largest collections will render this problematic from a cost standpoint, and it may increase the odds that one of the three graphics formats will be viewable decades from now. With digital video, of course, storage remains a serious and costly problem, making such parallelism less attractive and some kind of software solution seem more worthy of pursuit.[31]

The Future of Our Digital Past

If only robust, reliable storage were enough to ensure that our documents and other digital objects would be available and readable many years from now. As the Arts and Humanities Data Service at the University of Essex warns, "Backup is not preservation . . . in contrast [to backup], a preservation version of the data is designed to mitigate the effects of rapid technology change that might otherwise make the data unusable within a few years."[32] Technological change has indeed become a troubling constant in our world, and one that greatly erodes the reliability and durability of the data and documents on which we rely as both historians and modern human beings. It is already difficult to open WordStar documents from the 1980s or even many WordPerfect documents from the 1990s. Such continual change poses the greatest challenge to the preservation of digital records for posterity, and although much work has been done on this subject, we cannot currently offer solace that all of the issues have been solved.

Although almost every commentator waxes eloquent about the new forms of access to historical documents opened up by digitization, most view digitization's benefits for preserving the past skeptically. "The digital landscape looks bleak for preservation purposes," concludes Paula De Stefano, the head of the Preservation Department at New York University. "So far," agrees Abby Smith of the Council on Library and Information Resources, "digital resources are at their best when facilitating access to information and weakest when assigned the traditional library responsibility of preservation." We very well may face a future in which it is hard to retrieve large segments of the past.[33]

As we saw in Chapter 3, one reason that, in Smith's words, "digitization is not preservation" stems from the loss of information that comes in the move from analog to digital format. Digital copies can never be perfect copies—or at least not yet. Still, improved technology is making it easier to come closer to perfection, and recently the influential Association of Research Libraries (ARL, a coalition of major North American institutions) has acknowledged that digitization, though imperfect, presents some very real advantages as a preservation method. The main problem facing digitization as a preservation medium is that we have not yet figured out how to preserve digital objects—even cutting-edge programs like DSpace and Fedora are closer to repositories than true archives, which by definition ensure that valued objects are available in perpetuity (though these programs may certainly may grow into this role with further improvement). If digital objects are truly and irreparably impermanent, we are not saving anything by moving from a fading analog map to digital bits that may not be readable in twenty years because of hardware and software changes.[34]

On the other hand, as the recent ARL position on digitization shows, librarians and archivists are growing more optimistic about making digital forms more permanent. Several national and international initiatives are currently formulating a digital preservation architecture that will facilitate digital libraries and archives and confront many of the anxieties about obsolescence and nonstandardization. And despite these anxieties, digitization sometimes offers the best (albeit not the perfect) preservation approach. The "purist" strategy for preserving the 10,000 deteriorating reels of taped oral history interviews held by the Marine

Corps would require duplicating all the tapes. Instead, the Marines are putting the interviews on CDs and allowing the analog tapes to decay. Samuel Brylawski, the head of the Library of Congress Recorded Sound Section, quotes the assertion that "no one can prove any digital version will survive and be accessible beyond a few decades," but then adds that "in the case of audio preservation . . . there is no proven analog preservation practice" and concludes that "digital preservation is here to stay."[35]

Digitization is not yet the preservation silver bullet, but it can still extend the "preservation tool kit," as preservationists Anne R. Kenney and Paul Conway explain. The most obvious value is in creating digital surrogates that can be provided to users as an alternative to allowing more wear and tear on the originals. You no longer need to consult the original Beowulf manuscript in the British Library because you can more easily access a digital copy, which also happens to reveal more of the text. After the Chicago Historical Society finishes digitizing its 55,000 glass plate negatives from the *Chicago Daily News* photo morgue, it intends to retire the originals from use, "thus ensuring their longevity."[36]

But what about the longevity of the digital copies, or of digital materials in general? Caroline R. Arms of the Library of Congress's Office of Strategic Initiatives has summarized the five general avenues the library and others in the long-term preservation business are exploring to ensure the continuity of such valuable and growing collections of digital materials. The first two avenues have to do with solving problems related to the storage of digital files; the last three have to do with the more difficult matter of being able to understand and read those files in the distant future. The first avenue is "better media," or the search for media formats that will last longer and be more reliable throughout their lifetimes than existing media. The second approach is what Arms terms "refreshing bits" and is the process both of constantly backing up data onto storage media as well as transferring it to new computers over time, all the while making sure that no corruption of files has occurred.

The third and fourth avenues are often considered rival methods for accessing digital files for which the original "interpreters"—that is, the hardware and software used to read them during their initial creation and early life—are now gone. "Migration," as the name suggests, involves moving a file from one format to another to keep it up to date. So a file originally created in, and readable by, Microsoft Word 97 is updated to be a Word 2003 file, then a Word 2007 file, and so on. In this way, the latest version of the document is readable by the latest, current version of the software. "Emulation"—the approach taken with the seemingly doomed digital Domesday Project—takes the opposite tack:

rather than changing the original file, you try on modern hardware and software to re-create the original digital environment needed to read a very old file—in other words, making a version of Microsoft Word 97 that works on Windows 2050. As Arms puts it, emulation involves "using the power of a new generation of technology to function as if it were the technology of a previous generation." This sounds wonderful, especially because (at least in theory) a single Word 97 emulator could enable historians to read millions of once obsolete documents, unlike migration, which forces designated stewards to move each of those files through each intermediate file type over the decades. Although migration can be incredibly expensive—one estimate is that data migration of a digital library is equivalent to photocopying all of the books in a physical library of the same size every five years—it is a known, effective process. Businesses do it all the time, as does the federal government. But emulation remains unproven and untested. Keep in mind that in 2050 we will need to emulate not just the word processing program but elements of the operating system of yesteryear as well. And if emulation fails to work, we are in trouble. The final avenue is truly a last resort, only to be used if the prior four methods fail: "digital archaeology," in which it is no longer possible to read a file (due to an ancient file type or lack of proper hardware or software), and thus we must be satisfied with picking up pieces of the digital past and hoping to be satisfied with them (and with our ability to interpret them).[37]

Although historians should be aware of these various efforts to save digital materials for the long run and should be part of this crucial discussion about what will happen to the records of today and yesterday in a digital future, a large portion of this discussion and almost all of its implementation lies beyond our purview. Computer scientists, librarians, and archivists are the prime movers in this realm, and properly so, though they could certainly use our input as some of the most important end users of their products and as professional stewards of the future of the past. Most readers of this book will not become active participants in this work, but they should, to the degree possible, become engaged with the larger social and professional issues it raises. Keep an eye and an ear out for the themes and projects we have discussed, follow what they are trying to do, and connect with the librarians and archivists doing this critical work. We are still in the early stages of the creation of these archives, and many prototypes and methods will disappear like the failed dot-coms of the 1990s. While waiting for the dust to settle, historians should maintain their best individual preservation efforts by focusing on what we have emphasized earlier in this chapter.

*   *   *

At the present time, therefore, preservation of digital materials involves some modest, though not radical, steps. Until systems like DSpace or effective metadata schemas become essentially invisible— "click here to tag and archive your website"—our digital work faces an uncertain future. We cannot predict the likelihood that any of these projects will prove capable of easily accessioning websites whole and ensuring that such sites will be readable in fifty or a hundred years. We do know, however, that their overall success will have as much to do with social systems as technical ones. As Margaret Hedstrom perceptively notes, "The challenges of maintaining digital archives over long periods of time are as much social and institutional as technological. Even the most ideal technological solutions will require management and support from institutions that in time go through changes in direction, purpose, management, and funding."[38] Regardless of how sound the systems like DSpace are in the theory of library and computer sciences, they will need to be serviced and cared for over years, by definition, and thus stand at the whim of many human factors other than the technical elements their creators have labored over.

For now, you are the best preserver of your own materials. Pay attention to backing up, and try to create simple, well-documented, standardized code. After covering those basics, you might search for a preservation "partner," an institution that would be interested in saving your website or its constituent materials after you can no longer provide the attention (or financial resources) it needs. Only then take stock of more advanced preservation systems and methods yourself, or maintain an ongoing dialogue with a digitally savvy archivist. As Louis Pasteur astutely observed, "Chance favors the prepared mind," and the caprice of technological change as well as future efforts in digital preservation by smart librarians and computer scientists will likely reward the well-prepared website.

Some Final Thoughts

To preserve, of course, you must first create. Although we have emphasized the need for planning and have proceeded carefully through the steps of building your site's infrastructure, digitizing materials, designing your pages, launching your site, ensuring compliance with copyright laws, and protecting what you have developed, we would like—in closing—to warn you against the temptation to be overly deliberate in moving online. If historians are predisposed to a character flaw, being too deliberative is perhaps the most likely candidate. Deliberation is, to be sure, a great and worthy virtue in our profession. Diligent investigation of the historical record, the careful weighing of evidence, thoughtful dialogue with one's peers, and the detailed preparation of publications have formed the foundation of a discipline that has educated and enlightened generations.

We believe, however, that with so many details to think about, too much deliberation can be counterproductive, making some hesitant to contribute to the History Web—thus reducing the number and variety of online creators. To add the web to their means of expression and methods of research, all historians must shed the tentativeness that often accompanies an encounter with the new, and which our natural and sensible caution may exacerbate. Voltaire's observation that the perfect is the enemy of the good seems especially applicable to work in this new media. With a fairly simple and relatively forgiving underlying language, HTML, and a low barrier to entry—a computer connected to the Internet—the web encourages experimentation. By testing preliminary or partial versions of your site you can identify problems early on and make changes before you invest a lot of time and money. A site can always be changed or modified as it grows or you come across issues you were unable to anticipate in the planning stages. And, as you proceed, you can learn much of what we have covered in this book as well as other topics both historical and technical, as we have certainly done—and continue to do.

Encouraging broad participation is indeed part of the history of the web itself. Web inventor Tim Berners-Lee first developed his Internet technology for the computer-savvy members of CERN, the European

Organization for Nuclear Research, but he also hoped that the simplicity of adding pages to the system would encourage all kinds of people using all kinds of computers to participate in a World Wide Web. Berners-Lee set the bar for participation very low in his original 1989 proposal for the web, with the very brief section entitled "Bells and Whistles" only aiming at "storage of ASCII [plain] text, and display on 24 × 80 [character dimension] screens" with the "addition of graphics an optional extra."[1] Although 1989 may seem a long time ago, many quite advanced graphical computer systems existed by then—especially within CERN—so Berners-Lee's formulation shows he intended to have his method as widely adopted as possible. This intention remains in the relative ease with which you can enter the world of web production. Indeed, the recent spread of wikis and especially blogs has made it even easier for historians to put their words online. Despite the "bells and whistles" that the web has added since its first use at CERN, digital history can be not so dissimilar from history in print.

Although we have taken you through a series of topics that may be new and at times complex, we hope that our larger message—that all historians can use the web to make the past more richly documented, more accessible, more diverse, more responsive to future researchers, and above all more democratic—has risen above the occasional technical details. The ubiquity of digital media in our lives—a pervasiveness that will only grow in coming years—makes this message all the more important. We believe it would be a grave mistake to cede this new medium to commercial interests or to "techies." Surely, a wide range of historians—whether teachers or students, public or academic, professional or amateur—need to make their voices heard on the web. All of us have a responsibility to ensure that the new digital history is a democratic history, one that reflects many different voices of the past and the present, that encourages everyone to participate in writing their own histories, and that reaches diverse and multiple audiences in the present and future.

The great Southern historian C. Vann Woodward once declared, perhaps to the cheers of the neo-Luddites, that his #2 pencil was his computer. But in our new century most historians will consider the computer their pencil, and we hope this book will help them discover new and creative ways of gathering, preserving, and presenting the past with it.

Database Software, Scripting Languages, and XML

Chapter 2 outlined some of the basics of creating a website, but those contemplating more complex sites need to think about more involved technical infrastructures, especially the possibility of organizing expansive resources through databases or XML. If you plan on having more than a hundred digital objects in a historical archive, collecting more than a hundred historical artifacts or documents through your website, or are responsible for the membership roll of a historical society, you should consider attaching a web-enabled database to your site. If you are digitizing a similarly large number of historical documents that are mostly or completely text, you should consider the possibility of marking up those documents with XML. Using either a database or XML generally adds a few layers of technology to more basic website elements: additional software to encode or store materials, a way to deposit information into a database or mark up texts with XML, and a way to extract information from the database or XML archive to be displayed on a web page.

Databases

Most historians encounter simple databases when they use common software applications such as Access or Filemaker. Web databases differ from these "client," or desktop, programs. They run silently in the "background" of a web server and respond to specialized requests through small pieces of programming code rather than through the point-and-click actions that occur on a personal computer screen. These invisible database operators permit quick and complicated "queries," or instructions, from a web page.

Your budget and the other technologies you plan to use on your site will help you choose an appropriate database program. If you anticipate having more than 100,000 entries in the database and require no corruption or loss of information and a service-oriented company to go to with problems (in other words, if you are in charge of a large project like Ellis Island's website, which stores millions of names as well as associated documents), you may want to use software from Oracle, the high-end market leader, or similar products like DB2 from IBM. These expensive database products are often sold with technical support and cost thousands of dollars per year (or more) to buy and run.[1] Even then, many large historical sites with some in-house technical capabilities may be able to use a free high-end alternative called PostgreSQL, which has most of the same features as the commercial software with none of the eye-popping cost.[2] For example, the Eastern Illinois University students and professors behind the Coles County Legal History Project, which is cataloguing and making web searchable legal documents from the era of Abraham Lincoln, Esq., decided to move from Access to PostgreSQL as their collection and website grew rapidly over the years.[3] PostgreSQL, like Oracle's products, is "ACID" compliant, an acronym for a database checklist that ensures data integrity during fast-paced, high-volume usage.

For all but the most extensive historical archives, however, PostgreSQL, Oracle, DB2, and other robust databases are overkill, and many good alternatives for small- to medium-sized historical websites exist. Microsoft SQL Server sometimes comes bundled with Internet Information Services (IIS), Microsoft's web server software (beginning at around $1,500), and in certain ($20,000 and up) versions it can handle as much information as any database (educational versions of SQL Server cost considerably less). In addition, SQL Server includes administrative software that maintains the look and feel of Windows and thus may feel more comfortable than other database packages (though you may not see this administrative software if you do not own or run the server it is on).

Microsoft's low-end personal database, Access ($229 alone, and also available as part of the Office suite of programs), meant to run more on client computers than web servers, is inexpensive and can be pressed into service as a web database, but not without some software linkages that will require some technical knowledge. The University of Minnesota's Immigration History Research Center uses Access to store information about its thousands of documents and images, although they convert the Access data into another format to make it searchable via the web.[4]

More recently, with the widespread adoption of open source software, a good alternative to all of the preceding options has emerged: MySQL, the leading free database.[5] MySQL runs on virtually any type of server and ably handles ten or even hundreds of thousands of documents, as it does for our September 11 Digital Archive.[6] Although perhaps not as robust as PostgreSQL or Oracle, MySQL is extremely capable for most of the tasks historians will ask of it (e.g., finding a specific document quickly) and is slowly gaining many of the high-end features and stability of its rivals. MySQL will likely continue to proliferate, given its undeniably attractive price and large base of users ready to help out others. Most commercial web hosts (see below) provide MySQL for customers who want to attach a database to their site.

But how do you access the database software lurking on the server, either to put materials in or to get them out to display on your website? In general, putting things in is easier because it can be done through various interfaces without programming. Many database programs come with, or allow for, web-based interfaces to enter data—for instance, the popular phpMyAdmin for MySQL—though you may find such interfaces lacking many of the features you are used to with programs running on your personal computer (like Access, Excel, and FileMaker). But such web-based interfaces allow entry from any computer with an Internet connection and a browser and hence facilitate the distribution of data entry. Another possibility is using special linking software to open a web server database on your personal computer within Access, Excel, or FileMaker. The Open Database Connectivity protocol (ODBC) enables different client and server database software to function seamlessly together in this way. If you are planning to enter your data only once, it may be easier, however, just to record it as you would in one of the easy-to-use client programs (like Access) and then hand off a tab-delimited file (a text file with tabs separating each piece of information, which most databases like Access can easily create) to your web server administrator for ingest into a web database.

Scripting Languages

Unfortunately, getting information into the database is only half the battle to using a database on a historical website. You now need to be able to extract bits of this information, format them, and insert them into web pages as visitors to your site make requests. The database software is merely interested in storing and serving this data and cannot do this task for you. Neither can HTML, which is a fairly "dumb" set of text tags. Instead, you must rely on one of several "scripting" languages that know how to communicate with the database software. "Scripts," or little programs that you can place either inside the HTML pages you construct or in separate files linked to web pages, are processed on the fly by the web server and can fill a page with information from a database. There are as many scripting languages as databases, though you often see certain languages in combination with certain databases. For instance, one of Microsoft's scripting languages, Active Server Pages (ASP), is generally used with other Microsoft products, including SQL Server. PHP (a self-referential acronym for PHP: Hypertext Preprocessor), the open source community's answer to ASP, is most often used with the open source MySQL and PostgreSQL databases. In contrast, ColdFusion, a popular scripting system from Macromedia, can be found attached to a wide variety of databases.

The words "scripts" and "scripting" sound very humanities-like, but these languages are, for all intents and purposes, programming languages, meaning that they are more difficult to pick up than HTML and far less forgiving to human error. If you need scripts to access a database, you should consider hiring a programmer who knows one of these languages well. Go about designing and building your site without the materials from the database—leaving room in your design "templates" for those items—and then bring in a programmer for a day or two to write pieces of technical code that will add the database elements. A programmer who knows how to structure a database properly for your collection of historical items and how to write the scripts to place those items into your design templates should cost around $50–100 per hour (generally a minimum of $1,000 for a basic setup; complex websites like EllisIsland.org require weeks, if not months, of database and programming work).

Regardless of who does the technical work, you should start by outlining the specific "tables" for the information you want to store. Each table, similar to a spreadsheet in Excel, holds a particular kind of information—for instance, a list of a historical organization's members or the pieces of data about letters in an archive. Even without fully understanding database software, you can probably draft the fields of each table: last name, first name, membership renewal date, and so on, for a membership roll; author, date written, to whom the letter was sent, body of the text, and so on, for a letter. Once in the database, each of these fields will be searchable individually as well as in tandem with other fields. From this list of fields (or "columns"), you or your programmer can proceed to set up the framework of the database, into which specific records (also called "rows") will go. Remember you (or your staff) will spend most of your time filling the database rather than creating it in the first place, but you should start by thinking about which fields to separate out; you will have trouble if you decide later that members' last names should be in a separate field from their first names.

To be more specific, a historical society's membership roll in a database might look as follows:

first_name	last_name	member_since	dues
Charles	Beard	1986	$75
Frederick	Turner	1997	$75
Edward	Gibbon	1999	$75

. . .

Programming code, in this case PHP embedded in regular HTML, pulls entries out of the database and formats them for a "membership roll" web page:

```
<html>
<head>
<title>Membership Roll</title>
</head>
<body>
<h1>Membership Roll</h1>
. . .
<?php

// print out today's date
echo 'Generated on' . date ("F jS, Y") . '<br><br>';

// pull membership information out of the database
$result = mysql_query ("SELECT first_name, last_name,
member_since FROM membership ORDER BY last_name");

//format each member's information
while ($row = mysql_fetch_assoc ($result)) {
    echo $row['first_name'] . ' ' . $row['last_name'] . ' (member since
' . $row['member_since'] . ')<br>';
}

?>
. . .
</body>
</html>
```

The web server processes the programming code when a user requests the page and creates a pure HTML document in a split second as follows:

```
<html>
<head>
<title>Membership Roll</title>
</head>
<body>
<h1>Membership Roll</h1>

Generated on July 4th, 2005<br><br>

Charles Beard (member since 1986)<br>
Edward Gibbon (member since 1999)<br>
Frederick Turner (member since 1997)<br>
. . .
</body>
</html>
```

And, unaware of the process that went into its rapid assembly, users see this in their web browser:

Membership Roll

Generated on July 4th, 2005

Charles Beard (member since 1986)
Edward Gibbon (member since 1999)
Frederick Turner (member since 1997)
. . .

Although institutional or ISP web hosts rarely provide access to database systems or allow web pages to include programming languages in addition to basic HTML, an increasing number of commercial web hosts provide such amenities. As of this writing, the most popular scripting language among web hosts is PHP, and the most popular database is MySQL. (Note the trend toward free and open source products; you will have more trouble finding a host that uses commercial scripting languages like ASP or ColdFusion, or commercial databases like Microsoft SQL Server.) Most web host comparison sites allow you to list just the companies that offer these more advanced services.[7] If you have a small database or need modest scripting on your site, a commercial host can be a good choice, and they generally charge only a little bit more for these services than for basic HTML-only accounts. Decent web hosting with PHP and MySQL starts at around $10 per month with a single database. Many of these plans also offer access to bulletin board services for visitors to leave comments and engage in discussion about your site or the topic it covers.

XML

XML is a more recent technology with less of a track record than the database, but with a growing following in the digital humanities and among librarians and archivists who believe that it will stand the test of time—unlike database files. XML does not have the extensive built-in search features that database programs do, though with some additional fuss you can search XML documents in complex ways. XML is probably best for a historical website with a circumscribed, unchanging set of historical documents that are mostly text. For instance, the Virginia Center for Digital History used XML for their collection of primary documents (including poignant "runaway advertisements") in their project The Geography of Slavery.[8] XML is also a good choice for archives that want to share their contents with other related collections because the simple text format XML is written in is, like HTML, rapidly becoming a lingua franca on the web.[9] For example, the Cornell University Library, the University of Michigan Library, and the State and University Library of Göttingen combined their historical collections of mathematical works using XML.[10]

Getting started with XML is in some respects much easier—and in others much harder—than using a database. On the one hand, you can use a rudimentary text editor like Notepad to create XML documents (though more sophisticated text editors are very helpful) because XML is simply text with added tags. On the other hand, compared to databases, working with XML is a highly unstructured affair. Indeed, you create much of that structure yourself, which is both its beauty and its peril. Although you need to define columns in database programs, many common types of definitions often come preset—for example, database programs have built-in formats for dates and times, and ways to generate such information automatically. By contrast, in XML you have to define each of these elements yourself, although occasionally you can borrow a set of definitions, as with TEI (see Chapter 3). XML's flexibility—its ability to tag any bit of text in a document any way you like, highlighting words or phrases as you would with a set of differently colored highlighters on paper—can easily breed unwieldy complexity if you are not careful.

Just as databases require scripting languages like ASP and PHP to pluck information from the database and place it into a web page, XML documents require translators to convert them into HTML for web viewing. Although the very same scripting languages can take care of this task of "parsing" the XML into its constituent parts and putting those parts into a web template, the World Wide Web Consortium has two technologies specially designed for this task: XSL and XSLT. The Extensible Stylesheet Language (XSL) provides a set of codes for formatting XML elements; the related Extensible Stylesheet Language Transformations (XSLT) converts an XML document with an associated XSL stylesheet into an HTML file that can be viewed in any web browser. With XML/XSL/XSLT (a confusing alphabet soup, to be sure), you can create a formatting template for your XML documents—say, boldfacing the names of authors within each document, taking the date of each letter and right-justifying it—and the server will convert each XML document on request into that format for your web visitors. No need to create separate HTML pages for your web archive; merely create your XML documents and a translator will take care of the rest.

For example, a version of Frederick Jackson Turner's *The Frontier in American History* prepared in XML and made available for the web might have the following pieces. First, like any XML document, it must have a Document Type Definition (DTD), in this case defining different parts of the text such as the overall title to the work, the chapter titles, and paragraphs and notes:

```
<!ELEMENT doc (title, chapter*)>
<!ELEMENT chapter (title, (para|note)*)>
<!ELEMENT title (#PCDATA)*>
<!ELEMENT para (#PCDATA)*>
<!ELEMENT notenumber (#PCDATA)*>
<!ELEMENT note (#PCDATA)*>
```

XML tags are added to the raw text of Turner's *Frontier*:

```
<!DOCTYPE doc SYSTEM "doc.dtd">

<doc>
<title>The Frontier in American History</title>

<chapter>
<title>Chapter 2: The First Official Frontier of the Massachusetts
Bay</title>
<para>In "The Significance of the Frontier in American History," I took for
my text the following announcement of the Superintendent of the Census of
1890: "Up to and including 1880 the country had a frontier of settlement but
```

at present the unsettled areas has been so broken into by isolated bodies of settlement that there can hardly be said to be a frontier line. In the discussion of its extent, the westward movement, etc., it cannot therefore any longer have a place in the census reports." Two centuries prior to this announcement, in 1690, a committee of the General Court of Massachusetts recommended the Court to order what shall be the frontier and to maintain a committee to settle garrisons on the frontier with forty soldiers to each frontier town as a main guard.<notenumber>1</notenumber> In the two hundred years between this official attempt to locate the Massachusetts frontier line, and the official announcement of the ending of the national frontier line, westward expansion was the most important single process in American history.</para>
. . .
<note>1. Massachusetts Archives, xxxvi, p. 150.</note>
. . .
</chapter>
. . .

</doc>

An XSL stylesheet specifies how to take each part of this XML document and, by mixing its pieces (as defined in the DTD) with HTML tags, turn them into a new document (technically, an XHTML document) that a web browser can understand:

```
<xsl:stylesheet version = "1.0"
    xmlns:xsl = "http://www.w3.org/1999/XSL/Transform"
    xmlns = "http://www.w3.org/TR/xhtml1/strict">

<xsl:strip-space elements = "doc chapter"/>
<xsl:output
    method = "xml"
    indent = "yes"
    encoding = "iso-8859-1"
/>

<xsl:template match = "doc">
    <html>
      <head>
        <title>
          <xsl:value-of select = "title"/>
        </title>
      </head>
      <body>
        <xsl:apply-templates/>
      </body>
    </html>
</xsl:template>
```

```
<xsl:template match = "doc/title">
  <h1>
    <xsl:apply-templates/>
  </h1>
</xsl:template>

<xsl:template match = "chapter/title">
  <h2>
    <xsl:apply-templates/>
  </h2>
</xsl:template>

<xsl:template match = "para">
  <p>
    <xsl:apply-templates/>
  </p>
</xsl:template>

<xsl:template match = "notenumber">
  <sup>
    <xsl:apply-templates/>
  </sup>
</xsl:template>

<xsl:template match = "note">
  <p class = "note">
    <xsl:apply-templates/>
  </p>
</xsl:template>

</xsl:stylesheet>
```

The resulting document looks like this:

```
<?xml version = "1.0" encoding = "iso-8859-1"?>
<html xmlns = "http://www.w3.org/TR/xhtml1/strict">
   <head>
     <title>The Frontier in American History</title>
   </head>
<body>
   <h1>The Frontier in American History</h1>
   . . .
   <h2>Chapter 2: The First Official Frontier of the Massachusetts
Bay</h2>
<p>In "The Significance of the Frontier in American History," I took for
```
my text the following announcement of the Superintendent of the Census of 1890: "Up to and including 1880 the country had a frontier of settlement but at present the unsettled areas has been so broken into by isolated bodies of settlement that there can hardly be said to be a frontier line. In the discussion

of its extent, the westward movement, etc., it cannot therefore any longer have a place in the census reports." Two centuries prior to this announcement, in 1690, a committee of the General Court of Massachusetts recommended the Court to order what shall be the frontier and to maintain a committee to settle garrisons on the frontier with forty soldiers to each frontier town as a main guard.¹ In the two hundred years between this official attempt to locate the Massachusetts frontier line, and the official announcement of the ending of the national frontier line, westward expansion was the most important single process in American history.</p>
. . .
<p class = "note">1. Massachusetts Archives, xxxvi, p. 150.</p>

. . .
</body>
</html>

In a web browser, this XHTML document would render roughly like this:

The Frontier in American History

. . .

Chapter 2: The First Official Frontier of the Massachusetts Bay

In "The Significance of the Frontier in American History," I took for my text the following announcement of the Superintendent of the Census of 1890: "Up to and including 1880 the country had a frontier of settlement but at present the unsettled areas has been so broken into by isolated bodies of settlement that there can hardly be said to be a frontier line. In the discussion of its extent, the westward movement, etc., it cannot therefore any longer have a place in the census reports." Two centuries prior to this announcement, in 1690, a committee of the General Court of Massachusetts recommended the Court to order what shall be the frontier and to maintain a committee to settle garrisons on the frontier with forty soldiers to each frontier town as a main guard.[1] In the two hundred years between this official attempt to locate the Massachusetts frontier line, and the official announcement of the ending of the national frontier line, westward expansion was the most important single process in American history.

. . .

1. Massachusetts Archives, xxxvi, p. 150.

As you can see, compared to programming languages like ASP or PHP, XSL and XSLT are fairly straightforward text formats like XML and HTML—that is, they are written in plain English, with few embellishments other than colons and brackets. Their syntaxes still require an extra effort to learn, and that effort should not be underestimated, but XSL and XSLT do not require mastering sometimes complex mathematical elements that are found in web programming languages like ASP and PHP, such as arrays, functions, and logic, in addition to linguistic constructions. Nevertheless, if your head is spinning even slightly from this brief discussion of XML/XSL/XSLT, you will likely have to outsource the creation of these more complex documents and translators. Unfortunately, because databases have been around for so much longer than XML and especially XSLT, many more programmers know how to create websites with a database and scripting language than with these newer technologies. Furthermore, many more prepackaged (and often free) web tools using databases rather than XML currently exist. For instance, almost all forum software—which could use either XML or databases—is written for the latter. Tens of thousands of programmers who know how to create websites using the free database software MySQL and the programming language PHP are available; far fewer know XML and XSLT well. This situation will likely change in the coming years, and XML's large following in the digital humanities provides a source from which to draw strength—and, we hope, some advice about implementing this promising technology.

Notes

These notes include references to almost six hundred web pages. To save readers from having to type long web addresses into their browser and from experiencing the frustration of addresses having gone bad, we have created a web/page with links to all of the references here. At **http://chnm.gmu.edu/digitalhis tory/links**, you will find a list of web addresses organized by chapter and note numbers. The websites mentioned in the text are first listed serially. Then, there is a list for the endnotes from each chapter. For example, below you will be referred to "⇒ link 5.7a." (The symbol ⇒ indicates a web link.) That is the web address for Chapter 5, note 7, first reference (a; subsequent references in the same note are b, c, and so on), and you will find the link listed there. If the original link has disappeared, we will refer you to the best available reference for the material. Links in Introduction notes begin with 0 (0.1).

Introduction

1. Lewis J. Perelman, "School's Out: The Hyperlearning Revolution Will Replace Public Education;" John Browning, "Libraries Without Walls for Books Without Pages;" Louis Rosetto, "Why Wired?" all in *Wired Magazine* (March-April 1993), parts of which are available at ⇒ link 0.1.

2. Birkerts in "The Electronic Hive: Two Views," *Harper's Magazine*, May 1994, 17–21, 24–25. See also Birkerts, *The Gutenberg Elegies: The Fate of Reading in an Electronic Age* (Boston: Faber & Faber, 1994).

3. Gertrude Himmelfarb, "A Neo-Luddite Reflects on the Internet," *Chronicle of Higher Education* (1 November 1996), A56; Noble's essay was later reprinted in David Noble, *Digital Diploma Mills: The Automation of Higher Education* (New York: Monthly Review Press, 2001).

4. Even the Internet (and not the web) rates mention in only two articles: Bruce Sterling, "War Is Virtual Hell;" John Browning, "Libraries Without Walls for Books Without Pages," both in *Wired Magazine* (March-April 1993).

5. Phil Agre, "[RRE] Notes and Recommendations," email to "Red Rock Eater News Service" rre@lists.gseis.ucla.edu, 8 August 2000, ⇒ link 0.5.

6. Michael Lesk, "How Much Information Is There in the World?" *Michael Lesk*, ⇒ link 0.6a. See also Roy Rosenzweig, "Scarcity or Abundance? Preserving the Past in a Digital Era," *American Historical Review* 108 (June 2003): 735–62, ⇒ link 0.6b.

7. CHNM and ASHP, *The September 11 Digital Archive*, ⇒ link 0.7. Of course, a long-term increase in traffic of that scale will increase costs (for bandwidth and for support, for example), but not to the same degree as, say, printing ten times as many copies of a book.

8. Library of Congress, *American Memory: Historical Collections for the National*

Digital Library, ⇒ link 0.8a; Academic Affairs Library, University of North Carolina at Chapel Hill, *Documenting the American South,* ⇒ link 0.8b; Joe A. Hewitt, "Remarks," DocSouth 1000th Title Symposium, Chapel Hill, North Carolina, 1 March 2002, ⇒ link 0.8c.

9. See, for example, Kevin Roe's website *Brainerd, Kansas: Time, Place and Memory on the Prairie Plains,* ⇒ link 0.9.

10. Lev Manovich, *The Language of New Media* (Cambridge, Mass.: MIT Press, 2001), 36, 214. As Jim Sparrow has pointed out to us, this, in effect, reverses Walter Benjamin's famous argument in "The Work of Art in the Age of Mechanical Reproduction" that an "authentic" original is essential to our valuation of art as a "priceless" work of human creativity. For Benjamin, "mechanical reproduction" erased value, but here it unleashes the collective process of interpretation, debate, and memory from which genuine historical value flows. In other words, access harnesses and democratizes the collective work that undergirds the production of historical knowledge.

11. Amanda Lenhart, John Horrigan, and Deborah Fallows, *Content Creation Online* (Washington, D.C.: Pew Internet and American Life Project, 2004), ⇒ link 0.11a; *Technorati,* ⇒ link 0.11b counted 7,130,059 blogs on 17 February 2005.

12. Roger Norton, *Abraham Lincoln Research Site,* ⇒ link 0.12. Norton was first between June 2003 and July 2004 but has since slipped to number three.

13. Janet H. Murray, *Hamlet on the Holodeck: The Future of Narrative in Cyberspace* (New York: Free Press, 1997), 66.

14. Ethan Bronner, "You Can Look It Up, Hopefully," *New York Times,* 10 January 1999; Daniel J. Cohen, "By the Book: Assessing the Place of Textbooks in U.S. Survey Courses," *Journal of American History* 91 (March 2005): 1405-1415, ⇒ link 0.14.

15. Jerome McGann, *Radiant Textuality: Literature After the World Wide Web,* (New York: Palgrave, 2001), 84–85. For a brief overview of the state of content-based image retrieval, see Humanities Advanced Technology and Information Institute and National Initiative for a Networked Cultural Heritage, *The NINCH Guide to Good Practice in the Digital Representation and Management of Cultural Heritage Materials,* 45, ⇒ link 0.15.

16. Michael Frisch, *A Shared Authority: Essays on the Craft and Meaning of Oral and Public History* (Albany: State University of New York Press, 1990). See also Roy Rosenzweig and David Thelen, *The Presence of the Past: Popular Uses of History in American Life* (New York: Columbia University Press, 1998).

17. George P. Landow, *Hypertext 2.0* (Baltimore: Johns Hopkins University Press, 1997), 89, 2.

18. Himmelfarb, "A Neo-Luddite Reflects on the Internet"; James William Brodman, "E-Publishing: Prospects, Promises, and Pitfalls," *Perspectives* (February 2000), ⇒ link 0.18.

19. Kent Lassman, "Tech Bytes—Tid Bits in Tech News: Endangering Life and Limb . . . At Breakneck Speed," *Citizens for a Sound Economy,* ⇒ link 0.19a (In July 2004 Citizens for a Sound Economy and Empower America merged to form FreedomWorks, and the article is on their joint website); Bob McTeer, "The Great Trade Debates and What's at Stake" (remarks delivered at the World Affairs Council and Texas International Trade Alliance, Houston, Texas, 10 October 2000), ⇒ link 0.19b; David Bearman and Jennifer Trant, "Authentic-

ity of Digital Resources: Towards a Statement of Requirements in the Research Process," *D-Lib Magazine* 4, no. 6 (June 1998), ⇒ link 0.19c.

20. One website with this photo is *ArteMedia*, ⇒ link 0.20.

21. Rosenzweig, "Scarcity or Abundance?"; Jeffrey Benner, "Is U.S. History Becoming History?" *Wired News* (9 April 2001), ⇒ link 0.21a. Not until January 2005 did the National Archives finally issue guidelines on the archiving of the millions of government web pages. "NARA Guidance on Managing Web Records, January 2005," *NARA, U.S. National Archives and Records Administration,* ⇒ link 0.21b.

22. Birkerts, *The Gutenberg Elegies*; Roy Rosenzweig, "Crashing the System: Hypertext and American Studies Scholarship," *American Quarterly* 51 (June 1999): 237–46. Business historian Austin Kerr wrote in an online response to the online *AQ* essays: "a few moments was enough. . . . I certainly did not feel comfortable trying to read this one example." Sony's recently (2004) released Librie, which offers resolution of 600 x 800 dots at 170 dpi, provides a glimpse of things to come. J. Mark Lytle, "Library Without Books," *Guardian* (22 April 2004).

23. Espen J. Aarseth, *Cybertext: Perspectives on Ergodic Literature* (Baltimore: Johns Hopkins University Press, 1997); Philip J. Ethington, "Los Angeles and the Problem of Urban Historical Knowledge," *American Historical Review* 105 (December 2000), ⇒ link 0.23.

24. Rosenzweig, "Crashing the System."

25. ⇒ link 0.25; Lawrence Lessig, *The Future of Ideas: The Fate of the Commons in a Connected World* (New York: Random House, 2001), 7; Harold Bloom, *How to Read and Why* (New York: Scribner's, 2001).

26. On the digital divide, see Mark N. Cooper, *Does the Digital Divide Still Exist? Bush Administration Shrugs, But Evidence Says Yes* (Washington, D.C.: Consumer Federation of America, 2002), ⇒ link 0.26a; Jeffrey Benner, "Bush Plan 'Digital Distortion'," *Wired News* (7 February 2002), ⇒ link 0.26b; Eszter Hargittai, "Second-Level Digital Divide: Differences in People's Online Skills," *First Monday* 7, no. 4 (April 2002), ⇒ link 0.26c.

27. Roy Rosenzweig, "The Road to Xanadu: Public and Private Pathways on the History Web," *Journal of American History* 88 (September 2001): 548–79, ⇒ link 0.27a. For example, the list price for Thomson Corporation's eighteenth-century digital collection begins at $500,000: Kinley Levack, "Digital ECCOs of the Eighteenth Century," *EContentmag.com* (November 2003), ⇒ link 0.27b. Jeffrey Cymerint, interview, 1 August 2003. See also Barbara Quint, "Gale Group to Digitize Most 18th-Century English-Language Books, Doubles Info Trac Holdings," *Information Today* (17 June 2002), ⇒ link 0.27c.

28. *Budapest Open Access Initiative,* ⇒ link 0.28.

29. Roy Rosenzweig, Steve Brier, and Josh Brown, *Who Built America? From the Centennial of 1876 to the Great War of 1914,* multimedia CD-ROM (New York: Voyager, 1993). The CHNM home page (⇒ link 0.29) provides a portal to these different projects. Those done in collaboration with ASHP include the CD-ROM *Who Built America? From the Great War of 1914 to the Dawn of the Atomic Age in 1946* and the websites: *History Matters: The U.S. Survey Course on the Web; Liberty, Equality, Fraternity: Exploring the French Revolution;* and the *September 11 Digital Archive.* CHNM's other projects include *World History Matters,* the *Blackout History Project,* and *Echo: Exploring and Collecting History Online—Science, Technology, and Industry.*

CHNM also hosts projects which have been developed by others, including *DoHistory, History News Network,* and the *Business Plan Archive.*

Chapter 1. Exploring the History Web

1. Morris A. Pierce, email to Roy Rosenzweig, 23 June 2003; George Welling, "Information: About the Project," *From Revolution to Reconstruction,* ⇒ link 1.1; George Welling, email to Roy Rosenzweig, 22 June 2003.

2. Donald J. Mabry, "History of the HTA," *Historical Text Archive,* ⇒ link 1.2a; Lynn Nelson, "Before the Web: The Early Development of History On-line," *La Societa Italiana per lo Studio della Storia Contemporanea (SISSCO),* 19 May 2000, ⇒ link 1.2b; Lynn Nelson, "Gods, Heroes, & Legends: Lynn Nelson in His Own Words," *Gods, Heroes, & Legends,* ⇒ link 1.2c; Lynn Nelson, "HNSOURCE now open for business," email to Medieval History Listserv, 20 March 1993, ⇒ link 1.2d; *About the WWW-VL: United States History Network,* ⇒ link 1.2e; Lynn Nelson, "Carrie: A Full-Text Online Library," *ASSOCIATE: The Electronic Library Support Staff Journal,* ⇒ link 1.2f ; Lynn Nelson, email to Joan Fragaszy, 18 August 2003; Joni Makivirta, email to Roy Rosenzweig, 21 March 2004. See also Donald J. Mabry, "Electronic Mail and Historians," *Perspectives* (February 1991), 1, 4, 6.

3. National Digital Library Program, "A Periodic Report from the National Digital Library Program," *Library of Congress,* October 1995, ⇒ link 1.3a; Marilyn Parr, "American Memory—Then and Now" (paper presented at the Organization of American Historians Annual Meeting, Memphis, 4 April 2003). Our own involvement in digital history started with the "new media" of CD-ROM. One of us (Roy) began in 1990 to work with colleagues at the American Social History Project (especially Steve Brier and Josh Brown) and the Voyager Company on a CD-ROM history of the United States, *Who Built America?* which appeared in 1993. On CD-ROMs, see Roy Rosenzweig, "So, What's Next for Clio? CD-ROM and Historians," *Journal of American History* 81 (March 1995), ⇒ link 1.3b.

4. "The Rise and Rise of the Redmond Empire," *Wired Magazine* 6.12 (December 1998), ⇒ link 1.4a; "Netscape Through the Ages," *Wired News* (23 November 1998), ⇒ link 1.4b.

5. Andrew McMichael, Michael O'Malley, and Roy Rosenzweig, "Historians and the Web: A Guide," *Perspectives* (January 1996), 11–16.

6. Michael O'Malley and Roy Rosenzweig, "Brave New World or Blind Alley? American History on the World Wide Web," *Journal of American History* 84 (June 1997), ⇒ link 1.6a; Larry Stevens, *Ohio in the Civil War,* ⇒ link 1.6b; "Nicolas Pioch," *WebMuseum,* ⇒ link 1.6c; "Introduction," *Marxists Internet Archive,* ⇒ link 1.6d; Brian Basgen, email to Joan Fragaszy, 8 August 2003; "Constitution Society Home Page," *Constitution Society,* ⇒ link 1.6e.

7. George H. Hoemann, "The American Civil War Homepage," *The American Civil War,* ⇒ link 1.7.

8. On OpenCourseWare, see David Diamond, "MIT Everyware," *Wired News* (September 2003), ⇒ link 1.8.

9. *About the WWW-VL: United States History Network*; Ken Middleton, *American Women's History: A Research Guide,* ⇒ link 1.9a; Dennis Boals, *History/Social Studies for K-12 Teachers,* ⇒ link 1.9b; CHNM and ASHP, *History Matters: The U.S. Survey Course on the Web,* ⇒ link 1.9c; *Best of History Web Sites,* ⇒ link 1.9d.

10. O'Malley and Rosenzweig, "Brave New World or Blind Alley?"; "Discovery .com Workers Get Pink Slips," *Los Angeles Times,* 14 November 2000; Randy Rieland, email to Roy Rosenzweig, 4 August 2003.

11. Philip E. Agre, "Designing Genres for New Media: Social, Economic, and Political Contexts," in Steve Jones, ed., *CyberSociety 2.0: Revisiting Computer Media Community and Technology* (Thousand Oaks, Calif.: Sage, 1998), 79–81, 70.

12. See William J. Maher, "Society and Archives" (Presidential Address delivered at the 61st Annual Meeting of the Society of American Archivists, Chicago, 30 August 1997), ⇒ link 1.12a; "Cataloger's Reference Shelf: Definition: Provenance," *The Library Corporation,* ⇒ link 1.12b.

13. Caroline R. Arms, "Historical Collections for the National Digital Library: Lessons and Challenges at the Library of Congress," *D-Lib Magazine* (April 1996), ⇒ link 1.13.

14. Roy Rosenzweig, "The Road to Xanadu: Public and Private Pathways on the History Web," *Journal of American History* 88 (September 2001), ⇒ link 1.14.

15. *Gallica 2000,* ⇒ link 1.15a; *Picture Australia,* ⇒ link 1.15b; *Digital Imaging Project of South Africa,* ⇒ link 1.15c; *International Dunhuang Project,* ⇒ link 1.15d; "Japanese Old Photographs in Bakumatsu-Meiji Period," *Nagasaki University Old-Picture Database,* ⇒ link 1.15e.

16. Joe A. Hewitt, "Remarks," DocSouth 1000th Title Symposium, Chapel Hill, N.C., 1 March 2002, ⇒ link 1.16.

17. Humanities Advanced Technology and Information Institute (HATII) and National Initiative for a Networked Cultural Heritage, *The NINCH Guide to Good Practice in the Digital Representation and Management of Cultural Heritage Materials—Interview Reports* (Washington, D.C.: National Initiative for a Networked Cultural Heritage, 2002), ⇒ link 1.17; Gelber quoted in Rosenzweig, "The Road to Xanadu."

18. "The American Family Immigration History Center Fact Sheet," *American Family Immigration History Center,* ⇒ link 1.18a; Statue of Liberty–Ellis Island Foundation, *Annual Report, Year Ended March 31, 2003* (New York, 2003), 5; "Facts and Statistics," *FamilySearch Internet Genealogy Service,* ⇒ link 1.18b; "Free Internet Access to Invaluable Indexes of American and Canadian Heritage," *Church of Jesus Christ of Latter-day Saints,* ⇒ link 1.18c; ⇒ link 1.18d.

19. Edward Ayers, "Living in the Valley of the Shadow" (forthcoming book chapter in possession of authors); Edward Ayers, email to Roy Rosenzweig, 25 August 2003; Jerome McGann, *Radiant Textuality: Literature After the World Wide Web* (New York: Palgrave, 2001).

20. Jim Zwick, email to Roy Rosenzweig, 27 November 2000; Jim Zwick, email to Rosenzweig, 4 August 2003.

21. Jim Zwick, "'The White Man's Burden' and Its Critics," in *Anti-Imperialism in the United States, 1898–1935,* ⇒ link 1.21a; "Marxists Internet Archive History," *Marxists Internet Archive,* ⇒ link 1.21b. (Zwick's site was first when we wrote this in 2004, but it had dropped out of the top ranks by early 2005, possibly because of readjustments in Google's ranking system.)

22. Douglas Linder, "Goals and Purposes of the Famous Trials Site," *Famous Trials,* ⇒ link 1.22.

23. Paul Halsall, "Main Page," *Internet Modern History Sourcebook,* ⇒ link 1.23a; Paul Halsall, "Medieval Sourcebook: Introduction," *Internet Medieval Sourcebook,* ⇒ link 1.23b.

24. Peter Bakewell, "Culpepper Project Summary," *Culpepper/CTC Program in Teaching & Technology,* ⇒ link 1.24a; Eyler Robert Coates, Sr., "Information on

Eyler Robert Coates, Sr.," *Thomas Jefferson and His Writings,* ⇒ link 1.24b; "Web Server Statistics," *Electronic Text Center—University of Virginia Library,* ⇒ link 1.24c; Stefan Landsberger, *Chinese Propaganda Posters,* ⇒ link 1.24d; Omar Khan, Jim McCall, and Andrew Deonarine, *Harappa: The Indus Valley and the Raj in India and Pakistan,* ⇒ link 1.24e; Meeta Chaitanya Bhatnagar, "Omar Khan in Conversation," *HindustanTimes.com* (15 December 2002), ⇒ link 1.24f.

25. Deborah Markham, "Retirement Project Puts Historic Publications on the Web," *Hamptons Roads Business,* 24 March 2003, ⇒ link 1.25a. See also Randall Rothenberg, "HarpWeek Pitches U.S. History to Teens—and Marketers As Well," *Advertising Age,* 18 October 1999, ⇒ link 1.25b.

26. Jeffrey Cymerint, interview, 1 August 2003; "Gale's Biggest Digitization Project Ever Covers Eighteenth Century," *Gale Press Room,* ⇒ link 1.26a; Barbara Quint, "Gale Group to Digitize Most 18th-Century English-Language Books, Doubles Info Trac Holdings," *Information Today, Inc.* (17 June 2002), ⇒ link 1.26b.

27. Rosenzweig, "The Road to Xanadu"; "ProQuest Historical Newspapers Preview," *ProQuest Information and Learning,* ⇒ link 1.27a; "Google's Gigantic Library Project," *SPARC Open Access Newsletter,* 81 (2 January 2005), ⇒ link 1.27b.

28. National Portrait Gallery, *George Washington: A National Treasure,* ⇒ link 1.28a; Smithsonian American Art Museum, "Metropolitan Lives: The Ashcan Artists and Their New York," *Smithsonian American Art Museum,* ⇒ link 1.28b; New Jersey Historical Society in conjunction with ASHP, *What Exit? New Jersey and Its Turnpike,* ⇒ link 1.28c.

29. Rob Semper, "Bringing Authentic Museum Experience to the Web" (paper presented at the Museums and the Web 1998, Toronto, April 1998), ⇒ link 1.29.

30. James Allen, "Without Sanctuary: Lynching Photography in America," *Musarium.* We viewed this site a number of times between 2000 and 2004, but it was no longer available on the web as of August 2004.

31. Smithsonian Institution Office of Policy and Analysis, *September 11: Bearing Witness to History: Three Studies of an Exhibition at NMAH,* ⇒ link 1.31.

32. "Devices of Wonder," *The Getty Center Exhibitions,* ⇒ link 1.32a; Logan Museum of Anthropology, *A World of Art: Museum of Virtual Objects,* ⇒ link 1.32b; *The Antique Motorcycle Club of America,* ⇒ link 1.32c; John Kantner, "Sipapu— Chetro Ketl Great Kiva," *Sipapu—The Anasazi Emergence into the Cyber World,* ⇒ link 1.32d; Smithsonian National Museum of American History, *Bon Appétit: Julia Child's Kitchen at the Smithsonian,* ⇒ link 1.32e; Smithsonian National Museum of American History, *The Star-Spangled Banner,* ⇒ link 1.32f.

33. Chicago Historical Society and Northwestern University, *The Great Chicago Fire and the Web of Memory,* ⇒ link 1.33a. The same partners produced *The Dramas of Haymarket,* an even richer archive since the narrative site was produced in conjunction with the creation of the Haymarket Affair Digital Collection, a project supported by the Library of Congress/Ameritech National Digital Library Competition, ⇒ link 1.33b. Southern Utah University, *Voices of the Colorado Plateau,* ⇒ link 1.33c.

34. John Mack Faragher, "The Oregon Trail," *History Matters: The U.S. Survey Course on the Web,* ⇒ link 1.34a; Donald A. Ritchie, "The American President," *History Matters: The U.S. Survey Course on the Web,* ⇒ link 1.34b.

35. Robert B. Townsend, "Scholarship, History, and the New Media," unpublished paper submitted in fulfillment of New Media minor field requirement at George Mason University, in possession of authors.

36. Stefan Blaschke, "Periodicals Directory: Electronical Index: E-Journals," *The History Journals Guide*, ⇒ link 1.36a; Stephen Railton, "Common-Place: The Interactive Journal of Early American Life," *History Matters: The U.S. Survey Course on the Web*, ⇒ link 1.36b; data provided by Richard Shenkman, email to Roy Rosenzweig, 18 July 2003.

37. Robert Darnton, "An Early Information Society: News and the Media in Eighteenth-Century Paris," *American Historical Review* 105 (February 2000), ⇒ link 1.37.

38. Michael Katten, *Colonial Lists/Indian Power: Identity Politics in Nineteenth Century Telugu-Speaking India* (New York: Columbia University Press, 2001), ⇒ link 1.38a. Ignacio Gallup-Diaz, *The Door of the Seas and Key to the Universe: Indian Politics and Imperial Rivalry in the Darien, 1640–1750* (New York: Columbia University Press, 2001), ⇒ link 1.38b; Eileen Gardiner and Ronald Musto, "ACLS History E-Book Project," *OAH Newsletter* (August 2003), ⇒ link 1.38c.

39. Roy Rosenzweig, "Crashing the System: Hypertext and American Studies Scholarship," *American Quarterly* 51 (June 1999): 237–46; Louise Krasniewicz and Michael Blitz, "Why We Did Not Produce 'Dreaming Arnold Schwarzenegger' as a Book, Several Articles, an Encyclopedia, a Video, an Annotated Bibliography, and a Museum Installation (or Did We?)," *American Quarterly* 51 (June 1999): 258–67.

40. Philip J. Ethington, "Los Angeles and the Problem of Urban Historical Knowledge," *American Historical Review* 105 (December 2000), ⇒ link 1.40a; William G. Thomas III and Edward L. Ayers, "The Differences Slavery Made: A Close Analysis of Two American Communities," *American Historical Review* 108 (December 2003), ⇒ link 1.40b.

41. Jorn Barger, "Weblog Resources FAQ," *Robot Wisdom Weblog*, ⇒ link 1.41.

42. "History Blogs," *History News Network*, ⇒ link 1.42a; *POTUS*, ⇒ link 1.42b; *Invisible Adjunct*, ⇒ link 1.42c; *Epistemographer*, ⇒ link 1.42d; *Paleojudaica.com*, ⇒ link 1.42e. See also Scott Smallwood, "Disappearing Act: The Invisible Adjunct Shuts Down Her Popular Weblog and Says Goodbye to Academe," *Chronicle of Higher Education* (30 April 2004), ⇒ link 1.42f; *Wikipedia, The Free Encyclopedia*, ⇒ link 1.42g.

43. *TheHistoryNet.com*, ⇒ link 1.43.

44. William G. Thomas and Alice E. Carter, *The Civil War on the Web: A Guide to the Very Best Sites* (Wilmington, Del.: Scholarly Resources, 2001), xviii, 147–53.

45. Scott Alexander, *Red Hot Jazz Archive*, ⇒ link 1.45a; Kevin Roe, *Brainerd, Kansas: Time, Place and Memory on the Prairie Plains*, ⇒ link 1.45b.

46. Thomas and Carter, *The Civil War on the Web*, xvii, xix.

47. "The Learning Page," *American Memory from the Library of Congress*, ⇒ link 1.47a; U.S. National Archives and Records Administration, *Digital Classroom*, ⇒ link 1.47b; the Educational Resources Information Center (ERIC) lists more than twenty gateway sites for history lesson plans. Some of the notable compendia can be found at NEH's *Edsitement, History Matters: The U.S. Survey Course on the Web*, the National Park Service's *Teaching with Historic Places*, and the Dirksen Congressional Center's *CongressLink*.

48. See Paula Petrik, "Top Ten Mistakes in Academic Web Design," *History Computer Review* (May 2000), ⇒ link 1.48a; Daniel J. Cohen, "By the Book: Assessing the Place of Textbooks in U.S. Survey Courses," *Journal of American History* 91 (March 2005): 1405-1415, ⇒ link 1.48b.

49. Michael O'Malley, *Jacksonian Democracy*, ⇒ link 1.49a; *Between the Wars*, ⇒ link 1.49b; *History 120*, ⇒ link 1.49c; *Magic, Illusion, Detection*, ⇒ link 1.49d.

50. Center for the Historical Study of Women and Gender, *Women and Social Movements in the United States, 1775-2000*, ⇒ link 1.50a; National Humanities Center, *TeacherServe*, ⇒ link 1.50b. More recently, half of the Women and Social Movements site has been moved to a commercial and gated site run by Alexander Street Press.

51. Randy Bass and Roy Rosenzweig, "Rewiring the History and Social Studies Classroom: Needs, Frameworks, Dangers, and Proposals," *Journal of Education* 181.3 (1999), ⇒ link 1.51a; *History Matters: The U.S. Survey Course on the Web*, ⇒ link 1.51b; CHNM, *World History Matters*, ⇒ link 1.51c.

52. ASHP, *The Lost Museum*, ⇒ link 1.52a; Ruth Sandwell and John Lutz, *Who Killed William Robinson?* ⇒ link 1.52b.

53. Mark Kornbluh and Peter Knupfer, "H-Net Ten Years On: Usage, Impact and the Problems of Professionalization in New Media" (paper presented at the Annual Meeting of the American Historical Association, Chicago, January 2003), ⇒ link 1.53a; "soc.history," *Google Groups*, ⇒ link 1.53b. On early networks, see also Nelson, "Before the Web"; Mabry, "Electronic Mail and Historians," 1, 4, 6.

54. *American Historical Association*, ⇒ link 1.54a; *Wisconsin Historical Society*, ⇒ link 1.54b; *Third Regiment Infantry, Maryland Volunteers, Company A*, 2003, ⇒ link 1.54c; "Guide to History Departments," *Center for History and New Media*, ⇒ link 1.54d.

55. Thomas Jefferson Foundation, *Monticello: The Home of Thomas Jefferson*, ⇒ link 1.55a; National Park Service, "Links to the Past: National Park Service Cultural Resources," *National Park Service*, ⇒ link 1.55b.

56. Stephen Railton, "Preface-in-Progress," *Mark Twain in His Times*, ⇒ link 1.56a; Stephen Railton, "Credits," *Uncle Tom's Cabin & American Culture*, ⇒ link 1.56b; Film Study Center, Harvard University, *DoHistory: Martha Ballard's Diary Online*, ⇒ link 1.56c.

Chapter 2. Getting Started

1. Douglas County Historical Society, *Watkins Museum*, ⇒ link 2.1a; Rich Skrenta, "The Secret Source of Google's Power," *Topix.net Weblog*, ⇒ link 2.1b.

2. New Deal Network, *New Deal Network*, ⇒ link 2.2.

3. Jorge Luis Borges, *The Library of Babel* (Boston: David R. Godine, 2000).

4. Paula Petrik, "MS Word to Web Page: The Syllabus," ⇒ link 2.4.

5. "The Sixties-L Discussion List," *The Sixties Project*, ⇒ link 2.5a; MATRIX, *H-Net: Humanities and Social Sciences Online*, ⇒ link 2.5b.

6. Petrik, "MS Word to Web Page"; "Save Your Office 2000 File as a Web Page," *Microsoft*, ⇒ link 2.6a. Though it may be easy to convert Microsoft Office documents to web documents, the resulting HTML may not be especially concise or easy to maintain or update. Using a program like HTML Tidy (available at ⇒ link 2.6b) to "clean up" a converted document may be useful.

7. "Macromedia Dreamweaver MX," *Macromedia*, ⇒ link 2.7a; "Microsoft Office: FrontPage," *Microsoft*, ⇒ link 2.7b; Jeffrey Zeldman, *Designing with Web Standards* (Indianapolis: New Riders, 2003), 119–20; *Mozilla.org–Home of Mozilla, Firefox, Thunderbird, and Camino*, ⇒ link 2.7c.

8. *EditPlus Text Editor, HTML Editor, Programmers Editor for Windows*, ⇒ link 2.8a; "UltraEdit," *IDM Computer Solutions Inc.*, ⇒ link 2.8b; "BBEdit," *Bare Bone Software*, ⇒ link 2.8c. These programs can color-code and automatically generate

certain commonly used HTML tags, which greatly facilitates the web design process. If you or others are planning on doing some website programming with databases, XML, or scripting languages (see below), one of these advanced text editors is even more helpful, though Dreamweaver can handle modest chunks of such code. Notepad, the venerable free program that comes with all Windows computers, can also function as a rudimentary web editor for those who really know what they are doing or for those who just need to make a quick edit or two to web pages that have already been built in Dreamweaver or FrontPage.

9. Specific blogging programs and hosts are covered in Chapter 6. For a comprehensive list of both software and hosts, see "Blog Tools" and "Blog Hosting," *Weblogs Compendium*, ⇒ link 2.9a and ⇒ link 2.9b.

10. "Photoshop: Professional Photo Editing Software," *Adobe*, ⇒ link 2.10a; "Adobe Photoshop Elements: Photo Editing Software," *Adobe*, ⇒ link 2.10b; "Macromedia Fireworks MX," *Macromedia*, ⇒ link 2.10c.

11. Market share from one 2004 report shows Microsoft and Apple essentially tied for first place, followed by RealNetworks: Microsoft Media Player, 38.2%; Apple QuickTime, 36.8%; RealNetworks Real Player, 24.9%. Michael Singer, "Apple Readies Next-Gen MPEG-4 Part 10," *InternetNews*, 11 June 2004, ⇒ link 2.11a; *RealNetworks*, ⇒ link 2.11b; "Windows Media," ⇒ link 2.11c; "Quick-Time," *Apple*, ⇒ link 2.11d. Several open source multimedia formats, such as Ogg Vorbis (⇒ link 2.11e) for Audio, are free for both producers and end users, but very few people have downloaded the necessary programs to create, listen to, or watch these marginal formats.

12. Dan Arthurs, email to Dan Cohen, 20 August 2004.

13. "The Faws: What Streaming Video/Audio Formats Are Available?" *film-making.net*, ⇒ link 2.13a; "Designing Web Audio: Chapter 5: Introduction to Streaming Media," *O'Reilly Online Catalog*, ⇒ link 2.13b; "Tips and Tricks: Streaming Media Options for the World Wide Web," *Catalyst*, ⇒ link 2.13c.

14. Arthurs, email; Mary Ide, Dave MacCarn, Thom Shepard, and Leah Weisse, "Understanding the Preservation Challenge of Digital Television," in *Building a National Strategy for Preservation: Issues in Digital Media Archiving* (Washington, D.C.: Council on Library and Information Resources and the Library of Congress, 2002), 67–79, ⇒ link 2.14a; Howard D. Wactlar and Michael G. Christel, "Digital Video Archives: Managing Through Metadata," in *Building a National Strategy for Preservation*, 80–95, ⇒ link 2.14b.

15. *The Sonic Memorial Project*, ⇒ link 2.15.

16. "Macromedia Flash MX," *Macromedia*, ⇒ link 2.16a. Macromedia has recently tried to improve the accessibility of Flash. See "Accessibility and Macromedia Flash MX 2004," ⇒ link 2.16b, and Bob Regan's blog on accessibility for Macromedia products, ⇒ link 2.16c.

17. "Remembering Pearl Harbor," *National Geographic*, ⇒ link 2.17a; *Theban Mapping Project*, ⇒ link 2.17b.

18. "Not for Ourselves Alone: The Story of Elizabeth Cady Stanton and Susan B. Anthony," *PBS*, ⇒ link 2.18.

19. *Yahoo GeoCities*, ⇒ link 2.19a; *Web Host Directory*, ⇒ link 2.19b.

20. For instance, if a university's web server has 100 gigabytes of hard drive space, and the school gives 10 megabytes of website space to each student or faculty member, they can simultaneously host 10,000 people on that server. Although this is economical for the university, common sense dictates, however, that there may be problems with hosting so many sites on one machine. Not only do those 10,000 students and professors share hard drive space (not really

a problem), they also share the total speed, activity, and Internet connection of that computer. Powerful though it may be, if there are 100 very popular sites within the combined production of those 10,000 people (as one would hope at a thriving university), the "traffic" to *all* of the sites becomes slower, as if everyone in a large lecture hall asked a question of the professor at the same time and waited impatiently for an answer. Generally this is not a big issue given the "question-answering capacity" of modern servers, but it does matter in certain circumstances. If you are worried about the complications of sharing a server, be sure to ask your host (institution, ISP, company) about how many sites or individuals they house on a single server and what the overall server load ("traffic") is for that server. Also ask for the URLs of a few sites on the server and try them *at different times of the day* in your browser. How responsive do the sites seem? If you can't tell the difference and the sites load easily, you should be fine (unless you are planning a major site with major traffic).

21. A new protocol for Internet addresses, called IPv6, uses a longer set of numbers and letters, and will likely supplant the current IPv4 in the future. See *IPv6: The Next Generation Internet,* ⇒ link 2.21a; Hubert Feyrer, "Introduction to IPv6," *ONLamp,* ⇒ link 2.21b.

22. A constantly updated list of accredited registrars can be found on the InterNIC website, ⇒ link 2.22a, and the ICANN website, ⇒ link 2.22b.

23. *Dotster,* ⇒ link 2.23a; *GoDaddy.com,* ⇒ link 2.23b.

24. *The Sonic Memorial Project,* ⇒ link 2.24a; Stephen Railton, *Mark Twain in His Times,* ⇒ link 2.24b.

25. "AODL Grant Info," *National Gallery of the Spoken Word,* ⇒ link 2.25a; audio collections created by this project can be found at ⇒ link 2.25b.

26. "Libraries and Scholarly Communication," *The Andrew Mellon Foundation,* ⇒ link 2.26. Mellon also has a program in "teaching and technology" but it focuses on higher education.

Chapter 3. Becoming Digital

1. Barbara Quint, "Gale Group to Digitize Most 18th-Century English-Language Books, Doubles Info Trac Holdings," *Information Today, Inc.* (17 June 2002), ⇒ link 3.1a; Kinley Levack, "Digital ECCOs of the Eighteenth Century," *EContentmag.com* (November 2003), ⇒ link 3.1b; "Google's Gigantic Library Project," *SPARC Open Access Newsletter,* 81 (2 January 2005), ⇒ link 3.1c. An even more ambitious, multibillion-dollar digitization effort is proposed by the Digital Promise Project: *Creating the Digital Opportunity Investment Trust (DO IT), A Proposal to Transform Learning and Training for the 21st Century* (Washington, D.C., 2003).

2. Digital Library Forum, *A Framework of Guidance for Building Good Digital Collections* (Washington, D.C.: Institute of Museum and Library Services, 2001), ⇒ link 3.2a. This chapter is indebted to the many excellent digitization reports and handbooks, including especially Humanities Advanced Technology and Information Institute and National Initiative for a Networked Cultural Heritage, *The NINCH Guide to Good Practice in the Digital Representation and Management of Cultural Heritage Materials* (Washington, D.C.: National Initiative for a Networked Cultural Heritage, 2002) ⇒ link 3.2b, (hereafter cited as *NINCH Guide*); and Maxine K. Sitts, ed., *Handbook for Digital Projects: A Management Tool for Preservation and Access,* 1st ed. (Andover, Mass.: Northeast Document Conservation Cen-

ter, 2000), ⇒ link 3.2c. See also Western States Digital Standards Group Digital Imaging Working Group, *Western States Digital Imaging Best Practices, Version 1.0* (University of Denver and the Colorado Digitization Program; Denver, 2003), ⇒ link 3.2d (hereafter *Western States Digital Imaging*); Alan Morrison, Michael Popham, and Karen Wikander, *Creating and Documenting Electronic Texts: A Guide to Good Practice* (London: Arts and Humanities Data Service, 2000), ⇒ link 3.2e (hereafter *Creating and Documenting Electronic Texts*); and the various documents listed at "Digital Library Standards and Practices," *Digital Library Federation*, ⇒ link 3.2f.

3. Abby Smith, *Why Digitize?* (Washington, D.C.: Council on Library and Information Resources, 1999), 1. See similarly Paul Conway, "Overview: Rationale for Digitization and Preservation," in Sitts, ed., *Handbook for Digital Projects*, 16.

4. Smith, *Why Digitize?* 2. See also *NINCH Guide*, 227; "Analog Versus Digital: The Difference Between Signals and Data," Vermont Telecom Advancement Center, ⇒ link 3.4; Steven Puglia, "Technical Primer," in Sitts, ed., *Handbook for Digital Projects*, 93–95. Digital imaging cannot reproduce the chemical, biological, or textual makeup of the analog form, which allows, for example, carbon dating or fingerprint identification.

5. *NINCH Guide*, 228–30.

6. University of Georgia Language Laboratories, "The Great Analog Versus Digital Debate," *VoicePrint Online*, viewed online April 2004, but not available as of September 2004.

7. Nicholson Baker, "Discards: Annals of Scholarship," *New Yorker* (4 April 1994), 64–86.

8. "[Conversation in a Park]," *American Life Histories: Manuscripts from the Federal Writers' Projects, 1936–1940*, ⇒ link 3.8; *NINCH Guide*, 230.

9. Smith, *Why Digitize?* provides an excellent overview.

10. Steve Puglia, "Revisiting Costs" (paper presented at The Price of Digitization: New Cost Models for Cultural and Educational Institutions, New York City, 8 April 2003), ⇒ link 3.10a. See also Steven Puglia, "The Costs of Digital Imaging Projects," *RLG DigiNews* 3.5 (15 October 1999), ⇒ link 3.10b.

11. Joan Echtenkamp Klein and Linda M. Lisanti, *Digitizing History: The Final Report of the IMLS Philip S. Hench Walter Reed and Yellow Fever Collection Digitization Project* (Charlottesville: Claude Moore Health Sciences Library, University of Virginia Health System, 2001), ⇒ link 3.11a. For a detailed discussion of selection criteria and procedures, see Diane Vogt-O'Connor, "Selection of Material for Scanning," in Sitts, ed., *Handbook for Digital Projects*, 45–73; *Assessing the Costs of Conversion: Making of America IV: The American Voice 1850–1876* (Ann Arbor: University of Michigan Digital Library Services, 2001), 6, ⇒ link 3.11b.

12. Ricky L. Erway, "Options for Digitizing Visual Materials," in *Going Digital: Strategies for Access, Preservation, and Conversion of Collections to a Digital Format*, ed. Donald L. DeWitt (New York: Haworth Press, 1998), 124; Smith, *Why Digitize?* 8; "Original Plan of Washington, D.C.," *American Treasures of the Library of Congress*, ⇒ link 3.12. According to Franziska Frey, "Millions of negatives are never used only because their image content is not readily available to the user." "Working with Photographs," Sitts, ed., *Handbook for Digital Projects*, 122.

13. The library reported 8,890,221 "hits" from June to December 2003, but it appears that they really mean "visits." Marilyn K. Parr, email to Roy Rosenzweig, 7 May 2004; *Annual Report of the Librarian of Congress 2001* (Washington, D.C.: Library of Congress, 2001), 102, 121 ⇒ link 3.13.

14. Smith, *Why Digitize?* 12; Society of American Archivists Council, *The Preservation of Digitized Reproductions* (Chicago: Society of American Archivists, 1997), ⇒ link 3.14; Christina Powell, email to Roy Rosenzweig, 4 August 2004.

15. *NINCH Guide*, 40–41; Kevin Kiernan, "Electronic Beowulf," *University of Kentucky*, ⇒ link 3.15; Douglas Heingartner, "A Computer That Has an Eye for Van Gogh," *New York Times*, 13 June 2004, Arts & Leisure section, 1.

16. "The Safe Files," *Franklin D. Roosevelt Presidential Library and Museum*, ⇒ link 3.16. PDFs offer the ability to easily combine page images with either "dirty" or corrected text created by optical character recognition.

17. Lou Burnard, "Digital Texts with XML and the TEI," *Text Encoding Initiative*, ⇒ link 3.17.

18. See, for example, *NINCH Guide*, chapter 5 and appendix B; Digital Library Forum, "Metadata," in *A Framework of Guidance for Building Good Digital Collections*, ⇒ link 3.18; *Creating and Documenting Electronic Texts*, chapter 4.

19. Dennis G. Watson, "Brief History of Document Markup," *University of Florida, Electronic Data Information Source*, ⇒ link 3.19a; Harvey Bingham, "SGML: In Memory of William W. Tunnicliffe," *Cover Pages*, ⇒ link 3.19b; Watson, "Brief History of Document Markup"; SGML Users' Group, "A Brief History of the Development of SGML," *Charles F. Goldfarb's SGML Source Home Page*, ⇒ link 3.19c.

20. *Creating and Documenting Electronic Texts*, 5.1.1; Shermin Voshmgir, "XML Tutorial," *JavaCommerce*, ⇒ link 3.20.

21. *Text Encoding Initiative*, ⇒ link 3.21a. See also David Mertz, "An XML Dialect for Archival and Complex Documents," *IBM*, ⇒ link 3.21b.

22. Stephen Rhind-Tutt, "A Different Direction for Electronic Publishers—How Indexing Can Increase Functionality," *Technicalities* (April 2001), ⇒ link 3.22.

23. *Creating and Documenting Electronic Texts*, 5.2.2; Burnard, "Digital Texts with XML and the TEI." Not only are the TEI guidelines complex, but there have never been sufficiently easy tools for working in TEI. Moreover, scholars began creating SGML/TEI documents at about the same time as the web burst on the scene, and web browsers cannot read SGML. For detailed scholarly discussions of TEI, see the special issue of *Computers and the Humanities*, 33 (1999).

24. Michael Lesk, "The Future Is a Foreign Country" (paper presented at The Price of Digitization: New Cost Models for Cultural and Educational Institutions, New York City, 8 April 2003), ⇒ link 3.24a. Even projects with the intellectual, financial, and technical resources to implement SGML/TEI have bumped up against the fundamental limits of the coding schemes for representing complex electronic texts. Jerome McGann, the leading figure at the leading national center for digital scholarship in the humanities, the Institute for Advanced Technology in the Humanities (IATH) at the University of Virginia, has written about the frustrations in trying to integrate a visual and presentational approach (exemplified by hypertext) with one rooted in the logical and conceptual approach exemplified by SGML. Jerome McGann, "Imagining What You Don't Know: The Theoretical Goals of the Rossetti Archive," ⇒ link 3.24b.

25. "Text Encoding Initiative (TEI)," *Cover Pages*, ⇒ link 3.25a; Lou Burnard, "Prefatory Note," *Text Encoding Initiative*, ⇒ link 3.25b; "The TEI FAQ," *Text Encoding Initiative*, ⇒ link 3.25c. For a good brief overview of XML versus SGML, see Data Conversion Laboratory, "DCL's FAQ," *Data Conversion Laboratory*, ⇒ link 3.25d.

26. "Projects Using the TEI," *Text Encoding Initiative*, ⇒ link 3.26a. One of

the few TEI-compliant projects organized by historians is the "Model Editions Partnership: Historical Editions in the Digital Age," which is a consortium of several major historical papers projects. But even after nine years, the only visible result is the production of about a dozen "mini-editions"—not all of which work on all browsers and platforms. *The Model Editions Partnership*, ⇒ link 3.26b.

27. Stephen Chapman estimates that text mark-up doubles the cost of digitization, but mark-up can range from very light to full SGML. "Considerations for Project Management," in Sitts, ed., *Handbook for Digital Projects*, 42. For large and growing projects, descriptive mark-up in HTML may wind up costing more in the long run than structural mark-up in XML (e.g., TEI) because it is very expensive to repurpose such texts and to take advantage of more complex means of data mining.

28. Most consumer digital cameras, however, "do not have sufficient resolution for archival capture of cultural heritage materials." The lens in these cameras is "designed for capturing three-dimensional scenes and may introduce distortions to flat materials." But these problems are generally not important for the basic capture of texts. See *Western States Digital Imaging*, 15.

29. Sitts, ed., *Handbook for Digital Projects*, 96, 98–99. Scanning in grayscale may improve OCR in some cases and is required for simple readability in some cases (e.g., if photos are present). For scanning guidelines, see, for example, Steven Puglia and Barry Roginski, *NARA Guidelines for Digitizing Archival Materials for Electronic Access* (College Park, Md.: National Archives and Records Administration, 1998), ⇒ link 3.29a; California Digital Library, *Digital Image Format Standards* (Oakland: California Digital Library, 2001) ⇒ link 3.29b.

30. Sitts, ed., *Handbook for Digital Projects*, 115–16; Nicholson Baker, *Double Fold: Libraries and the Assault on Paper* (New York: Random House, 2001). Note that you should select a scanner based on actual optical resolution and not "interpolated resolution," which is a method of increasing resolution through a mathematical algorithm. And make sure that the scanner transfers data quickly (e.g., through FireWire or USB 2.0). See *Western States Digital Imaging*, 12–14. Another approach, which is being piloted at Stanford University but is currently feasible only for very large projects, uses an expensive robot that can automatically scan one thousand pages per hour. John Markoff, "The Evelyn Wood of Digitized Book Scanners," *New York Times*, 12 May 2003, C1.

31. Sitts, ed., *Handbook for Digital Projects*, 123.

32. Kendon Stubbs and David Seaman, "Introduction to the Early American Fiction Project," *Early American Fiction*, ⇒ link 3.32a; "Equipment and Vendors," *Early American Fiction*, ⇒ link 3.32b; *NINCH Guide*, 40–41. Microfilm scanners run between $650 and $53,000 and up, depending on scanning quality and other processing capabilities. Generally, projects using cameras for digital images use "digital scan back" cameras, which attach a scanning array in place of a film holder on a 4" x 5" camera. *Western States Digital Imaging*, 15.

33. *NINCH Guide*, 46; Sitts, ed., *Handbook for Digital Projects*, 130–31. As demand for non-Latin character recognition has grown, so has the amount of available software that recognizes non-Latin and other stylized text. OmniPage, for example, lists 119 languages it supports. See ⇒ link 3.33a. "Unconstrained machine translation of handwriting appears particularly far off, and may be unachievable." "FAQ," *RLG DigiNews* 8.1 (15 February 2004), ⇒ link 3.33b.

34. "Why Images?" *JSTOR*, ⇒ link 3.34a; Douglas A. Bicknese, *Measuring the Accuracy of the OCR in the Making of America* (Ann Arbor: University of Michigan, 1998), ⇒ link 3.34b; LDI Project Team, *Measuring Search Retrieval Accuracy of*

Uncorrected OCR: Findings from the Harvard-Radcliffe Online Historical Reference Shelf Digitization Project (Cambridge, Mass.: Harvard University Library, 2001), ⇒ link 3.34c; "Product Pricing," *Prime Recognition,* ⇒ link 3.34d. As the University of Michigan report points out, the additional costs for PrimeOCR are most readily justified by higher volumes of digitizing such as at Michigan, which digitizes millions of pages per year. *Assessing the Costs of Conversion,* 27. Our understanding of this and a number of other points was greatly aided by Roy's conversation with David Seaman, 10 May 2004.

35. These very rough figures are based on talking to vendors, digitizers, and reading *Assessing the Costs of Conversion.* For a good discussion of the complexity of pricing digitization, see Dan Pence, "Ten Ways to Spend $100,000 on Digitization" (paper presented at The Price of Digitization: New Cost Models for Cultural and Educational Institutions, New York City, 8 April 2003), ⇒ link 3.35a. A vendor who works in the United States told us he could automatically OCR a typescript page for about 10 cents (at 95 to 98 percent accuracy) but that the price would rise to $1.70 to $2.50 for fully corrected text. Michael Lesk maintains that "you can get quotes down to 4 cents a page or $10/book if you're willing to disbind, you are willing to ship to a lower-cost country, and you're not so fussy about the process and quality." Lesk, "Short Report" (paper presented at The Price of Digitization: New Cost Models for Cultural and Educational Institutions, New York City, 8 April 2003), ⇒ link 3.35b. Brewster Kahle is working on getting the cost of scanning a book down to $10 as part of a massive project to digitize all the books in the Library of Congress. Matt Marshall, "Internet Archivist Has Modest Goal: Store Everything," *SiliconValley.com* (4 August 2004), ⇒ link 3.35c.

36. "Executive Notes," *JSTORNews* 8.1 (February 2004), ⇒ link 3.36a; Bicknese, *Measuring the Accuracy of the OCR in the Making of America;* "Why Images?" *JSTOR.* JSTOR hand keys bibliographic citation information, key words, and abstracts. "The Production Process," *JSTOR,* ⇒ link 3.36b. JSTOR also makes available TIFFs and PDFs, which can be used with more sophisticated assistive technologies. JSTOR also limits users to the page views, probably for legal reasons that have to do with its rights to make use of content that is still under copyright. Reformatted content might be considered a new publication and might require them to go back to authors for permission.

37. Chapman, "Working with Printed Text and Manuscripts" in Sitts, ed., *Handbook for Digital Projects,* 114.

38. *Creating and Documenting Electronic Texts,* 23–24; John Price-Wilkin, "Access to Digital Image Collections: System Building and Image Processing," in *Moving Theory into Practice,* 110–16. That offshore typists don't know the subject matter or even, in some cases, the language is seen as aiding in accuracy because it makes them less likely to subconsciously modify the text.

39. A good, but somewhat dated, introduction is Howard Besser and Jennifer Trant, *Introduction to Imaging: Issues in Constructing an Image Database* (Santa Monica, Calif.: Getty Art History Information Program, 1995). See also *NINCH Guide,* 102–19; Puglia and Roginski, *NARA Guidelines for Digitizing Archival Materials for Electronic Access;* Erway, "Options for Digitizing Visual Materials"; Council on Library and Information Resources, "File Formats for Digital Masters," in *Guides to Quality in Visual Resource Imaging,* ⇒ link 3.39a; CDL Technical Architecture and Standards Workgroup, *Best Practices for Image Capture* (Berkeley: California Digital Library, 2001), ⇒ link 3.39b; Steven Puglia, "Technical Primer," in Sitts, ed., *Handbook for Digital Projects,* 93–111; Colorado Digitization Project Scanning

Working Group (hereafter CDP), *General Guidelines for Scanning* (Denver: Colorado Digitization Project, 1999), ⇒ link 3.39c.

40. Erway, "Options for Digitizing Visual Materials," 127.

41. JPEG works better for photos with a large range of hues and compresses photos better than GIF, but it loses its compression advantages over GIF at small sizes (e.g., 200 × 200 pixels). A check of Google's image search tool confirms the large number of photos rendered as GIFs on the web. In 1995, Unisys, which owns the compression algorithm used in GIFs, announced that it would charge royalties for software programs that output into GIFs. As a result, PNG (Portable Network Graphics) was developed as a nonproprietary alternative to GIF and one with some attractive additional features. But so far it has failed to attract a wide following, and the recent expiration of the patents on the compression used in GIF suggests that PNG will never become a major graphics format for the web. Paul Festa, "GIF Patent to Expire, Will PNG Survive?" *CNET News.com* (9 June 2003), ⇒ link 3.41a. Another image format that you might encounter is the proprietary "MrSID" (.sid) format used with very large digital images such as maps. The compression used allows for the "zoom in" capability that you can see in the Library of Congress map projects in American Memory. See David Yehling Allen, "Creating and Distributing High Resolution Cartographic Images," *RLG DigiNews* 4.1 (15 April 1998), ⇒ link 3.41b.

42. See ⇒ link 3.42. Corbis charges $1,000 per year for you to use a relatively low resolution JPEG of the Migrant Mother photo on your website, but you can download a better quality version from the Library of Congress for free. According to the *Western States Digital Imaging* guide (p. 23), electronic watermarks "can be easily overcome through manipulation."

43. *NINCH Guide*, 108; CDP, *General Guidelines for Scanning*, 21–24; Puglia and Roginski, *NARA Guidelines for Digitizing Archival Materials for Electronic Access*, 2–3; CDL Technical Architecture and Standards Workgroup, *Best Practices for Image Capture*; William Blake Archive, "The Persistence of Vision: Images and Imaging at the William Blake Archive," *RLG DigiNews* 4.1 (15 February 2000), ⇒ link 3.43.

44. Conversion from one file format to another can be done easily with commonly available software like Adobe Photoshop. If you have many images to convert, you can use batch-processing tools such as Tif2gif, DeBabelizer, or ImageMagick.

45. Blake Archive, "The Persistence of Vision." The inclusion of "targets"— grayscales and color bars—in every scanned image or at least in every scanned batch can make this process more efficient. CDP, *General Guidelines for Scanning*, 25, 27. See also Anne R. Kenney, "Digital Benchmarking for Conversion and Access," in *Moving Theory into Practice: Digital Imaging for Libraries and Archives*, ed. Anne R. Kenney and Oya Y. Rieger (Mountain View, Calif.: Research Libraries Group, 2000), 24–60. In some cases, however, it may be more efficient to do color correction in the scanning process. CDP, *General Guidelines for Scanning*, 3, ⇒ link 3.45.

46. This information can either sit in stand-alone text files or databases or, as the Blake Archive has done, can be incorporated into the "header information" of the image files themselves. In all cases, image files should be logically and consistently named, for instance by incorporating existing catalog numbers directly into the filenames of digital counterparts. Blake Archive, "The Persistence of Vision."

47. *NINCH Guide*, 140. See also CDP Digital Audio Working Group, *Digital*

Audio Best Practices, Version 1.2 (Denver: Colorado Digitization Project, 2003), ⇒ link 3.47a; MATRIX, "Audio Technology / A/D Conversion and Digital Audio Signal Transfer," *Oral History Tutorial*, ⇒ link 3.47b.

48. *NINCH Guide*, 122–24.

49. CDP, *Digital Audio Best Practices*, 19–22; MATRIX, "Audio Technology"; Carl Fleischhauer, "The Library of Congress Digital Audio Preservation Prototyping Project" (paper presented at Sound Savings: Preserving Audio Collections, Austin, Texas, 24–26 July 2003), ⇒ link 3.49a. For sound editing, Sound Forge and Cool Edit Pro are PC only and Bias Peak is Mac only; Pro Tools has versions for both platforms.

50. See, for example, Virginia Danielson, "Stating the Obvious: Lessons Learned Attempting Access to Archival Audio Collections," in *Folk Heritage Collections in Crisis*, ed. Council on Library and Information Resources (Washington, D.C.: CLIR, 2001), ⇒ link 3.50a. Initially, sound digitizers were more likely to use 44 kHz and 16 bits, and some still see that as adequate. For 96 kHz, see Fleischhauer, "The Library of Congress Digital Audio Preservation Prototyping Project"; Michael Taft, "The Save Our Sounds Project" (paper presented at Sound Savings: Preserving Audio Collections, Austin, Texas, 24–26 July 2003), ⇒ link 3.50b; Bartek Plichta and Mark Kornbluh. "Digitizing Speech Recordings for Archival Purposes"; *NINCH Guide*, 126, 133; MATRIX, "Audio Technology." Macintosh computers tend to use AIFF (Audio Interchange File Format) for audio, but WAV (which was developed for Windows) files generally also play on that operating system.

51. EVIA Digital Archive, "Ethnomusicological Video for Instruction and Analysis (EVIA) Digital Archive Project Development Phase," proposal to Andrew W. Mellon Foundation, ⇒ link 3.51a; Melitte Buchman, email to Roy Rosenzweig, 19 July 2004. See also E-MELD (Electronic Metastructure for Endangered Languages Data) Project, "Digitization of Video Files," *E-Meld School of Best Practices in Digital Language Documentation*, ⇒ link 3.51b.

52. *NINCH Guide—Interview Reports*.

53. Ibid., 2.2, 6.2, 9.2; 14.2, 17.2, 19.2, 21.2, 22.2; Janet Gertz, "Vendor Relations," in Sitts, ed., *Handbook for Digital Projects*, 151–52. See similarly Stephen Chapman and William Comstock, "Digital Imaging Production Services at the Harvard College Library," *RLG DigiNews* 4.6 (15 December 2000), ⇒ link 3.53.

54. *NINCH Guide—Interview Reports*, 4.2, 13.2, 15.2. See English Heritage National Monuments Record, *Images of England*, ⇒ link 3.54.

55. Paula De Stefano, "Digitization for Preservation and Access," in *Preservation: Issues and Planning*, eds. Paul N. Banks and Roberta Pilette (Chicago: American Library Association, 2000), 318–19; David Seaman, interview, 10 May 2004; Peter Kaufman, interview, 30 April 2004; Rhind-Tutt, interview; Pence, "Ten Ways to Spend $100,000 on Digitization."

56. Gertz, "Vendor Relations," 155–57; *Assessing the Costs of Conversion*, 13, 20.

57. Erway, "Options for Digitizing Visual Materials," 129–30. See ⇒ link 3.57 for RLG listings.

58. Ashok Deo Bardhan and Cynthia Kroll, "The New Wave of Outsourcing," *Research Report: Fisher Center for Real Estate and Urban Economics* (Fall 2003), 5, ⇒ link 3.58a; Patrick Thibodeau, "U.S. History Moves Online, with Offshore Help," *Computerworld* (16 January 2004), ⇒ link 3.58b. Such jobs, although poorly paid by American standards, are generally viewed as desirable in India and other locations outside the United States. See John Lancaster, "Outsourcing Delivers Hope to India: Young College Graduates See More Options for Better

Life," *Washington Post* (8 May 2004), ⇒ link 3.58c; Katherine Boo, "Best Job in Town," *New Yorker* (5 July 2004), 54ff. In addition to Innodata, the largest companies working in data conversion for cultural heritage organizations are probably Apex, Data Conversion Laboratory, Inc. (DCL), and TechBooks.

59. Seaman, interview; *Assessing the Costs of Conversion;* "Frequently Asked Questions About the Million Book Project," *Carnegie Mellon University Libraries,* ⇒ link 3.59; Thibodeau, "U.S. History Moves Online."

60. Jim Zwick, interview, 30 March 2004.

Chapter 4. Designing for the History Web

1. David Hume, "Of the Standard of Taste," in David E. Cooper, ed., *Aesthetics: The Classic Readings* (Oxford: Blackwell, 1997), 80.

2. Jakob Nielsen, *Designing Web Usability: The Practice of Simplicity* (Indianapolis: New Riders, 1999); Jakob Nielsen, *Homepage Usability: Fifty Websites Deconstructed* (Indianapolis: New Riders, 2001); Jakob Nielsen, *Alertbox,* ⇒ link 4.2; Steve Krug, *Don't Make Me Think: A Common Sense Approach to Web Usability* (Indianapolis: New Riders, 2000), 14.

3. Young-Hae Chang, "Artist's Statement No. 45,730,944: The Perfect Artistic Web Site," *yhchang.com,* ⇒ link 4.3.

4. Michael O'Malley, "Building Effective Course Sites: Some Thoughts on Design for Academic Work," *Inventio* 2.1 (Spring 2000), ⇒ link 4.4.

5. Keith Whittle, *Atomic Veterans History Project,* ⇒ link 4.5a; "Atomic Veterans History Project," *Korean War Educator,* ⇒ link 4.5b.

6. Douglas Linder, "Goals and Purposes of the Famous Trials Site," *Famous Trials,* ⇒ link 4.6.

7. *Wisconsin Historical Society,* ⇒ link 4.7.

8. To get a sense of how much web projects cost (and possibly to get bids on your own), see the web design services section of Elance, an online auction service for outsourcing jobs. *Elance,* ⇒ link 4.8a; for ways to save on your web design, see Carrie Bickner, *Web Design on a Shoestring* (Upper Saddle River, N.J.: Pearson Education, 2003); for many examples of high-end exhibit sites, see the design firm Second Story's website, ⇒ link 4.8b; National Museum of American History, *September 11: Bearing Witness to History,* ⇒ link 4.8c. Many of the web design firms serving historical museums and societies attend the annual Museums and the Web conference and can be found through the registration list for that conference. For the most recent list of companies and institutions, see ⇒ link 4.8d. Some of the best-known design firms are Second Story, Terra Incognita (⇒ link 4.8e), Interactive Knowledge (⇒ link 4.8f), and New Tilt (⇒ link 4.8g).

9. O'Malley, "Building Effective Course Sites."

10. Also, see Morris's typographical and illustrative work for the Kelmscott Press, e.g., the individual head pages for each work in William Shakespeare, *The Poems* (London: Kelmscott Press, 1893) or the dense artistry found on Morris's title page for Raoul Lafevre, *The Recuyell of the Historyes of Troye* (London: Kelmscott Press, 1892); Robert Strassler, ed., *The Landmark Thucydides* (New York: Free Press, 1996).

11. Edward R. Tufte, *The Visual Display of Quantitative Information* (Cheshire, Conn.: Graphics Press, 1983); Edward R. Tufte, *Envisioning Information* (Cheshire, Conn.: Graphics Press, 1990); Edward R. Tufte, *Visual Explanations: Images and Quantities, Evidence and Narrative* (Cheshire, Conn.: Graphics Press, 1997).

12. Tufte, *Visual Display of Quantitative Information*, 40, ⇒ link 4.12.

13. Larry Gales, "Web Page Design Inspired by Edward Tufte," and "Graphics and Web Design Based on Edward Tufte's Principles," *Larry Gales*, ⇒ links 4.13a and 4.13b.

14. Jeffrey Zeldman, *Designing with Web Standards* (Indianapolis, Ind.: New Riders, 2003), 25; "About: Mission," *The Web Standards Project*, ⇒ link 4.14a; Simon Paquet, Marcio Galli, Ian Oeschger, Jim Ley, Daniel Ulrich, and Mike Cowperthwaite, "Using Web Standards in Your Web Pages," *Mozilla*, ⇒ link 4.14b; Apple Developer Connection, "Web Page Development: Best Practices," *Apple*, ⇒ link 4.14c.

15. Robin Williams and John Tollett, *The Non-Designers Web Book: An Easy Guide to Creating, Designing, and Posting Your Own Web Site* (2nd ed.; Berkeley, Calif.: Peachpit, 2000), ch. 6.

16. Macquarie University, *Journeys in Time, 1809–1822: The Journals of Lachlan and Elizabeth Macquarie, 1809–1822*, ⇒ link 4.16.

17. Patrick Lynch and Sarah Horton, *Web Style Guide* (2nd ed., New Haven, Conn.: Yale University Press, 2001), 38 and 144–45. This preference for terseness when writing for the web is widespread, including in many academic settings. See, for example, Office of Communications and Marketing, "Writing and Editing for the Web," *Santa Clara University*, ⇒ link 4.17a, and "Writing for the Web: Guidelines for MIT Libraries," *Massachusetts Institute of Technology*, ⇒ link 4.17b. Jakob Nielsen's mid-1990s web usability studies led to much of this thinking about web prose. See Jakob Nielsen, "How Users Read on the Web," *Alertbox*, ⇒ link 4.17c.

18. To ensure that your pages will print well, use an HTML table of less than 500 pixel width, or CSS layout, to confine the text within an $8\frac{1}{2}$-by-11-inch page (at 72 dpi, an $8\frac{1}{2}$-by-11-inch sheet of paper is 612 pixels wide; you must leave room for margins). We should note, however, that you will have even less control of the look of a print-out than you have over how your website will look on different computers and in different browsers. "Design Tip: Build Print-friendly Pages," *NetMechanic*, ⇒ link 4.18.

19. Chronicle of Higher Education, *Arts and Letters Daily*, ⇒ link 4.19.

20. Lynch and Horton, *Web Style Guide*, 183–84.

21. Tufte, *Envisioning Information*, 90ff.; Larry Gales, "Graphics and Web Design Based on Edward Tufte's Principles—Color," *Larry Gales*, ⇒ link 4.21.

22. This was due to the 8-bit video cards installed on most computers, PCs as well as Macs. See Lynda Weinman, "Non-Dithering Colors in Browsers," *lynda .com*, ⇒ link 4.22a. Weinman provides a good palette, organized by hue rather than hexadecimal code, for choosing web-safe colors. See ⇒ link 4.22b.

23. There are two ways of doing thumbnails. The first, and simplest, is to simply shrink the entire image (using graphics software like Photoshop Elements) to a smaller, more manageable size. The second, more time-intensive, manner is to choose a representative portion of the image and crop and zoom into that area of the original. Some web designers advocate using this second method exclusively. However, it is in part a matter of taste and a function of what you are thumbnailing. It is true that small images of maps, for instance, can be almost indecipherable, but other images shrink remarkably well. Try both methods to see which one works best for your project. For the Formosa site, see the Reed Institute, *Formosa: Nineteenth Century Images*, ⇒ link 4.23.

24. Media Center for Art History, *Amiens Cathedral Project*, ⇒ link 4.24a; *Harappa: The Indus Valley and the Raj in India and Pakistan*, ⇒ link 4.24b; Dana

Leibsohn and Barbara Mundy, "Vistas Main Gallery," *Vistas: Spanish American Visual Culture, 1520–1820,* ⇒ link 4.24c.

25. The Flint Sit-Down Strike Audio Gallery, *Historicalvoices.org,* ⇒ link 4.25.

26. Jakob Nielsen, "Search: Visible and Simple," *Alertbox,* ⇒ link 4.26a; Michael Bernard, "Developing Schemas for the Location of Common Web Objects," *Usability News,* 3.1, (2001), ⇒ link 4.26b.

27. Mint Museum, *The Mesoamerican Ballgame,* ⇒ link 4.27a; Archives & Museum Informatics, "Best Museum Web Site,*" Museums and the Web 2002: The Best of the Web,* ⇒ link 4.27b.

28. Gwendolyn Midlo Hall, *Afro-Louisiana History and Genealogy 1719–1820,* ⇒ link 4.28.

29. Albert Van Helden and Elizabeth Burr, *The Galileo Project,* ⇒ link 4.29a; "Galileo's Early Life," ⇒ link 4.29b; "Pope Urban VIII," ⇒ link 4.29c.

30. Louis Rosenfeld and Peter Morville, *Information Architecture for the World Wide Web* (Cambridge, Mass.: O'Reilly, 1998), 10; Aaron West, "The Art of Information Architecture," *iBoost Journal,* ⇒ link 4.30.

31. Note the lack of ".html" here—most web servers will automatically look for the file "index.html" or "home.html" in a folder or directory, which means that for home pages you can just use a short form of the URL if you name it one of those options. In other words, the full URL for McCann's site is actually http://www.bu.edu/africa/envr/index.html, but the abridged form is perfectly acceptable.

32. These plainer URLs can be created using some technical capabilities that most web server software programs have, such as mod_rewrite for the most popular web server software, Apache. In general, try to avoid query strings, those ungainly strings of numbers and symbols after the question mark in a URL. The History Cooperative uses an addressing system of the sort we advocate. For example, Kenneth Cmiel's essay on "The Recent History of Human Rights" in volume 109, issue number 1 of the *American Historical Review* is found at http://www.historycooperative.org/journals/ahr/109.1/cmiel.html.

33. Koninklijke Bibliotheek, *Medieval Illuminated Manuscripts,* ⇒ link 4.33.

34. Web Accessibility Initiative, ⇒ link 4.34a; "WAI Resources," ⇒ link 4.34b.

35. For those who do need to comply with the federal laws, the United States Access Board has placed the full law and its interpretation of how to enact the law at ⇒ link 4.35a. The law itself, with all of the technical language, is at ⇒ link 4.35b, with the critical passages for web design in subsection 1194.22: "Web-based intranet and Internet information and applications." It is notable that this subsection closely follows the first edition of the Web Content Accessibility Guidelines from the World Wide Web Consortium (W3C), which does a much better job of explaining some of the principles and the technical ways in which web designers can conform to these principles. The full text of the W3C guidelines is at ⇒ link 4.35c.

36. Rehabilitation Engineering & Assistive Technology Society of North America, ⇒ link 4.36a; Information Technology Technical Assistance and Training Center, "Overview of State Accessibility Laws, Policies, Standards and Other Resources Available On-line," ⇒ link 4.36b; Information Technology Technical Assistance and Training Center, "A National Assessment of State E&IT Accessibility Initiatives," ⇒ link 4.36c.

37. Kathy Cahill, email to Joan Fragaszy, 30 June 2003.

38. "Section 508 Standards," *Jimthatcher.com,* ⇒ link 4.38.

Chapter 5. Building an Audience

1. Very little has been written about marketing for history or nonprofit websites. There are many business-oriented works such as Simon Collin, *Work the Web, E-marketing* (West Sussex, England: John Wiley & Sons, 2000); Susan Sweeney, *101 Ways to Promote Your Website: Filled with Proven Internet Marketing Tips, Tools, Techniques, and Resources to Increase Your Web Site Traffic* (4th ed.; Gulf Breeze, Fla.: Maximum Press, 2003).

2. Randy Rieland, interview, 17 May 2004.

3. Philip E. Agre, "Designing Genres for New Media: Social, Economic, and Political Contexts," in Steve Jones, ed., *CyberSociety 2.0: Revisiting Computer Media Community and Technology* (Thousand Oaks, Calif.: Sage, 1998), 79, 95.

4. CHNM and American Social History Project, *Liberty, Equality, Fraternity: Exploring the French Revolution,* ⇒ link 5.4; Drew VandeCreek, interview, 10 June 2004.

5. CHNM, *Echo: Exploring and Collecting History Online—Science, Technology, and Industry,* ⇒ link 5.5. The National Center for Education Statistics (NCES) reports 118,570 teachers in secondary school and 15,436 in combined secondary and primary. Kelly Gruber, email to Emily Bliss, 10 June 2004.

6. Matthew Nickerson, interview, 9 June 2004.

7. For *Best of the Web,* see ⇒ link 5.7a; for *Muse,* see ⇒ link 5.7b; for *Edsitement,* see ⇒ link 5.7c. The American Library Association gives Katharine Kyes Leab & Daniel J. Leab American Book Prices Current Exhibition Awards "for excellence in the publication of catalogs and brochures that accompany exhibitions of library and archival materials, as well as for electronic exhibitions of such materials." See ⇒ link 5.7d.

8. Rieland, interview.

9. Timothy Messer-Kruse, interview, 9 June 2004.

10. Richard Shenkman, email to Emily Bliss, 10 June 2004.

11. For registering your website with major search engines, see Adam Shannon, *Building an Effective Website: A Guide for Nonprofit Organizations* (Washington, D.C.: Oxygen Communications, 2000), 29–32. See also "Search Engine Submission Tips," *SearchEngineWatch,* ⇒ link 5.11.

12. For the basic principles, see Sergey Brin and Lawrence Page, "The Anatomy of a Large-Scale Hypertextual Web Search Engine" (proceedings of the Seventh International World Wide Web Conference, Brisbane, Australia, 14–18 April 1998), ⇒ link 5.12.

13. Jill Whalen, "All About Title Tags," *High Rankings Advisor,* 96 (28 April 2004); David Callan, "Google Ranking Tips," *PowerHomeBiz.Com;* Ralph F. Wilson, "The Web Marketing Checklist: 29 Ways to Promote Your Site," *Web Marketing Today,* 125 (4 June 2003); Shannon, *Building an Effective Website,* 29–32.

14. Alice Sheehy, email to Emily Bliss, 16 June 2004. Google ad prices are estimates for getting your ad at or near the top of the listings.

15. Most web users tend to make a "habit" of certain sites. See John B. Horrigan and Lee Rainie, *Counting on the Internet* (Washington, D.C.: Pew Internet and American Life Project, 2002); John Carey, "The Web Habit: An Ethnographic Study of Web Usage," *OPA White Papers* 2.1 (January 2004); "Internet Metrics: The Loyal Audience," *OPA White Papers* 1.1 (May 2002).

16. "Guide to History Departments," *Center for History and New Media,* ⇒ link 5.16.

17. Harry Butowsky, interview, 14 June 2004; National Park Service, "Ask a Question," *Links to the Past*, ⇒ link 5.17.

18. Rieland, interview.

19. For a good overview of logs, see Michael Calore, "Log File Lowdown," *WebMonkey*, ⇒ link 5.19.

20. As with most other things, you can outsource your log analysis to a service provider, which installs some programming code on your web pages and then provides continuously updated reports online. Such services can run $100,000 to $250,000 per year—well beyond the budget of a typical nonprofit history site. Jim Rapoza, "Vital Web Stats—And More," *eWeek* (26 August 2002), ⇒ link 5.20a; "Web Log Analyzers," *GlobalSecurity.Org*, ⇒ link 5.20b.

21. If you redesign your site, your hits can decrease while your number of visitors increases, as seems to be the case for the American Family Immigration History Center, which saw its hits drop from 3.4 billion to 2.5 billion while its visitors grew from 1.7 to 2.4 million. Statue of Liberty–Ellis Island Foundation, *Annual Report, Year Ended March 31, 2003* (New York, 2003), 5.

22. Robin Good, "Monitoring Your Web Traffic Online—Part II Log Analysis Tools," *Master Mind Explorer* (31 August 2001), ⇒ link 5.22a. You can control how your site is cached by AOL, however: "AOL Caching Info," *AOL.Webmaster. Info*, ⇒ link 5.22b; "AOL Proxy Info," *AOL.Webmaster.Info*, ⇒ link 5.22c.

23. Jon Weisman, "Not All Page Views Are Created Equal," *E-Commerce Times* (4 October 2002), ⇒ link 5.23a; ⇒ link 5.23b.

24. Shannon, *Building an Effective Website*, 27.

25. Kate Fitzgerald, "Debate Grows Over Net Data; NetRatings, ComScore Numbers Diverge," *Advertising Age* (15 March 2004). See also "Can We Get an Accurate Accounting of Website Visitors?" *DSstar* 4.38 (19 September 2000), ⇒ link 5.25a. Another system of ranking is offered by Alexa (owned by Amazon), which tracks usage of computers with the Alexa toolbar. They claim "millions" of users, but their sample is not a scientific one. See ⇒ link 5.25b.

26. Statue of Liberty–Ellis Island Foundation, *Annual Report, Year Ended March 31, 2003*, 5.

27. Angela O'Neal, interview, 9 June 2004; Butowsky, interview.

28. Mary Stutz, interview, 11 June 2004.

29. Even anonymously, cookies can be used for more sophisticated tracking of web traffic. See Sane Solutions, *Analyzing Web Site Traffic: A Sane Solutions White Paper* (North Kingstown, R.I.: Sane Solutions, 2003). Cookies cannot damage your computer or make you vulnerable to hackers. Nonetheless, some web users view them suspiciously and do not allow them on their hard drives. Most reputable sites have privacy policies that state that they will not sell information about you to someone else. But the company could be bought by less privacy-minded owners. Even if you haven't registered, cookies can gather information on your surfing habits. Advertising companies like DoubleClick place advertisements on hundreds of sites across the Internet and then distribute cookies though each of the ad banners they operate. The reach and breadth of their banners allow their cookies to gather data on web surfers. In effect, you become an unpaid participant in their marketing studies. *Pbs.org* offers a good model of a privacy policy for a nonprofit organization. See "About This Site, Privacy," ⇒ link 5.29a. For more information about cookies and how they work see "Persistent Client State HTTP Cookies," *Netscape.com*, ⇒ link 5.29b.

30. Bruce Tognazzini, *Tog on Interface* (Boston: Addison-Wesley Professional, 1992), 79.

31. Katherine Khalife, "Nine Common Marketing Mistakes Museum Websites Make," *Museum Marketing Tips*, 2001, ⇒ link 5.31; O'Neal, interview.

32. Phil Agre, "[RRE] Notes and Recommendations," email to "Red Rock Eater News Service" rre@lists.gseis.ucla.edu, 8 August 2000, ⇒ link 5.32.

Chapter 6. Collecting History Online

1. MATRIX, *H-Net: Humanities and Social Sciences Online*, ⇒ link 6.1.

2. Quoted in Lee Dembart, "Go Wayback," *International Herald Tribune*, 4 March 2002, ⇒ link 6.2.

3. Linda Shopes, "The Internet and Collecting the History of the Present" (paper presented at September 11 as History: Collecting Today for Tomorrow, Washington, D.C., 10 September 2003). For more on this "rapport" and the way rich historical accounts arise during the live interaction of interviewer and interviewee, see Alessandro Portelli, *The Battle of Valle Giulia: Oral History and the Art of Dialogue* (Madison: University of Wisconsin Press, 1997) and Michael Frisch, *A Shared Authority: Essays on the Craft and Meaning of Oral and Public History* (Albany: State University of New York Press, 1991). It may also be worth comparing (or supplementing) the practical advice of this chapter with the offline advice of Donald A. Ritchie in *Doing Oral History* (Oxford: Oxford University Press, 2003), and Judith Moyer, "Step-by-Step Guide to Oral History," ⇒ link 6.3.

4. *Moving Here: Two Hundred Years of Migration to England*, ⇒ link 6.4a; BBC, *WW2 People's War*, ⇒ link 6.4b.

5. National Park Foundation, "Rosie the Riveter Stories," *Ford Motor Company Sponsored Programs*, ⇒ link 6.5a; National Geographic, *Remembering Pearl Harbor*, ⇒ link 6.5b; *Voices of Civil Rights*, ⇒ link 6.5c; Alfred P. Sloan Foundation, "History of Science and Technology," ⇒ link 6.5d; *C250 Perspectives: Write Columbia's History*, ⇒ link 6.5e; *The Vietnam Project: The Oral History Project—How to Participate*, ⇒ link 6.5f.

6. Spencer Weart, "Icedrilling: History of Greenland Ice Drilling," *Discovery of Global Warming*, ⇒ link 6.6.

7. Computer History Museum, *Apple Computer History Weblog*, ⇒ link 6.7a; Andy Hertzfeld, *Folklore.org: Macintosh Stories*, ⇒ link 6.7b; David Kirsch, *Electronic Vehicle History Online Archive*, ⇒ link 6.7c; CHNM, *Echo: Exploring and Collecting History Online—Science, Technology, and Industry*, ⇒ link 6.7d.

8. Kevin Roe, *Brainerd, Kansas: Time, Place and Memory on the Prairie Plains*, ⇒ link 6.8a; Rowville Lysterfield History Project, *Rowville Lysterfield History Project*, ⇒ link 6.8b; Exploratorium, *Remembering Nagasaki: Atomic Memories*, ⇒ link 6.8c; SeniorNet, *World War II Living Memorial*, ⇒ link 6.8d; "Veteran's Forums," *History Channel*, ⇒ link 6.8e.

9. Joshua Greenberg, *Video Store Project*, ⇒ link 6.9. The resulting dissertation was entitled "From Betamax to Blockbuster: Medium and Message in the Video Consumption Junction" (Ph.D. diss., Cornell University, 2004).

10. National Park Foundation, "Rosie the Riveter Stories"; BBC, "Associate Centres," *WW2 People's War*, ⇒ link 6.10.

11. Keith Whittle, *Atomic Veterans History Project*, ⇒ link 6.11.

12. Sixties Project, *The Sixties-L Discussion List*, ⇒ link 6.12.

13. National Institute of Technology & Liberal Education, "Market Share," *NITLE Weblog Census*, ⇒ link 6.13a; *Blogger*, ⇒ link 6.13b; *Live Journal*, ⇒ link 6.13c; *AOL Hometown*, ⇒ link 6.13d; *Movable Type Publishing Platform*, ⇒ link

6.13e; *TypePad: Hosted Weblog Service,* ⇒ link 6.13f; "Blog Tools," *Weblogs Compendium,* ⇒ link 6.13g; "Blog Hosting," *Weblogs Compendium,* ⇒ link 6.13h. There are many other blog software packages and hosts, and some offer advanced features that may be useful for certain collecting efforts. A full list of software packages can be found at ⇒ link 6.13i, and hosts for a variety of blog packages can be found at ⇒ link 6.13j. In general, however, the top four systems will be suitable in most cases. Two of the more sophisticated blogging systems are the free *Nucleus CMS* (⇒ link 6.13k) and pMachine's *ExpressionEngine* (⇒ link 6.13l).

14. *Phpbb.com: Creating Communities,* ⇒ link 6.14a; *Infopop,* ⇒ link 6.14b; *Bulletin – Instant Community,* ⇒ link 6.14c.

15. "Tell Your Story," *Moving Here: Two Hundred Years of Migration to England,* ⇒ link 6.15.

16. See ⇒ link 6.16.

17. Several companies offer inexpensive voicemail services that allow contributors to contact the collecting institution via a toll-free telephone number and record a message according to prompts you provide. These services can be configured so that recordings are emailed to you as digital audio attachments, complete with date, time, and incoming number stamp. From your email inbox, these recordings can be easily archived, made available on your website, or edited for other kinds of public presentation. UReach, Onebox, MaxEmail, and many other telecommunications companies provide such services for less than 10 cents per minute. Burgeoning technologies for making phone calls via the Internet, including so-called VoIP (Voice over Internet Protocol) services from most of the large telecommunications companies as well as start-ups such as Vonage and Skype, also hold promise for conducting and recording historical interviews cheaply, since the sound from these calls is already digital and can be stored on your hard drive using special software.

18. Jewish Museum, "The Jewish Lads' Brigade," *Moving Here: Two Hundred Years of Migration to England,* ⇒ link 6.18.

19. CHNM, "Claude Shannon: The Man and His Impact," *Echo: Exploring and Collecting History Online—Science, Technology, and Industry,* ⇒ link 6.19a. For the Siberia entry, see the submission dated 5 August 2001, ⇒ link 6.19b.

20. Kirsch, *Electric Vehicle History Online Archive.*

21. National Institutes of Health, *A Thin Blue Line: The History of the Pregnancy Test Kit,* ⇒ link 6.21.

22. James Sparrow, *Blackout History Project,* ⇒ link 6.22.

23. A couple of years ago it seemed as if oral history had successfully won an exemption from the stricter IRB rules. See Bruce Craig, "Oral History Excluded from IRB Review," *Perspectives* (December 2003), ⇒ link 6.23a; American Historical Association, *Questions Regarding the Policy Statement on Institutional Review Boards,* Press Release 10 November 2003, ⇒ link 6.23b; Donald A. Ritchie and Linda Shopes, "Oral History Excluded from IRB Review," *Oral History Association,* ⇒ link 6.23c. More recent developments have put this exemption in question. See Robert B. Townsend and Mériam Belli, "Oral History and IRBs: Caution Urged as Rule Interpretations Vary Widely," *Perspectives* (December 2004), ⇒ link 6.23d. For general guidelines for ethically conducting interviews (online or off), see Oral History Association, *Oral History Evaluation Guidelines,* Pamphlet Number 3, September 2000, ⇒ link 6.23e; American Historical Association, *Statement on Standards of Professional Conduct,* May 2003, ⇒ link 6.23f.

24. For good examples of short, clear terms of contribution and use, see the submission page for the Voice of Civil Rights project at ⇒ link 6.24a or the Echo

project policies page at ⇒ link 6.24b; for further guidance on building a policies page, see "TRUSTe Model Privacy Disclosures," *TRUSTe: Make Privacy Your Choice,* ⇒ link 6.24c.

25. "Tell Your Story," ⇒ link 6.25a; National Park Foundation, "Rosie the Riveter Stories—Your Contact Information," *Ford Motor Company Sponsored Programs,* ⇒ link 6.25b; National Park Foundation, "Rosie the Riveter Stories—'Your Stories' Terms of Submission and Disclaimer," *Ford Motor Company Sponsored Programs,* ⇒ link 6.25c.

26. See R. Tourangeau, L. J. Rips, and K. Rasinski, *The Psychology of Survey Response* (New York: Cambridge University Press, 2000) for an overview of the subject. For more on web surveys from the social science perspective, see M. P. Couper, M. Traugott, and M. Lamias, "Web Survey Design and Administration," *Public Opinion Quarterly,* 65, 2 (2001), 230–53, and M. P. Couper, "Web Surveys: A Review of Issues and Approaches," *Public Opinion Quarterly,* 64, 4, (2000), 464–94. A full bibliography of survey design is available from the Laboratory for Automation Psychology and Decision Processing at the Human/Computer Interaction Laboratory at the University of Maryland, ⇒ link 6.26.

27. Quotation from Don A. Dillman, "Internet Surveys: Back to the Future," *The Evaluation Exchange,* 10, 3 (2004), 6. See also Don A. Dillman, *Mail and Internet Surveys: The Tailored Design Method* (New York: Wiley and Sons, 2000), and related papers at ⇒ link 6.27.

28. "Web Newspaper Registration Stirs Debate," *CNN.com,* 14 June 2004, ⇒ link 6.28a. Online collecting projects that focus on sensitive topics obviously may encounter more resistance to revealing accurate personal information. See R. Coomber, "Using the Internet for Survey Research," *Sociological Research Online,* 2, 2 (1997), ⇒ link 6.28b.

29. The American Registry for Internet Numbers has a free IP lookup service at ⇒ link 6.29a. Non-U.S. domains (those with two-letter country codes at the end) can be located through Uwhois.com, ⇒ link 6.29b. Domains that end in .aero, .arpa, .biz, .com, .coop, .edu, .info, .int, .museum, .net, and .org can be located through the governing body for the web, the Internet Corporation for Assigned Names and Numbers (ICANN), at ⇒ link 6.29c. Several commercial services scan worldwide IP addresses, e.g., Network-tools.com, ⇒ link 6.29d, and Network Solutions, ⇒ link 6.29e.

30. Michael Kazin, "12/12 and 9/11: Tales of Power and Tales of Experience in Contemporary History," *History News Network,* 11 September 2003, ⇒ link 6.30.

31. Pew Internet and American Life Project, "One Year Later: September 11 and the Internet" (Washington, D.C.: Pew Internet and American Life Project, 2002). See also Bruce A. Williams and Michael X. Delli Carpini, "Heeeeeeeeeeeere's Democracy!" *Chronicle of Higher Education,* 19 April 2002, 14.

32. Lane Collins, Geoffrey Hicks, and Marie Pelkey, *Where Were You: September 11th, 2001,* ⇒ link 6.32.

33. Both the September 11 project and the 2000 election project were launched under the auspices of the Library's larger web preservation effort named MINERVA (Mapping the INternet Electronic Resources Virtual Archive). See ⇒ link 6.33a. For the projects, see Library of Congress, *The September 11 Web Archive,* ⇒ link 6.33b; Library of Congress, *Election 2002 Web Archive,* ⇒ link 6.33c. For an overview of collection statistics, see Library of Congress, "Welcome," *The September 11 Web Archive,* ⇒ link 6.33d.

34. CHNM and the American Social History Project, *The September 11 Digital Archive*, ⇒ link 6.34.

35. *Here Is New York: A Democracy of Photographs*, ⇒ link 6.35.

36. Pew Internet and American Life Project, *The Commons of the Tragedy* and *How Americans Used the Internet After the Terror Attack* (Washington, D.C.: Pew Internet and American Life Project, 2001); quotation from *The Commons of the Tragedy*. See also Amy Harmon, "The Toll: Real Solace in a Virtual World: Memorials Take Root on the Web," *New York Times*, 11 September 2002, G39. For more on the growth of Internet usage, especially as a place for communication, expression, and dialogue, see Deborah Fallows, *The Internet and Daily Life* (Washington, D.C.: Pew Internet and American Life Project, 2004).

37. Herodotus, *The History*, trans. David Grene (Chicago: University of Chicago Press, 1987), 35.

Chapter 7. Owning the Past?

1. Some of the tensions between museums, which are worried about protecting revenue from reproduction and rights fees, and other cultural workers are evident in David Green, *The NINCH Copyright and Fair Use Town Meetings 2000 Report* (Washington, D.C.: NINCH, 2001), 11–12. We are greatly indebted to Rebecca Tushnet and Peter Jaszi for their patient and invaluable help on the complex legal issues raised by this chapter, although neither is responsible for our interpretations.

2. For Lessig, see *Free Culture: How Big Media Uses Technology and the Law to Lock Down Culture and Control Creativity* (New York: Penguin Press, 2004). Lessig's important book appeared after our book was written, but it provides a lucid discussion of many of the issues covered in this chapter.

3. See, for example, Brad Templeton, *Ten Big Myths About Copyright Explained*, ⇒ link 7.3a; Linda Starr, "Part 2: Is Fair Use a License to Steal?" *Education World*, ⇒ link 7.3b.

4. Siva Vaidhyanathan, *Copyrights and Copywrongs: The Rise of Intellectual Property and How It Threatens Creativity* (New York: New York University Press, 2001), 37–44; Edward Samuels, *The Illustrated Story of Copyright* (New York: Thomas Dunne Books, 2000), 12–13. Sometimes the Statute of Anne is dated to 1709—the date on the law itself. At the time of the law, however, the new year began on March 25, meaning that, based on the 1752 calendar (which reinstituted January 1 as the start of the new year), it was actually 1710. For more on history of copyright, see also Lyman Ray Patterson, *Copyright in Historical Perspective* (Nashville, Tenn.: Vanderbilt University Press, 1968); L. Ray Patterson and Stanley W. Lindberg, *The Nature of Copyright: A Law of Users' Rights* (Athens: University of Georgia Press, 1991); William W. Fisher, III, "The Growth of Intellectual Property: A History of the Ownership of Ideas in the United States," ⇒ link 7.4. Massachusetts Bay Colony enacted a copyright law as early as 1672; the Connecticut law was the first passed after the Revolution. Our brief summary of copyright history is particularly indebted to Vaidhyanathan's fine book.

5. Vaidhyanathan, *Copyrights and Copywrongs*, 45; Samuels, *The Illustrated Story of Copyright*, 14–15.

6. Vaidhyanathan, *Copyrights and Copywrongs*, 45; *Circular 1a: United States Copyright Office: A Brief History and Overview* (Washington, D.C.: U.S. Copyright Office, 2005), ⇒ link 7.6.

7. Vaidhyanathan, *Copyrights and Copywrongs*, 46–47; L. Ray Patterson, "*Folsom v. Marsh* and Its Legacy," *Journal of Intellectual Property Law* 5.2 (Spring 1998): 431–52. It can be argued that the Folsom decision has been misunderstood as establishing a fair use defense and that Justice Story did not use "fair use" in a modern sense. But, regardless of the original intent, the case has been used by courts to establish fair use.

8. Vaidhyanathan, *Copyrights and Copywrongs*, 50–55. The rationale for allowing the translation was that the translator had produced a new and useful work rather than simply pirating it. The domestic manufacturing clause, which mandated that foreign works had to be produced from plates made in the United States if they were to receive copyright protection and which remained in effect until relatively late in the twentieth century, limited the degree to which foreign authors actually benefited from the treaty. Over time, however, the expense of creating plates in the United States diminished. On this, see Bill Colitre, "House Report No. 94-1476," *The Hypertext Annotated Title 17*, ⇒ link 7.8.

9. Vaidhyanathan, *Copyrights and Copywrongs*, 35–80 (quote on p. 79); Jessica Litman, "Copyright As Myth," *University of Pittsburgh Law Review* (Fall 1991), 36, 51–52.

10. Patterson argues that the law actually narrowed fair use by defining it because in specifying the terms of fair use for the first time, the law ruled out broader possible interpretations. But others maintain that the provisions are broad and not closely defined, and hence offer significant protection. Patterson, "*Folsom v. Marsh* and Its Legacy," 450.

11. Jonathan D. Salant, "Disney Locks in Copyrights to Mickey, Goofy and Gang," *San Francisco Chronicle*, 17 October 1998, ⇒ link 7.11a; Dennis S. Karjala, "Some Famous Works and Year of First Publication (Subverted Public Domain List)," *Value of the Public Domain*, ⇒ link 7.11b. Digital Archives are, however, allowed to put work online in the final twenty years of copyright if that work is not being commercially exploited. But the law does not establish a procedure for establishing whether or not a work falls into that category, and it does not apply to musical works and pictorial, graphic, and sculptural works. Senator Orrin Hatch was actually the author of the CTEA; Bono's name was attached to the legislation after his death.

12. Vaidhyanathan, *Copyrights and Copywrongs*, 79; "Nina Clemens Gabrilowitsch, 55, Twain's Last Direct Heir, Dies," *New York Times*, 19 January 1966, ⇒ link 7.12. The American Cancer Society now holds the Twain copyrights.

13. Jonathan Band, "Digital Millennium Copyright Act Guide," *American Library Association*, ⇒ link 7.13a; *The Digital Millennium Copyright Act of 1998 U.S. Copyright Office Summary* (Washington, D.C.: U.S. Copyright Office, 1998), ⇒ link 7.13b. For strong warnings on the threat of DMCA, see Siva Vaidhyanathan, "The State of Copyright Activism," *First Monday* 9.4 (April 2004), ⇒ link 7.13c. For a good discussion of the implications for historians of DMCA (and other copyright provisions), see Gerald Herman, "Roundtable: Intellectual Property and the Historian in the New Millennium," *Public Historian* 26.2 (Spring 2004): 23-48.

14. Richard Stim, *Getting Permission: How to License and Clear Copyrighted Material Online and Off* (Berkeley, Calif.: Nolo, 2001), 7/2.

15. See Board of Regents of the University System of Georgia Office of Legal Affairs, *Regents Guide to Understanding Copyright & Educational Fair Use*, 37 (hereafter *Regents Guide*); Stephen Fishman, *The Copyright Handbook: How to Protect and Use Written Work*, 2nd ed. (Berkeley, Calif.: Nolo, 1994), 14/11–15. Another

recent case that suggests that factual compilations lack the "minimal creativity" needed for copyright is *Matthew Bender & Co. v. West Publishing Co.*, 158 F.3d 674 (2d Cir. 1998), ⇒ link 7.15a. The European Union, however, has enacted a "database right" that might protect such compilations. Randal C. Picker and Alan Charles Raul, "European Union Database Developments: An Update on the Status of Intellectual Property Protections for Factual Compilations," *Cyberlaw@Sidley*, ⇒ link 7.15b; Jordan M. Blanke, "Vincent Van Gogh, 'Sweat of the Brow,' and Database Protection," *American Business Law Journal* 39 (Summer 2002).

16. Linda Greenhouse, "The Supreme Court; Protected Works; 20-Year Extension of Existing Copyrights Is Upheld," *New York Times*, 16 January 2003; Amy Harmon, "The Supreme Court: The Context; A Corporate Victory, But One That Raises Public Consciousness," *New York Times*, 16 January 2003. For detailed coverage, see ⇒ link 7.16.

17. *Who Built America? From the Great War of 1914 to the Dawn of the Atomic Age in 1946*, a multimedia CD-ROM (New York: Worth Publishers, 2000), produced by ASHP in collaboration with CHNM.

18. Linda Starr, "Part 5: District Liability and Teaching Responsibility," *Education World*, ⇒ link 7.18. Whether this copying actually violates fair use would, however, depend on various factors, including whether it was done once and at the last minute rather than repeatedly and with enough advance planning so that permission could have been obtained.

19. Lawrence Levine, email to Roy Rosenzweig, 3 January 2004. For another recent case, where a publisher had to withdraw a published book from circulation because of alleged copyright infringement, see Richard Byrne, "Silent Treatment: A Copyright Battle Kills an Anthology of Essays About the Composer Rebecca Clarke," *Chronicle of Higher Education* (16 July 2004), ⇒ link 7.19.

20. United States Copyright Office, *Circular 1: Copyright Basics* (Washington, D.C.: U.S. Copyright Office, 2000), ⇒ link 7.20. At least as far back as 1909, copyright *registration* has not been a condition of protection. See *Washingtonian Publishing Co. v. Pearson*, 306 U.S. 30, 36 (1939). The one exception was that if the Registrar of Copyright asked you to register (in connection with copyright deposit) and you refused, you could also lose your rights. The 1976 law liberalized notice requirements (starting in 1978), but they remained in effect until 1989.

21. According to Peter Vankevich of the Copyright Office, only putting the copyright notice on your home page is roughly analogous to the standard practice of only putting a copyright notice at the front of a book. But though only posting a notice on your home page is sufficient, he believes it is a good idea to put the notice on every page of your site. Peter M. Vankevich, interview, 24 November 2003.

22. Fishman, *The Public Domain*, 17/11, 14, and 6/10. See also *Regents Guide*. On Corbis, see Kathleen Butler, "The Originality Requirement: Preventing the Copy Photography End-Run Around the Public Domain" (paper presented at the NINCH Copyright Town Meeting: The Public Domain: Implied, Inferred and In Fact, San Francisco, 5 April 2000), ⇒ link 7.22a, which challenges the Corbis claims of copyright and the contrary position at the same NINCH town meeting presented by Dave Green of the Corbis legal department. "NINCH Copyright Town Meeting: The Public Domain: Implied, Inferred and In Fact, San Francisco, 5 April 2000," NINCH, Meeting Report, 2000, ⇒ link 7.22b. Kathleen Butler, "Keeping the World Safe from Naked-Chicks-in-Art Refrigera-

tor Magnets: The Plot to Control Art Images in the Public Domain Through Copyrights in Photographic and Digital Reproductions," *Hastings Communications and Entertainment Law Journal* 21 (Fall 1998), 55–128. There are ethical and legal issues involved in taking digital copies of public domain documents that others have posted on the web. The legal issues involve whether they have made significant editorial changes that would entitle them to copyright. The ethical issues involve the credit that someone deserves for the "sweat of brow" in scanning the documents. For a long debate on this, see E-DOCS: Exchanges Among Jon Roland, Paul Halsall, and Jerome Arkenberg ⇒ link 7.22c.

23. Fishman, *The Public Domain*, 17/10–11. Some significant enhancements of the original data might be entitled to protection; let's say you provided annotations explaining the occupations listed in the census records. The proposed "Database and Collections of Information Misappropriation Act (HR 3261)," which is being advocated by large information conglomerates like Reed Elsevier, could change this situation by making the facts assembled in a database eligible for copyright-like protection and making it illegal to make commercially available "quantitatively substantial" portions of a database, although it could be subject to constitutional challenge if passed. See Lisa Vaas, "Putting a Stop to Database Piracy," *eWeek* (24 September 2003), ⇒ link 7.23a; "Your Right to Get the Facts Is at Stake," *Public Knowledge*, ⇒ link 7.23b; Sebastian Rupley, "Critics Assail Proposed Database Law," *PC Magazine* (3 March 2004), ⇒ link 7.23c. Note that "database" is an expansive concept, which includes websites themselves, as computer programmer David Brooks found out when another site—legally— appropriated much of his site on Vincent Van Gogh. Nancy Matsumoto, "When the Art's Public, Is the Site Fair Game?" *New York Times*, 17 May 2001, G6; Blanke, "Vincent Van Gogh, 'Sweat of the Brow,' and Database Protection."

24. *Circular 1: Copyright Basics*; *Engel v. Wild Oats, Inc.*, 644 F. Supp. 1089 (S.D.N.Y. Oct. 3, 1986), ⇒ link 7.24a; Michael Landau, " 'Statutory Damages' in Copyright Law and the MP3.com Case," *GigaLaw.com*, ⇒ link 7.24b. Statutory damages currently range from $750 to $30,000 per work infringed, with a maximum of $150,000 per work for willful infringement.

25. U.S. Copyright Office, *Circular 66: Copyright Registration for Online Works* (Washington, D.C.: U.S. Copyright Office, 2002), ⇒ link 7.25a. The case for registering is made at "Copyright Registration: Why Register?" *Copyright Website*, ⇒ link 7.25b. This is not unbiased, however, in its encouragements to register because the site offers to register your website for you for $99. According to Vankevich, the U.S. Copyright Office regularly receives several thousand applications each year to copyright websites. It has not decided how to respond to the constantly changing content inherent to the medium. Vankevich, interview.

26. Fishman, *The Copyright Handbook*, 2/11, 14/14, 17/15; Mary Case in "NINCH Copyright Town Meeting: The Changing Research and Collections Environment: The Information Commons Today, St. Louis, March 23, 2002," NINCH, Meeting Report, 2002, ⇒ link 7.26a. For example, HarpWeek requires you to consent to a "web access agreement," which says you will not "store the downloaded Content in any electronic/magnetic/optical or other format now known or hereinafter created for more than ninety (90) days." Although some question the enforceability of such licenses, they are valid in Virginia and Maryland, which have passed the Uniform Computer Information Transactions Act (UCITA) giving priority to licensing over copyright. See, for example, "NINCH Copyright Town Meeting: Copyright Perspectives, Rice University, Houston, April 25, 2001," NINCH, Meeting Report, 2001, ⇒ link 7.26b. On UCITA, see

"UCITA," *American Library Association,* ⇒ link 7.26c. Peter Jaszi describes efforts to protect databases through licenses as "quasi-copyright." Herman, "Roundtable," 39.

27. Townsend writes "the growing trend is to see the 'teacher exception' as created not by judge-made law [its previous basis] but by individual university policies." In other words, whether or not your work as a teacher is considered "work for hire" depends on what your employer says. Elizabeth Townsend, "Legal and Policy Responses to the Disappearing 'Teacher Exception,' or Copyright Ownership in the 21ˢᵗ Century University," *Minnesota Intellectual Property Review* 2.3 (2003): 210, 272, 277, 279–80, ⇒ link 7.27. Recent cases suggest the persistence of the exception for "books and articles," although textbooks based on course materials could be an ambiguous case. The "teacher exception" apparently does not exist within the European Union.

28. Corynne McSherry, *Who Owns Academic Work? Battling for Control of Intellectual Property* (Cambridge, Mass.: Harvard University Press, 2001); Jeffrey Young, "Law Student Warns That Professors' Quest for Rights to Lectures Could Backfire," *Chronicle of Higher Education* (6 November 2001), ⇒ link 7.28. Townsend's article offers a sharp rejoinder to McSherry, whom she sees as discouraging "academics and from using the law and court systems to protect their work, demonizing those who do and accusing them of changing the tone of the university into a space fearing litigation." Townsend, "Legal and Policy Responses to the Disappearing 'Teacher Exception,'" 209.

29. "GNU General Public License," *GNU Operating System—Free Software Foundation,* ⇒ link 7.29.

30. D. C. Denison, "For Creators, An Argument for Alienable Rights," *Boston Globe,* 22 December 2002, E2; Kendra Mayfield, "Making Copy Right for All," *Wired News* (17 May 2002), ⇒ link 7.30.

31. "The Founders' Copyright," *Creative Commons,* ⇒ link 7.31.

32. Peter B. Hirtle, "When Works Pass into the Public Domain in the United States: Copyright Term for Archivists," *Cornell Institute for Digital Collections,* ⇒ link 7.32, originally published in Peter B. Hirtle, "Recent Changes to the Copyright Law: Copyright Term Extension," *Archival Outlook,* January–February 1999; updated on 15 January 2003.

33. Not, however, according to the Sixties Project, which includes this dubious warning: "This text, made available by the Sixties Project, is copyright (c) 1993 by the Author or by Viet Nam Generation, Inc., all rights reserved." See ⇒ link 7.33a. On Port Huron statement, see Kirkpatrick Sale, *SDS* (New York: Random House, 1973), 69. In 1996 the estate of Rev. Dr. Martin Luther King, Jr., sued CBS News after the network began selling a five-part documentary called "The Twentieth Century with Mike Wallace," which contained excerpts of King's famous 1963 Lincoln Memorial oration. The King estate claimed the speech was copyrighted; CBS, on the other hand, argued that it had the right to use the original footage, such as that of the King speech, that it records at news events. In 2000, CBS and the King estate reached a settlement in which CBS paid the estate an undisclosed sum. Because the case ended with a settlement, the larger legal issues in this case have not been resolved. David Firestone, "King Estate and CBS Settle Suit over Rights to Famous Speech," *New York Times,* 14 July 2000, A12. The Martin Luther King, Jr., Papers Project at Stanford University presents the "I Have a Dream" speech on its website but only in an encrypted PDF format and with an indication at the top (an unusually prominent spot): "©The Estate of Martin Luther King, Jr." See ⇒ link 7.33b.

34. A. N. Wilson, *Tolstoy* (London: Hamish Hamilton, 1988), 492–95. The Guthrie quotation is widely disseminated (see, for example, ⇒ link 7.34a), but we have been unable to find (including through correspondence with the Guthrie Archives) any direct confirmation that such a songbook exists. Joe Klein, *Woody Guthrie: A Life* (New York: Alfred A. Knopf, 1980), 355–57. For a depressing tale about Richmond that shows why copyright laws do not always benefit "creators," see Rian Malan, "In the Jungle," *Rolling Stone* (25 May 2000), ⇒ link 7.34b.

35. Dennis S. Karjala, "How to Determine Whether a Work is in the Public Domain," *Value of the Public Domain,* ⇒ link 7.35a; U.S. Copyright Office, *Circular 22: How to Investigate the Copyright Status of a Work* (Washington, D.C.: U.S. Copyright Office, 2002), ⇒ link 7.35b; Hirtle, "When Works Pass into the Public Domain in the United States," *Cornell Institute for Digital Collections.* According to historian Paul Halsall, smaller publishers were particularly unlikely to renew, as were publishers who had picked up a book from another imprint. Paul Halsall to E-DOCS, 22 November 1998.

36. "Copyright Renewal Records," *Lesk SCILS Website* ⇒ link 7.36a. For a careful set of rules for determining whether an item is in the public domain, see "Project Gutenberg Copyright HOW TO," *Project Gutenberg,* ⇒ link 7.36b. Also see John Mark Ockerbloom, "Frequently Asked Questions: How Can I Tell Whether a Book Can Go Online?" *Online Books Page,* ⇒ link 7.36c; and "Information About the Catalog of Copyright Entries," ⇒ link 7.36d. See also "Books from 1923 with U.S. Copyright Not Renewed," ⇒ link 7.36e. As of June 2004, the Copyright Office is considering digitizing its pre-1978 records; the records since 1978 are currently available.

37. Fishman, *The Public Domain*, 16/11. For a summary of laws, see Ockerbloom, "Frequently Asked Questions."

38. "NINCH Copyright Town Meetings 2002: Creating Museum IP Policy in a Digital World," NINCH, Conference Announcement and Agenda, ⇒ link 7.38a; Project Gutenberg, "Project Gutenberg of Australia: A Treasure-Trove of Literature," ⇒ link 7.38b; June M. Besek, *Copyright Issues Relevant to the Creation of a Digital Archive: A Preliminary Assessment* (Washington, D.C.: Council on Library and Information Resources and the Library of Congress, 2003), 16. Commercial operations with a legal presence in another country have further reasons to be cautious. In November 2000, Judge Jean-Jacques Gomez of the Paris Tribunal de Grande Instance ruled that Yahoo had to block French residents from viewing auctions of Nazi memorabilia or face fines of $13,000 per day because French law bans the sale or display of items that incite racism. But, a year later, a California court ruled that the French court could not tell Yahoo what to do. Lori Enos, "Yahoo! Ordered to Bar French from Nazi Auctions," *E-Commerce Times* (20 November 2000), ⇒ link 7.38c; "Yahoo! Bans Nazi Sales," *BBC News*, 3 January 2001, ⇒ link 7.38d; "eBay Bans All Hate Item Auctions," *ADLAW by Request* (7 May 2001), ⇒ link 7.38e; Troy Wolverton, "Court Shields Yahoo from French Laws," *CNET News.com*, 8 November 2001, ⇒ link 7.38f; Besek, *Copyright Issues Relevant to the Creation of a Digital Archive*, 13–16.

39. Fishman, *The Public Domain*, 16/14–15. In the United States, the Visual Artists Rights Act (Section 106a of the Copyright Act) provides some limited and narrowly framed "moral" rights. See "NINCH Copyright Town Meeting: Copyright Perspectives, Rice University, Houston, April 25, 2001," NINCH, Meeting Report, 2001, ⇒ link 7.39a. See also Melissa Smith Levine, "Overview of Legal Issues for Digitization," in *Handbook for Digital Projects: A Management Tool for Pres-*

ervation and Access, ed. Maxine K. Sitts, 1st ed. (Andover, Mass.: Northeast Document Conservation Center, 2000), 76–77, ⇒ link 7.39b.

40. Fishman, *The Public Domain,* 15/2; Paul Halsall, "GATT and Copyright Checking," email to E-DOCS, 2 April 1998. One crucial exception to the GATT rules is that it does not apply to books published at the same time in the United States. But, Halsall observes, "virtually no one can prove this one way or other." As attorney Besek concludes more generally, the "issues are complicated and worthy of more detailed study. A current court case, *Golan v. Ashcroft,* challenges the constitutionality of having works that were once in the public domain being returned to copyright. See Stanford Law School, "Golan v. Ashcroft Case Page," *Center for Internet and Society,* ⇒ link 7.40.

41. *Regents Guide,* 3. The rejection of a fair use request does not, however, mean that you are not able to go ahead if you think you are exercising your legal rights. But it does mean that your actions are more likely to be scrutinized closely by the ostensible rights holder. On short phrases, see Richard Stim, "I May Not Be Totally Perfect But Parts of Me Are Excellent: Copyright Protection for Short Phrases," *Copyright & Fair Use: Stanford University Libraries,* ⇒ link 7.41.

42. Paul Halsall to E-DOCS, 22 November 1998; Jon Roland also reports good experiences in getting permission: Jon Roland, "Re: E-DOCS: Paul Halsell on Copyright," email, 11 February 1999. Lynn Nelson similarly notes that he has had good responses from copyright holders for materials he wanted to include in his Kansas-related collections after he explained the public service nature of the collections. Lynn Nelson, interview, 24 August 2003.

43. Leigh Gensler, email to Joan Fragaszy, 6 August 2003. On the issue of difficulty of getting long-term rights, see "NINCH Copyright Town Meeting 2003: Digital Publishing: The Rights Issues," NINCH, Conference Summary Report, 2003, ⇒ link 7.43.

44. David Kirsch, interview, 2 September 2003. In France and Canada, you can simply pay a fixed fee to deal with these grey areas. Unfortunately no equivalent exists in the United States. But some publishers will accept your efforts as "good faith." On Canada, see Canadian Copyright Licensing Agency, "Unlocatable Copyright Holders," *Access,* ⇒ link 7.44a. Two current legal efforts are attempting to deal with the problem of the "orphan works": the court case *Kahle v. Ashcroft,* which argues that the current system of unconditional copyright, which leads to orphan works, is unconstitutional, and the proposed Public Domain Enhancement Act, which would push unused works into the public domain by imposing a very small renewal fee. Stanford Law School, "Kahle v. Ashcroft Case Page," *Center for Internet and Society,* ⇒ link 7.44b.

45. Jon Roland, "Re: E-DOCS: Paul Halsell on Copyright," email, 11 February 1999. On Roland, see ⇒ link 7.45a; on society, see ⇒ link 7.45b. Fishman, *The Public Domain,* 1/11 gives detailed advice on record keeping.

46. Mary Minow, "How I Learned to Love FAIR USE," *Copyright & Fair Use: Stanford University Libraries,* ⇒ link 7.46a. Probably the best (but also the most complex) of those online copyright guides comes from the University of Georgia and reflects the influence of L. Ray Patterson, a leading copyright expert who teaches at Georgia's Law School and was also a member of the committee that drew up the guide. *Regents Guide.* Stanford University Libraries have recently revamped their pages on copyright and fair use, which contain some excellent materials. See, for example, Mary Minow's valuable discussion of fair use. See also Linda Starr, "Part 2: Is Fair Use a License to Steal?" Minow also offers valuable coverage of issues concerning libraries and the law (especially copyright

issues) on her *LibraryLaw Blog,* ⇒ link 7.46b, which also has Peter Hirtle and Ralzel Liebler as contributing authors.

47. Minow, "How I Learned to Love FAIR USE"; *Regents Guide, Chicago Manual of Style,* 15th ed. (Chicago: University of Chicago Press, 2003), 135. *Chicago Manual of Style,* 14th ed. (Chicago: University of Chicago Press, 1993), 144–48. Compare *A Manual of Style,* 10th ed. (Chicago: University of Chicago Press, 1949), 199. Questions of what is permissible in terms of critical commentary and parody continue to be litigated, as in, for example, the suit against Alice Randall's novel, *The Wind Done Gone,* which rewrote *Gone with the Wind* from a black perspective, for infringing the copyright of the Margaret Mitchell estate. Randall's publisher, Houghton Mifflin, lost in the District Court, won in the Court of Appeals, and then settled. David Kirkpatrick, "Mitchell Estate Settles 'Gone with the Wind' Suit," *New York Times,* 10 May 2002, C6.

48. *Regents Guide,* 9.

49. Kenneth D. Crews, *New Copyright Law for Distance Education: The Meaning and Importance of the TEACH Act* (Chicago: American Library Association, 2002), ⇒ link 7.49a; Kristine H. Hutchinson, "The TEACH Act: Copyright Law and Online Education," *New York University Law Review* 78.6 (December 2003), 2224, ⇒ link 7.49b. As Hutchinson notes, some administrators believe that this requirement about unauthorized retention would require universities to develop new technology to track what students do with the copyrighted material after it is downloaded. As a result, some universities have been reluctant to take advantage of the law and have continued to license materials, as they had done before (pp. 2233–34).

50. David W. Stowe, "Just Do It: How to Beat the Copyright Racket," *Lingua Franca* 6.9 (November–December 1995): 32–42; *Chicago Manual of Style,* 15th ed., 137.

51. Fishman, *The Public Domain,* 5/6. If you walk into a museum and take a photograph of a painting created before 1923, you own that photograph and can use it as you like. Some museums argue, however, that your admission ticket is a contract that can include a clause restricting what you can do with a photograph. See "NINCH Copyright Town Meeting: Chicago, March 3, 2001," NINCH, Meeting Report, 2001, ⇒ link 7.51.

52. *Bridgeman Art Library, Ltd. v. Corel Corp.,* 36 F. Supp. 2d 191 (S.D.N.Y. 1999), ⇒ link 7.52. If the book was published before 1923, you are probably in the clear in any case.

53. Fishman, *The Public Domain,* 5/31-3. University of Oregon Professor Christine Sundt describes this as a question "desperately seeking" an answer: "If a work of art is clearly in the public domain—let's imagine for the moment a reasonably well-known (e.g., published) seventeenth-century painting by an Italian artist—but the museum owning the canvas requires that a fee be paid before the work can be illustrated in a publication, could the author ignore the requirement and bypass the museum if she already possesses a good quality illustration without publication rights?" Christine Sundt, "Permission Denied . . . Questions Desperately Seeking Answers" (paper presented at the Digital Publishing: A Practical Guide to the Problem of Intellectual Property Rights in the Electronic Environment for Artists, Museums, Authors, Publishers, Readers and Users, College Art Association, New York, N.Y., 2003), ⇒ link 7.53a. Kathleen Butler argues forcefully, however, that "photographic and digital reproductions are not original and therefore not copyrightable" in "The Originality Requirement: Preventing the Copy Photography End-Run Around the Public Domain" (paper

presented at the NINCH Copyright Town Meeting: The Public Domain: Implied, Inferred and in Fact, San Francisco, 5 April 2000), ⇒ link 7.53b. But Dave Green of the Corbis legal department argued at the same town meeting that the Bridgeman case was misleading and it was only a "narrow holding." Keep in mind that generally speaking a work of art like a painting would be treated like an unpublished manuscript in determining whether or not it was in the public domain.

54. Stowe, "Just Do It," 33.

55. Fishman, *The Public Domain*, 4/44-7; Music Library Association, "What Impact Do Differences Between U.S. and European Copyright Laws Have on Peer to Peer (P2P) File Sharing?" *Copyright for Music Librarians*, ⇒ link 7.55a; Robert Clarida, "Who Owns Pre-1972 Sound Recordings?" *Greater Philadelphia Old Time Radio Club*, ⇒ link 7.55b; Public Domain Information Project, "Sound Recordings," *PD Info: Public Domain Music*, 2003, ⇒ link 7.55c; Georgia Harper, "Copyright Law and Audio Preservation" (paper presented at Sound Savings: Preserving Audio Collections, Austin, Texas, 24–26 July 2003), ⇒ link 7.55d. A more confusing question involves whether music also benefits from the exemption granted in the CTEA for works not in commercial exploitation and in the last twenty years of their copyright. Harper points out that the law is ambiguous and poorly drafted on this point.

56. "Okeh Records," *Wikipedia*, ⇒ link 7.56a; David Edwards and Mike Callahan, *Okeh Album Discography*, ⇒ link 7.56b.

57. "Information About Red Hot Archive," *Red Hot Jazz Archive*, ⇒ link 7.57a; Scott Alexander, interview, 10 February 2004; Linda Tadic, "Intellectual Property Versus the Digital Environment: Rights Clearance," NINCH, Town Meeting Report, 2001, ⇒ link 7.57b. When Charles Haddix set up *Club Kaycee*, ⇒ link 7.57c, a website that "serves up the sights and sounds of the Golden Age of Kansas City Jazz," the Harry Fox Agency waived any claims and ASCAP agreed to charge a flat annual fee as long as they didn't provide any music produced after 1970. Haddix told us that the deal he got with ASCAP wouldn't be possible now: "We kind of got into it under different circumstances than today. There was no file sharing at the time. It was not a big issue. Now they wouldn't have cooperated with us, not in this environment." Haddix, interview, 12 February 2004. Even so, Haddix may not be entirely covered because he would need the performance rights for the sound recording, which need to come from the record company, and ASCAP provides only the performance rights for musical work. As with *Red Hot Jazz*, record companies are less likely to pursue *Club Kaycee* because it is not presenting recordings that are currently being sold. The royalty rates for webcasting of music have been the subject of much contention, although few historians are likely to be affected by this issue. See ⇒ link 7.57d.

58. These issues have been litigated in some of the lawsuits over "sampling." For example, a court ruled in 2003 that a six-second flute sample used by the Beastie Boys was permissible. Stan Soocher, "Song Sampling Is Found De Minimis," *Entertainment Law & Finance* (8 December 2003).

59. Mark Carnes, "Beyond Words: Reviewing Motion Pictures," *Perspectives* (May–June 1996), ⇒ link 7.59a; Kristin Thompson, "Fair Usage Publication of Film Stills: Report of the Ad Hoc Committee of the Society for Cinema Studies," *Cinema Journal* 32.2 (Winter 1993), 3–20, ⇒ link 7.59b; Kristin Thompson to Editor, *Perspectives* (October 1996), 19. For a number of egregious cases of using permissions as a form of censorship, see Stowe, "Just Do It," 34–35. Two court cases do suggest possible fair uses in music. In a political ad, a candidate used

fifteen seconds of his opponent's campaign jingle. The opponent sued: *Keep Thomson Governor Comm. v. Citizens for Gallen Comm.,* 457 F. Supp. 957 (D. N.H. 1978). The judge ruled it was fair use because only a small fraction of the song was used and the purpose of using it was to further political debate. In Manhattan, a TV crew shot footage of an Italian festival, and their taping included a band's performance of "Dove sta Zaza." The ensuing news broadcast included a portion of the song. (*Italian Book Corp, v. American Broadcasting Co.,* 458 F. Supp. 65 (S.D. N.Y. 1978)). The judge ruled that this was fair use because only a small part of the song was used, the song was relevant to the news event, and the broadcast did not damage the composer or the market for the work. See "Summaries of Fair Use Cases," *Copyright & Fair Use: Stanford University Libraries,* ⇒ link 7.59c. Carnes rejects Thompson's argument and says that he checked with top executives and editors at leading commercial publishers and reports that "none said that he or she would publish a book with film stills and enlargements without first acquiring permission from the studios." Mark C. Carnes to Editor, *Perspectives* (October 1996), 35.

60. Larry McCalister, Executive Director, Licensing, Paramount, to Roy Rosenzweig, 12 February 2004; Julie Heath to Roy Rosenzweig, 2 December 2003. (Information on Fox is from recorded message on the Fox Still and Clip Licensing Department's telephone line.)

61. Thompson, "Fair Usage Publication of Film Stills," 5; Robert Clarida in "NINCH Copyright Town Meeting 2003." Whether an excerpt is "at the heart of the work" can be an important determinant of fair use. For example, a court ruled in 1982 that a one-minute-and-fifteen-second clip from a Chaplin film that was used in a television news report was not fair use because it was part of the "heart" of the film. Thus a compilation of "great moments" in film would be more likely to transgress fair use than a compilation that showed how films interpret American history. See "Summaries of Fair Use Cases;" Minow, "How I Learned to Love FAIR USE." Some relatively recent court cases suggest that using brief film clips is fair use.

62. Carlyn Kolker, "Employing Trademark Violation Detectives," *Internet Newsletter including legal.online* 7.3 (June 2002). See also Steven Anderson, "Law Departments Wrestle with Internet Infringement Issues," *Corporate Legal Times* (December 2000). Robert G. Gibbons and Lisa M. Ferri, "IP Policing a Priority Amid Profusion of Online Piracy," *National Law Journal* (4 October 1999), IN FOCUS; Legal Tech; B7; Chilling Effects Clearinghouse, *Chilling Effects,* ⇒ link 7.62. Companies like Coca-Cola, which values its brand name at $34 billion, take a very dim view of trademark infringement. American Memory's website on Coca-Cola ads carries the warning: "Unlike most of the materials presented on the Internet as part of American Memory, materials in *Fifty Years of Coca-Cola Television Advertisements: Highlights from the Motion Picture Archives at the Library of Congress* are subject to copyright and other legal concerns such as publicity rights. These materials are presented here with the permission of The Coca-Cola Company for private educational, scholarly, and research uses."

63. Privacy and defamation are complex and vast topics, and you should consult more detailed sources if your work touches on these issues. For a brief summary, see Levine, "Overview of Legal Issues for Digitization," 83–86. For a summary of legal cases on linking (many of which involve trademark issues of no concern to historians), see "The Link to Liability," *Mondaq Business Briefing* (20 January 2004). See also Richard Poynter, "Reasons to Think Before You Link," *Financial Times,* 24 June 2002.

64. *The On-Line Guitar Archive,* ⇒ link 7.64.

65. If you do find yourself looking for legal help, American University, Harvard, and Stanford all have student law projects focusing on intellectual property.

66. Attorney quoted in Anderson, "Law Departments Wrestle with Internet Infringement Issues"; Starr, "Part 2: Is Fair Use a License to Steal?"; Minow, "How I Learned to Love FAIR USE."

Chapter 8. Preserving Digital History

1. Fred R. Byers, *Care and Handling of CDs and DVDs: A Guide for Librarians and Archivists,* (Washington, D.C.: Council on Library and Information Resources, 2003), ⇒ link 8.1a; Peter Svensson, "CDs and DVDs Not So Immortal After All," Associated Press, 5 May 2004, ⇒ link 8.1b; Basil Manns and Chandrui J. Shahani, *Longevity of CD Media, Research at the Library of Congress* (Washington, D.C.: Library of Congress, 2003), ⇒ link 8.1c; Eva Orbanz, ed., *Archiving the Audio-Visual Heritage: A Joint Technical Symposium* (Berlin: Stiftung Deutsche Kinemathek, 1988); Diane Vogt-O'Connor, "Care of Archival Compact Discs," *Conserve O Gram,* 19/19 (Washington, D.C.: National Park Service, 1996), ⇒ link 8.1d.

2. Charles Arthur, "The End of History," *Independent* (London), 30 June 2003, 4; Jonathan Tisdall, "Hackers Solve Password Mystery," *Aftenposten Norway,* 10 June 2002, ⇒ link 8.2.

3. University of Michigan School of Information, "CAMiLEON Project Cracks Twentieth-Century Domesday Book," news release, December 2002, ⇒ link 8.3a; John Elkington, "Rewriting William the Conqueror / Focus on a computer project to update the Domesday Book," *Guardian* (London), 25 April 1985; Arthur, "The End of History." See also CAMiLEON Project, "BBC Domesday," *CAMiLEON Project,* ⇒ link 8.3b; Margaret O. Adams and Thomas E. Brown, "Myths and Realities about the 1960 Census," *Prologue: Quarterly of the National Archives and Records Administration* 32, 4 (Winter 2000), ⇒ link 8.3c.

4. Laura McLemore quotation from WGBH, "Migration," *Universal Preservation Format,* ⇒ link 8.4a; Margaret Hedstrom quotation from *It's About Time: Research Challenges in Digital Archiving and Long-Term Preservation* (Washington, D.C.: National Science Foundation and the Library of Congress, 2003), 8, ⇒ link 8.4b. For more on the challenges libraries and archives currently face with the proliferation of digital artifacts and collections, see Daniel Greenstein, Bill Ivey, Anne R. Kenney, Brian Lavoie, and Abby Smith, *Access in the Future Tense* (Washington, D.C.: Council on Library and Information Resources, 2004), ⇒ link 8.4c, and *Building a National Strategy for Preservation: Issues in Digital Media Archiving* (Washington, D.C.: Council on Library and Information Resources and the Library of Congress, 2002), ⇒ link 8.4d.

5. *How Much Information? 2003,* ⇒ link 8.5a; "Built to Last," *New York Times,* 5 December 1999. The Long Now Foundation has done similar thinking about how to send information deeply into the future, ⇒ link 8.5b.

6. Hedstrom, *It's About Time,* 9.

7. U.S. National Archives and Records Administration, "Records Management: Strategic Directions: Appraisal Policy," ⇒ link 8.7a. The Pitt Project, an influential, early effort at developing an approach to archiving electronic records, takes a very different approach, focusing on "records as evidence" rather than "information." "Records," David Bearman and Jennifer Trant

explain, "are that which was created in the conduct of business" and provide "evidence of transactions." Data or information, by contrast, Bearman "dismisses as non-archival and unworthy of the archivist's attention." See David Bearman and Jennifer Trant, "Electronic Records Research Working Meeting, 28–30 May 1997: A Report from the Archives Community," *D-Lib Magazine* 3, nos. 7–8 (July–August 1997), ⇒ link 8.7b. Linda Henry offers a sweeping attack on Bearman and other advocates of a "new paradigm" in electronic records management and a defense of the approach of Theodore Schellenberg, who shaped practice at NARA during his long career there, in "Schellenberg in Cyberspace," *American Archivist* 61 (Fall 1998): 309–27.

8. Adrienne M. Woods, "Building the Archives of the Future," *Quarterly* 2, no. 6 (December 2001), ⇒ link 8.8a; "Internet," *How Much Information? 2000,* ⇒ link 8.8b; Steve Gilheany, "Projecting the Cost of Magnetic Disk Storage Over the Next 10 Years," *Burghell Associates – Content Management Integrators,* ⇒ link 8.8c.

9. Roy Rosenzweig, "Scarcity or Abundance? Preserving the Past in a Digital Era," *American Historical Review* 108 (June 2003): 735–62, ⇒ link 8.9.

10. Center for History and New Media and American Social History Project, *The September 11 Digital Archive,* ⇒ link 8.10; Joseph Menn, "Net Archive Turns Back 10 Billion Pages of Time," *Los Angeles Times,* 25 October 2001.

11. Since 1996, the Internet Archive (IA) has been saving copies of millions of websites approximately once every month or two. Visiting the IA's Wayback Machine interface (⇒ link 8.11), you can explore what a site looked like a month, a year, or several years ago. Coverage is quite spotty (for less popular sites just the home page is saved, some images and other pieces may be missing from early snapshots, and the IA's computers have trouble getting inside some database-driven websites), but it is already useful if you need to retrieve information that you may have posted on the web but that is long deleted from your own hard drive. On a similar scale, the search engine giant Google has cached versions of most websites it indexes. Because the spidering of sites by commercial entities such as Google raises copyright concerns, many people argue that the Library of Congress should declare that it has the right to archive all websites in the name of copyright deposit, as has been done in some other countries. See Rosenzweig, "Scarcity or Abundance?"

12. *Preserving Digital Information: Report of the Task Force on Archiving of Digital Information,* (Washington, D.C.: Commission on Preservation and Access, and Mountain View, Calif.: Research Libraries Group, 1996), ⇒ link 8.12.

13. Thomas Jefferson Foundation, *Monticello: The Home of Thomas Jefferson,* ⇒ link 8.13.

14. Film Study Center, Harvard University, *DoHistory,* ⇒ link 8.14. Many computer operating systems ignore standard alphabetizing rules and put the README file at the top of an alphabetized file list of a website so that it is the first thing you encounter in a sea of website-related files (the capitalization also helps to make it stand out).

15. Dollar Consulting, *Archival Preservation of Smithsonian Web Resources: Strategies, Principles, and Best Practices* (Washington, D.C.: Smithsonian Institution, 2001), ⇒ link 8.15.

16. Library of Congress, *Metadata Encoding and Transmission Standard,* ⇒ link 8.16a; Library of Congress, *Metadata Object Description Schema,* ⇒ link 8.16b; Dublin Core Metadata Initiative, ⇒ link 8.16c; Library of Congress and the Society of American Archivists, *Encoded Archival Description (EAD),* ⇒ link 8.16d.

17. Cory Doctorow, "Meta-crap: Putting the Torch to the Seven Straw-Men of the Meta-Utopia," *The WELL*, ⇒ link 8.17.

18. Daniel J. Cohen, "Digital History: The Raw and the Cooked," *Rethinking History* 8 (June 2004): 337–40; Online Computer Library Center, *Open WorldCat Pilot*, ⇒ link 8.18a; Barbara Quint, "OCLC Project Opens WorldCat Records to Google," *Information Today*, ⇒ link 8.18b. Our thanks to Abby Smith for pointing out the successful metadata cases of the Human Genome Project and MIDI.

19. See ⇒ link 8.19a for W3C's full documentation on the XHTML standard. For the importance of web standards like XHTML, see Dollar Consulting, *Archival Preservation of Smithsonian Web Resources*; Jeffrey Zeldman, *Designing with Web Standards* (Indianapolis: New Riders, 2003); Dan Cederholm, *Web Standards Solutions* (Berkeley, Calif.: Apress, 2004). As the W3C puts it, much more opaquely: "Alternate ways of accessing the Internet are constantly being introduced. The XHTML family is designed with general user agent interoperability in mind. Through a new user agent and document profiling mechanism, servers, proxies, and user agents will be able to perform best effort content transformation. Ultimately it will be possible to develop XHTML-conforming content that is usable by any XHTML-conforming user agent." See ⇒ link 8.19b.

20. Douglas O. Linder, email to Joan Fragaszy, 30 June 2004.

21. Cornell University Library, "Chamber of Horrors: Obsolete and Endangered Media," *Digital Preservation Tutorial*, ⇒ link 8.21a; Tom Mainelli, "Dell Drops Floppy Drives in New PCs," *PCWorld.com*, 5 February 2003, ⇒ link 8.21b.

22. Byers, *Care and Handling of CDs and DVDs*, ⇒ link 8.22.

23. National Institute of Standards and Technology, "Digital Data Preservation Program CD and DVD Archiving: Quick Reference Guide for Care and Handling," *Digital Data Preservation Program*, ⇒ link 8.23; Kimberly A. Tryka, email to Joan Fragaszy, 20 July 2004.

24. Ibid.

25. Helen Meredith, "Learning All About Disaster Recovery," *Australian Financial Review*, Supplement, 1 May 2002, 16. The principle of mirroring is at the center of the digital preservation strategy advanced by the LOCKSS program (Lots of Copies Keep Stuff Safe), which hopes to sustain digital documents and artifacts through a federation of library servers with redundant copies of accessioned files. For an overview of LOCKSS, see ⇒ link 8.25.

26. "Error 404: Page Not Found," *H-GIG*, ⇒ link 8.26.

27. Shareware link checkers can be downloaded from ⇒ link 8.27a. Alert LinkRunner is a good program for PCs, and can be found at ⇒ link 8.27b. W3C's link checker is at ⇒ link 8.27c.

28. Douglas O. Linder, email.

29. DSpace Federation, *DSpace*, ⇒ link 8.29.

30. On Fedora, see "Fedora: The Flexible Extensible Digital Object Repository Architecture," *The Fedora Project: An Open-Source Digital Repository Management System*, ⇒ link 8.30a. Because of a trademark dispute with Red Hat Inc., the Fedora project may have to change its name, even though it has used it since 1998, five years before Red Hat adopted it for one of its software releases. See ⇒ link 8.30b and also Thornton Staples, Ross Wayland, and Sandra Payette, "The Fedora Project: An Open-source Digital Object Repository System," *D-Lib Magazine*, April 2003, ⇒ link 8.30c. Outside of the United States, Greenstone software, which grew out of the New Zealand Digital Library Project at the University of Waikato, offers another turnkey solution for setting up a digital library. With support from UNESCO and with documentation in five languages and an

interface that can be modified to more than thirty other languages, Greenstone has gained a modest following worldwide, including in the United States. It seems more popular as a display and search technology for finite digitization projects (e.g., New York Botanical Garden's rare book collection at ⇒ link 8.30d) than a continuously updated archival system like DSpace. On OAI compliance, see Don Sawyer, "ISO 'Reference Model for an Open Archival Information System (OAIS)'" (paper presented to USDA Digital Publications Preservation Steering Committee, 19 February 1999), ⇒ link 8.30e. Originally postulated by the Consultative Committee for Space Data Systems, a coalition of international space agencies (including NASA) that was trying to figure out how to store digital data from space missions for the long term, OAIS provides a framework of both systems and people and an associated set of common definitions (such as what a "data object" is) that should be applicable (CCSDS claims) to any archive, from small, personal ones to international, nearly boundless ones. OAIS provides a model that should enable individual digital archives to store materials effectively and sustain themselves over the long run. Note that this is, by CCSDS's own admission, a high-level conceptual framework, not a ground-level working model. See ⇒ link 8.30f.

31. See Mary Ide, Dave MacCarn, Thom Shepard, and Leah Weisse, "Understanding the Preservation Challenge of Digital Television," and Howard D. Wactlar and Michael G. Christel, "Digital Video Archives: Managing Through Metadata," in *Building a National Strategy for Preservation: Issues in Digital Media Archiving* (Washington, D.C.: Council on Library and Information Resources and the Library of Congress, 2002), 67–79 and 80–95, ⇒ link 8.31a and ⇒ link 8.31b. For an example of the challenges of digital video, see the EVIA Digital Archive, a joint effort of Indiana University and the University of Michigan to archive approximately 150 hours of ethnomusicological video, ⇒ link 8.31c.

32. Arts and Humanities Data Service, "Planning Historical Digitisation Projects—Backup," *Planning Historical Digitisation Projects*, ⇒ link 8.32.

33. Paula de Stefano, "Digitization for Preservation and Access," in *Preservation: Issues and Planning*, ed. Paul N. Banks and Roberta Pilette (Chicago: American Library Association, 2000), 319; quotation from Abby Smith, *Why Digitize?* (Washington, D.C.: Council on Library and Information Resources, 1999), 3; Rosenzweig, "Scarcity or Abundance?"

34. Smith, *Why Digitize?* 3; Kathleen Arthur, Sherry Byrne, Elisabeth Long, Carla Q. Montori, and Judith Nadler, "Recognizing Digitization as a Preservation Reformatting Method," Association of Research Libraries, ⇒ link 8.34a; Hartmut Weber and Marianne Dörr, *Digitization as a Means of Preservation?* (Amsterdam: European Commission on Preservation and Access, 1997), ⇒ link 8.34b.

35. Among the larger, more elaborate initiatives are the Library of Congress National Digital Information Infrastructure and Preservation Program (NDIIPP) (⇒ link 8.35a), the National Archives and Records Administration's Electronic Records Archive (ERA) (⇒ link 8.35b), and the International Research on Permanent Authentic Records in Electronic Systems (InterPARES) (⇒ link 8.35c); Frederick J. Graboske and Christine T. Laba, "Field History, the War on Terrorism, and the United States Marine Corps Oral History Program" (paper presented at the International Oral History Association, Rome, Italy, 23–26 June 2004); Samuel Brylawski, "Review of Audio Collection Preservation Trends and Challenges" (paper presented at Sound Savings: Preserving Audio Collections, Austin, Texas, 24–26 July 2003), ⇒ link 8.35d.

36. Anne R. Kenney and Paul Conway, "From Analog to Digital: Extending the Preservation Tool Kit," in *Going Digital: Strategies for Access, Preservation, and Conversion of Collections to a Digital Format*, ed. Donald L. DeWitt (New York: Haworth Press, 1998), 67–79; Matthew Cook, "Economies of Scale: Digitizing the Chicago Daily News," *RLG DigiNews* 4.1 (15 February 2000), ⇒ link 8.36.

37. Warwick Cathro, Colin Webb, and Julie Whiting, "Archiving the Web: The PANDORA Archive at the National Library of Australia" (paper presented at Preserving the Present for the Future, Copenhagen, June 18–19, 2001). See also Diane Vogt-O'Connor, "Is the Record of the 20th Century at Risk?" *CRM: Cultural Resource Management* 22, 2 (1999): 21–24; Caroline R. Arms, "Keeping Memory Alive: Practices for Preserving Digital Content at the National Digital Library Program of the Library of Congress," *RLD DigiNews* 4, 3 (June 15, 2000), ⇒ link 8.37a. For the argument in favor of emulation, see Jeff Rothenberg, *Avoiding Technological Quicksand: Finding a Viable Technical Foundation for Digital Preservation* (Washington, D.C.: Council on Library and Information Resources, 1999), ⇒ link 8.37b. For other comparisons of digital preservation strategies, as well as what leading institutions, such as the U.S. National Archives and Records Administration (NARA) and the San Diego Supercomputing Center (SDSC), are doing to address the technological challenges, see NARA's Electronic Records Archives home page, ⇒ link 8.37c; SDSC's Methodologies for Preservation and Access of Software-dependent Electronic Records home page, ⇒ link 8.37d; Kenneth Thibodeau, "Overview of Technological Approaches to Digital Preservation and Challenges in Coming Years," *The State of Digital Preservation: An International Perspective* (Washington, D.C.: Council on Library and Information Resources, 2002), ⇒ link 8.37e; Raymond A. Lorie, "The Long-Term Preservation of Digital Information," ⇒ link 8.37f; *Preserving Digital Information*, ⇒ link 8.37g.

38. Hedstrom, *It's About Time*, 9.

Some Final Thoughts

1. Tim Berners-Lee, "Information Management: A Proposal," March 1989, ⇒ link F.1.

Appendix. Database Software, Scripting Languages, and XML

1. The Statue of Liberty–Ellis Island Foundation, *American Family Immigration History Center*, ⇒ link A.1.

2. *PostgreSQL*, ⇒ link A.2.

3. Localités/Localities, *Coles County Legal History Project*, ⇒ link A.3.

4. University of Minnesota, *Immigration History Research Center*, ⇒ link A.4.

5. *MySQL*, ⇒ link A.5.

6. Center for History and New Media and American Social History Project, *The September 11 Digital Archive*, ⇒ link A.6.

7. For example, see *Web Host Directory*, ⇒ link A.7.

8. Tom Costa, *The Geography of Slavery in Virginia: Virginia Runaways*, ⇒ link A.8.

9. Daniel J. Cohen, "History and the Second Decade of the Web," *Rethinking History* 8 (June 2004): 297–98, ⇒ link A.9.

10. Cornell University Library, *Distributed Digital Library of Mathematical Monographs*, ⇒ link A.10.

Index

Aarseth, Espen, 11
Aasen Centre (Ivar Aasen Centre of Language and Culture), 223
About.com, 24
Abraham Lincoln Historical Digitization Project, 145
academic institutions. *See* colleges and universities
Access database software, 249, 250, 251
accessibility: as feature of digital media, 4–5, 84–85; obstacles to, for some users, 64, 94, 101, 137–40
"ACID" (Atomicity Consistency Isolation Durability) compliance, 250
acid-free paper, 222, 241
Active Server Pages (ASP) scripting language, 252, 254, 260
Adler, John, 33–34
Adobe Corporation, 234. *See also* Photoshop; Photoshop Elements
advertising, 150–51, 156, 176, 281n29
Afro-Louisiana History and Genealogy, 1718–1820 (online archive), 131–32
Agre, Phil, 3, 25, 144, 159
Alexa Internet, Inc., 281n25
Alexander, Scott, 43, 215
Alexander Street Press, 89, 94
Alfred P. Sloan Foundation, 48, 76, 77, 164, 167, 185
"alt" attribute, 139–40
AltaVista search engine, 148–49
Amazon.com, 110, 158
Ambrose, Stephen, 200
American Association of Museums, 146
American Council of Learned Societies, 39, 78
American Experience websites, 37–38
American Family Immigration History Center website, 281n21
American Historical Association (AHA),

20, 73–74, 78, 142, 145. See also *American Historical Review*
American Historical Review, 9, 11, 39, 40–41
American Memory (website), 26–27, 44, 204, 275n41, 294n62; as database, 22; large audience for, 4, 84–85; size of, 22, 26, 80
American Presidency website (The American Presidency: A Glorious Burden), 44–45
American Quarterly, 39
American Social History Project, 16, 17, 46, 47, 263n29. *See also* History Matters; Lost Museum; September 11 Digital Archive; *Who Built America?;* World History Matters
American University, 295n65
Amiens Cathedral Project, 128, 129
Andreessen, Marc, 20
animation files, 128
Anti-Imperialism in the United States, 1898–1935 (website), 31–32, 93, 107
AOL, Inc., 155, 173
Apache software, 202, 235
Apple Computers, 61, 103, 166, 173, 235. *See also* Macintosh Computers; QuickTime; QuickTime VR
archival websites, 25–35
Arms, Caroline R., 244
Arthurs, Dan, 62–63
Arts & Letters Daily, 125, 126
ASCII, 242
ASHP. *See* American Social History Project
ASP (Active Server Pages) scripting language, 252, 254, 260
Association of Research Libraries (ARL), 243
Atlantic Monthly, 198, 207
Atomic Memories (website), 167
Atomic Veterans History Project (website), 112, 170, 174

"attribution" license, 202–3
audience, 32, 85, 141–44; as community of
    interest, 144–47, 159; defining, 143;
    methods of building, 144–44, *see also*
    promotion; and return traffic, 151–52;
    tracking of, 152–59, 281n20
audiences, historians' multiple, 4–5,
    143–44
audio browsers, 101
audio files, 128–30, 139; digitization of,
    101–2. *See also* multimedia
Austin College, 224
Authentic software, 86
Autodesk Cleaner, 102, 103
Ayers, Edward, 30, 32, 41. *See also* Valley of
    the Shadow

background images, 127
backup, 235–39
Baker, Nicholson, 83, 92
Bakewell, Peter, 33
Ballard, Martha, 143. *See also* DoHistory
Barger, Jorn, 41
Basic Books, Inc. v. Kinko's Graphic Corp.
    (1991), 194
Bass, Randy, 47
BBC (British Broadcasting Corporation),
    164, 169, 223–24, 235
Bearman, David, 295–96n7
Benjamin, Walter, 262n10
Beowulf project, 92
Berners-Lee, Tim, 8, 137, 247–48
Besek, June, 208
Best of History Web Sites, 23, 146
Bibliothèque Nationale de France, 27
Binghamton University, 46
Birkerts, Sven, 1, 11
bit depth, 82, 96, 102
BlackBerry messages, 169–70
Blackboard software, 23, 45, 59
Blackout History Project (website), 176
Blake Archive (William Blake Archive), 100
Bleecker, Julian, 63
Blitz, Michael, 39–40
blogs, 41–42, 148, 161, 170–72, 248; growth
    in number of, 6; hosting systems for,
    171; software for, 41, 59, 171, 282–83n13
Bloom, Harold, 12
Boals, Dennis, 23
books: design principles for, 113–16; digiti-
zation of, 34, 35, 80, 85, 92, 93–94; elec-
    tronic (e-books), 39, 78
Borges, Jorge Luis, 54
Boston University, 135–36
"bots," 155
Brainerd, Kansas: Time, Place and Memory
    on the Prairie Plains (website), 43, 44
Bridgeman Art Library, 212–13
Brier, Steve, 17, 264n3
Brin, Sergey, 149
British Broadcasting Corporation (BBC),
    164, 169, 223–24, 235
British Library, 134, 164
broadband connection, 61
Brodman, James William, 8
Brown, David E., 74–75
Brown, Glenn Otis, 202
Brown, Joshua, 17, 39, 264n3
Browning, John, 1
browsers, 20, 54–55, 58, 118, 157–58;
    audio, 101
"browser-safe" colors, 127
Brylawski, Samuel, 244
Budapest Open Access Initiative, 13
bulletin board discussions, 146. *See also*
    online discussions
Burnard, Lou, 88, 90
Bush, George W., 220
Butler, Kathleen, 292–93n53
Butowsky, Harry, 157
Byers, Fred R., 222

Cahill, Kathy, 138
camcorders, digital, 103
cameras, digital, 273n28
Carnegie Mellon University, 86, 106, 207
Carnes, Mark, 216
Carter, Alice, 43
Cascading Style Sheets (CSS), 120, 234
Case, Mary, 200
CD-R storage format, 238
CD-ROMs, 20, 237, 264n3
CDs, 222, 237
census records, 29
Center for History and New Media
    (CHNM), 4, 7, 16, 20, 151, 172–73, 263–
    64n29; authors' involvement with, 17;
    and digital preservation, 235; goal of, 16.
    See also Blackout History project; Echo
    project; History Matters; History News
    Network; Liberty, Equality, Fraternity;

September 11 Digital Archive; *Who Built America?;* World History Matters

CERN (European Organization for Nuclear Research), 247–48

Chang, Young-Hae, 110–11

Chapman, Stephen, 273n27

Chicago Daily Tribune, 209

Chicago Fire website (The Great Chicago Fire and the Web of Memory), 37

Chicago Historical Society, 37, 119–20, 244

Chicago Manual of Style, 211, 212

ChillingEffects.org website, 218

China, 105

Chronicle of Higher Education, 125

"chunking" of text, 124–25

Church of Jesus Christ of Latter-day Saints, 29, 199

City University of New York, 185. *See also* American Social History Project

client computer: defined, 54. *See also* computer screens

Clinton, Bill, 137, 193

Coates, Eyler Robert, Sr., 33

ColdFusion scripting language, 252, 254

Coles County Legal History Project, 250

collaboration, importance of, 90

collecting. *See* online collecting

colleges and universities, 22–23, 138–39; copyright policies of, 194, 201–2, 292n49; web hosting by, 67–68, 74, 239. *See also* institutional review boards

Colonial Williamsburg website, 158

colors, 126–27, 139

Columbia University, 128, 164

Columbia University Press, 39, 78

column width, 123, 131–32

comment tags, 230

Commission on Preservation and Access, 229

Common-Place: The Interactive Journal of Early American Life, 39

"commons," web as, 186–87, 190, 197. *See also* Creative Commons; open source software

communities of interest, 143, 144–47, 150, 159

Composer HTML editor, 58

Computer History Museum, 166

computer screens, 11, 86–87, 117–18, 132, 181

Computerworld, 105

comScore Media Matrix rating service, 156

Constitution Society, 210

Conway, Paul, 244

"cookies," 158, 281n29

copyright law, 12–13, 189–90, 195–97, 217–19, 288n23; and copyright notice, 197–99, 204, 287n21; and databases, 194–95, 199; and "fair use," 209, 210–12, 215–16, 217; and film, 216–17, 294n61; history of, 191–95, 286nn7,8,10,11; and images, 212–13, 292–93n53; and music, 203, 213–15, 218–19, 293nn55,57, 293–94n59; and non-U.S. works, 192, 207–9; and public domain, 203–10; and registration, 199, 287n20, 288n25; and "teacher exception," 201–2, 289n27. *See also* Sonny Bono Copyright Term Extension Act

copyright radicalism, 203

Corbis image library, 99, 293n53; misleading claims by, to copyright, 197–98, 204, 275n42

Corel Corporation, 212–13

Cornell University, 29, 104, 237, 241, 255

costs: for database software, 249–50; for digitization, 83–84, 90, 91, 93–95, 104–6, 273nn27,32, 274n35; for discussion software, 172; for graphics software, 60; and increased traffic, 4, 261n7; for log analysis, 281n20; for permissions, 196, 209, 213, 214, 216; for storage, 3–4, 100, 102, 227, 237, 242; for web design, 58, 59, 60, 113; for web hosting, 68–70. *See also* funding

Council on Library and Information Resources, 229

course websites, 45–46. *See also* syllabi

Creative Commons, 190, 202–3

CTEA. *See* Sonny Bono Copyright Term Extension Act

Cuneiform Digital Library, 147

Daccord, Thomas, 23

Darnton, Robert, 39

databases, 5, 22, 249–51, 260, 288n23; advantages of, 66–67; and copyright law, 194–95, 199; "gated," 22, 24–25; scripting languages for, 251–55; software for, 249–50, 251

Davila, James R., 41, 42

"deep linking," 218

"deep web," 22
democracy, 187–88, 248. *See also* "commons," web as
"density of data," 82, 83
design. *See* web design
De Stefano, Paula, 104, 243
Dickens, Charles, 192
DigiBeta tapes, 102
"digital archaeology," 245
digital camcorders, 103
digital cameras, 273n28
Digital Classroom (website), 44
digital divide, 12
Digital Imaging Project of South Africa, 27
Digital Library Federation, 104
Digital Library Forum, 81
Digital Library Production Service, 28–29
digital media: advantages of, 3–8; hazards of, 8–13; prophecies about, 1–2. *See also* digital preservation; digitization; World Wide Web
Digital Millennium Copyright Act (1998), 193–94
digital photographs, 170
digital preservation, 9–11, 220–22, 233–35, 239–46; and backups, 235–39; challenges to, 10–11, 220–25, 233–34, 239–40, 241–43; and choices made during website construction, 229–35; of federal government records, 10–11, 226–27; and low storage costs, 227, 237; of multimedia, 62–63, 222, 224–25; selectivity in, 225–29; and website documentation, 229–33
Digital Vault Initiative, 34
digitization, 80–81; of audio and moving images, 101–3; of books, 34, 35, 80, 85, 92, 93–94; costs and benefits of, 81–86; of handwriting, 83, 242; of images, 95–101; in-house vs. outsourced, 103–7; of text, 86–95
Dillman, Don, 181–82
Discovery Communications, 24, 152, 158
discussions, online. *See* online discussions
Disney Corporation, 13, 207
distance education, 211–12
DjVu format, 234–35
Doctorow, Cory, 232–33
documentary films, 37–38
documentation: defined, 229; efforts to standardize, 232–33; importance of, for digital preservation, 229–32

Documenting the American South (website), 4, 27–28
Document Type Definition (DTD), 89, 256
DoHistory (website), 49, 77, 143, 231, 240–41, 242
"do-it-yourself" spirit, 106–7, 184
Dollar Consulting, 231
domain names, 71–73; masking of, 73; registration of, 72–74
Domain Name System (DNS), 71–72
Domesday Project, 223–24, 235, 244
Donald, David, 6
Dotster domain registrar, 72
DoubleClick, Inc., 281n29
Douglas County Historical Society website, 52, 72, 73
downloading (vs. streaming), 61
"Dreaming Arnold Schwarzenegger" (online article), 39–40
Dreamweaver web design software, 58–59, 60, 269n8
DSpace repository software, 241, 243, 246
Dublin, Thomas, 46
Dublin Core Metadata Initiative, 101, 232
durability. *See* digital preservation
DVDs, 193–94, 237, 238

Early American Fiction Project, 92
Eastern Illinois University, 250
EBSCO, 106
Echo project (Echo: Exploring and Collecting History Online—Science, Technology, and Industry), 48, 77, 145, 167, 168, 185
EDSITEment directory, 146
Education World, 219
Eighteenth Century Collections Online, 34, 80
Eldred, Eric, 195
Eldred v. Ashcroft (2003), 195
Eldritch Press website, 195
Electric Vehicle History Online Archive, 175–76
electronic books (e-books), 39, 78
Electronic Frontier Foundation, 232
Ellis Island website (Statue of Liberty–Ellis Island Foundation), 29, 70, 157, 250
email, 18, 19–20, 47, 56–57, 145, 187; and online collecting, 169, 170
Emory University, 33
"emulation," 244–45

Encoded Archival Description (EAD), 232
Erikson, Joakim, 223
Eskandari-Qajar, M. M., 73
Ethington, Philip J., 11, 41
EVIA (Ethnomusicological Video for Instruction and Analysis) Digital Archive, 102–3
Excel, 58
Excite search engine, 148–49
exhibits, online, 35–37, 186; by Smithsonian Institution, 35, 36, 37, 44–45, 113
"exit pages," 157
expenses. See costs
Exploratorium (San Francisco), 167
Extensible Stylesheet Language (XSL), 256, 257, 260
Extensible Stylesheet Language Transformations (XSLT), 256, 260

"fair use," 192, 197, 209, 210–12, 219, 291n41, 294n61; defined, 192; and *Folsom* case, 192, 286n7; importance of upholding, 197, 212; legal tests for, 196, 210–11; and multimedia, 215–16, 217, 219, 293–94n59, 294n61; and 1976 Copyright Act, 193, 210–11, 286n10
FamilySearch Internet Genealogy Service, 29
Famous Trials (website), 33, 112, 236
"fanzine" websites, 43
FAQ (frequently asked questions) page, 151
Faragher, John Mack, 38
Fasulo, Thomas, 43
Fedora project, 241, 243, 297n30
Feist Publications, Inc. v. Rural Telephone Co. (1991), 194, 198
Ferris, William, 220
file size, 61, 97–98, 100
Fireworks graphics software, 60
Fishman, Stephen, 197–98, 213
Flash, 36, 63–65, 128, 130; and accessibility issues, 64
Flint Sit-Down Strike website (Remembering the Flint Sit-Down Strike, 1936–1937), 128, 130
focus groups, 159
Folklore.org website, 166, 167
Folsom v. Marsh (1841), 192, 286n7
fonts, 123–24
Ford Motor Company, 164

forums. See online discussions
"Founders' Copyright," 203
fragility of digital objects, 222–25
frames, 136–37
Franklin D. Roosevelt Presidential Library and Museum website, 87
free software movement, 202. See also open source software
From Revolution to Reconstruction (website), 19
FTP sites, 20
funding, 27, 76–79, 220

Gales, Larry, 116–17
Galileo Project website, 132–33
games, 152
"gated" websites, 22, 24–25, 45
Gates, Bill, 197–98
gateways, 23, 146
GATT (General Agreement on Tariffs and Trade), 208, 291n40
Gelber, Steven M., 29
genealogy, 5, 29
General Agreement on Tariffs and Trade (GATT), 208, 291n40
Generalized Markup Language (GML), 88
"General Public License" (GPL), 202
genres, 25, 37–44, 47–50, 144. See also archival websites; online exhibits; teaching websites; topical websites
GeoCities web host, 68
Geography of Slavery, The (website), 255
George Catlin and His Indian (online exhibit), 45
George Mason University, 45, 76. See also Center for History and New Media
Georgia Institute of Technology, 138
Gertz, Janet, 103, 104
Getty Research Institute, 36
GIF (Graphics Interchange Format), 96–100, 127, 242, 275n41
Ginsburg, Justice Ruth Bader, 195
Glasgow University, 103
GML (Generalized Markup Language), 88
GoDaddy.com domain registrar, 72–73
Goldfarb, Charles, 88
Google search engine, 6, 64, 90, 148–50, 156, 171, 233; methods used by, 52, 101, 136, 148–50, 296n11; online book project of, 34, 35, 80; primacy of, 22, 148
Gopher navigational system, 20

Gould Foundation, 77
grants. *See* funding
graphical navigation, 140
Great Chicago Fire and the Web of Memory, The (website), 37
Green, Dave, 293n53
Greenberg, Joshua, 42, 169
Greenstone software, 297–98n30
Grier, Justice Robert, 192
Grossman, Loyd, 224
guestbooks, 151, 158
Gutenberg-e project, 39, 78
Guthrie, Woody, 206

Haddix, Charles, 293n57
Hale, Christopher, 207
Hall, Gwendolyn, 131–32
Halsall, Paul, 33, 74, 75, 209
handicapped users, 94. *See also* visually impaired users
handwriting, 83, 242
Hanrahan, Michael, 128
Harappa: The Indus Valley and the Raj in India and Pakistan (website), 33, 128
Harper, Georgia, 214
HarpWeek online archive, 34, 200, 201, 288n26
Harvard University, 93, 231, 295n65
HD-Rosetta disk, 225
Hedstrom, Margaret, 224–25, 246
Hemispheric Institute of Performance and Politics, 102
Henriques, Peter R., 27
Henry, Linda, 296n7
Here Is New York (online exhibit), 186
Herodotus, 187–88
Hertzfeld, Andy, 166, 167
Hewitt, Joe, 4
Hewlett-Packard, 241
H-GIG website, 239
high school students and teachers, 4, 5, 143, 145, 155
Himmelfarb, Gertrude, 1, 8, 9
"historians": defined, 3
Historical Newspapers (ProQuest commercial service), 80
historical organizations, 49. *See also* American Historical Association
historical societies, 5. *See also specific societies*
Historical Voices (website), 78, 128
historic sites, 142

History Channel, 9, 12; website of, 24, 48, 152, 160, 168
History Cooperative, 9, 38, 279n32
history department websites, 49, 151
History E-Book project, 78
History Matters: The U.S. Survey Course on the Web, 46–47, 145, 146, 148, 152, 157; as gateway, 23. *See also* World History Matters
History News Network (HNN), 39, 41, 148, 151, 152, 158
History Sourcebooks, 209
History Web, 18, 50; diversity of, 22–25, *see also* genres; dramatic growth of, 2; origins of, 18–22
"hits," 153–55, 281n21
H-Net, 47, 48, 57, 145, 160
HNSource (website), 20
Horton, Sarah, 124–25, 126
hosting. *See* web hosting
HotBot search engine, 148–49
Hotmail, 172
HTML (HyperText Markup Language), 52, 54–55, 87, 127, 234, 240; and browsers, 118; and databases, 251; and more sophisticated mark-up languages, 88, 91, 234; "translators" for, 58
HTML Tidy software, 268n6
HTTP (HyperText Transfer Protocol), 8, 54
Human Genome Project, 233
Humanities Advanced Technology and Information Institute, 103
hypertext, 8, 130; as foundational principle of web, 8, 130. *See also* HTML; HTTP; mark-up languages

IBM, 88, 250
images, 60, 85–86; as background, 127; and copyright law, 212–13, 292–93n53; different file formats for, 96–100, 275n44; file size of, 96, 97–98, 100; and issues of accessibility, 139; printing of, 99; in web design, 125–28. *See also* photographs; "thumbnails"
Images of England project, 104
Immigration History Research Center website, 250
India, 105
Indiana University, 102
Innodata Isogen, 105

instant messaging (IM), 169, 173
Institute for Advanced Technology in the Humanities (IATH), 30, 76, 77, 272n24
Institute of Museum and Library Services, 27, 78, 90–91
institutional review boards (IRBs), 179, 283n23
interactivity, 42, 160, 172–73, 187; and community-making, 187; in courses, 53; as feature of digital media, 7–8; and History Channel website, 48, 152, 160, 168; and online exhibits, 36–37. *See also* communities of interest; online collecting; online discussions
International Copyright Treaty (1891), 192
International Dunhuang Project, 27
Internet: decentralized nature of, 54
Internet2, 102
Internet Archive, 161, 184–85; and digital preservation, 220–21, 228, 296n11
Internet Corporation for Assigned Names and Numbers (ICANN), 72
Internet Explorer web browser, 20, 118
Internet History Sourcebooks Project, 33
Internet Information Services (IIS), 250
Internet Protocol (IP) addresses, 71, 183, 200
Invisible Adjunct, The (blog), 42
ISPs (Internet service providers), 68, 239
Ivar Aasen Centre of Language and Culture, 223

Jensen, Richard, 20
Jewish Museum (London), 174
Journal of American History, 9, 45, 145, 146, 217
Journal of Multimedia History, 38
Journal of the Association for History and Computing, 38
journals, scholarly, 2, 38–39, 42. See also *American Historical Review; Journal of American History;* JSTOR
Journeys in Time, 1809–1822: The Journals of Lachlan & Elizabeth Macquarie (website), 123, 124
JPEG (Joint Photographic Experts Group) files, 96, 98–99, 100, 127, 242, 275n41
JSTOR, 7, 38, 136, 274n36; and accuracy of scanning, 87, 93, 94; as "gated" database, 22
JT Imaging software company, 234

Kahle, Brewster, 163, 228, 274n35
Kalfatovic, Martin, 105
Kaplan, Judge Lewis A., 213
Katten, Michael, 39
Kazin, Michael, 183–84
Kelly, Kevin, 1
Kenney, Anne R., 244
Kerr, Austin, 263n22
keywords, 149, 150
Khan, Omar, 33
King, Rev. Dr. Martin Luther, Jr., 204, 289n33
Kirsch, David, 166, 175–76, 210
Koninklijke Bibliotheek, 137
Korean War Educator (website), 112
Krasniewicz, Louise, 39–40
Krug, Steve, 109

Landow, George, 8
Landsberger, Stefan, 33
language translation software, 5
laserdiscs, 20
learning disabled users, 94
Leibsohn, Dana, 128
Lesk, Michael, 3–4, 90, 207, 274n35
Lessig, Lawrence, 12, 190
Levine, Lawrence, 197
liability. *See* copyright law
Liberty, Equality, Fraternity: Exploring the French Revolution (website), 77, 144–45, 214
Library of Congress, 24, 198, 214; and digital preservation, 222, 224–25, 232, 233, 244, 284n33; digitization methods used by, 83, 97–98, 102, 103; expanded access to holdings of, 4, 84–85, 143; free access to photographs held by, 99, 198, 275n42; impetus given by, to digital history, 20, 27; and September 11 collecting, 161, 185. *See also* American Memory
licenses, 200, 202–3, 213
Lifton, Fred, 127–28
Linder, Douglas, 33, 112, 236, 240
links, 149–50, 240
Links to the Past (website), 49
Linux, 118, 120, 202, 235
listservs, 146, 170
Litman, Jessica, 192
LOCKSS program (Lots of Copies Keep Stuff Safe), 297n25
log analysis, 152–58, 281n20

logins, 177
long-term preservation. *See* digital preservation
Looksmart web directory, 150
Lorie, Raymond, 88
Los Angeles Times, 80
Lost & Found Sound, 76
Lost Museum, The (website), 47
Luna Imaging, 106
Lynch, Patrick, 124–25, 126

Mabry, Donald, 20
machine-readable text, 87, 92–95
Macintosh Computer, 118, 120, 166, 238, 276n50
Macromedia Corporation, 60, 98, 252. *See also* Dreamweaver; Flash
Mahlberg, George, 9, 10
mailing lists, 158–59
Making of America project, 28–29, 93, 94, 104–5, 106
Makivirta, Joni, 19
Manovich, Lev, 5
maps, 140, 275n41
MARC (MAchine-Readable Cataloging), 233
Marine Corps, 243–44
marked-up text, 87–91
marketing. *See* promotion
Mark Twain in His Times (website), 49, 76
mark-up languages, 87–91; TEI standards for, 89–91. *See also* HTML; SGML; XML
Massachusetts Institute of Technology (MIT), 22, 60, 138, 241
MATRIX, 102
McCann, James C., 135–36
McGann, Jerome, 7, 30, 272n24
McLemore, Laura, 224
McSherry, Corynne, 202, 289n28
Medieval Illuminated Manuscripts (website), 137
Mellon Foundation, 29, 78
messaging, instant, 169, 173
Messer-Kruse, Timothy, 147
"metadata," 83–84, 87, 100–101, 177, 232–33
Metadata Encoding and Transmission Standard (METS), 101, 232
Metadata Object Description Schema (MODS), 232
"meta" tags, 149

Michigan State University, 77, 102. *See also* Historical Voices; National Gallery of the Spoken Word
microfilm, 92
Microsoft Corporation, 58–59, 156, 250, 252, 254; market strength of, 118, 235, 238. *See also* Internet Explorer; Microsoft Word; Windows Media Player
Microsoft Word, 58, 87, 242
Middleton, Ken, 23
MIDI (Musical Instrument Digital Interface), 233
"migration," 244–45
Million Book project, 106
Minard, Charles Joseph, 116, 117
MINERVA (Mapping the INternet Electronic Resources Virtual Archive), 284n33
Minow, Mary, 210, 211, 219
mirroring, 239, 297n25
MIT (Massachusetts Institute of Technology), 22, 60, 138, 241
Model Editions Partnership: Historical Editions in the Digital Age, 272–73n26
modems, 61
monitors, 99. *See also* computer screens
Montgomery Advertiser, 209
Monticello website, 49, 230–31
Mormons (Church of Jesus Christ of Latter-day Saints), 29, 199
Morris, William, 114, 115
Morville, Peter, 134
Mosaic, 19, 20, 30
Mosher, Edward, 88
Movable Type blogging system, 171
movies, 216–17
Moving Here (website), 164, 172, 174, 179, 180
Mozilla web browser, 58
MP3 audio standard, 63
MP3 music files, 102, 203
multimedia, 61–65, 128–30, 196; and accessibility issues, 64, 139, 196; and digital preservation, 62–63, 222, 224–25, 242; digitization of, 101–3. *See also* audio files; Flash; music; video files
Mundy, Barbara, 128
Murray, Janet, 6
MUSE Awards, 146
Museum of London, 164
museums, 99, 142; online exhibits by, 35–37, 113. *See also specific museums*

Museums and the Web conference, 146
music: and copyright law, 203, 213–15, 218–19, 293nn55,57, 293–94n59
Musical Instrument Digital Interface (MIDI), 233
My History Is America's History (website), 220–21
MySQL database program, 250–51, 252, 255; and digital preservation, 235; as free software, 202, 254; widespread use of, 251, 254, 260

Nagasaki University Library, 27
National Archives (U.S. National Archives and Records Administration), 10–11, 44, 226–27, 263n21
National Center for Supercomputing Applications (NCSA), 19
National Council for Social Studies, 145
National Digital Library Program, 26
National Endowment for the Arts (NEA), 76
National Endowment for the Humanities (NEH), 27, 46, 90–91, 146, 220–21
National Gallery of the Spoken Word, 77, 78. See also Historical Voices
National Geographic, 64–65, 164
National Humanities Center, 46
National Institute of Standards and Technology (NIST), 222, 238
National Institutes of Health, 176
National Monuments Record, 104
National Museum of American History, 113, 186
National Park Foundation, 164
National Park Service, 24, 49, 151–52, 157, 164
National Public Radio, 76
National Science Foundation (NSF), 77, 78, 224
navigation, 117, 130, 140
Nelson, Lynn, 20, 23, 291n42
Netscape web browser, 20, 58
Network Solutions domain registrar, 72
New Deal Network online archive, 53
New Jersey Historical Society, 35–36
newsgroups, 47
newsletters, online, 151
newspapers, 117–18; websites of, 161, 182. See also specific newspapers
New York Times, 80, 86, 209, 225

New York University, 102
Nickerson, Matthew, 145–46
Nielsen, Jakob, 109
Nielsen/NetRatings, 156
NINCH Guide to Good Practice in the Digital Representation and Management of Cultural Heritage Resources, 82, 101
1976 Copyright Act, 192–93, 201, 207, 214; and "fair use," 193, 210–11, 286n10
NIST (National Institute of Standards and Technology), 222, 238
Noble, David, 1–2
"noncommercial license," 202
Northwestern University, 37
Norton, Roger, 6
Notepad text editor, 255, 269n8

OAI compliance, 241
OAIS (Reference Model for an Open Archival Information System), 232, 298n30
OCR (optical character recognition) software, 92, 93–95, 105, 106, 107
Ogg Vorbis audio format, 269n11
Ohio Memory (website), 157, 159
Okeh Records, 215
OLGA (On-Line Guitar Archive), 218–19
O'Malley, Michael, 45, 46, 111, 113–14, 122
OmniPage OCR software, 93, 107
O'Neal, Angela, 157, 159
online collecting, 161–65, 187–88; attracting contributors to, 173–80, 185–86; as democratic form of history, 187–88; technologies for, 169–73; good and poor candidates for, 165–69; and oral history, 163–64; quality of, 181–84; and September 11 events, 36, 113, 178, 181, 183–87. See also September 11 Digital Archive
online discussions, 146, 152, 160, 172; software for, 172
OpenCourseWare, 60
Open Database Connectivity (ODBC) protocol, 251
Open Directory Project, 150
open source software, 13, 59, 202, 252, 254, 269n11. See also free software movement
optical character recognition (OCR) software, 92, 93–95, 105, 106, 107
Optical Disk Pilot Project, 20
Oracle software, 250, 251
oral history, 163–64, 179, 283n23

Oral History Association, 179
organizational websites, 49
Organization of American Historians, 145.
    See also *Journal of American History*
Oriental Institute, 103
"orphan works," 210
Oswald, Lee Harvey, 9, 10
outsourcing, 103–7, 274n38; and workers'
    pay, 105, 276–77n58
Oxford University Press, 197

Page, Larry, 149
page images, 86; limitations of, 86–87
page views, 155–56
PaleoJudaica.com blog, 42
paper, acid-free, 222, 241
Paramount Pictures, 216
passwords, 200
Patterson, L. Ray, 291n46
PBS (Public Broadcasting Service), 113
PDF files, 234–35, 242
Pence, Dan, 104
Perleman, Lewis J., 1
permissions fees, 99, 196, 209, 213, 214,
    216, 275n42
Perseus Digital Library, 77
Pew Charitable Trusts, 185
Pew Internet and American Life Project,
    161, 184, 186–87
Philippines, 105
phone calls, Internet-based, 283n17
photographs: digital, 170; fake, 9, 10; in
    public domain, 197–98, 199, 204,
    275n42
Photoshop, 10, 60, 98, 100, 275n44
Photoshop Elements, 60, 100
PHP scripting language, 202, 240, 252, 254,
    255, 260
PictureAustralia project, 27
Pierce, Morris, 19
Pioch, Nicolas, 21
Pitt Project, 295–96n7
plagiarism, 200
PNG (Portable Network Graphics), 275n41
Port Huron Statement, 204
PostgreSQL database, 250, 251, 252
postmodernists, 8
PowerPoint, 58
preservation. *See* digital preservation
Preserving Digital Information (1996 report),
    229

press releases, 148, 176
Primedia Inc., 24
PrimeOCR software, 93
*Princeton University Press v. Michigan Docu-
    ment Services* (1996), 194
printouts, 241–42, 278n18
privacy concerns, 177–80
Project Gutenberg of Australia, 207–8
Project MUSE, 38
promotion: by appealing to community of
    interest, 143, 144–47, 159; by mass mar-
    keting, 147–51; need for, 141–42; of
    online collecting projects, 175–76; and
    return traffic, 151–52
ProQuest Company, 12, 24–25, 34, 80, 106
"public domain," 203–9, 288n22; efforts to
    restrict, through licenses, 200; need for
    broadened definition of, 190; photo-
    graphs in, 197–98, 199, 204, 275n42;
    U.S. government documents in, 203–4.
    See also copyright law
public historians, 7–8
Puglia, Steve, 83–84
puzzles, 152

QuickTime, 61–63, 102, 103, 269n11
QuickTime VR, 36, 38
quizzes, 152

Railton, Stephen, 49, 76
"README" file, 231, 296n14
RealAudio, 215
RealMedia, 61–63, 102, 103
RealNetworks, 61, 62, 63, 269n11
Red Hot Jazz Archive, 43, 215
Reed College, 128
Reed Elsevier, 12
Reference Model for an Open Archival
    Information System (OAIS), 232,
    298n30
referrers, 157. *See also* search engines
registrars, 72–73, 270n22
Rehabilitation Act Amendments (1988),
    137–39
Rehabilitation Engineering and Assistive
    Technology Society of North America
    (RESNA), 138
rekeying, 94–95
Remembering Nagasaki (online exhibit),
    36
Remembering Pearl Harbor (website), 64–
    65, 164, 165

Remembering the Flint Sit-Down Strike, 1936–1937 (website), 128, 130
repository software, 241
Research Libraries Group, 105, 229
resolution, 96
return traffic, 151–52
Rhind-Tutt, Stephen, 89
Rice, Stanley, 88
Rice University, 132–33
Richmond, Howie, 206
Rich Text Format (RTF), 242
Rieland, Randy, 144, 146, 152
"right of publicity," 218
Ritchie, Donald, 38
Roe, Kevin, 43, 44
Rogers, Richard P., 240
Rosenfeld, Louis, 134
Rosie the Riveter/World War II Home Front National Historical Park (website), 164, 169, 179–80
Rossetto, Louis, 1
Ruby, Jack, 9, 10

Sakai software, 59
"sampling," 95–96, 102
San Francisco Exploratorium, 36
scanning, 91–92, 273nn29,30,32; degree of accuracy of, 87, 93–95
Schellenberg, Theodore, 296n7
scholarly journals. See journals, scholarly
Schultz, Stanley, 45
Scout Report, 146
screens, computer, 11, 86–87, 117–18, 132, 181
scripting languages, 240, 251–55, 256, 260
scrolling, 181
Seaman, David, 104
search engines, 136, 148–50. See also Google
searching, 85–86, 87, 101, 130. See also search engines
second-level domain (SLD), 72
Second Story, 37, 113
Section 508, 137–39
self-publishing, 196–97
SeniorNet, 48, 168
September 11, 2001 events, 239. See also Here Is New York; September 11: Bearing Witness to History; September 11 Digital Archive; September 11 Web Archive; Sonic Memorial Project

September 11: Bearing Witness to History (website), 36, 113
September 11 Digital Archive, 76, 147, 161, 185–86, 251; collection of stories for, 178, 185–86; uses made of, 183–84, 228
September 11 Web Archive, 185
"server": defined, 54
servers. See web servers
"server-side" software, 59–60
SGML (Standardized Generalized Markup Language), 88–90, 272nn23,24
Shannon, Claude, 175
Shapiro, Fred, 7
Shenkman, Rick, 42, 148, 158
SHOAH Visual History Foundation, 102
Shopes, Linda, 163–64
site structure, 133–37
Six Apart, Ltd., 171
Sixties-L discussion group, 56–57, 170
Sixties Project, 289n33
Sklar, Kathryn Kish, 46
Sloan Foundation (Alfred P. Sloan Foundation), 48, 76, 77, 164, 167, 185
"small multiples," 128
Smith, Abby, 81–82, 243
Smith, Carl, 37
Smithsonian Institution, 105, 231, 234; online exhibits by, 35, 36, 37, 44–45, 113. See also National Museum of American History
Social Education, 145
Society for Cinema Studies (SCS), 216
Society for French Historical Studies (SFHS), 145
Society of American Archivists, 85, 232
Someone In Time (online quiz), 152
Sonic Memorial Project, 63, 64, 76
Sonny Bono Copyright Term Extension Act (CTEA, 1998), 34–35, 193, 195, 207, 214, 286n11, 293n55; bolstering of "gated" archives by, 12–13, 35
Sparks, Jared, 192
Sparrow, James, 147, 176
Sport of Life and Death, The: The Mesoamerican Ballgame (website), 130, 131
SQL Server database, 250, 252, 254
Stallman, Richard, 202
Stanford University, 273n30, 295n65
Star-Spangled Banner, The (Smithsonian online exhibit), 37
Statue of Liberty-Ellis Island Foundation, 157; website of, 29, 70, 157, 250

Stevens, Larry, 21, 23
storage, 235–39; cost of, 3–4, 100, 102, 227, 237, 242; formats for, 236–39; space for, 101, 102
Story, Justice William, 192
Stowe, David, 212
Stowe, Harriet Beecher, 192
Strassler, Robert, 114
streaming, 61, 103
StreamingCulture (website), 62
Structured Query Language (SQL) standard, 235
Students for a Democratic Society, 204
submission pages, 283–84n24
Sundt, Christine, 292n53
Survey Builder software, 172–73
surveys, 181
"suspicious characters," 93
syllabi, 2, 7, 22, 45, 56, 59–60
Syllabus Finder, 7

Tadic, Linda, 215
TEACH Act (Technology, Education and Copyright Harmonization Act, 2002), 211–12
"teacher exception," 201–2, 289n27
teachers: and copyright law, 201–2, 289n27; high school, 5, 143, 145; resources for, 44–47, 53, 60. See also History Matters; syllabi
TeacherServe (website), 46
teaching websites, 32–33, 44–47. See also syllabi
technical support, 68, 70
"techno-realists," 3
TEI (Text Encoding Initiative), 89–91, 272nn23,24, 272–73nn26,27
TEI tags ("TEI Lite"), 90
templates, 59–60
Texas Tech University, 164
text: "chunking" of, 124–25; digitization of, 86–95; and web design, 121–25
text editors, 255, 269n8
Text Encoding Initiative (TEI), 89–91, 272n23,24, 272–73n26, 273n27
Thatcher, Jim, 139
Theban Mapping Project, 65
TheHistoryNet (website), 24, 42
Thin Blue Line, A (website), 176
Thomas, William G., III, 41, 43
Thompson, Kristin, 216

Thomson Corporation, 12, 24–25, 34, 80, 106, 263n27
"thumbnails," 100, 127–28, 278n23
Tichi, Cecelia, 213
TIFF (Tagged Image File Format) files, 96–100, 127, 242
TimeWarner, 171
Tognazzini, Bruce, 159
Toledo's Attic: A Virtual Museum of Toledo, Ohio (website), 147
Tollett, John, 118–21
Tolstoy, Leo, 204–6
topical websites, 49–50
top-level domain (TLD), 72
Townsend, Elizabeth, 201, 289nn27,28
trademarks: vigorous enforcement of, 217–18
traffic patterns, 158
transcription, 101, 163
Trant, Jennifer, 295–96n7
Truman Presidential Library, 209
TRUSTe, 179
Tufte, Edward, 114–15, 118, 125, 127, 128
Tufts University, 77
Tunnicliffe, William, 88
Twain, Mark, 192, 193
typing, 94–95

Ulrich, Laurel Thatcher, 49. See also DoHistory
UMG Recordings v. MP3.com (2000), 199
Uncle Tom's Cabin & American Culture (website), 49, 76
Unicode, 242
Uniform Computer Information Transactions Act (UCITA), 288n26
uniform resource locators. See URLs
Unisys, 275n41
United States Access Board, 279n35
Universal Library, 86
Universal Studios, 216
universities. See colleges and universities
University of California, Berkeley, 225
University of California, Riverside, 239–40
University of Chicago, 103
University of Essex, 242
University of Georgia, 211, 291n46
University of Groningen, 19
University of Illinois, 19
University of Leeds, 224
University of Maastricht, 86

University of Michigan, 28–29, 85, 102, 106, 224, 255, 274n34. *See also* Making of America project
University of Minnesota, 250
University of Missouri-Kansas City, 240
University of North Carolina, 4, 27–28
University of Virginia, 76, 84, 92, 100, 170, 241. *See also* Institute for Advanced Technology in the Humanities; Valley of the Shadow; Virginia Center for Digital History
University of Wisconsin, 45, 146
Upham, Rev. Charles, 192
URLs (uniform resource locators), 71–74, 134–37, 150; relative, 234
"usability" school, 109–10, 124
U.S. Census Bureau, 224
U.S. Constitution, 191
U.S. Copyright Office, 52, 199, 288n25
Usenet discussion groups, 172
U.S. National Archives and Records Administration (NARA), 10–11, 44, 226–27, 263n21
U.S. Supreme Court, 191–92, 194–95, 211, 286n7

Valley of the Shadow (website), 29–31, 77, 238
Vankevich, Peter, 287n21
Veterans' Forum (website), 168
Victoria and Albert Museum, 164
video files, 101, 102, 103, 128–30, 139, 242. *See also* multimedia
Video Store Project, 169
Vietnam War Internet Project, 122
Virginia Center for Digital History (VCDH), 238–39, 255. *See also* Valley of the Shadow
"visitors," 153–55, 281n21
Vistas: Visual Culture in Spanish America, 1520–1820 (website), 128, 129
Visual Artists Rights Act (1990), 290n39
visually impaired users, 64, 94, 101, 139
Voices of Civil Rights (website), 164, 166
Voices of the Colorado Plateau (website), 37, 146
VoIP (Voice over Internet Protocol) services, 283n17
Voyager Company, 17, 264n3

W3C. *See* World Wide Web Consortium
Walsh, Robin, 123, 124

Warner Brothers, 216–17
WAV (waveform audio), 102
web. *See* World Wide Web
WebArchivist.org, 161
Web Content Accessibility Guidelines, 279n35
WebCT database, 23, 45, 59
web design, 108–9, 151, 170, 277n8, 278n18; and accessibility, 137–40; and artistic conventions, 121; basic principles of, 116–21; and book design, 113–16; differing approaches to, 109–12; and images, 125–28, *see also* "thumbnails"; and multimedia, 128–30; for online collecting, 176–77; by outside firms, 112–13, 277n8; and site structure, 133–37; and text, 121–25
Web Host Directory, 68
web hosting, 67–75, 269–70n20; commercial, 68–69, 70–71, 239, 254–55; "dedicated," 68–69; for discussions, 172; institutional, 67–68, 74; by ISPs, 68, 74–75, 254
Web Museum (website), 21
web pages, nature of, 51–52
"web-safe" colors, 127
web servers, 69–71; defined, 19, 54; growth in number of, 19. *See also* web hosting
"website": defined, 54
web standards, 58, 118, 120, 234
Webster, Noah, 191
Web Style Guide (Lynch and Horton), 124
Web Trends log analysis software, 153
Weinman, Lynda, 127
Welling, George, 19, 20
Western Society for French History, 145
Wheaton v. Peters (1834), 191–92
Wherewereyou.org website, 184
Whittle, Keith, 170, 174
Who Built America? From the Great War of 1914 to the Dawn of the Atomic Age in 1946 (CD-ROM), 195–96, 214
WHOIS search, 183
Who Killed William Robinson? Race, Justice and Settling the Land (website), 47
Wikipedia, 42
Wiki software, 42, 248
William Blake Archive, 100
Williams, Robin, 118–21
Windows Media, 61–63, 102
Wired magazine, 1, 2

Wisconsin Historical Society, 112
Without Sanctuary: Photographs and Post-
    cards of Lynching in America (website),
    36
Women and Social Movements in the
    United States, 1775–2000 (website), 46
Woodward, C. Vann, 248
Word (Microsoft Word), 58, 87, 242
WordPerfect, 243
WordPress blog program, 171
WordStar, 243
Workforce Investment Act (1988), 137–39
"work for hire" doctrine, 201
Works Progress Administration (WPA) Life
    Histories (website), 83
World History Matters, 23, 46–47, 146
World War II Living Memorial (website),
    168
World Wide Web, 2, 71; importance of hyp-
    ertext to, 8; interconnectedness of, 228;
    origins of, 18–19, 248; standards for, 58,
    118, 120, 234; structure of, 71–75;
    threatened balkanization of, see "gated"
    archives. See also "commons," web as;
    History Web; HTML; HTTP; web design;
    web hosting
World Wide Web Consortium (W3C), 137,
    139, 240, 256, 279n35, 297n19
World Wide Web Virtual Library, 23
WW2 People's War collection, 164, 169
WYSIWYG ("what you see is what you
    get"), 58

XHTML, 234, 257, 297n19; and long-term
    preservation, 234
XML, 5, 66–67, 90, 232, 234, 241, 255–60;
    compared to databases, 66–67, 255–56,
    260
XSL (Extensible Stylesheet Language),
    256, 257, 260
XSLT (Extensible Stylesheet Language
    Transformations), 256, 260

Yahoo, 101, 118, 156, 172, 233, 290n38;
    web directory of, 2, 22, 23, 150; web host-
    ing by, 68; and web's interactivity, 160,
    173

Zielke, Thomas, 20
Zwick, Jim, 31–32, 93, 107

Acknowledgments

This book grew out of a project at the Center for History and New Media (CHNM) at George Mason University (GMU) entitled Echo: Exploring and Collecting History Online—Science, Technology, and Industry, which has been funded by the Alfred P. Sloan Foundation. One of the key goals of that project has been to foster the online collecting of history of the sort described in Chapter 6. In working with those interested in this emerging practice, we saw the need for a straightforward introduction to all aspects of digital history, and this book is the result. We are deeply grateful to the Sloan Foundation for its generous support and especially to our program officer, Jesse Ausubel, for his vital encouragement of the work of CHNM and, more generally, for his visionary commitment to using new digital technology to collect, present, and preserve the past.

Our work in Echo would not have been possible without our wonderful colleagues at CHNM and, especially, two close collaborators in this book. Very early on, Jim Sparrow began thinking about many of the issues discussed herein, and his inspiration and energy were central to creating and sustaining Echo and to conceptualizing this volume. We were also tremendously lucky to have Tom Scheinfeldt join us in the summer of 2002, and he played a key role in making the September 11 Digital Archive the great success described in Chapter 6 as well as in the further development of Echo. Tom not only helped plan this book (as did Jim); he also drafted early versions of two of the chapters. We could not ask for better colleagues and friends.

Other staff members at Echo and CHNM played essential roles in the writing of this book. Emily Bliss, Rustin Crandall, Joan Fragazy, and Jim Safley provided thoughtful, energetic, and invaluable assistance— locating articles and documents, interviewing digital historians, organizing references, finding and preparing illustrations, and helping us work through difficult technical and conceptual issues. They also offered valuable and perceptive feedback on portions of the manuscripts as did other colleagues at CHNM, including Stephanie Hurter, Rikk Mulligan, Mike O'Malley, Elena Razlogova, Kelly Schrum, Amanda Shuman, and Tom Scheinfeldt. As we note in the introduction, the "we" that is often invoked in this book includes our collaborators at CHNM as well as those at the American Social History Project (ASHP) at the City University of New York, especially Steve Brier and Josh Brown, with whom we have worked on a wide range of digital history projects stretching back over more than fifteen years and whose deep democratic commitments and extraordinary creativity have taught us so much. We hope that our dedication adequately conveys our deep debt to the wonderful collaborators we have had at ASHP and CHNM. We are also indebted to our department chair, Jack Censer, and our dean, Daniele Struppa, for the enthusiastic support they have given to CHNM.

We benefited greatly from astute readings of the whole or parts of the manuscript. We received insightful comments on the entire manuscript from Steve Brier, Robert Chazan, Abbie Grotke, Giles Hudson, and Jim Sparrow. In addition to those already named, we also received valuable comments on particular chapters from Josh Brown, Peter Jaszi, Terence Ross, David Seaman, Abby Smith, and Rebecca Tushnet.

Bob Lockhart's enthusiasm for this project has been indispensable, particularly his willingness to take a chance on an open access model of publishing, which will make a digital version of the book available for free online. We are also grateful to the University of Pennsylvania Press for its support of this approach, as well as its willingness to publish the print edition under the Founders' Copyright, as we advocate in Chapter 7. Noreen O'Connor provided clear and timely editorial assistance. It is a delight to have an index prepared by Jim O'Brien.

Our most profound thanks go to our families—Deborah Kaplan, Rachel Chazan Cohen, and Eve and Arlo Cohen—for cheerfully tolerating the distractions of this project and for providing many wonderful reasons to look up from our computers.